PRAISE FOR
Self Improvement: The Top 1
Who Help Us Improve Our Lives

"This is the most impressive collection of the best-of-the-best advice from the world's top success experts. You can invest the next 30-40 years searching for answers or can buy this book now."

Jack Canfield – Co-Author, *Chicken Soup for the Soul* best-selling series
http://www.jackcanfield.com

"*The Top 101 Experts* holds the most valuable lessons from people who have achieved remarkable success. Each expert lived to make a positive and pro-found impact in other people's lives in a way that will last throughout time. This book has the potential to change your life in a very enlightening way."

John Gray – Author, *Men Are from Mars, Women Are from Venus*
http://www.marsvenus.com

"This is an inspirational, informative and power-packed book, full of valuable insights and ideas for personal success. It is easy to read and apply. Everyone should have a copy at their fingertips."

Brian Tracy – Author, *Maximum Achievement*
http://www.briantracy.com

"David Riklan's book, *Self Improvement: The Top 101 Experts*, is a fantastic collection of the thoughts of some of the most influential motivational and inspirational leaders of our day. Each and every interview, resource and rec-ommendation is filled with the wisdom of the ages. Turn to a page—any page—and you'll find guidance and sage advice to help you along this journey of life. This is a brilliant testimony to the dignity of the human spirit. Read it and grow."

John Harricharan – Award-Winning and Best-Selling Author, *When You*
**   *Can Walk on Water, Take the Boat***
**   http://www.insight2000.com**

"Here are 101 Experts who have a tremendous impact on the world. Their lives challenge you to live your life at your best. A valuable book that provides a powerful road map for a successful life."

Jim Rohn – America's Foremost Business Philosopher
   http://www.jimrohn.com

"*101 Experts* is an absolute masterpiece! The enormous amount of valuable content in this book simply astounded me. Make an investment in this book and you've made one of the smartest investments in your life."

Peggy McColl – Author, *On Being a Dog with a Bone*
   http://www.destinies.com

"An outstanding treasure chest of vital information that will benefit everyone who uses it. I'd love to have had access to this 30 years ago!"

Les Hewitt – Co-Author, *The Power of Focus* and *The Power of Focus for Women*
   http://www.achievers.com

"What a delight! I love this book. It contains an entire education in self-improvement. This giant book on the self-help leaders is a crash course in the best of personal growth wisdom. Inspiring and priceless material here. Well done!"

Joe Vitale – #1 Best-Selling Author, *Spiritual Marketing*
   http://www.MrFire.com

"In one volume, I was able to gain insights from Tony Robbins, Zig Ziglar, Dale Carnegie, Deepak Chopra, Wayne Dyer, Les Brown, and Stephen Covey. The list goes on and on. *The Top 101 Experts* will save you an enormous amount of time and effort...the two most precious assets you have. I refer to it constantly."

Mike Brescia – President, Think Right Now! International
   http://www.ThinkRightNow.com

"An extraordinary array of shakin' and bakin' success secrets that will turbo-charge and skyrocket your income! So much insight, from so many people, and so affordable. A winning product, get it now!"

Mike Litman – #1 Best-Selling Co-Author, *Conversations with Millionaires*
   http://www.mikelitman.com

"Without a doubt, this is the definitive work on the self improvement industry. I guarantee that no where else will you find such comprehensive information about both the experts and their work! Before you even consider buying ANY personal development material you must get this book. The attention to detail spread over hundreds of pages is staggering. *Self Improvement: The Top 101 Experts* has now redefined the standard of personal development books…and I would strongly suggest that you read it from cover to cover with a pen and notebook by your side."

Gary Vurnum – Founder, Our Success Partnership
   http://www.oursuccesspartnership.com

"Reading Riklan's comprehensive self improvement guide is like sitting down for coffee with some of the wisest voices of our time. If you're ready to embrace the highest vision for your life, this mini-encyclopedia of key people and resources will both inspire you and show you how."

Amara Rose – "Midwife for the Soul" and Creator of Live Your Light
   Foundation
   http://www.liveyourlight.com

"*Self Improvement: Top 101 Experts* is a fantastic compilation of wisdom, practical guidance and resources needed to tackle any problem and enhance your life. The book includes important contributions by top modern day experts in all aspects of human development, so that the reader can easily find material that deals with whatever issue he is dealing with. I highly recommend this wonderful book. No bookshelf should be without it."

Dr. Brenda Shoshanna – Author, *Why Men Leave* and *Zen and the Art of*
   Falling in Love
   http://www.brendashoshanna.com

"Congratulations to David Riklan and a sincere thank you for expending the considerable effort that went into this needed and wanted book. The serious student of personal growth and development will find a valuable overview of the self improvement arena with Riklan's thoughtful personal evaluations of the role and impact of 101 experts."

Robert White – Author, *Living an Extraordinary Life*, and Chairman/CEO, ARC Worldwide
http://www.arcworldwide.com

"This book will become a classic in the field and allow wonderful interconnections between the leaders in the self-help field. It is well-written and organized and stimulates creative thought and positive action. I will be sending my clients and colleagues to its resources for years to come."

Gail McMeekin – Author, *The 12 Secrets of Highly Creative Women: A Portable Mentor*
http://www.creativesuccess.com

"[David,] you have created the 'guru bible' for the 21st century. Everything anyone would need to learn about the best of the best is here. I commend you for the massive undertaking and making it so simple and easy for anyone to use."

John Assaraf – *The New York Times* and *Wall Street Journal* Best-Selling Author, *The Street Kid's Guide to Having It All*
http://www.thestreetkid.com

"This book uniquely chronicles many of the individual leaders and cutting edge thinkers in the area of personal training and development. As the CEO of Landmark Education Business Development, and a person committed to breakthrough thinking, I acknowledge SelfGrowth.com for making this collection available."

Steve Zaffron – CEO, Landmark Education Business Development
http://www.lebd.com, http://www.landmarkeducation.com

SELF IMPROVEMENT

THE TOP 101 EXPERTS

Who Help Us Improve Our Lives

– DAVID RIKLAN –

Self Improvement Online, Inc.
Marlboro, New Jersey

Self Improvement: The Top 101 Experts
Who Help Us Improve Our Lives – by David Riklan

Published by:
Self Improvement Online, Inc.
http://www.selfgrowth.com
20 Arie Drive, Marlboro, N.J. 07746

Copyright © 2004 by David Riklan
ISBN 0-9745672-3-X
Manufactured in the United States

Cover Design:
Peri Poloni
Knockout Design
http://www.knockoutbooks.com

This book is dedicated to my wife Michelle and our three children: Joshua, Jonathan, and Rachel.

ACKNOWLEDGEMENTS

This book was truly created through a team effort that took countless hours of research, revisions, and updates to create. It could not have been created alone. There were several hundred people involved with this project including many of the experts themselves, but there were four people involved that deserve a special acknowledgement.

Todd Lesser was involved in this project from the very beginning. He was responsible for countless hours of research and editing that went into the development of this book.

Joe De Palma was responsible for contacting each of the experts and working with them or their companies to verify the accuracy of the information included in this book.

Gary Dong was our prime webpage designer, involved with the design and creation of all of the webpages on http://www.SelfGrowth.com that support this project.

Many special thanks are due to my friends and family, who have provided much needed support and encouragement throughout.

Finally, a special thanks to my wife Michelle, who is a continual source of motivation for everything that I do.

TABLE OF CONTENTS

APPENDICES

INTRODUCTION

THE PURPOSE OF THIS BOOK

The purpose of this book is to assist you with that wonderful journey we call life!

Our goal was to create a single resource that would open up the doors to the Top 101 Self Improvement Experts in the world who can help us improve our lives. Through the use of Internet technology, this book provides detailed biographical information, product information, key thoughts and beliefs, book excerpts, audio clips, and articles for the Top 101 Experts (i.e. Gurus) in the Self Improvement Industry. This fact-filled book is a guide to help us determine which experts are best for us and what products will help us improve our lives.

Our first challenge was to define the Self Improvement Industry. What is Self Improvement and how does it differ from Self Help or Personal Growth? Our research indicated that the term "Self Help" was coined by Samuel Smiles in a book that he wrote in 1859 titled *Self-Help*. The terms Self Improvement and Personal Growth appeared to have evolved over time. Due to the nuances of each of these terms, we decided to limit the definition of Self Improvement to the categories that we cover. These categories enabled us to define Self Improvement.

The six different general categories that define Self Improvement include:

- Personal Empowerment (Phil McGraw, Anthony Robbins, et al.)
- Spirituality (Marianne Williamson, Dan Millman, et al.)
- Business (Spencer Johnson, Ken Blanchard, Stephen Covey, et al.)
- Relationships (John Gray, Harville Hendrix, Barbara De Angelis, et al.)
- Personal Finance (Robert Kiyosaki, Robert Allen, et al.)
- Professional & Academic Skills (Dale Carnegie, Og Mandino, Brian Tracy, et al.)

WHO SHOULD READ THIS BOOK?

This book is a must-read for absolutely anybody connected to, or interested in, Self Improvement. It is a clear, concise, and handy Self Improvement reference guide, with rankings for the industry's top experts. Finally, all of the world's top experts in one place, ready to inspire you now!

WHAT ARE THE TOP TEN QUESTIONS TO DETERMINE IF THIS BOOK IS FOR YOU?

We have included a series of questions you should ask yourself. If you answer "yes" to at least three of these questions, then this is the book for you.

1.　　　Do you feel drawn to the Self Help section of your local bookstore?
2.　　　Have you ever taken a continuing education course or seminar on any of the following topics: personal growth, empowerment, goal setting, speed reading, public speaking, communication, relationships, stress management, time management, writing skills, or sales skills?
3.　　　Have you ever tried to find or contact any of the top Self Improvement Experts or their companies?
4.　　　Have you ever wished there was one meeting place for every major expert in the industry with instructions for how to get started with your favorites?
5.　　　Have you every watched a Tony Robbins infomercial or an episode of Dr. Phil's TV show?
6.　　　Have you ever picked up a copy of the book by Dale Carnegie called *How to Win Friends and Influence People*?
7.　　　Do you want to know who the Top 101 Experts in the Self Improvement Industry are and their rankings?
8.　　　Have you ever listened to an audio program by a motivational speaker?
9.　　　Have you ever searched the Internet looking for Self Improvement information?
10.　　Do you want to improve your career, make more money, meet Mr. or Ms. Right, feel better, or be happier?

If you answered "no" to all of the above questions, you probably need this book more than anyone else. Start reading it immediately.

WHY WRITE A BOOK ABOUT SELF IMPROVEMENT EXPERTS?

This is a very valid question. Why should a Self Improvement book cover information about the experts? We based the premise of this book around the concept of "modeling." We believe that if you want something, anything, the best way to get it is to find somebody else who already has it and figure out how they got it. It doesn't matter what that is; it could be anything from:

- A Better Job
- A Higher Level of Education
- A Great Tennis Game
- More Fulfilling Relationships
- A Happy Outlook on Life
- Inner Peace

SO WHICH EXPERT DO YOU GO TO?

The experts featured in this book are all people who specialize in helping people get something they want. That something could be tangible or intangible. This book is about the Top 101 Self Improvement Experts who teach us how to improve our lives. In many cases, they are showing us how to teach ourselves.

WHY DID WE WRITE THIS BOOK?

We were looking to create a guidebook for anybody interested in Self Improvement, or more importantly, anyone interested in improving their lives. Originally, we wanted to buy a Self Improvement reference guide and couldn't find one. So we wrote one ourselves. Our hope is that we can all use it as a guide to help us improve our lives.

HOW TO USE THIS BOOK

This reference guide can be used in many different ways. Here is a short list of ways this book might be helpful to you:

1. AS A REFERENCE GUIDE

This book can be used as a traditional reference guide. You can look up any of the Top 101 Experts in Self Improvement and immediately get their contact information, their websites, a list of their best-sellers, information about their businesses, their most notable quotes or ideas, their biographies, and a quick place to get started with them. You can then proceed to the URL at the end of each "Getting Started" section and immediately read additional excerpts from their books or listen to audio excerpts from their programs when they are available.

2. SELF IMPROVEMENT 101 COURSE

This book can be read cover-to-cover. Each chapter functions like a course in the beliefs, background, and experiences of the expert. The book can be described as a mini-encyclopedia for the Self Improvement Industry.

3. A QUICK DOSE OF EMPOWERMENT AND ENLIGHTENMENT

For each of the 101 Experts, we tried to identify their key concepts or key thoughts for helping us improve our lives. You can read chapter-by-chapter and gain insights from the people that helped create the Self Improvement movement (Napoleon Hill, Dale Carnegie, et al.) or from the people who are leading the charge today (Phil McGraw, Tony Robbins, et al.).

** A WORD OF CAUTION FOR OUR READERS **

As part of our personal Self Improvement belief system, we stress the positive in the descriptions for each of these experts. This book is perfect if you want to find out who the experts are, what they have to say, what products they have to learn from, and how to contact them. If you are just looking for "dirt" on any of these gurus, you're looking in the wrong place.

The experts included in this book also provide a wide diversity of opinions, backgrounds, and perspectives. In many cases, their programs, recommendations, and ideas clash with each other. We don't expect anybody to agree with all of the diverse opinions of the experts.

HOW IS THIS BOOK ORGANIZED?

The main section of the book is broken into 101 chapters, one for each of our Self Improvement Experts. The chapters are in order based on their rankings.

We provide eight sections of information on each of the Self Improvement Experts. They include the following:

- Quick Facts
- Biography
- Favorite Quotes and Thoughts
- The Best Way to Get Started
- Books
- Audio and Video Programs
- Other Programs and Highlights
- Contact Information

In addition, for each of our experts, we provide a URL to private web pages that contain the following:

1. Audio samples from our experts. You can listen to the majority of the gurus talk and teach in their own words. We have over 50 hours of supplemental audio samples for our readers and listeners. Access to a computer (with speakers) is required.

2. Book excerpts and articles. You can read material from the experts themselves and get a taste of what their writing is like. In total, there are over 1,500 pages of supplemental Self Improvement material for our readers. Again, access to a computer is required.

So, how exactly did we come up with this list of 101 Experts and how did we rank them?

WHO IS AN EXPERT and HOW ARE THEY RANKED?

THE MISSION

We wanted to identify the top Self Improvement Experts in the industry—the "best of the best"—and rank them from 1 to 101. Who are the top people that are helping us help ourselves? It turned out to be quite a challenge! It appeared to be an exercise in subjectivity. How do you rank and compare what Anthony Robbins does with what Deepak Chopra does with what Zig Ziglar does? They are all different. How could anyone be objective?

THE SOLUTION

We reviewed our options and identified several "objective methodologies" for determining the "Best of the Best." Next, we combined these methodologies with an analysis of the Internet search habits of the Self Improvement community. This resulted in the theory that the more important an expert was, the more that expert would be searched for on the Internet. But with that came questions:

Are the people most searched for the most effective Self Improvement Experts for you?
- Maybe not.

Are the people most searched for the wealthiest experts?
- Maybe not.

Are the people most searched for the most popular Self Improvement Experts?
- They might not be the most popular, but they are the most popular on the Internet, and the Internet provides us with the most objective venue that we can find.

OUR SYSTEM

The more frequently an expert's name would be typed into search engines on the Internet, like Yahoo and Google, the higher their ranking would be. We did our best to crunch the numbers for the whole universe of Self Improvement Experts. The person with the most searches was our #1 expert.

WHAT WE FOUND

Phillip McGraw (or Dr. Phil) was the most commonly searched name on our Self Improvement list. Oprah Winfrey is actually searched for more on the Internet than Dr. Phil, but we consider Oprah to be in a class of her own. As for topics, there were three times as many people searching for "health" as there were for "money." Maybe our society is not as "money-centric" as we think.

CHALLENGES ALONG THE WAY

This system for ranking experts had it problems. Our first and most important challenge was how we would define a Self Improvement Expert. We came up with a list of questions that needed to be answered.

THE QUESTIONS AND ANSWERS

1.   Which topics fall under Self Improvement?

We included the following areas for Self Improvement: Personal Empowerment, Spirituality, Business, Relationships, Personal Finance, and Professional & Academic Skills.

2.   Should we only include living Self Improvement Experts? What about ones from the past like Dale Carnegie?

We decided to include present and past leaders in the Self Improvement Industry. We let the Internet search criteria define those leaders for us. Dale Carnegie is included. This shows that an expert's legacy and contribution can have a lasting effect even after he/she is gone.

3.   Are religious leaders Self Improvement Experts? (Jesus, Muhammad, Moses, Buddha, the Pope, etc.)

We excluded most religious leaders. Even though we personally feel that religious leaders help us improve our lives, we left them out. However, if we felt certain religious leaders were mostly well-known for their contribution to the Self Improvement Industry, they were included. Reverend Norman Vincent Peale is a prime example. He is the author of *The Power of Positive Thinking*, an important book in the Self Improvement arena.

4.   Are leading psychologists from the past Self Improvement Experts? (Abraham Maslow, Sigmund Freud, Milton Erickson, Carl Rogers, Carl Jung, William James, Alfred Adler, Alfred Kinsey, Jean Piaget, etc.)

We made a judgment call on each of these. We asked ourselves the question, "What are they best known for?" Are they known for their research or their contribution to the Self Improvement Industry?

5.   What about great philosophers? Are they included?

No, they are not included. Socrates, Plato, and Aristotle cannot be found in this book. They are more suited for the Philosophy section in your local bookstore.

6.   What about people whose name is not well-known but whose work is? For example, *What Color is Your Parachute* is a very popular book on finding your ideal career, but the author, Richard N. Bolles, is not searched for very frequently.

We decided to go with name recognition only. Those who are primarily known for a certain book, product, or company did not make the list. However, we did include many of these people in Appendix A-C for other valuable Self Improvement resources. *Self Improvement: The Top 101 Experts* is about the experts and their message, rather than what they are known for.

7.   Should we include health and dieting experts?

We decided to exclude health and dieting experts. Those experts would take up a complete book on their own. Health and dieting is such a large area that we think it should stand by itself, separate from what we're including here.

8.   Should we include people who are primarily entertainers that became Self Improvement Experts?

In general, we excluded experts who are primarily entertainers. For example, Marlo Thomas (*That Girl* television show) wrote a book titled *The Right Words at the Right Time*. It can be considered a Self Help book, but Marlo Thomas did not make the list.

9.   What about psychics and psychic mediums? Where do they fit in?

Many people believe that psychics and psychic mediums have added tremendously to their lives, providing them with inner peace, closure in their lives, and a better understanding of where they fit into the universe. Some names that come to mind are Edgar Cayce, John Edward, James Van Praagh, and Rosemary Altea. We only included one person that fits under this heading, Sylvia Browne, due to the all of the work she has done on the Spirituality side of Self Improvement.

10.   What about other famous people that didn't make the list?

There are quite a few other people that we believe contribute substantially to Self Improvement, even though the Self Improvement Industry isn't their primary focus. Some of these people are Ralph Waldo Emerson, Ann Landers, Dear Abby, C. S. Lewis, Viktor Frankl, Joyce Brothers, Joseph Campbell, Robert Bly, Benjamin Franklin, and Horatio Alger.

WHAT ABOUT ALL of the OTHER EXPERTS?

The Self Improvement Industry is vast and is made up of people and organizations. We realized that defining the Self Improvement area by a mere 101 experts was extremely limiting. In order to provide a more comprehensive resource, we included several appendices that cover a wealth of additional resources available to improve your life.

Appendix A   Other Valuable Self Improvement Experts

We provided this appendix with additional experts who did not make our Top 101 list. We feel they provide great material to help us improve our lives, and these people deserve to be mentioned in this book.

Appendix B   Other Valuable Self Improvement Companies and Resources

We included this appendix because some of the main Self Improvement companies do not have a leader who made our Top 101 list. These companies are absolutely worth looking at.

Appendix C   Other Valuable Self Improvement Books

This appendix lists some extraordinary books that have helped countless people improve their lives. Although the authors of these books did not make the Top 101, these works are truly inspirational.

WHERE IS OPRAH?

Our book contains 101 Self Improvement Experts from Dr. Phil to Dr. Laura, from Anthony Robbins to the Dalai Lama. But where is Oprah? Many people have asked, "How can you not include Oprah Winfrey?" They demand to know why Oprah isn't on the list. Well, we made the decision that Oprah isn't best labeled as a Self Improvement Expert; she should really have her own category.

Oprah can best be described as a supporter of the Self Improvement and Self Help Industry. We like to describe Oprah as the "Patron Saint of Self Improvement." Why is she the Patron Saint? Very simply, Oprah has given millions of people the opportunity to see and hear what the experts have to say. Over 30 of the people on our list have been on *The Oprah Winfrey Show*, including our #1 expert, Dr. Phil McGraw.

We believe that Oprah has done more for providing access to Self Improvement and Self Help tools than anybody else alive today. And we're not just saying that to get her to invite us on the show. Although…Oprah, if you do want us as guests, we won't turn you down.

We even love to quote Oprah. One of our favorite Self Improvement quotes from Oprah is: "Everyone wants to ride with you in the limo, but what you need is someone who will take the bus with you when the limo breaks down."

Since Oprah has demonstrated her importance to the Self Improvement Industry, we would like to share some additional information on her:

Oprah Winfrey is the first woman in history to own and produce her own talk show. Born in Kosciusko, Mississippi, Oprah's broadcasting career began at age 17, when she was hired by WVOL radio in Nashville. In 1984, she went to the Midwest to host WLS-TV's *A.M. Chicago*, a faltering local talk show that she turned completely around in less than a year. The format of the show soon expanded to one hour and was renamed *The Oprah Winfrey Show*. Today, it is the #1 talk show in national syndication.

In 1986, Oprah formed her own production company, HARPO Productions, Inc., which two years later, acquired ownership and all production responsibilities for *The Oprah Winfrey Show*. Based in Chicago, HARPO Entertainment Group includes HARPO Productions, Inc., HARPO Films, and HARPO Video, Inc. Oprah is also one of the partners in Oxygen Media, Inc., a cable channel designed primarily for women.

Oprah was named one of the "100 Most Influential People of the 20th Century" by *Time* magazine, and in 1998, received a Lifetime Achievement Award from the National Academy of Television Arts and Sciences. When she started

Oprah's Book Club, selected publications became instant best-sellers. In 1999, she received the National Book Foundation's 50th anniversary gold medal for her service to books and authors.

If you wish to find out additional information on Oprah, you can watch her television show or visit her website at www.oprah.com.

SELF IMPROVEMENT MINI-COURSE

THE PURPOSE OF THIS MINI-COURSE

The purpose of this section is to assist with our primary task: TO IMPROVE OUR LIVES! Everybody that I speak to wants to improve their life, but many of them are faced with the same questions:

    A.   What is the best way to start improving my life?
    B.   What are the best resources for me?
    C.   Which book should I read first?
    D.   Which seminar should I go to?
    E.   Should I listen to an audio program from my car?
    F.   What is the best website to go to?

This book is going to help you answer these questions. This mini-course will help you to answer them correctly.

The following three lessons are:

- The 31 Absolute Best Resources for Self Improvement
- The Untold Truth About Mentors, and Why You Don't Need "ONE"
- The "Ten Commandments" of Self Improvement

Read, learn, and enjoy!

The 31 Absolute Best Resources for Self Improvement

This section is designed as a brainstorming session to help you think about and understand all of the different resources available. Here I provide you with a complete list of 31 resources, and for each section, I include the pros and cons of using that particular resource. Basically, I want you to use this for two reasons:

- To get you thinking about all of the different resources available to you.
- To get you thinking about the advantages and disadvantages for each of the resources.

After you've had additional time to digest these, we will get back to helping you identify the best resources to improve your life. I have divided the resources into five different areas to get you thinking, and in some cases I have provided very specific examples. So, how many of these resources have you used to improve your life?

YOUR IMMEDIATE CIRCLE OF CONTACTS (1-4)

As a general rule, the people in this group are more likely to give you personal attention, and they are more likely to sincerely care about your needs. There are two things to look out for. These people are not necessarily experts in the areas where you need to improve, and they might have their own agenda, but they are generally easily accessible and can be great resources to help you improve your life.

1. Your Friends
2. Your Family
3. Co-workers
4. Your Employer (boss or manager)

INFORMATION RESOURCES (5-12)

There is an unbelievable wealth of information out there to improve your life. On the Internet alone, there are over five million websites with the exact phrases of "Self Help" or "Self Improvement." On Amazon.com, there are over 190,000 books with references to Self Help and Self Improvement. Almost all of the information you are looking for can be found here, but it could take hundreds of lifetimes to find the right information for you. Which of these resources do you currently use to help improve your life?

5. Internet Websites
6. Books (Library, Bookstore)

7.   Seminars, Retreats
8.   High School, College, or Continuing Education Courses
9.   Audio Programs
10. Television and Video Programs
11. Radio
12. Other Media, Magazines, Movies, Music

TRAINED PROFESSIONALS (13-22)

A trained professional can help you survive and to thrive in many areas of your life. Many have worked with people in your exact circumstances and helped them find the answers they were looking for. As a general rule, professionals can provide you with more objectivity than you would get from a friend or a family member.

One of the challenges of working with trained professionals is finding the right one for you. It is important to find the right type of trained professional (i.e.— therapist or personal coach) and then the best person based on your background, needs, and personality. Trained professionals can also be very expensive to work with and in some instances have a stigma attached to them. In many cases, the benefits of working with a trained professional far outweigh the costs and the risk, but this is something that you need to evaluate.

13. Therapists (Professional Counselors, Psychologists)
14. Personal Coaches, Life Coaches
15. Clergy (i.e.—Priest, Minister, Rabbi)
16. Accountant, Attorney, Stockbroker, Financial Planner
17. Self Improvement Experts (Tony Robbins, Dr. Phil)
18. Librarians
19. Personal Trainer
20. Doctors and Other Health Care Professionals
21. Employment Experts (Job Placement Experts)
22. Psychics, Spiritualist, Yogis

ORGANIZATIONS (23-25)

I am using the term "organizations" in a very broad sense. These can include non-profit and for-profit organizations and both professional and social organi-zations. The biggest benefit that many of these organizations provide is the ability to work with, network with, and share experiences with people in the same boat, on the same mission, or with the same problem. These organizations frequently have "trained professionals," frequently have people who are our friends and family, and use "Known Information Resources" to help each of us grow. These types of organizations are not for everybody, and the benefits that you get back are tied directly into what you are contributing. The wrong group could be a waste of time, but the right group could change your life forever.

23.　Non-Profit Support Groups (i.e.—AA, Child Support Groups)
24.　Social and Professional Organizations (i.e.—Toastmasters, MENSA)
25.　Spas, Health Clubs
26.　Personal Support Network (Master Mind Groups)

OTHERS POTENTIAL AREAS (27-31)

The above areas covered countless resources to improve your life. I have included a few other areas that others have found helpful in the past. As you can see, there is a tremendous amount of overlap between the different resources.

27.　Free Government Resources (Hotlines, Brochures, Help Centers)
28.　Inner Guidance (Asking and Giving Yourself Help)
29.　Pets for other wisdom (Great listeners)
30.　Mentors
31.　God

Each and every one of us has used at least one of these resources to improve our lives. Your assignment is to evaluate each of the areas above and try to determine which of these has helped you the most in the past. Once this is done, I am sure you'll be able to determine which resource will work best for you in the future.

The Untold Truth About Mentors, and Why You Don't Need "ONE"

I think there is a misconception about what a mentor truly is. A mentor is someone who guides you, someone wise, someone you trust. A mentor can be your confidant, advisor, coach, or even your role model. Many people swear by their mentors and frequently credit them with much of their success.

Yet you do not have to choose just one! The mentor-protégé bond is certainly a special one, but this does not mean you are limited to the knowledge of only a single source. In the early years of my adult life, I was hoping to find just one person to guide me and direct me, but I never did find that person.

Over time, a few things became clear to me:

1. There is no single person who can provide us with every answer. So why abide by one mentor who you know cannot meet every requirement? I discovered that I could learn more, not by following the advice of a single person but by observing a multitude of people.

2. There is no perfect role model. I used to believe there was such a person and that I would simply model myself after him. All I would have to do is watch and do the things he did. Unfortunately, I haven't met that person yet.

3. There is no perfect person. Very few people possess all of the qualities that I think define success and happiness: great friends, career, health, family life, finances, social life, leisure, spiritual life, community involvement, etc. Most of the very successful people I've met had one or some of these, but hardly any had all of them. So why compare myself to the perfect person who doesn't exist?

4. I didn't have all of the answers, and I never will. I knew that I was going to make mistakes, but what I discovered was that it was much easier to learn from other people's mistakes than to make all of the mistakes myself.

To me, my mentor had to:

*   Take a personal interest in my development and support me in the avenues I take.
*   Help me strive toward the highest of aspirations, not only in career but in the satisfaction of life.

- Want to share his knowledge and experiences, in hope that I reach a high level of achievement.
- Show me the need to fulfill all responsibilities, both at home and away from it.
- Care about the well-being of himself and his family.
- Be a great overall example.

Needless to say, I still haven't found that one mentor yet.

Since I couldn't find that one special person to guide me, I needed to create a mentor. Now, how does one go about doing something like that? Well, it's not as hard as it seems. You first have to determine what you want. That is most important, not only because it's part of the mentor process but because it directly concerns what will make you happy in life.

Once you figure out what you want, find the people that have it or know how to get it and make sure they are willing to teach you how to get it. You don't even have to know them personally. As your mentors, they can teach you through a variety of ways: books, audio tapes, lectures, seminars, etc. A mentor then can have millions of protégés.

Here is some additional advice in finding mentors:

1. You can learn from practically anybody. In essence, anybody can be your mentor. Not only can you learn what to do or how to behave, you can also learn to avoid the wrong paths that others have followed.

2. Identify the key people in your life. Mentors can be close family members like parents or siblings, and they can also be public figures. Again, don't believe that you have to have a close relationship with your mentors. Public figures can be key people in your life because they can have a profound effect on how you live it.

3. Find people with specialized knowledge. If certain people have written an insightful book on a particular subject or have inspirational life experiences to share, then they might be possible mentors who can help in motivating you. Plus, if they are famous, they are easy to watch via television or the Internet, and their material is not difficult to find.

4. Try to ask as much as possible. Ask people for advice, ask them how they got where they are, ask them how you can get the same things. Also ask yourself what certain people would say or how they would act in specific situations. The more prepared you are, the less likely you'll make a mistake in the future.

5.   Mentors can simply be people who are happy in life! Salary and position don't matter as long as there is contentment and commitment. Mentors can range from athletes and politicians to religious figures and stay-at-home mothers.

I have hundreds of mentors. So how many do you have?

The "Ten Commandments" of Self Improvement

What does it really take to change your life? Let me begin by giving you a little background. Here are some guidelines, what I like to call the pre-commandments of Self Improvement:

- There is no single book, tape, seminar, expert, or system that will work equally well for everybody.
- There is no master plan for everybody. We are all unique.
- There is no panacea (a remedy for all diseases, evils or difficulties; a cure-all).
- There are many people with products and information that can help you.
- There are also a lot of books, tapes, and programs out there that will provide you with very little benefit.

Now let me share with you some ideas that I believe will stick with you throughout your time as a Self Improvement seeker.

The following are ten steps or "Commandments" you can use as you scan the aisles, check the Web sites, and read the books trying to improve your life. For each of these "Ten Commandments," I have included quotes that support that belief from a variety of experts in the field of Self Improvement and beyond.

You are probably familiar with many of these "Commandments." If so, please look at them as a refresher course to remind you of the basics. The "Ten Commandments" of Self Improvement are as follows:

#1: Thou Shalt Take Responsibility for Your Life

Dr. Phil: "Life Law: You Create Your Own Experience. Acknowledge and Accept Responsibility for your life."

Stephen Covey: "Taking initiative does not mean being pushy, obnoxious, or aggressive. It does mean recognizing our responsibility to make things happen."

Les Brown: "Accept responsibility for your life. Know that it is you who will get you where you want to go, no one else."

Denis Waitley: "There are two primary choices in life: to accept conditions as they exist, or accept the responsibility for changing them."

#2: Thou Shalt Take Action

Dr. Phil McGraw: "Life Rewards Action. Make Careful Decisions."

Tony Robbins: "Take Massive Action."

Dale Carnegie: "The man who goes farthest is generally the one who is willing to do and dare. The sure-thing boat never gets far from shore."

Jack Canfield: "Everything you want is out there waiting for you to ask. Everything you want also wants you. But you have to take action to get it."

#3: Thou Shalt Have Desire

Napoleon Hill: "Desire is the starting point of all achievement."

Muhammad Ali: "Champions aren't made in the gyms. Champions are made from something they have deep inside them—a desire, a dream, a vision."

Mario Andretti: "Desire is the key to motivation, but it's the determination and commitment to an unrelenting pursuit of your goal—a commitment to excellence—that will enable you to attain the success you seek."

Earl Nightingale: "The key that unlocks energy is 'Desire.' It's also the key to a long and interesting life. If we expect to create any drive, any real force within ourselves, we have to get excited."

#4: Thou Shalt Set Goals

Tony Robbins: "Setting goals is the first step in turning the invisible into the visible."

Aristotle: "First, have a definite, clear practical ideal; a goal, an objective. Second, have the necessary means to achieve your ends; wisdom, money, materials, and methods. Third, adjust all your means to that end."

Maxwell Maltz: "People who say that life is not worthwhile are really saying that they themselves have no personal goals which are worthwhile. Get yourself a goal worth working for. Better still, get yourself a project. Always have something ahead of you to 'look forward to'—to work for and hope for."

Brian Tracy: "Every single life only becomes great when the individual sets upon a goal or goals which they really believe in, which they can really commit themselves to, which they can put their whole heart and soul into."

Zig Ziglar: "A goal properly set is halfway reached."

#5: Thou Shalt Create a Plan

Unknown: "If You Fail to Plan, You Plan to Fail."

Napoleon Hill: "When defeat comes, accept it as a signal that your plans are not sound, rebuild those plans, and set sail once more toward your coveted goal."

Mark Victor Hansen: "The majority of people meet with failure because they lack the persistence to create new plans to take the place of failed plans."

#6: Thou Shalt Pay the Price

Vince Lombardi: "The price of success is hard work, dedication to the job at hand, and the determination that whether we win or lose, we have applied the best of ourselves to the task at hand."

Orison Swett Marden: "Success is the child of drudgery and perseverance. It cannot be coaxed or bribed; pay the price and it is yours."

#7: Thou Shalt Have Persistence

Calvin Coolidge: "Nothing in the world can take the place of persistence. Talent will not; nothing is more common than unsuccessful men with talent. Genius will not; unrewarded genius is almost a proverb. Education will not; the world is full of educated derelicts. Persistence and determination alone are omnipotent."

Orison Swett Marden: "There is genius in persistence. It conquers all opposers. It gives confidence. It annihilates obstacles. Everybody believes in a determined man. People know that when he undertakes a thing, the battle is half won, for his rule is to accomplish whatever he sets out to do."

#8: Thou Shalt Believe

Denis Waitley: "If you believe you can, you probably can. If you believe you won't, you most assuredly won't. Belief is the ignition switch that gets you off the launching pad."

Anthony Robbins: "If you develop the absolute sense of certainty that powerful beliefs provide, then you can get yourself to accomplish virtually anything."

Maxwell Maltz: "Realizing that our actions, feelings and behavior are the result of our own images and beliefs gives us the level that psychology has always needed for changing personality."

David J. Schwartz: "The size of your success is determined by the size of your belief. Think little goals and expect little achievements. Think big goals and win big success." Remember this, too! Big ideas and big plans are often easier—certainly no more difficult—than small ideas and small plans."

#9: Thou Shalt Learn From Thy Mistakes

Winston Churchill: "All men make mistakes, but only wise men learn from their mistakes."

Oprah Winfrey: "There are no failures, only lessons to be learned."

John Sculley: "I have found that I always learn more from my mistakes than from my successes. If you aren't making some mistakes, you aren't taking enough chances."

10: Thou Shalt Create A Clear Picture of Your Future and Visualize It

Earl Nightingale: "Picture yourself in your mind's eye as having already achieved this goal. See yourself doing the things you'll be doing when you've reached your goal."

Stephen Covey: "Create a clear, mutual understanding of what needs to be accomplished, focusing on what, not how; results not methods. Spend time. Be patient. Visualize the desired result."

Robert L Schwartz: "The entrepreneur is essentially a visualizer and an actualizer. He can visualize something, and when he visualizes it he sees exactly how to make it happen."

These "Ten Commandments" are designed to enable you to springboard yourself to success. But are these the only commandments? Absolutely not!

Can you improve your life without using these? Yes, but it's not easy. Whatever the case may be, I wish you the best of luck in all that you pursue.

And now…

THE TOP 101 EXPERTS!

This book contains 101 chapters for each of the experts. We hope you enjoy your journey of learning and Self Improvement.

THE TOP 101 EXPERTS

PHIL McGRAW
(Expert #1)

PHIL McGRAW QUICK FACTS	
Main Area:	Personal Empowerment
NY Times Best-Sellers:	"Life Strategies"; "Self Matters"; "Relationship Rescue"; "The Ultimate Weight Solution"
Profile:	Author; Psychologist; Life Strategist; TV Host
Affiliation:	Courtroom Sciences, Inc.

❑ *Phil McGraw Biography*

Dr. Phil McGraw is a life strategist and host of the nationally syndicated series, *Dr. Phil*. He is also known as the human behavior expert from *The Oprah Winfrey Show*. With 25 years of experience in psychology and human functioning, Dr. Phil deals with real issues in his signature "tell-it-like-it-is" style. He is the author of many *New York Times* best-sellers.

Dr. Phil grew up in Oklahoma and Texas and was awarded a football scholarship to the University of Tulsa. He then finished his degree at Midwestern State University in Wichita Falls, Texas. Later, Dr. Phil earned his doctorate in psychology at the University of North Texas and in 1979, opened a practice with his father, who got his psychology degree at the age of 40.

After years of practicing, Dr. Phil realized that traditional therapy was not his calling. In 1989, he co-founded Courtroom Sciences, Inc. (CSI), a company that assists the legal profession by conducting mock trials, behavioral analysis, jury selection, and mediation. Dr. Phil met Oprah Winfrey when she hired CSI to help with her case against cattlemen who claimed she defamed the beef industry on one of her shows.

❑ *David Riklan's Favorite Phil McGraw Quotes and Thoughts*

- Sometimes it's hard to see your face without a mirror!

- Instead of asking whether the way you are living, behaving, and thinking is "right," I want you to ask if the way you are living, behaving, and thinking is working or not working.

- You cannot play the game of life with sweaty palms.

- You must demand nothing less than the best of yourself and for yourself. You must tell yourself that it is not wrong to want it all.

From *Life Strategies: Doing What Works, Doing What Matters:*

- Life Law #1: You either get it, or you don't.
  Strategy: Become one of those who gets it.

- Life Law #2: You create your own experience.
  Strategy: Acknowledge and accept accountability for your life.

- Life Law #3: People do what works.
  Strategy: Identify the payoffs that drive your behavior and that of others.

- Life Law #4: You cannot change what you do not acknowledge.
  Strategy: Get real with yourself about your life and everybody in it.

- Life Law #5: Life rewards action.
  Strategy: Make careful decisions and then pull the trigger.

- Life Law #6: There is no reality; only perception.
  Strategy: Identify the filters through which you view the world.

- Life Law #7: Life is managed; it is not cured.
  Strategy: Learn to take charge of your life.

- Life Law #8: We teach people how to treat us.
  Strategy: Own, rather than complain, about how people treat you.

- Life Law #9: There is power in forgiveness.
  Strategy: Open your eyes to what anger and resentment are doing to you..

- Life Law #10: You have to name it before you can claim it.
  Strategy: Get clear about what you want and take your turn.

❑ *The Best Way to Get Started with Phil McGraw*

Dr. Phil McGraw has created a dynasty. If I told you five years ago that Dr. Phil was an important part of the Self Improvement Industry, you would have probably responded in complete disbelief, asking, "Who is Dr. Phil?" Yet in a short time, he has become a household name.

One reason for Dr. Phil's success is his stint on *The Oprah Winfrey Show.* Oprah gave him the opportunity to shine, and he did so with his wisdom, skills, and personality. Dr. Phil provides a practical, no-nonsense type of self-help that is truly effective for those listening.

There are two ways to get started with Dr. Phil. One is to simply turn on your television and watch his show, which is both helpful and entertaining. The best way to understand his philosophy, though, is read his book *Life Strategies: Doing What Works, Doing What Matters*. Dr. Phil's son, Jay McGraw, adapted his father's book for teenage readers and published *Life Strategies for Teens*, which became a *New York Times* best-seller.

TO READ ADDITIONAL BOOK EXCERPTS or ARTICLES or to LISTEN TO PHIL McGRAW RIGHT NOW, VISIT
http://www.selfgrowth.com/experts

❏ *Books*

- Life Strategies: Doing What Works, Doing What Matters
- Self Matters: Creating Your Life from the Inside Out
- Relationship Rescue: A Seven-Step Strategy for Reconnecting With Your Partner
- The Ultimate Weight Solution: The 7 Keys to Weight Loss Freedom

❏ *Audio and Video Programs*

- Dr. Phil Getting Real: Lessons in Life, Marriage, and Family
- Life Strategies; Self Matters; Relationship Rescue (each on audio cassette or audio CD)

❏ *Other Programs and Highlights*

After five weeks of testimony in her "Mad Cow" case, Dr. Phil helped Oprah Winfrey show the world that she was merely hosting a public debate about the beef industry's role in a deadly medical mystery. Dr. Phil's other clients at Courtroom Sciences, Inc. have included Exxon, ABC, *The New York Times,* and other Fortune 500 companies.

❏ *Contact Information*

ADDRESS: Dr. Phil Show
P.O. Box 1902
5482 Wilshire Boulevard
Los Angeles, CA 90036

PHONE: 323-461-PHIL *(to make reservations to attend a show taping)*
1-866-4-DRPHIL *(to purchase a videotape/transcript of the show)*

EMAIL: Go to www.drphil.com/email/email_landing.jhtml
WEBSITE: www.drphil.com

ANTHONY ROBBINS
(Expert #2)

ANTHONY ROBBINS QUICK FACTS

Main Areas:	Empowerment; Personal and Business Success
Best-Sellers:	"Unlimited Power"; "Awaken the Giant Within" (over 1 million copies sold)
Profile:	Author; Speaker; Entrepreneur; Business Leader
Affiliations:	Anthony Robbins Companies; Anthony Robbins Foundation

---

❏ *Anthony Robbins Biography*

Anthony Robbins is an authority on the psychology of leadership, negotiations, organizational turnaround, and peak performance. He has impacted the lives of nearly 50 million people from 80 countries with his public speaking engagements and live appearances, along with his audiotape products and best-selling books like *Unlimited Power*. He is called upon by leaders from all walks of life, including presidents, CEOs, athletes, and entertainers.

Robbins is a successful entrepreneur and chairman of six companies. He has been honored by Accenture as one of the "Top 50 Business Intellectuals in the World" and by American Express as one of the top six business leaders in the world to coach their entrepreneurial clients. A much sought-after speaker, he has addressed such distinguished audiences as the British Parliament and Harvard Business School.

Robbins was one of the founding strategists in the creation of the Presidential Summit for America's Promise, which has helped generate over 2 million mentors for young people throughout the United States. His non-profit Anthony Robbins Foundation provides assistance to the homeless, elderly, and inner-city youth, feeding more than one million people each year through its international holiday, "Basket Brigade."

❏ *David Riklan's Favorite Anthony Robbins Quotes and Thoughts*

- The truth of the matter is that there's nothing you can't accomplish if: (1) you clearly decide what it is that you're absolutely committed to achieving, (2) you're willing to take massive action, (3) you notice what's working or not, and (4) you continue to change your approach until you achieve what you want, using whatever life gives you along the way.

- Action is the foundational key to all success.

- If you develop the absolute sense of certainty that powerful beliefs provide, then you can get yourself to accomplish virtually anything, including those things that other people are certain are impossible.

- If you want to be successful, find someone who has achieved the results you want and copy what they do and you'll achieve the same results.

- We are the only beings on the planet who lead such rich internal lives that it's not the events that matter most to us, but rather, it's how we interpret those events that will determine how we think about ourselves and how we will act in the future.

- Any time you sincerely want to make a change, the first thing you must do is to raise your standards. When people ask me what really changed my life eight years ago, I tell them that absolutely the most important thing was changing what I demanded of myself. I wrote down all the things I would no longer accept in my life, all the things I would no longer tolerate, and all the things that I aspired to becoming.

- Once you have mastered time, you will understand how true it is that most people overestimate what they can accomplish in a year—and underestimate what they can achieve in a decade!

- I discovered a long time ago that if I helped people get what they wanted, I would always get what I wanted and I would never have to worry.

❑ *The Best Way to Get Started with Anthony Robbins*

If one thinks of Dale Carnegie as the grandfather of the 20th century Self Improvement movement, then Anthony Robbins is his successor. Robbins has a tremendous ability to excite people and motivate them to action. And Self Improvement is, in many ways, about taking action. Robbins's main focus is helping us achieve peak performance. He shows us effective strategies and techniques for mastering our emotions, our body, our relationships, our finances, and our life, and he provides step-by-step programs, teaching the fundamental lessons of self-mastery.

To gain an understanding of Anthony Robbins, you need to listen to him speak, either on tape or by going to one of his live events. He has written several very successful books, but his true power comes in is ability to captivate an audience with his spoken words. If you are looking for an easy way to get started, I would recommend listening to one of his audio tapes, either *Get the Edge* or the

Personal Power II program. One quick way to actually see Tony is to watch his infomercial for *Get the Edge*, which is his newest program.

TO READ ADDITIONAL BOOK EXCERPTS or ARTICLES or to LISTEN
TO ANTHONY ROBBINS RIGHT NOW, VISIT
http://www.selfgrowth.com/experts

❑ *Books*

- Unlimited Power: The New Science Of Personal Achievement
- Awaken The Giant Within: How To Take Immediate Control Of Your Mental, Emotional, Physical and Financial Destiny!
- Notes From A Friend: A Quick And Simple Guide To Taking Control Of Your Life

❑ *Audio and Video Programs*

- Get the Edge
- Personal Power
- Live with Passion!: Stategies for Creating a Compelling Future
- Anthony Robbins' "Powertalk!": The Six Master Steps to Change
- Lessons in Mastery

❑ *Other Programs and Highlights*

Anthony Robbins has met with, consulted, or advised a number of international leaders and currently serves as Vice Chairman of Health, Education, and Science for the United Nations/Research Center for the International Council for Caring Communities (ICCC) NGO. He has developed and produced four award-winning television infomercials, and his work has been featured in major media worldwide. He had an acting role in the hit movie, *Shallow Hal.*

❑ *Contact Information*

ADDRESS: Anthony Robbins Companies
9888 Carroll Centre Road
San Diego, CA 92126
PHONE: 800-445-8183
EMAIL: tony@tonyrobbins.com
WEBSITE: www.tonyrobbins.com

SYLVIA BROWNE
(Expert #3)

SYLVIA BROWNE QUICK FACTS

Main Areas:	Spirituality; Psychic Abilities; Dreams; Counseling
NY Times Best-Sellers:	"The Other Side and Back"; "Life on the Other Side"; "Adventures of a Psychic"
Profile:	Author; Psychic; Lecturer; Teacher; Researcher
Affiliations:	Sylvia Browne Corporation; Society of Novus Spiritus

---

❑ *Sylvia Browne Biography*

Sylvia Browne is world renowned for her psychic talent, her counseling ability, and her research into parapsychology. She lectures, teaches, and counsels people from around the world. Sylvia manifested her psychic ability at the age of three in her hometown of Kansas City. For many years, she shared her gift with friends and family and became known for helping people to see their future.

To further her research into the paranormal, Sylvia incorporated The Nirvana Foundation for Psychic Research, a professional, legally sanctioned, non-profit organization, which is now known as Society of Novus Spiritus. Since then, Sylvia has helped thousands of people gain control of their lives. She has written a number of books, including *New York Times* best-sellers like *The Other Side and Back.*

Sylvia's philosophy of life is based upon research into past lives via hypnosis and through the information obtained via her deep trance channeling ability. From thousands of hypnotic regressions and hundreds of trance sessions, the fact of reincarnation was established as the key to understanding life. Sylvia accepts reincarnation as a central theme in her philosophy, yet this belief is never forced upon anyone who does not want to hear it.

❑ *David Riklan's Favorite Sylvia Browne Quotes and Thoughts*

- The Odyssey you are about to embark upon is probably the most glorious journey you will ever take. It is a spiritual banquet of knowledge that fills the soul with realization and truth.

- There is nothing more fascinating, more intensely personal, and more uniquely ours than the voyages our minds and spirits take while we sleep. These dreams and other adventures confuse us, alarm us, preoccupy us, relieve us, amuse us, comfort us, inform us, enlighten us, and above all, keep us more sane and whole than we could ever hope to be without them. Our sleep journeys, even the nightmares, are gifts, our allies, to embrace rather than dread, and worth every effort it takes to unravel their mysteries and cherish every valuable lesson they have to offer.

- I believe in the other side and the eternity of the soul. I believe our spirits make the round-trip from this world to The Other Side many times, by our own choice, to learn and experience for the ongoing advancement of the souls God gave each one of us. I believe that only a thin veil separates our earthly dimension from the dimension of The Other Side. I believe that The Other Side is Home, where we all came from and where we will all go again, and that we carry very real memories of it in our spirit minds. And I believe it is on The Other Side, between what we call "lifetimes," that we are really at our most alive.

- A person in grief is a person who's in pure survival mode. Breathing, eating, and sleeping may be about the best they can do for a while. Taking care of the basics for them without their having to ask—grocery shopping, tidying up, doing their laundry, whatever you can manage without making a pest of yourself—can make an enormous difference until they care enough to start wanting to do those things for themselves again.

❏ *The Best Way to Get Started with Sylvia Browne*

Sylvia Browne has a tremendous impact on many people's lives and has opened people up to a whole new world. She has written several best-sellers and makes many public appearances. But the best way to get started with Sylvia Browne is to read her book, *The Other Side and Back: A Psychic's Guide to Our World and Beyond*. She opens her book with the following:

> HELP FROM THE OTHER SIDE: OUR ANGELS AND SPIRIT GUIDES
>
> Almost every religion on Earth accepts the fact that our spirits survive death. But tell people you can communicate with those spirits and they will think you are nuts. So spirits exist, but we can't communicate with them? I think *that's* nuts. Of course we can! And we do, all the time, whether we are aware of it or not.

Sylvia's book takes us on a fascinating journey to the "other side" and functions like a comprehensive manual on living a spiritual life. Her twofold purpose, she states, is to help readers use their psychic abilities to create health and to reveal the nature of the "other side," the place where spirits reside after death and before they are reborn into new selves that retain programming and memories from previous existences.

In her book, *The Other Side and Back*, she shares information and answers a variety of questions, including:

- How spirit guides and angels "talk" to us—and how we can nurture them.
- How ghosts differ from spirits—and why hauntings occur.
- How the dead communicate with the living—and what they can teach us.
- Reincarnation and how we can reunite with our past lives.
- The three simple steps to developing your own psychic skills.
- Must-read predictions for the coming years.

Sylvia Browne frequently discusses her spirit guide, Francine, who has helped her grow along her personal journey. *The Other Side and Back* has the ability to draw you in and keeps you thinking about your own journey toward greater spirituality.

TO READ ADDITIONAL BOOK EXCERPTS or ARTICLES or to LISTEN TO SYLVIA BROWNE RIGHT NOW, VISIT
http://www.selfgrowth.com/experts

❏ *Books*

- The Other Side and Back: A Psychic's Guide to Our World and Beyond
- Life on the Other Side: A Psychic's Tour of the Afterlife
- Sylvia Browne's Book of Dreams
- Sylvia Browne's Book of Angels
- Adventures of a Psychic: The Fascinating and Inspiring True-Story of One of America's Most Successful Clairvoyants
- Blessings from the Other Side: Wisdom and Comfort from the Afterlife for This Life
- Prayer Book
- Meditation Book
- Contacting Your Spirit Guide Book & CD
- Conversations with the Other Side

❏ *Audio and Video Programs*

- Angels and Spirit Guides
- Sylvia Browne's Tools for Life

- Making Contact with the Other Side: How to Enhance Your Own Psychic Powers

❑ *Other Programs and Highlights*

Sylvia's talents have been showcased on national programs such as the *Montel Williams Show* and *Larry King Live*. She does many public appearances each year, such as her two-hour one-woman show and charitable benefits, especially for AIDS-related organizations. She is involved with community activities and donates many hours to help find missing children and also working with police to solve crimes.

❑ *Contact Information*

ADDRESS: Sylvia Browne Corporation
Society of Novus Spiritus
35 Dillon Avenue
Campbell, CA 95008
PHONE: (408) 379-7070
EMAIL: office@sylvia.org
WEBSITE: www.sylvia.org

THE DALAI LAMA
(Expert #4)

THE DALAI LAMA QUICK FACTS	
Main Areas:	Peace; Happiness; Spirituality; Buddhist Philosophy
NY Times Best-Sellers:	"The Art of Happiness"; "Ethics for the New Millennium"
Profile:	Author; Spiritual Leader

❑ *The Dalai Lama Biography*

The Dalai Lama is a spiritual and temporal leader of the Tibetan people, known worldwide as a tireless worker for peace. Born Lhamo Dhondrub to a peasant family in 1935, he was recognized at age two, in accordance with Tibetan tradition, as the reincarnation of his predecessor, the 13th Dalai Lama, and an incarnation of Avalokitesvara, the Buddha of Compassion. The Dalai Lamas are the manifestations of the Buddha of Compassion.

In 1950, the Dalai Lama assumed full political power after Tibet was invaded by the People's Liberation Army. He sought to bring about a peaceful solution to Sino-Tibetan conflict. After a national Tibetan uprising, which was crushed by the Chinese army, the Dalai Lama escaped to India, where he was given political asylum. Tens of thousands of Tibetan refugees followed him into exile. The Dalai Lama saw that he needed to save the Tibetan exiles and their culture alike.

The Dalai Lama appealed to the United Nations on the question of Tibet, resulting in three resolutions adopted by the General Assembly, calling on China to respect the human rights of Tibetans. Since his first visit to the West, he has received numerous peace awards, including the 1989 Nobel Peace Prize, and honorary doctorate degrees for his writings on Buddhist philosophy and his leadership in the solution of international conflicts and global environmental problems.

❑ *David Riklan's Favorite Dalai Lama Quotes and Thoughts*

- In the practice of tolerance, one's enemy is the best teacher.

- Be kind whenever possible. It is always possible.

- Awareness of death is the very bedrock of the entire path. Until you have developed this awareness, all other practices are obstructed.

- Pain is inevitable. Suffering is optional.

- I believe all suffering is caused by ignorance. People inflict pain on others in the selfish pursuit of their happiness or satisfaction. Yet true happiness comes from a sense of peace and contentment, which in turn must be achieved through the cultivation of altruism, of love and compassion, and elimination of ignorance, selfishness, and greed.

- If you want others to be happy, practice compassion. If you want to be happy, practice compassion.

- Love and compassion are necessities, not luxuries. Without them humanity cannot survive.

- My religion is very simple. My religion is kindness.

- Sleep is the best meditation.

- Old friends pass away, new friends appear. It is just like the days. An old day passes, a new day arrives. The important thing is to make it meaningful: a meaningful friend—or a meaningful day.

- Learn the rules well, so you can break them properly.

- You can transplant a heart, but you cannot transplant a warm heart.

❑ *The Best Way to Get Started with the Dalai Lama*

The best place to get started with the Dalai Lama is to read or listen to *The Art of Happiness: A Handbook for Living*. Howard C. Cutler, a Western psychiatrist, wanted to find out the secrets of happiness that the Dalai Lama appeared to have inside of him. He was able to set up a series of interviews with the Dalai Lama that became the basis for this book. Dr. Cutler's goal was to question the Dalai Lama about a wide variety of topics, gaining insight into how to live a happy life.

Some of the questions that Dr. Cutler poses include:

- Why are so many people unhappy?
- How can I abjure loneliness?
- How can we reduce conflict?
- Is romantic love true love?
- Why do we suffer?
- How should we deal with unfairness and anger?
- How do you handle the death of a loved one?

The Dalai Lama initially provides some simple answers that grow into more involved responses and then evolve into a more complete philosophy for living.

He discusses relationships, health, family, work, spirituality, the pursuit of wealth, and how to find inner peace while facing these struggles. He also talks about how to defeat depression, anxiety, anger, and jealousy through meditation.

When Dr. Cutler asks the Dalai Lama if he is happy, the answer is yes, and when he asks if he is ever lonely, the answer is no. The Dalai Lama says this is because he always looks at others positively and experiences a "feeling of affinity, a kind of connectedness." The audio version of this enlightening work is read by Dr. Cutler and Ernest Abuba.

TO READ ADDITIONAL BOOK EXCERPTS or ARTICLES or to LISTEN TO THE DALAI LAMA RIGHT NOW, VISIT
http://www.selfgrowth.com/experts

❑ **Books**

- The Art of Happiness: A Handbook for Living (co-authored with Howard C. Cutler, M.D.)
- Destructive Emotions: How Can We Overcome Them? (narrated by Daniel Goleman)
- How to Practice: The Way to a Meaningful Life (translated and edited by Jeffery Hopkins Ph.D.)
- Healing Anger: The Power of Patience from a Buddhist Perspective
- Stages of Meditation (translated by Venerable Geshe Lobsang Jordhen, Losang Choepel Ganchenpa, and Jeremy Russell)
- Ethics for the New Millennium

❑ **Audio and Video Programs**

- The Four Nobel Truths (book or audio cassette or DVD)
- Advice on Dying (translated and edited by Jeffery Hopkins Ph.D.) (book or audio cassette or audio CD)
- An Open Heart: Practicing Compassion in Everyday Life (book or audio cassette)
- The Art of Happiness; How to Practice; Stages of Meditation; Ethics for the New Millennium (each on audio cassette or audio CD)

❑ **Other Programs and Highlights**

The Dalai Lama began his education at age six and completed the Geshe Lharampa Degree (Doctorate of Buddhist Philosophy) when he was 25. He pursues an ongoing schedule of administrative meetings, private audiences, and religious teachings and ceremonies. Following the life of a Buddhist monk, he lives in a small cottage, rises at 4 a.m. to meditate, and ends each day with further prayer.

❑ *Contact Information*

ADDRESS:	Tibet House U.S.	The Office of Tibet
	22 West 15th Street	Tibet House, 1 Culworth Street
	New York, NY 10011	London NW8 7AF
PHONE:	(212) 807-0563	0044-20-7722 5378
EMAIL:	info@tibethouse.org	info@tibet.com
WEBSITE:	www.dalailama.com	www.tibet.com
	www.tibethouse.org	

LAURA SCHLESSINGER
(Expert 5)

LAURA SCHLESSINGER QUICK FACTS

Main Areas:	Empowerment; Motivation; Relationships
NY Times Best-Sellers:	Ten Stupid Things Women Do to Mess Up Their Lives"; "Ten Stupid Things Men Do to Mess Up Their Lives"; "Ten Stupid Things Couples Do To Mess Up Their Relationships"; "Parenthood by Proxy"; "The Ten Commandments"; "How Could You Do That?!"; "The Proper Care and Feeding of Husbands"
Profile:	Author; Speaker; Children's Writer; Radio Host; Ph.D. in Physiology from Columbia University
Affiliation:	The Dr. Laura Schlessinger Foundation

❑ Laura Schlessinger Biography

Dr. Laura Schlessinger is a radio personality, known for her no-nonsense philosophy of personal responsibility and self-motivation. The *Dr. Laura Schlessinger Show* on KFI-AM Radio in Los Angeles started in 1990 and has been syndicated since 1994, reaching more than 315 stations and 12 million listeners. Schlessinger's on-air radio career spans over 25 years. Her fans admire her humor and curt style, all of which cut to the root of their problems.

Schlessinger is also a best-selling author, children's writer, and sought-after public speaker. Her best-selling books include *The Ten Commandments* and the *Ten Stupid Things* series. She is a member of the National Association of At-Home Mothers Board of Advisors and is president of The Dr. Laura Schlessinger Foundation, which helps abused and neglected children.

Schlessinger has been a faculty member at USC and Pepperdine University and has taught at UCLA. She was in private practice for 12 years before turning her attention to a national audience. In 1997, Schlessinger was the first woman to win the Marconi Award for Network/Syndicated Personality of the Year. In 2000, she was the first non-Christian to receive the Chairman's Award from the National Religious Broadcasters.

❑ David Riklan's Favorite Laura Schlessinger Quotes and Thoughts

- Victimization status is the modern promised land of absolution from personal responsibility.

[45]

- Because it's possible to do, and you have the right to do it, doesn't mean it's the right thing to do.

- Values are principles and ideas that bring meaning to the seemingly mundane experience of life. A meaningful life that ultimately brings happiness and pride requires you to respond to temptations as well as challenges with honor, dignity, and courage.

From *Ten Stupid Things Couples Do to Mess Up Their Relationships:*

- Stupid Secrets
  Withholding important information for fear of rejection.

- Stupid Egotism
  Asking not what you can do for the relationship but only what the relationship can do for you.

- Stupid Pettiness
  Making a big deal out of the small stuff.

- Stupid Power
  Always trying to be in control.

- Stupid Priorities
  Consuming all your time and energies with work, hobbies, errands, and chores instead of focusing on your relationship.

- Stupid Happiness
  Seeking stimulation and assurance from all the wrong places to satisfy the immature need to feel good.

- Stupid Excuses
  Not being accountable for bad behavior.

- Stupid Liaisons
  Not letting go of negative attachments to friends and relatives who are damaging to your relationship.

- Stupid Mismatch
  Not knowing when to leave and cut your losses.

- Stupid Breakups
  Disconnection for all the wrong reasons.

❑ *The Best Way to Get Started with Laura Schlessinger*

To get started with Dr. Laura, just turn on your radio and tune to the *Dr. Laura Schlessinger Show.* She is known for her blunt advice about life, relationships, careers—basically anything a caller asks about. If you cannot listen to her show from your hometown, you can always listen to Dr. Laura live on her website at DrLaura.com. The site provides streaming audio while the show is broadcast live.

If you prefer to read, Dr. Laura has a wide variety of successful books on relationships and living a successful life. The "Quotes and Thoughts" section above will give you a taste of her book, *Ten Stupid Things Couples Do to Mess Up Their Relationships*.

TO READ ADDITIONAL BOOK EXCERPTS or ARTICLES or to LISTEN TO LAURA SCHLESSINGER RIGHT NOW, VISIT
http://www.selfgrowth.com/experts

❑ *Books*

- The Ten Commandments: The Significance of God's Laws in Everyday Life
- Ten Stupid Things Women Do to Mess Up Their Lives
- Ten Stupid Things Men Do to Mess Up Their Lives
- Ten Stupid Things Couples Do to Mess Up Their Relationships
- The Proper Care and Feeding of Husbands

❑ *Audio and Video Programs*

- Parenthood by Proxy: Don't Have Them If You Won't Raise Them (book or audio cassette or audio CD)
- How Could You Do That?! The Abdication of Character, Courage, and Conscience (book or audio cassette)
- But I Waaannt It! (book or audio cassette)

❑ *Other Programs and Highlights*

Dr. Laura Schlessinger has been featured on a wide variety of television programs, including *The Oprah Winfrey Show*, *A&E Biography*, and *Lifetime's Intimate Portrait*. She has also been highlighted in such publications as *Time*, *People*, and *USA Today* and has been a featured speaker on PBS and at the Museum of Radio and Television.

❑ *Contact Information*

ADDRESS: Dr. Laura Schlessinger   The Dr. Laura Schlessinger
P.O. Box 8120   Foundation
Van Nuys, CA 91409   5347 Sterling Center Dr.
Westlake Village, CA 91361
866-3MY-STUFF

PHONE: 1-800-DRLAURA
(to call Dr. Laura on the radio and ask a question)
818-461-5140
(fax number to make comments to Dr. Laura)

EMAIL: webmaster@drlaura.com
(Dr. Laura herself does not have email.)
WEBSITE: www.drlaura.com

DALE CARNEGIE
(Expert #6)

DALE CARNEGIE QUICK FACTS

Main Areas:	Public Speaking; Sales Training; Empowerment
Best-Seller:	"How to Win Friends and Influence People" (over 15 million copies sold)
Profile:	Author; Trainer; 1888-1955
Affiliation:	Dale Carnegie Training

❏ *Dale Carnegie Biography*

Dale Carnegie was a best-selling author, prominent lecturer, and sought-after counselor. Born in 1888 in Maryville, Missouri, he was devoted to public speaking from his teenage years. An aspiring actor and unsuccessful salesman, he moved to New York City and began teaching communications classes to adults at the YMCA. In 1912, the world-famous Dale Carnegie Course was born.

After serving in the army in World War I, Carnegie turned to a tour to promote his ideas about success through public speaking. In 1936, he wrote *How to Win Friends and Influence People*, which became an immediate success and one of the biggest sellers of all time. He also authored the best-seller *How to Stop Worrying and Start Living*. Over 50 million copies of Carnegie's books have been printed in 38 languages.

In demand as a lecturer and writer, Carnegie began a syndicated newspaper column, had his own daily radio show, and organized the Dale Carnegie Institute for Effective Speaking and Human Relations with branches all over the world. Carnegie was convinced that it is never too late for people to realize their full potential.

❏ *David Riklan's Favorite Dale Carnegie Quotes and Thoughts*

- You can make more friends in two months by becoming interested in other people than you can in two years by trying to get other people interested in you.

- You have it easily in your power to increase the sum total of this world's happiness now. How? By giving a few words of sincere appreciation to someone who is lonely or discouraged. Perhaps you will forget tomorrow the kind words you say today, but the recipient may cherish them over a lifetime.

- Be more concerned with your character than with your reputation. Your character is what you really are, while your reputation is merely what others think you are.

- The man who goes farthest is generally the one who is willing to do and dare. The sure-thing boat never gets far from shore.

- Are you bored with life? Then throw yourself into some work you believe in with all your heart, live for it, die for it, and you will find happiness that you had thought could never be yours.

- Remember, happiness doesn't depend upon who you are or what you have. It depends solely upon what you think.

- If you want to win friends, make it a point to remember them. If you remember my name, you pay me a subtle compliment; you indicate that I have made an impression on you. Remember my name, and you add to my feeling of importance.

❑ *The Best Way to Get Started with Dale Carnegie*

Dale Carnegie is best known for his book, *How to Win Friends and Influence People*, so this is the perfect place to get started. I believe this book defines him and is the reason that he is a household name in the Self Improvement Industry. If you haven't read it, go out and read it today. It should be a part of every Self Improvement library.

How to Win Friends and Influence People is as useful today as it was in the 1930s because Dale Carnegie had an understanding of human nature that will never be outdated. A complete industry has sprung up around it. The book emphasizes the importance of being able "to express ideas, to assume leadership, and to arouse enthusiasm among people." Carnegie also emphasizes fundamental techniques for handling people without making them feel manipulated.

If you want to gain the full Dale Carnegie experience, I would suggest contacting one of the Dale Carnegie Training offices in your area and signing up for the Dale Carnegie Course, or any other public speaking programs they offer. Through the use of public speaking, the Dale Carnegie Course teaches you how to communicate more effectively and can help you increase your confidence tremendously. Visit www.dalecarnegie.com for more information.

TO READ ADDITIONAL BOOK EXCERPTS or ARTICLES or to LISTEN
TO DALE CARNEGIE RIGHT NOW, VISIT
http://www.selfgrowth.com/experts

❑ *Books*

- How to Win Friends and Influence People
- How to Stop Worrying and Start Living: Time-Tested Methods for Conquering Worry
- The Quick and Easy Way to Effective Speaking: Modern Techniques for Dynamic Communication
- How to Develop Self-Confidence and Influence People by Public Speaking

❑ *Audio and Video Programs*

- The Dale Carnegie Leadership Mastery Course: How to Challenge Yourself and Others to Greatness
- The Sales Advantage: How to Get it, Keep it, and Sell More Than Ever

❑ *Other Programs and Highlights*

Dale Carnegie Training has helped individuals become successful professionals for nearly a century. Its courses, like The Dale Carnegie Course, enable people to move beyond their comfort zone and achieve real performance improvement. Its programs encourage interaction and participation.

❑ *Contact Information*

ADDRESS: Dale Carnegie Training
290 Motor Parkway
Hauppauge, NY 11788-5102
PHONE: 1-800-231-5800
EMAIL: customer_service@dalecarnegie.com
WEBSITE: www.dalecarnegie.com

PAULO COELHO
(Expert #7)

PAULO COELHO QUICK FACTS

Main Areas:	Inspiration; Following Your Dreams
Best-Seller:	"The Alchemist" (over 27 million copies sold)
Profile:	Author; Journalist; Songwriter
Affiliation:	Paulo Coelho Institute

❑ *Paulo Coelho Biography*

Paulo Coelho has touched millions of readers searching for their own path for understanding the world. He is the founder of the Paulo Coelho Institute, a non-profit institution that gives opportunities to the underprivileged members of Brazilian society, especially children and the elderly. Born in 1947, Paulo entered the Jesuit school of San Ignacio in Rio de Janeiro at age 7 but hated the obligatory nature of religious practice.

Paulo began to break the family rules, and his father, who took this behavior as a sign of mental illness, had him committed to a psychiatric hospital three different times. Paulo was a hippie and wrote popular song lyrics for some of Brazil's famous popular music stars. Shortly after, he worked as a journalist. He decided at age 26 that he had had enough experience of "life" and wanted to be "normal."

In 1987, a year after walking the Road to Santiago, a medieval pilgrim's route between France and Spain, Paulo wrote his first book, *The Pilgrimage*. The book describes his discovery that the extraordinary occurs in the lives of ordinary people. In 1988, Paulo wrote *The Alchemist*, a highly symbolic book that went on to sell more copies than any other book in the history of Brazil. Sales of his books have totaled almost 61 million copies in 140 countries.

❑ *David Riklan's Favorite Paulo Coelho Quotes and Thoughts*

- There is only one thing that makes a dream impossible to achieve: the fear of failure.

- At this moment, many people have stopped living. They do not become angry, nor cry out; they merely wait for time to pass. They did not accept the challenges of life, so life no longer challenges them. You are running that same risk; react, face life, but do not stop living.

- But there is suffering in life, and there are defeats. No one can avoid them. But it's better to lose some of the battles in the struggles for your dreams than to be defeated without ever knowing what you're fighting for.

- Everyday God gives us the sun and also the moment in which we have the ability to change everything that makes us unhappy. Our magic moment helps us to change and send us off in search of our dreams.

- Follow your dreams, transform your life, take the path that leads to God. Perform your miracles. Cure. Make prophecies. Listen to your guardian angel. Transform yourself. Be a warrior, and be happy as you wage the good fight. Take risks.

- Have courage, be capable of loving...Be happy in love. Be joyful in victory. Follow the dictates of your heart.

- Tell your heart that the fear of suffering is worse than the suffering itself. And that no heart has ever suffered when it goes in search of its dreams.

- You can become blind by seeing each day as a similar one. Each day is a different one; each day brings a miracle of its own. It's just a matter of paying attention to this miracle.

❑ ***The Best Way to Get Started with Paulo Coelho***

The Alchemist is one of the biggest-selling inspirational books of all times, and this it clearly the best place to get started. To begin with, *The Alchemist* is well-written, entertaining, and thought-provoking. It is a charming fable, based on simple truths about following one's dreams.

In the book, Brazilian storyteller Paulo Coehlo introduces Santiago, an Andalusian shepherd boy who dreams of a distant treasure in the Egyptian pyramids. Shortly thereafter, he leaves his home in Spain to follow his dream. During his journey, he meets many spiritual messengers, including a camel driver, a well-read Englishman, and of course, an alchemist.

Santiago learns many lessons along the way, including the true nature of the alchemists. The following dialogue between Santiago and Alchemist illustrates one of the many insights from the book:

> "My heart is afraid that it will have to suffer," the boy confides to the alchemist one night as they look up at a moonless night. "Tell your heart that the fear of suffering is worse than the suffering itself," the alchemist replies. "And that no heart

has ever suffered when it goes in search of its dreams because every second of the search is a second's encounter with God and with eternity."

The Alchemist is the type of book that many people have read over and over, and for many, it has changed their lives forever. An international best-seller for years, it has become a modern classic.

TO READ ADDITIONAL BOOK EXCERPTS or ARTICLES or to LISTEN TO PAULO COELHO RIGHT NOW, VISIT
http://www.selfgrowth.com/experts

❑ *Books*

- The Alchemist: A Fable About Following Your Dream
- The Pilgramage
- By the River Piedra, I Sat Down and Wept
- The Valkyries
- The Fifth Mountain
- Veronika Decides to Die
- Manual of the Warrior of the Light
- The Devil and Miss Prym
- Eleven Minutes

❑ *Audio and Video Programs*

- The Alchemist (on audio CD)

❑ *Other Programs and Highlights*

In July 2002, Paulo Coelho became a member of the prestigious Brazilian Academy of Letters. Paulo writes weekly journalistic columns syndicated throughout the world to several notable organizations. He has also appeared in various documentaries about his life and about various aspects of Brazilian life.

❑ *Contact Information*

EMAIL: autor@paulocoelho.com.br
WEBSITE: www.paulocoelho.com

DEEPAK CHOPRA
(Expert #8)

DEEPAK CHOPRA QUICK FACTS

Main Areas:	Spirituality; Mind-Body Medicine; Healing
Best-Seller:	"The Seven Spiritual Laws of Success" (over 2 million copies sold)
Profile:	Author; Speaker; M.D.; Endocrinologist
Affiliation:	Chopra Center for Well Being

❏ *Deepak Chopra Biography*

Dr. Deepak Chopra is a leader in the field of mind-body medicine. He created the Chopra Center for Well Being in California in 1995 and serves as its director of education. The Center, which offers training programs in mind-body medicine, is a vehicle for expanding his healing approach and integrating the best of western medicine with natural healing traditions.

Dr. Chopra is the former chief of staff at Boston Regional Medical Center and built a successful endocrinology practice in the 1980s. He realized that perfect health is more than just the absence of disease. He has discovered practical skills to ensure perfect health and total well-being that enable people to take control of their lives. In 1992, he served on the National Institutes of Health Ad Hoc Panel on Alternative Medicine.

Dr. Chopra is the author of more than 35 books, including *The Seven Spiritual Laws of Success*, and over 100 audio, video, and CD-ROM titles. He has sold more than 20 million copies of his books worldwide. Dr. Chopra is a fellow of the American College of Physicians and a member of the American Association of Clinical Endocrinologists.

❏ *David Riklan's Favorite Deepak Chopra Quotes and Thoughts*

- If you and I are having a single thought of violence or hatred against anyone in the world at this moment, we are contributing to the wounding of the world.

- Most people think that aging is irreversible and we know that there are mechanisms even in the human machinery that allow for the reversal of aging, through correction of diet, through anti-oxidants, through removal of toxins from the body, through exercise, through yoga and breathing techniques, and through meditation.

- The physical world, including our bodies, is a response of the observer. We create our bodies as we create the experience of our world.

- The way you think, the way you behave, the way you eat, can influence your life by 30 to 50 years.

- There is always one moment in childhood when the door opens and lets the future in.

- We are not victims of aging, sickness, and death. These are part of scenery, not the seer, who is immune to any form of change. This seer is the spirit, the expression of eternal being.

- You and I are essentially infinite choice-makers. In every moment of our existence, we are in that field of all possibilities where we have access to an infinity of choices.

- You believe that you live in the world, when in fact the world lives within you.

- Perfect health, pure and invincible, is the state we have lost. Regain it, and we regain a world.

- From a pure heart anything can be accomplished. If you ask what the universe is doing, it is eavesdropping on your every desire.

- Silence is the great teacher, and to learn its lessons you must pay attention to it. There is no substitute for the creative inspiration, knowledge, and stability that come from knowing how to contact your core of inner silence.

- The possibility of stepping into a higher plane is quite real for everyone. It requires no force or effort or sacrifice. It involves little more than changing our ideas about what is normal.

- In the midst of movement and chaos, keep stillness inside of you.

❑ *The Best Way to Get Started with Deepak Chopra*

Deepak Chopra has contributed considerably to teaching us about spiritual growth, the mind-body connection, and healing. His impact makes it difficult to decide how to get started. His seminars probably have the greatest impact, his books contain the greatest details, and his audio programs provide a quick, easy way to get a sense of what Dr. Chopra has to say.

Dr. Chopra has a soothing, reassuring voice that instills a sense of well-being in the listener. With all of the information that he provides, I would suggest starting with the *The Seven Spiritual Laws of Success*, in either book or audio form. In it, he discusses natural laws which govern all of creation.

Dr. Chopra teaches us that after we understand our true nature and learn to live in harmony with natural law, we can develop a better sense of good health and improved relationships. We can gain an increased energy and enthusiasm for life. These benefits will then lead us to greater material abundance.

The Seven Spiritual Laws of Success contains practical steps that we can start applying immediately to our lives. The seven laws include "The Law of Pure Potentiality," "The Law of Giving," "The Law of 'Karma' or Cause and Effect," "The Law of Least Effort," "The Law of Intention and Desire," "The Law of Detachment," and "The Law of 'Dharma' or Purpose in Life."

Some specific suggestions from Dr. Chopra include the following:

- Listen with your heart.
- Evaluate consequences of your choices.
- Take responsibility for actions, not blaming others/things.
- Give something to everyone you meet (i.e.—a compliment, a silent blessing, a gift).
- Be open to receive from others.
- Practice silent meditation.
- Commune with nature—appreciate the beauty.
- Serve others. Ask yourself, "How can I help?"

Deepak Chopra has a unique spiritual quality and a tremendous ability to teach and communicate this spirituality to others.

TO READ ADDITIONAL BOOK EXCERPTS or ARTICLES or to LISTEN TO DEEPAK CHOPRA RIGHT NOW, VISIT
http://www.selfgrowth.com/experts

❑ *Books*

- The Seven Spiritual Laws of Success: A Practical Guide to the Fulfillment of Your Dreams
- How to Know God: The Soul's Journey into the Mystery of Mysteries
- The Path to Love: Spiritual Strategies for Healing

❑ *Audio and Video Programs*

- Magical Mind, Magical Body
- Sacred Verses, Healing Sounds

- The Way of the Wizard: Twenty Spiritual Lessons for Creating the
    Life You Want

❑ *Other Programs and Highlights*

Dr. Chopra is an international presenter and keynote speaker. *Esquire* magazine named him as one of the top ten motivational speakers in the country, and in 1995, he joined four others as recipients of the Toastmasters International Top Five Outstanding Speakers award. Dr. Chopra has been a keynote speaker at several academic institutions.

❑ *Contact Information*

ADDRESS: The Chopra Center at La Costa Resort and Spa
                 2013 Costa del Mar Rd.
                 Carlsbad, CA 92009
PHONE: 888-424-6772
WEBSITE: www.chopra.com

STEPHEN COVEY
(Expert #9)

STEPHEN COVEY QUICK FACTS

Main Area:	Personal and Business Effectiveness
NY Times Best-Seller:	"The 7 Habits of Highly Effective People" (over 13 million copies sold)
Profile:	Author; Lecturer; College Professor; Leadership Mentor
Affiliation:	FranklinCovey Company

❑ *Stephen Covey Biography*

Dr. Stephen R. Covey is the co-founder and vice-chairman of FranklinCovey Company, a leading global professional services firm. He is respected internationally as an author, lecturer, teacher, and leadership mentor. His *New York Times* best-selling book, *The 7 Habits of Highly Effective People*, has sold more than 13 million copies in 36 languages, and the audio book on tape has sold over 1.5 million copies.

Dr. Covey earned his B.S. degree from the University of Utah, his M.B.A. from Harvard University, and his doctorate degree from Brigham Young University. He has served as an administrative assistant to the president of B.Y.U. and a visiting professor at the University of Utah and Belfast Technical College. He has also been an officer and board member of several corporations.

Dr. Covey teaches principle-centered living and is the founder of Covey Leadership Center. In 1997, a merger with Franklin Quest created the new Franklin-Covey Company with over 3,000 employees and $350 million in annual revenue. FranklinCovey offers learning and performance solutions to assist professionals in increasing their effectiveness in productivity, leadership, communications and sales.

❑ *David Riklan's Favorite Stephen Covey Quotes and Thoughts*

- Each of us tends to think we see things as they are, that we are objective. But this is not the case. We see the world, not as it is, but as we are—or as we are conditioned to see it.

- Effective people are not problem-minded; they're opportunity minded. They feed opportunities and starve problems.

- Without involvement, there is no commitment. Mark it down, asterisk it, circle it, underline it. No involvement, no commitment.

From *The 7 Habits of Highly Effective People:*

1. Be Proactive
"Taking initiative does not mean being pushy, obnoxious, or aggressive. It does mean recognizing our responsibility to make things happen."

2. Begin With the End in Mind
"(This habit)...is based on imagination—the ability to envision, to see the potential, to create with our minds what we cannot at present see with our eyes..."

3. Put First Things First
"Create a clear, mutual understanding of what needs to be accomplished, focusing on what, not how; results not methods. Spend time. Be patient. Visualize the desired result."

4. Think Win-Win
"Win-Win is a frame of mind that constantly seeks mutual benefit in all human interactions. Win-Win means that agreements or solutions are mutually beneficial and satisfying."

5. Seek First to Understand, Then to Be Understood
"'Seek First to Understand' involves a very deep shift in paradigm. We typically seek first to be understood. Most people do not listen with the intent to understand; they listen with the intent to reply. They're either speaking or preparing to speak. They're filtering everything through their own paradigms, reading their autobiography into other people's lives."

6. Synergize
"Synergy works; it's a correct principle. It is the crowning achievement of all the previous habits. It is effectiveness in an interdependent reality—it is teamwork, team building, the development of unity and creativity with other human beings."

7. Sharpen the Saw
"This is the habit of renewal...It circles and embodies all the other habits. It is the habit of continuous improvement...that lifts you to new levels of understanding and living each of the habits."

❑ *The Best Way to Get Started with Stephen Covey*

The 7 Habits of Highly Effective People was a popular book when it was first published in 1990, and it continues to be a business best-seller 13 years later. It is the best place to start with Stephen Covey. The book was already extremely successful when I first started reading it, and Stephen Covey was highly respected in personal and business development. Initially, I expected to read it quickly and walk away with some random, quick tips. But the book really provides detailed information to enable anyone to change their life.

The "7 Habits" are included in the "Quotes and Thoughts" section above, but the magic comes in the implementation of these habits, not in the reading of them. Dr. Covey writes about the "paradigm shift" required to truly change your life. According to Dr. Covey, you need to actually change your perception and interpretation of how your world works. His system and habits work to enhance both your personal and professional life and provide a holistic, integrated, principle-centered approach for solving problems. Bottom line—the habits work.

TO READ ADDITIONAL BOOK EXCERPTS or ARTICLES or to LISTEN TO STEPHEN COVEY RIGHT NOW, VISIT
http://www.selfgrowth.com/experts

❑ *Books*

- The 7 Habits of Highly Effective People: Powerful Lessons in Personal Change
- Principle Centered Leadership:
- The 7 Habits of Highly Effective Families

❑ *Audio and Video Programs*

- First Things First (co-authored with A. Roger Merrill and Rebecca R. Merrill) (book or audio cassette or audio CD)
- Focus: Achieving Your Highest Priorities
- Beyond the 7 Habits

❑ *Other Programs and Highlights*

Dr. Covey is the recipient of a number of awards, including the Thomas More College Medallion for continuing service to humanity and the 1994 International Entrepreneur of the Year Award. He has also received seven honorary doctorate degrees and has been recognized as one of *Time*'s 25 most influential Americans.

❑ *Contact Information*

ADDRESS: FranklinCovey
2200 W Parkway Blvd.
Salt Lake City, UT 84119

PHONE: 800-819-1812
EMAIL: comments@franklincovey.com
WEBSITE: www.franklincovey.com

ZIG ZIGLAR
(Expert #10)

<table>
<tr><td colspan="2" align="center">ZIG ZIGLAR QUICK FACTS</td></tr>
<tr><td>Main Areas:</td><td>Motivation/Inspiration; Self-Image; Goals; Empowerment</td></tr>
<tr><td>Best-Sellers:</td><td>"Over the Top"; "See You at the Top"; "Zig Ziglar's Secrets of Closing the Sale"; "Courtship After Marriage"; "Top Performance"; "Raising Positive Kids in a Negative World"</td></tr>
<tr><td>Profile:</td><td>Author; Speaker</td></tr>
<tr><td>Affiliation:</td><td>Ziglar Training Systems</td></tr>
</table>

❏ Zig Ziglar Biography

Zig Ziglar is an author and speaker who delivers powerful life improvement messages. Since 1970, he has traveled over five million miles across the world, cultivating the energy of change. Zig is the author of 23 books, including the best-seller *Over the* Top. He has written on such topics as personal growth, leadership, sales, faith, family, and success.

Zig has shared the speaking platform with United States presidents, military generals, members of Congress, governors, and other prestigious people. He has been recognized three times in the Congressional Record of the United States for his work with youth in the drug war and for his dedication to America and the free enterprise system.

His corporation, Ziglar Training Systems, offers public seminars, customized educational programs, workshops, and keynote speakers—all focused on personal and professional development. Zig has a client list that includes thousands of small and mid-sized businesses, like Fortune 500 companies, U.S. government agencies, churches, schools, and non-profit associations. The corporation has had a profound effect on the lives of many people.

❏ David Riklan's Favorite Zig Ziglar Quotes and Thoughts

- You can have everything in life you want if you will just help enough other people get what they want.

- It's your attitude, not your aptitude, that determines your altitude.

- You have to "be" before you can "do" and do before you can "have."

- You cannot climb the ladder of success dressed in the costume of failure.

- You don't pay the price for success. You enjoy the price for success.

- If you go looking for a friend, you're going to find they're very scarce. If you go out to be a friend, you'll find them everywhere.

- People often say that motivation doesn't last. Well, neither does bathing—that's why we recommend it daily.

- What you get by achieving your goals is not as important as what you become by achieving your goals.

- You cannot make it as a wandering generality. You must become a meaningful specific.

- I believe that persistent effort, supported by a character-based foundation, will enable you to get more of the things money will buy and all of the things money won't buy.

❑ *The Best Way to Get Started with Zig Ziglar*

Zig Ziglar's career in the Self Improvement Industry has spanned over 35 years, and he is clearly one of its leaders. For me, his philosophy can be summed up with the quote, "You can have everything in life you want if you will just help enough other people get what they want. " It is a belief that many people have incorporated into their lives.

To get a good sense of who Zig Ziglar is, I would suggest starting with one of his audio tape programs. One of the tapes that personally inspired me is his *Goals* tape. Zig's preacher style is ideal for anyone looking for true inspiration. He incorporates old fashioned good sense with strong Christian ethics.

One of Zig's strengths is in the sales arena. If you are a salesperson or need to sell internally to promote your business, his new book, *Selling 101*, is the best place to start. I would also recommend *See You at the Top*, an inspiring book with a straight forward approach to success. It has sold two million copies since 1975.

TO READ ADDITIONAL BOOK EXCERPTS or ARTICLES or to LISTEN TO ZIG ZIGLAR RIGHT NOW, VISIT
http://www.selfgrowth.com/experts

❑ *Books*

- Over the Top
- See You at the Top
- Zig Ziglar's Secrets of Closing the Sale
- Courtship After Marriage
- Top Performance: How to Develop Excellence in Yourself & Others
- Raising Positive Kids in a Negative World
- Selling 101: What Every Successful Sales Professional Needs to Know
- Confessions of a Happy Christian
- Success for Dummies

❑ *Audio and Video Programs*

- Goals: Setting and Achieving Them on Schedule
- 5 Steps to Successful Selling
- Success and the Self-Image
- How to Stay Motivated
- Christian Motivations for Daily Living
- Secrets of Closing the Sale
- Closes, Closes, Closes
- Strategies for Success
- Changing the Picture

❑ *Other Programs and Highlights*

Zig Ziglar's autobiography, *Zig*, was published in July 2002. In addition to the line of printed books, audio cassettes, and video tapes, Ziglar Training Systems offers the opportunity of attending workshops and seminars. To view Zig's updated schedule and to receive his free weekly e-zine, visit www.zigziglar.com.

❑ *Contact Information*

ADDRESS: Ziglar Training Systems
2009 Chenault Drive, Suite 100
Carrollton, TX 75006
PHONE: 800-527-0306
EMAIL: info@ziglartraining.com
WEBSITE: www.ziglartraining.com

WAYNE DYER
(Expert #11)

WAYNE DYER QUICK FACTS

Main Areas:	Self Esteem; Healing; Empowerment
NY Times Best-Sellers:	"Your Erroneous Zones" (over 6 million copies sold); "10 Secrets for Success and Inner Peace"
Profile:	Author; Speaker; Psychotherapist

❑ *Wayne Dyer Biography*

Wayne Dyer, Ph.D, is a psychotherapist, lecturer, and inspirational speaker on spiritual growth and personal development. He is the author of the best-selling book, *Your Erroneous Zones*. In it, he reveals how you can take charge of yourself and break free of the facets of life that act as barriers to success and happiness. Dr. Dyer has written many other Self Help classics, including the best-seller *10 Secrets for Success and Inner Peace*.

Just after he was born, his father walked away from his family. Dr. Dyer spent his childhood in orphanages and foster homes, but he sees this as the way he learned the valuable lesson of self-reliance. He has overcome many obstacles to make his dreams come true and today spends much of his time showing others how to do the same. His message is that as spiritual beings, we possess unlimited power to recreate our lives.

Dr. Dyer received his doctorate in counseling psychology from Wayne State University. When he's not traveling the globe lecturing and delivering his uplifting message, he is writing from his home in Maui. He contributes to a number of professional journals and is affectionately called the "father of motivation" by his fans.

❑ *David Riklan's Favorite Wayne Dyer Quotes and Thoughts*

- Everything you need you already have. You are complete right now. You are a whole, total person, not an apprentice person on the way to someplace else. Your completeness must be understood by you and experienced in your thoughts as your own personal reality.

- I will grow. I will become something new and grand but no grander than I now am. Just as the sky will be different in a few hours, its present perfection and completeness is not deficient, so am I presently perfect and not deficient because I will be different tomorrow. I will grow and I am not deficient.

- Go for it now. The future is promised to no one.

- Did you ever notice how difficult it is to argue with someone who is not obsessed with being right?

- People who want the most approval get the least, and people who need approval the least get the most.

- The measure of your life will not be in what you accumulate but in what you give away.

- You are always a valuable, worthwhile human being—not because anybody says so, not because you're successful, not because you make a lot of money—but because you decide to believe it and for no other reason.

- When you squeeze an orange, orange juice comes out—because that's what's inside. When you are squeezed, what comes out is what is inside.

- Love is the ability and willingness to allow those that you care for to be what they choose for themselves without any insistence that they satisfy you.

- You cannot be lonely if you like the person you're alone with.

- Your children will see what you're all about by what you live rather than what you say.

❑ *The Best Way to Get Started with Wayne Dyer*

Dr. Wayne Dyer is a legend in the Self Improvement arena and has touched millions of lives. His blockbuster book, *Your Erroneous Zones*, first published in 1976, is still hugely popular and what I believe to be the best place to start. This best-seller provides a truly profound message—avoid the trap of negative thinking and self-rejection and focus on authentic self-acceptance.

In the introduction of the book, Dr. Dyer provides a list of 25 questions designed to measure your capacity to choose happiness and fulfillment. A few of the questions in the introduction include: "Are you capable of controlling your own feelings?", "Can you accept yourself and avoid complaining?", and "Have you eliminated procrastination as a lifestyle?".

Your Erroneous Zones expands, articulates, and instructs us in each area, and the chapters are written like a counseling session, providing us with valuable tools and insights. Six million copies of the book have been sold. If you prefer listening to Dr. Dyer on tape, *Your Erroneous Zones* is also available on audio cassette.

TO READ ADDITIONAL BOOK EXCERPTS or ARTICLES or to LISTEN TO WAYNE DYER RIGHT NOW, VISIT
http://www.selfgrowth.com/experts

❑ *Books*

- Your Erroneous Zones
- Pulling Your Own Strings: Dynamic Techniques for Dealing With Other People and Living Your Life As You Choose
- Real Magic: Creating Miracles in Everyday Life
- Your Sacred Self: Making the Decision to be Free
- 10 Secrets for Success and Inner Peace
- Wisdom of the Ages: 60 Days to Enlightenment
- The Power of Intention: Learning to Co-create Your World Your Way

❑ *Audio and Video Programs*

- Meditations for Manifesting
- 101 Ways to Transform Your Life

❑ *Other Programs and Highlights*

Dr. Dyer has appeared on thousands of television and radio shows and has been interviewed in dozens of popular magazines. To view his updated schedule, visit his website at www.drwaynedyer.com.

❑ *Contact Information*

ADDRESS: Hay House, Inc.
                 P.O. Box 5100
                 Carlsbad, CA 92018-5100
PHONE: (800) 654-5126
EMAIL: info@hayhouse.com
WEBSITE: www.drwaynedyer.com
                 www.hayhouse.com

KAHLIL GIBRAN
(Expert #12)

KAHLIL GIBRAN QUICK FACTS

Main Area:	Spirituality
Best-Seller:	"The Prophet" (over 11 million copies sold)
Profile:	Author; Artist; Philosophical Essayist; Novelist; Poet; 1883-1931

❑ *Kahlil Gibran Biography*

Kahlil Gibran was a Lebanese-American philosophical essayist, novelist, mystical poet, and artist. He believed that if a sensible way of living and thinking could be found, people would have mastery over their lives. His work influenced American popular culture in the 1960s, and his style, a combination of beauty and spirituality, became known as "Gibranism."

Born in Bechari (Bsharri), Lebanon in 1883, Gibran was modeling, drawing, and writing at an early age. After coming to the United States, Gibran was introduced to F. Holland Day, a photographer, who tutored him in art and literature. In 1904, Gibran had his first art exhibition in Boston, and in 1912, he settled in New York, where he devoted himself to writing and painting. The basic subject in Gibran's art was naked human bodies, tenderly intertwined.

Gibran's early works were written in Arabic, but he wrote mostly in English from 1918 and managed to revolutionize the language of poetry in the 1920s and 30s. Gibran typically used prophetic tone to condemn the evils that tormented his homeland or threatened the humankind. After his death in 1931, the Gibran Museum was established, and in his will, he left all the royalties of his books to his native village.

❑ *David Riklan's Favorite Kahlil Gibran Quotes and Thoughts*

- Advance and never halt, for advancing is perfection. Advance and do not fear the thorns in the path, for they draw only corrupt blood.

- An eye for an eye, and the whole world would be blind.

- I have learnt silence from the talkative, toleration from the intolerant, and kindness from the unkind; yet strange, I am ungrateful to these teachers.

- If you reveal your secrets to the wind, you should not blame the wind for revealing them to the trees.

- You give but little when you give of your possessions. It is when you give of yourself that you truly give.

- To understand the heart and mind of a person, look not at what he has already achieved but at what he aspires to do.

- I prefer to be a dreamer among the humblest, with visions to be realized, than lord among those without dreams and desires.

- And forget not that the Earth delights to feel your bare feet, and the winds long to play with your hair.

❑ *The Best Way to Get Started with Kahlil Gibran*

Gibran's book, *The Prophet*, first published in 1932, has sold over 11 million copies, and this is the place to start. This beloved classic has been translated into over 20 languages. The book contains his philosophy on major concepts in human life, such as love, joy, self-knowledge, freedom, and friendship.

The emphasis of *The Prophet* is on the individual's quest for enlightenment and inner peace. The book opens up in the twelfth year, on the seventh day of Ielool, in the city of Orphalese. It begins with the story of Almustafa, a mysterious prophet who is leaving the city after spending 12 years there. Before he leaves, the people of the city ask him to share his wisdom, and the book is the wisdom that he shares.

The Prophet speaks about 26 topics in a poetic, inspiring way, sharing wisdom for the ages. Some examples of his wisdom are below:

- On Love:
  When love beckons to you follow him, though his ways are hard and steep.

- On Giving:
  You give but little when you give of your possessions. It is when you give of yourself that you truly give.

- On Talking:
  You talk when you cease to be at peace with your thoughts. And when you can no longer dwell in the solitude of your heart, you live in your lips, and sound is a diversion and a pastime.

- On Work:
  You work that you may keep pace with the Earth and the soul of the earth. For to be idle is to become a stranger unto the seasons and to step out of life's procession, that marches in majesty and proud submission towards the infinite.

- On Reason and Passion:
  Your soul is oftentimes a battlefield, upon which your reason and your judgment wage war against passion and your appetite.

The Prophet has been described as a classical treasury of mystical insight; the words of this book are inspiring, powerful, and magical. It is a gift for all of us.

TO READ ADDITIONAL BOOK EXCERPTS or ARTICLES or to LISTEN TO KAHLIL GIBRAN RIGHT NOW, VISIT
http://www.selfgrowth.com/experts

❑ **Books**

- The Prophet
- The Madman
- Sand and Foam
- The Garden of the Prophet
- The Broken Wings

❑ **Audio and Video Programs**

- The Prophet (on audio cassette)

❑ **Other Programs and Highlights**

In 1904, Gibran started to contribute articles to the Arabic-speaking émigré newspaper called *Al-Mouhajer* (The Emigrant), marking his first published written work. In 1920, he founded a society for Arab writers called "Aribitah" (the pen bond) and supported the struggle to revolutionize the classically conservative Arabic literature.

❑ **Contact Information**

(There is no official website or affiliation for Kahlil Gibran. For additional information, we recommend the email address and website listed below.)

EMAIL: mira@leb.net
WEBSITE: www.leb.net/gibran

RICK WARREN
(Expert #13)

RICK WARREN QUICK FACTS

Main Areas:	A Purpose Driven Life; Strong Christian Values
NY Times Best-Seller:	"The Purpose-Driven Life"
Profile:	Author; Pastor; Church Leader
Affiliations:	Saddleback Church in Lake Forest, California; Pastors.com

---

❑ *Rick Warren Biography*

Rick Warren is the pioneer of the Purpose-Driven paradigm for church health. He is the founding pastor of Saddleback Church in Lake Forest, California, which he and his wife began in their home with one family in 1980. Saddleback is now one of America's largest and best-known churches with 16,000 in attendance each weekend.

Warren is the best-selling author of *The New York Times* best-seller, *The Purpose-Driven Life*, which sold 7.5 million copies in its first year of print. His classic book, *The Purpose-Driven Church*, has sold over one million copies in 20 languages. It is used as a textbook in most seminaries and was named as one of the 100 Christian books that changed the 20th century. More than 300,000 pastors and church leaders from over 125 countries have attended Purpose-Driven Church seminars.

Born in San Jose, California, Warren earned a Bachelor of Arts degree from California Baptist College, a Master of Divinity from Southwestern Theological Seminary, and a Doctor of Ministry degree from Fuller Theological Seminary. He has been honored with the Biblical Preaching Award and several honorary doctorates.

❑ *David Riklan's Favorite Rick Warren Quotes and Thoughts*

- The moment you stop learning, you stop leading.

- To make the best use of your life, you must never forget two truths: first, compared with eternity, life is extremely brief; second, Earth is only a temporary residence.

- In our final moments, we all realize that relationships are what life is all about. Wisdom is learning that truth sooner rather than later.

- God, whether I get anything else done today, I want to make sure that I spend time loving you and loving other people—because that's what life is all about.

- If you don't release those who hurt you, you will begin to resemble them.

- Don't be afraid to repeat yourself. Nobody gets it the first time.

❏ *The Best Way to Get Started with Rick Warren*

The New York Times best-seller, *The Purpose-Driven Life*, is clearly the book to get started with. To get a quick sense of what Rick Warren is about, all you need to do is start with Chapter 1, entitled "It All Starts with God":

> For everything, absolutely everything, above and below, visi-ble and invisible...everything got started with him, and finds its purpose in him.
> -- Colossians 1:16 (Msg)
>
> Unless you assume a God, the question of life's purpose is meaningless.
> -- Bertrand Russell, atheist.
>
> It's not about you.
>
> The purpose of your life is far greater than your own personal fulfillment, your peace of mind, or even your happiness. It's far greater than your family, your career, or even your wildest dreams or ambitions. If you want to know why you were placed on this planet, you must begin with God.

According to Warren, Self Help books often suggest that you try to discover the meaning and purpose of your life by looking within yourself. He says that is the wrong place to start. You must begin with God, your Creator, and his reasons for creating you. You were made by God and for God, and until you understand that, life will never make sense. Warren believes that discerning and living five God-ordained purposes—worship, community, discipleship, ministry, and evangelism—is key to effective living.

The Purpose-Driven Life has been described as a "blueprint for Christian living in the 21st century." It has 40 short chapters that are intended to be read over 40 days, taking you on a personal spiritual journey. The purpose of the book is to enable you to answer life's most important question, "What on Earth am I here for?"

TO READ ADDITIONAL BOOK EXCERPTS or ARTICLES or to LISTEN
TO RICK WARREN RIGHT NOW, VISIT
http://www.selfgrowth.com/experts

❑ *Books*

- The Purpose-Driven Life: What On Earth Am I Here For?
- The Purpose-Driven Church: Growth without Compromising Your Message & Mission
- Planned for God's Pleasure: Meditations on the Purpose-Driven Life
- Answers to Life's Difficult Questions: Encouragement for Your Most Common Fears and Struggles
- The Power to Change Your Life: Exchanging Personal Mediocrity for Spiritual Significance

❑ *Audio and Video Programs*

- Songs for a Purpose-Driven Life

(All of Rick Warren's sermons and training materials are available through Pastors.com.)

❑ *Other Programs and Highlights*

Rick Warren is the founder of Pastors.com, a global Internet community that serves and mentors those in ministry worldwide. Over 110,000 pastors subscribe to Rick Warren's Ministry Toolbox, a free weekly email newsletter.

Churches across America are using "40 Days of Purpose" to revitalize their congregations. "40 Days" allows an entire congregation to go through "The Purpose-Driven Life" together, helping people discover why God placed them on Earth. More information about this life-transforming even can be found at www.purposedriven.com.

❑ *Contact Information*

ADDRESS: Pastors.com
20 Empire Drive
Lake Forest, CA 92630
PHONE: 866-829-0300
EMAIL: info@pastors.com
WEBSITE: www.purposedrivenlife.com
www.pastors.com
www.purposedriven.com

JOHN C. MAXWELL
(Expert #14)

JOHN C. MAXWELL QUICK FACTS

Main Areas:	Leadership
NY Times Best-Sellers:	"The 21 Irrefutable Laws of Leadership"; "Failing Forward"
Profile:	Author; Company Leader
Affiliations:	Maximum Impact; EQUIP

❑ *John C. Maxwell Biography*

Dr. John C. Maxwell is a cutting-edge entrepreneur, best-selling author, and dynamic speaker, who has cultivated an extensive following among the most highly respected and influential business leaders across the globe. Reaching more than 350,000 people a year through speaking engagements alone and over a million through resources, Dr. Maxwell is committed to developing leaders of excellence and integrity by providing the finest resources and training for personal and professional growth.

Maxwell's philosophy that "everything rises and falls on leadership" motivates every endeavor to help individuals reach their highest potential, both in the home office and abroad through conferences, books, and audio and video resources. His passion has quickly caught on, and countless organizations have benefited from his training and on-going support, including such renowned groups as Books-a-Million, AFLAC, Wal-Mart, Sam's Club, and many more.

Author of more than 30 books with more than 7 million copies sold, he works diligently to make leadership tools easily accessible and convenient for the busy business leader. Both a Time Warner and Thomas Nelson author, some of Maxwell's hottest titles have landed on the best-seller lists of noted publications like *The New York Times*. His book, *The 21 Irrefutable Laws of Leadership*, surpassed the 1 million shipped/sold mark early in 2003. Maxwell resides in Atlanta with his wife Margaret.

❑ *David Riklan's Favorite John C. Maxwell Quotes and Thoughts*

- A leader is one who knows the way, goes the way, and shows the way.

- The pessimist complains about the wind. The optimist expects it to change. The leader adjusts the sails.

- Leaders must be close enough to relate to others but far enough ahead to motivate them.

- Nobody cares how much you know until they know how much you care.

- The greatest mistake we make is living in constant fear that we will make one.

- The whole idea of motivation is a trap. Forget motivation. Just do it. Exercise, lose weight, test your blood sugar, or whatever. Do it without motivation. And then, guess what. After you start doing the thing, that's when the motivation comes and makes it easy for you to keep on doing it.

- Where there is no hope in the future, there is no power in the present.

- As you begin changing your thinking, start immediately to change your behavior. Begin to act the part of the person you would like to become. Take action on your behavior. Too many people want to feel, then take action. This never works.

❑ *The Best Way to Get Started with John C. Maxwell*

John C. Maxwell is world renowned for his knowledge of leadership, and his book, *The 21 Indispensable Qualities of a Leader* (published by Thomas Nelson, 1999), is clearly the place to get started. But first, let's start with a simple question: Why do some people consistently inspire others to follow their lead? According to John C. Maxwell, it is the "character qualities" they possess. In *The 21 Indispensable Qualities of a Leader*, he identifies these top traits and then defines them in ways that readers can absorb and utilize.

Each character trait is covered in a separate chapter and contains relevant quotes and anecdotes, details on its meaning, suggestions for further reflection, and exercises for improvement. In essence, John provides a mini-course in each quality. So what are the 21 indispensable qualities? They are listed below:

1. CHARACTER: Be a Piece of the Rock
2. CHARISMA: The First Impression Can Seal the Deal.
3. COMMITMENT: It Separates Doers from Dreamers.
4. COMMUNICATION: Without It You Travel Alone.
5. COMPETENCE: If You Build It, They Will Come.
6. COURAGE: One Person with Courage Is a Majority.
7. DISCERNMENT: Put an End to Unsolved Mysteries.
8. FOCUS: The Sharper It Is, the Sharper You Are.

9.   GENEROSITY: Your Candle Loses Nothing When It Lights Another.
10. INITIATIVE: You Won't Leave Home Without It.
11. LISTENING: To Connect with Their Hearts, Use Your Ears.
12. PASSION: Take This Life and Love It.
13. POSITIVE ATTITUDE: If You Believe You Can, You Can.
14. PROBLEM SOLVING: You Can't Let Your Problems Be a Problem.
15. RELATIONSHIPS: If You Get Along, They'll Go Along.
16. RESPONSIBILITY: If You Won't Carry the Ball, You Can't Lead the Team.
17. SECURITY: Competence Never Compensates for Insecurity.
18. SELF-DISCIPLINE: The First Person You Lead Is You.
19. SERVANTHOOD: To Get Ahead, Put Others First.
20. TEACHABILITY: To Keep Leading, Keep Learning.
21. VISION: You Can Seize Only What You Can.

© 1999 Thomas Nelson

The real value of the 21 indispensable qualities comes in learning how to incorporate them into your life. That is where the power of John C. Maxwell's book steps in.

TO READ ADDITIONAL BOOK EXCERPTS or ARTICLES or to LISTEN TO JOHN C. MAXWELL RIGHT NOW, VISIT
http://www.selfgrowth.com/experts

❏ *Books*

- The 21 Indispensable Qualities of a Leader: Becoming the Person Others Will Want to Follow
- The 21 Irrefutable Laws of Leadership
- Thinking for a Change: 11 Ways Highly Successful People Approach Life and Work
- Failing Forward: Turning Your Failures into Stepping Stones for Success
- Leadership 101
- Attitude 101
- There's No Such Thing as "Business" Ethics
- Running With the Giants
- The 21 Most Powerful Minutes in a Leader's Day

❏ *Audio and Video Programs*

- Learning the 17 Indisputable Laws of Teamwork
- Learning the 21 Irrefutable Laws of Leadership

- Developing The Leader Within You
- Developing The Leaders Around You
- The Five Levels of Leadership
- Becoming a Person of Influence

❑ *Other Programs and Highlights*

John C. Maxwell has a following in business, industry, professional sports, and public service. Maxwell's unique brand of coaching has proven effective for sports organizations, where he has spoken to and mentored such groups as the NCAA Coaches, Green Bay Packers, Atlanta Hawks, San Diego Padres, USC Trojans, and the Indianapolis 500 drivers. He has logged over 4 million miles traveling and thousands of hours speaking to audiences as large as 105,000 people.

❑ *Contact Information*

ADDRESS:	Maximum Impact P.O. Box 7700 Atlanta, GA 30357-0700	EQUIP P.O. Box 1808 Duluth, GA 30096
PHONE:	678-225-3100	678-225-3300
EMAIL:	webmaster@maximumimpact.com	equipinfo@iequip.org *(with no attachments)*
WEBSITE:	www.maximumimpact.com www.livingleadership.com	www.iequip.org

ROBERT KIYOSAKI
(Expert #15)

ROBERT KIYOSAKI QUICK FACTS

Main Areas:	Personal Finances; Investing
NY Times Best-Seller:	"Rich Dad, Poor Dad" (over 15 million copies sold)
Profile:	Author; Speaker; Businessman; Investor
Affiliation:	Rich Dad Organization (CASHFLOW Technologies, Inc.)

❑ *Robert Kiyosaki Biography*

Robert Kiyosaki is an investor, businessman, and best-selling author. Born and raised in Hawaii, he is a fourth-generation Japanese-American who comes from a prominent family of educators. After high school, Kiyosaki was educated in New York, and upon graduation, he joined the U.S. Marine Corps and went to Vietnam as an officer and helicopter gunship pilot.

Returning from war, Kiyosaki went to work for the Xerox Corporation. In 1977, he started a company that brought to market the first nylon and Velcro "surfer" wallets, which grew into a mega-million-dollar worldwide product. In 1985, Kiyosaki founded an international education company that taught business and investing to tens of thousands of students worldwide.

Kiyosaki retired at age 47 but continued with his love of investing. It was during his retirement that he wrote the *New York Times* best-seller, *Rich Dad, Poor Dad*. Although Kiyosaki's business is in trading and real estate, his true passion is teaching. He is a highly acclaimed speaker on financial education, and his work has inspired audiences around the globe.

❑ *David Riklan's Favorite Robert Kiyosaki Quotes and Thoughts*

- The rich don't work for money. The poor and middle class work for money. The rich have money work for them.

- The rich buy assets. The poor only have expenses. The middle class buys liabilities they think are assets.

- The primary reason people seek job security is because that is what they are taught to seek, at home, and at school....then with debt loads, they must cling even tighter to a job, or professional security, just to pay the bills.

- My rich dad taught me to focus on passive income and spend my time acquiring the assets that provided passive or long-term residual income...passive income from capital gains, dividends, residual income from business, rental income from real estate, and royalties.

- Job security is a myth...it is also risky for self-employed people in my opinion. If they get sick, injured, or die, their income is directly impacted.

- It is vitally important for parents to identify the child's native geniuses early in life, encourage those geniuses to grow strong, and protect those geniuses from a "single-genius" educational system.

- A job is really a short-term solution to a long-term problem.

- The reason so many financial advisors are called brokers is because they are often broker than you.

- Be sure to have friends who demand more of you rather than tell you why you cannot do what you want to do.

❑ *The Best Way to Get Started with Robert Kiyosaki*

There is only one place to start with Robert Kiyosaki, and that is with his book *Rich Dad, Poor Dad*. It became a *New York Times* best-seller, then the basis of seminars and a board game, and now it is truly a phenomenon. The story behind *Rich Dad, Poor Dad* is very clever. When Kiyosaki was growing up in Hawaii, he had two "dads"—a well-educated but fiscally challenged biological dad ("Poor Dad"), and the multimillionaire eighth-grade dropout father of his closest friend ("Rich Dad").

Kiyosaki watched his "poor dad" live his life with continuous monetary struggles. Yet he balanced that with the wisdom of his "rich dad," who believed "the poor and the middle class work for money [while] the rich have money work for them." The rich are different from you and me, Kiyosaki says, in that they teach their children how to be rich. By following his "rich dad's" message, Kiyosaki was able to retire before age 50.

Rich Dad, Poor Dad describes the philosophy behind his relationship with money. The book is based primarily on the principle that income-generating assets provide a healthier outcome than even the best of traditional jobs. Kiyosaki discusses concepts like investing with leverage, protecting one's investments with insurance, and taking advantage of tax laws. In the book, he teaches you how to acquire assets so that the job can eventually be discarded.

While you're reading this book, you have to ask yourself if you want to live the life of "Rich Dad" or "Poor Dad," or for that matter, "Rich Mom" or "Poor Mom." If I had to choose between being rich or poor, I would opt for being rich. I want my money working for me.

TO READ ADDITIONAL BOOK EXCERPTS or ARTICLES or to LISTEN TO ROBERT KIYOSAKI RIGHT NOW, VISIT
http://www.selfgrowth.com/experts

❑ *Books*

- Rich Dad, Poor Dad: What the Rich Teach Their Kids About Money—That the Poor and Middle Class Do Not!
- Rich Dad's Guide to Investing: What the Rich Invest in, That the Poor and the Middle Class Do Not!
- CASHFLOW Quadrant: Rich Dad's Guide to Financial Freedom

❑ *Audio and Video Programs*

- Rich Dad's Roads to Riches: 6 Steps to Becoming a Successful Real Estate Investor
- How To Increase The Income From Your Real Estate Investments
- Rich Dad's Classic Audio Books

❑ *Other Programs and Highlights*

Concerned about the growing gap between the "haves" and "have-nots," Robert Kiyosaki created the patented board game CASHFLOW 101. The game teaches individuals the same financial strategies his "rich dad" spent years teaching him. Kiyosaki has made media appearances on *The Oprah Winfrey Show* and other top national television and radio shows.

❑ *Contact Information*

PHONE: 800-308-3585
EMAIL: service@richdad.com
WEBSITE: www.richdad.com
www.richdadseminars.com

CARLOS CASTANEDA
(Expert #16)

CARLOS CASTANEDA QUICK FACTS	
Main Areas:	Reality; Viewing the World; Mysticism; Magical Passes
Best-Sellers:	"The Teachings of Don Juan" (over 10 million copies sold); "Journey to Ixtlan"; "A Separate Reality"; "The Art of Dreaming"
Profile:	Author; Anthropologist
Affiliation:	Cleargreen, Incorporated

❏ *Carlos Castaneda Biography*

Carlos Castaneda, Ph.D. was the author of *The Teachings of Don Juan* and 11 other best-selling books about his apprenticeship with don Juan Matus, a Yaqui Indian from Sonora, Mexico. Don Juan was a *nagual* or leader of a group of men and women shamans whose lineage began in ancient Mexico. Dr. Castaneda was a graduate student in anthropology at UCLA seeking a native expert on medicinal plants of the American Southwest when he met don Juan in Yuma, Arizona. His field guide became his teacher, and Castaneda's books chronicle his transformation from student to shaman apprentice.

While his initiation via hallucinogenic plants was a cultural keystone of the 60s, galvanizing the hearts and minds of a generation and spurring a breakthrough in anthropological research, Dr. Castaneda later eschewed the use of those plants, choosing alternate methods to break the boundaries of normal perception. He came to believe that one could most effectively access "separate realities" through the discipline of self-examination and physical movements he called Tensegrity.

Dr. Castaneda's readers number millions worldwide, and his books are in continuous print in 17 languages. His first book, *The Teachings of Don Juan: A Yaqui Way of Knowledge*, appeared in 1968 and was an immediate best-seller. Dr. Castaneda maintained that shamanism is an evolutionary journey of return— to the spirit, and the freedom to perceive not only the world taken for granted but everything else that is humanly possible: "the known, the unknown, and the unknowable."

❏ *David Riklan's Favorite Carlos Castaneda Quotes and Thoughts*

- To seek freedom is the only driving force I know. Freedom is to fly off into that infinity out there. Freedom is to dissolve, to lift off, to be like the flame of a candle, which, in spite of being up against the light of a billion stars, remains intact because it never pretended to be more than what it is: a mere candle. *(Art of Dreaming)*

- To be impeccable means to put your life in the line to back up your decisions and then do quite a lot more than your best to realize those decisions. *(Art of Dreaming)*

- The trick is in what one emphasizes. We either make ourselves miserable or we make ourselves strong. The amount of work is the same. *(Journey to Ixtlan)*

- A man of knowledge lives by acting, not by thinking about acting. *(Separate Reality)*

- Look at every path closely and deliberately, then ask ourselves this crucial question: Does this path have a heart? If it does, then the path is good. If it doesn't, it is of no use. *(Teachings of don Juan)*

To be angry at people means that one considers their acts to be important. It is imperative to cease to feel that way. The acts of men cannot be important enough to offset our only viable alternative: our unchangeable encounter with infinity. *(Teachings of don Juan)*

- A rule of thumb for a warrior is that he makes his decisions so carefully that nothing that may happen as a result of them can surprise him, much less drain his power. *(Tales of Power)*

- The basic difference between an ordinary man and a warrior is that a warrior takes everything as a challenge, while an ordinary man takes everything as a blessing or a curse. *(Tales of Power)*

- The most effective way to live is as a warrior. A warrior may worry and think before making any decision, but once he makes it, he goes his way, free from worries or thoughts; there will be a million other decisions still awaiting him. That's the warrior's way. *(Separate Reality)*

❑ *The Best Way to Get Started with Carlos Castaneda*

The Teachings of Don Juan, Carlos Castaneda's first book, remains a magical touchstone for millions of readers. It is a marvelous introduction to his work, setting the pace and tone for the volumes to come. I recommend it as the place to get started.

In *The Teachings of Don Juan*, Dr. Castaneda describes Don Juan's perception and mastery of the "non-ordinary reality" and how peyote and other plants sacred to the Mexican Indians were used as gateways to the mysteries of dread, clarity, and power. Dr. Castaneda uses a storytelling technique to introduce you to Don Juan's teachings and wealth of knowledge.

The Wheel of Time, written much later, is another good place to begin. It is a compendium of quotations from many of his books, with the author providing invaluable commentary from the view of a lifetime on the warrior's path. Other important sources include two books written by don Juan's female apprentices: *Being-in-Dreaming* by Florinda Donner-Grau and *The Sorcerers' Crossing* by Taisha Abelar.

The practical aspects of Carlos Castaneda's teachings are delineated in the book, *Magical Passes,* and four videos that demonstrate the physical movements he called Tensegrity (a term coined by R. Buckminster Fuller). These movements, taught to Dr. Castaneda by his own teacher, consist of an elegant tensing and relaxing of one's tendons and muscles in a way that promotes physical and energetic vitality. For more information, visit www.castaneda.com and click on "Tensegrity."

TO READ ADDITIONAL BOOK EXCERPTS or ARTICLES or to LISTEN TO CARLOS CASTANEDA RIGHT NOW, VISIT
http://www.selfgrowth.com/experts

❑ *Books*

- The Teachings of Don Juan: A Yaqui Way of Knowledge
- A Separate Reality: Further Conversations with Don Juan
- Journey to Ixtlan: The Lessons of Don Juan
- Tales of Power
- The Second Ring of Power
- The Eagle's Gift
- The Fire from Within
- The Power of Silence: Further Lessons of Don Juan
- The Art of Dreaming
- The Wheel of Time
- Magical Passes: The Practical Wisdom of the Shamans of Ancient Mexico
- The Active Side of Infinity

❑ *Audio and Video Programs*

- The Teachings of Don Juan (on audio cassette)
- A Separate Reality (on audio cassette)
- The Active Side of Infinity (on audio cassette)
- Tensegrity, Volumes 1, 2 and 3 *(video produced by Cleargreen, Inc.)*

- Magical Passes: Unbending Intent *(video produced by Cleargreen, Inc.)*

❑ *Other Programs and Highlights*

Cleargreen, Incorporated, is the organization Carlos Castaneda established in 1995 to promote seminars and workshops throughout the world. These include the teaching of Tensegrity, a series of light and focused movements that require no special equipment and can be performed by practitioners of all ages. Announcements regarding upcoming workshops and feedback from participants are continuously updated on the company's web site at www.castaneda.com.

❑ *Contact Information*

ADDRESS: Cleargreen, Incorporated
10812A Washington Blvd.
Culver City, CA 90232
PHONE: (310) 839-7150
EMAIL: Go to www.castaneda.com and click on "Contact."
WEBSITE: www.castaneda.com
(also reached by typing www.cleargreen.com)

ROBERT ALLEN
(Expert #17)

ROBERT ALLEN QUICK FACTS	
Main Areas:	Real Estate Investment; Income Building; Prosperity
NY Times Best-Sellers:	"Nothing Down"; "Multiple Streams of Income"; "The One Minute Millionaire"
Profile:	Author; Real Estate Trainer; Seminar Leader
Affiliation:	Robert Allen Institute

❑ *Robert Allen Biography*

Robert Allen is one of the most influential and recognized financial experts of all time. He is the author of several #1 *New York Times* best-selling books, three of which have become the largest selling financial books ever. His work, *Creating Wealth*, helps readers to discover the ways of financial success. Allen says the first step in creating wealth is to stop thinking poor.

Allen has helped to create a countless number of millionaires in the United States. He wants people to actually create wealth for themselves, rather than just *know* how to create it. People from around the world have recognized the truth of what Allen has written about in his books, including the essential, powerful, and simple ways everyday people can become wealthy.

Allen developed his science of real estate training back in 1981. His seminars have led thousands of new real estate investors to successful careers and have provided trainees with the strategies and tools that started a real estate revolution. He has returned with new training for our times when real estate is the best investment for everyone.

❑ *David Riklan's Favorite Robert Allen Quotes and Thoughts*

- Don't let the opinions of the average man sway you. Dream, and he thinks you're crazy. Succeed, and he thinks you're lucky. Acquire wealth, and he thinks you're greedy. Pay no attention. He simply doesn't understand.

- There is no failure. Only feedback.

- You don't drown by falling in the water. You drown by staying there.

❏ *The Best Way to Get Started with Robert Allen*

Robert Allen provided me with a challenge because he has several best-selling books, most of which would provide a great way to get started. The book that you start with should depend on your area of interest:

If you are interested in <u>real estate investing</u>, start with *Nothing Down for the 90s*. This is an update of the original classic on real estate investing called *Nothing Down*. This book and his successful program put Robert Allen on the map.

If you are interested in <u>becoming a millionaire</u>, start with *The One Minute Millionaire*. This is a new book that he wrote with Mark Victor Hansen, co-author of the *Chicken Soup for the Soul* series. *The One Minute Millionaire* provides a step-by-step guide for earning seven figures in a short period of time.

If you want to learn about <u>making money through a variety of sources</u>, Allen's book, *Multiple Streams of Income*, is the best place to start. He provides advice on everything from controlling spending to increasing savings and includes chapters on stock market and real estate investing.

If you want to learn about <u>making money on the Internet</u>, I recommend his book *Multiple Streams of Internet Income*. Allen teaches you everything you need to know to get started on the web, including website marketing, email promotion, placing ads on your web page, identifying products to sell, affiliate marketing, and much more.

Robert Allen has helped thousands of people become rich and successful by using his systems. Many of these people keep coming back for more.

TO READ ADDITIONAL BOOK EXCERPTS or ARTICLES or to LISTEN TO ROBERT ALLEN RIGHT NOW, VISIT
http://www.selfgrowth.com/experts

❏ *Books*

- Creating Wealth
- The One Minute Millionaire: The Enlightened Way to Wealth (co-authored with Mark Victor Hansen)
- Nothing Down for the 90s
- Multiple Streams of Income
- Multiple Streams of Internet Income

❑ *Audio and Video Programs*

- The One Minute Millionaire; Multiple Streams of Income (each on audio cassette or audio CD)

❑ *Other Programs and Highlights*

Robert Allen has been featured in such publications as *The Wall Street Journal*, *USA Today*, *Newsweek*, *Redbook*, *Barron's*, *People*, and *Reader's Digest*. He has also appeared on hundreds of radio and television programs nationwide, including *Good Morning America*, *Live with Regis*, and *Larry King Live*.

❑ *Contact Information*

ADDRESS: Robert Allen Institute
255 South Orange Ave.
Suite 600
Orlando, FL 32801
PHONE: 1-800-809-1281, then press 2
EMAIL: info@robertalleninstitute.com
WEBSITE: www.robertalleninstitute.com
www.oneminutemillionairechallenge.com

JOHN GRAY
(Expert #18)

JOHN GRAY QUICK FACTS

Main Areas:	Relationships; Marriage; Communication; Health
NY Times Best-Seller:	"Men Are from Mars, Women Are from Venus" (over 15 million copies sold)
Profile:	Author; Certified Family Therapist; Columnist; Editor; Speaker; Seminar Leader
Affiliations:	The Mars Venus Institute; Ask Mars Venus relationship coaching; John Gray's Mars Venus LLC; MarsVenus.com

---

❏ *John Gray Biography*

John Gray, Ph.D. is a best-selling relationship author and expert. In his book, *Men Are from Mars, Women Are from Venus*, he provides a useful and proven way for men and women to communicate better by acknowledging the differences between them. The book has been transformed into a musical comedy revue and was made into a daytime TV talk show. This and Dr. Gray's other books have sold more than 40 million copies in 43 different languages throughout the world

For over 30 years, Dr. Gray has conducted public and private seminars for thousands of people. In his books, audiotapes, and videotapes, as well as in his seminars, he inspires audiences with his practical insights and easy-to-use communication techniques that can be immediately applied to enhance relationships.

Dr. Gray is a certified family therapist, consulting editor of *The Family Journal*, a member of the Distinguished Advisory Board of the International Association of Marriage and Family Counselors, and a member of the American Counseling Association. His nationally syndicated column reaches 30 million readers in a variety of newspapers.

❏ *David Riklan's Favorite John Gray Quotes and Thoughts*

- The number one way a man can succeed in fulfilling a woman's primary love needs is through communication. By learning to listen to a woman's feelings, a man can effectively shower a woman with caring, understanding, respect, devotion, validation, and reassurance.

- A woman under stress is not immediately concerned with finding solutions to her problems but rather seeks relief by expressing herself and being understood.

- To offer a man unsolicited advice is to presume that he doesn't know what to do or that he can't do it on his own.

- One of the things that's so hard for women to understand is that there are certain differences and you can't change them. If you try to change them it will not work. And that basic difference is the man needs to be the pursuer. If you pursue a man more than he pursues you, he becomes the pursued and he loses touch with his ability to hunger for her, to want her, to be motivated to do things to get her. Men have to be driven, they have to find that there's a distance, and I have to cross over that distance. I have to get to her. I have to win her over.

❑ *The Best Way to Get Started with John Gray*

John Gray is synonymous with the *Mars Venus* series of books, tapes, and programs. To know John Gray is to start where *Mars Venus* begins and that is with the first book, *Men Are from Mars, Women Are from Venus: A Practical Guide for Improving Communication and Getting What You Want in Your Relationships*. My wife and I both read the book before we met and both gained tremendous insight into ourselves and relationships in general.

Dr. Gray often speaks in generalities or stereotypes, but more often than not, these generalities are accurate, provide insight, and can assist us in understanding relationships. An example would include how Martians (men) play Mr. Fix-It while Venusians (women) run the Home-Improvement Committee; when upset, Martians "go to their caves" (to sort things out alone) while Venusians "go to the well" (for emotional cleansing).

John Gray's audio, video, and live programs provide the added benefit of his soothing, compassionate, and sensitive demeanor. His brand of relationship counseling has spread through the Mars Venus Counseling Centers, and most recently, they added a Mars Venus telephone hotline at 866-628-8858. With this service, you can get Mars Venus relationship coaching by phone seven days a week.

TO READ ADDITIONAL BOOK EXCERPTS or ARTICLES or to LISTEN TO JOHN GRAY RIGHT NOW, VISIT
http://www.selfgrowth.com/experts

❑ *Books*

- Men are from Mars, Women are from Venus: A Practical Guide for Improving Communication and Getting What You Want in Your Relationships
- Mars and Venus on a Date
- Mars and Venus in the Bedroom
- Mars and Venus Diet and Exercise Solution: Create the Brain Chemistry of Health, Happiness, and Lasting Romance

❑ *Audio and Video Programs*

- Secrets of Successful Relationships
- Personal Success
- Positive Parenting

❑ *Other Programs and Highlights*

John Gray is a popular speaker on the national lecture circuit and often appears on television and radio programs to discuss his work. He has made guest appearances on a number of shows, including *The Oprah Winfrey Show, Good Morning America*, the *Today Show*, and *The View*. He has also been profiled in *Time, Forbes, USA Today*, and many other major publications across the United States. Dr. Gray established The Mars Venus Institute in 1996.

❑ *Contact Information*

PHONE: 888-627-7836 *(Customer service)*
               866-628-8858 *(To talk to a Mars Venus coach.)*
EMAIL: info@marsvenus.com
WEBSITE: www.marsvenus.com

IYANLA VANZANT
(Expert #19)

IYANLA VANZANT QUICK FACTS	
Main Areas:	Spirituality; Personal Growth; Love; Women's Empowerment
NY Times Best-Sellers:	"In the Meantime"; "Until Today!"; "Yesterday, I Cried"
Profile:	Author; Lecturer; Counselor; Ordained Minister; Attorney
Affiliations:	Inner Visions Worldwide Network, Inc.

❑ *Iyanla Vanzant Biography*

Iyanla Vanzant is an empowerment specialist, Spiritual Life Counselor, and ordained minister. She is the founder and president of the Inner Visions Institute for Spiritual Development in Silver Spring, Maryland and regularly conducts personal growth classes and workshops for men and women. She has built the foundation for transformation after a less-than-inspiring background.

Born in Brooklyn in the back of a taxi, Vanzant was given to her grandmother at age 2 after her mother died. A troubled childhood was followed by teen pregnancy, abusive marriages, and welfare. Yet Vanzant went on to become a practicing attorney, serving nearly four years as a public defender in Philadelphia. She earned a B.S. degree from Medgar Evers College and a J.D. degree from Queens College Law School.

While working with a group of women on public assistance and creating lectures about changing their lives, Vanzant wrote a book called, *Tapping the Power Within*, which contained basic spiritual principals, self-affirmations, and personal rituals. It became a best-seller and started a new career for her. The award-winning author of several other books, including *In the Meantime*, she assists in the empowerment of people everywhere. She married her life-long love, her husband Adeyemi Bandele, after spending many years *in the meantime*.

❑ *David Riklan's Favorite Iyanla Vanzant Quotes and Thoughts*

- Anger is a little thing. Hate is a little thing. Order is a little thing. Each of these little things has a major impact on the big picture. Right thinking, right action, and right response to the little things will help us conquer the big things, like injustice, inequality, poverty, and disorder.

Until we are each able to conquer and master the little things in our lives, the big things will remain undone.

- Challenges come so we can grow and be prepared for things we are not equipped to handle now. When we face our challenges with faith, prepared to learn, willing to make changes, and if necessary, to let go, we are demanding our power be turned on.

- Learning, understanding, or practicing spiritual disciplines will not immunize you against any of the lessons you must "grow through" in your life.

- Remember that you can trust life to give you the courage that is required to do anything or face anything. Giving up is not an option!

- The process of living encourages you to leap and to fly, to run and to soar, to meander and to piddle, to embrace and to release. What you tell yourself about your ability to do one or all of these things at any given time determines how hard life will be for you.

- Worry is the vampire that drains life of its force. Worry stagnates the mind, creates an imbalance in the immune system; weakens the throat, your power, and authority center; impairs the ability to see beyond the thing being worried about. We worry about things we cannot control. We worry about the past and future. We worry about those things we cannot do or have not done and how they will affect what we are doing right now. We worry about what we do not have, cannot get and things we have lost. Worry creates confusion, disorder, and helplessness. Then we worry because we cannot figure things out. We must eliminate the tendency to worry without worrying if it will work out. Take the situation creating the worry, briefly and concisely write it down. Place the paper on which you have written in a window, facing the sun. Make a commitment to yourself to let it go and move on. Everyone knows that when sunlight hits a vampire, it shrivels up and then it is gone.

❑ *The Best Way to Get Started with Iyanla Vanzant*

The best place to get started is with Vanzant's book, *In the Meantime*. But what exactly is the "meantime"? According to Vanzant, being "in the meantime" means being in a state of limbo. She explains, "When you are not happy where you are and you are not quite sure if you want to leave or how to leave, you are in the meantime."

In her book, Vanzant uses the metaphor of getting your house in order for getting your life in order. The chapters, including "Spring Cleaning," "Doing the Laundry," "Cleaning Out the Refrigerator," and "Let's Do a Little Dusting," are all designed to provide solid advice and inspiration, and they succeed. Vanzant helps you clean out your most destructive thoughts, clarify your vision, and define your purpose.

How can you tell if you are "in the meantime"? Vanzant says you are "in the meantime" if:

- You know what is wrong with all your ex-lovers, but you are blind to your own weaknesses.
- You are crying for no apparent reason, and you do not want anyone to know you are crying.
- You have been fired or laid off.
- You are separated or recently divorced.
- You were recently robbed or ripped off, sentenced to prison, or recently released from prison.
- You have had six dates with five different people in the last nine months.
- You haven't had any dates in the last nine months.
- You are married and share toothpaste with another person, and you are still looking for a date.
- You are not married but have been sharing toothpaste and closet space and still aren't sure this is what you want to be doing.
- You are not married, do not share toothpaste, and have given up on dating.
- Your mother keeps asking when are you going to have children.
- Your mother keeps asking when was the last time you saw your children.
- You have forgotten how children come into being.

If you fit into any of the descriptions above, then this book is for you. Iyanla Vanzant created a great life for herself and wants to help create a great life for you.

TO READ ADDITIONAL BOOK EXCERPTS or ARTICLES or to LISTEN TO IYANLA VANZANT RIGHT NOW, VISIT
http://www.selfgrowth.com/experts

❑ *Books*

- In the Meantime: Finding Yourself and the Love You Want
- Until Today! Daily Devotions for Spiritual Growth and Peace of Mind
- Yesterday, I Cried: Celebrating the Lessons of Living and Loving
- One Day My Soul Just Opened Up: 40 Days and 40 Nights Towards Spiritual Strength and Personal Growth

- Tapping the Power Within: A Path to Self-Empowerment for Black Women
- The Value in the Valley: A Black Woman's Guide Through Life's Dilemmas
- Faith in the Valley: Lessons for Women on the Journey to Peace
- Every Day I Pray: Prayers for Awakening to the Grace of Inner Communion
- The Spirit of a Man: A Vision of Transformation for Black Men and the Women Who Love Them
- Up from Here: Reclaiming the Male Spirit: A Guide to Transforming Emotions into Power and Freedom

❑ *Audio and Video Programs*

- Iyanla Live! Collection
- Acts of Faith: Meditations for People of Color
- Faith in the Valley: Lessons For Women on the Journey to Peach

❑ *Other Programs and Highlights*

Iyanla Vanzant makes regular appearances on radio and national television and has given numerous lectures at such events as African American Women on Tour, the Essence Music Festival, Howard University, and the Apollo Theater. She was the host of her own daytime talk show called *Iyanla!*.

❑ *Contact Information*

ADDRESS: Inner Visions Worldwide Network, Inc.
Inner Visions Institute for Spiritual Development
926 Philadelphia Avenue
Silver Spring, MD 20910
PHONE: (301) 608-8750
EMAIL: ivisd@innervisionsworldwide.com
WEBSITE: www.innervisionsworldwide.com

LES BROWN
(Expert #20)

LES BROWN QUICK FACTS

Main Areas:	Empowerment; Success
Profile:	Author; Motivational Speaker
Affiliation:	Les Brown Enterprises, Inc

❑ *Les Brown Biography*

Les Brown is a renowned professional speaker, author, and television personality. He delivers a high energy message that tells people how to shake off mediocrity and live up to their greatness. Born a twin and adopted at six weeks old, Les was labeled a slow learner as a child. This damaged his self-esteem to such an extent that it took years to overcome.

Les has had no formal education beyond high school, yet his passion to learn has helped him to achieve greatness. He has continued a process of unending self-education, distinguishing him as an authority on harnessing human potential. In 1986, he entered the public speaking arena on a full-time basis. In 1989, he received the National Speakers Association's highest honor, The Council of Peers Award of Excellence.

Les is the founder and CEO of Les Brown Enterprises, Inc. The company provides motivational tapes and materials, workshops, and development programs targeting individuals, companies, and organizations. Les is the former host of *The Les Brown Show*, a nationally syndicated daily TV talk show, and has written such highly acclaimed books as *Live Your Dreams*.

❑ *David Riklan's Favorite Les Brown Quotes and Thoughts*

- Shoot for the moon. Even if you miss, you will land among the stars.

- You are never too old to set another goal or to dream a new dream.

- Other people's opinion of you does not have to become your reality.

- Change is difficult but often essential to survival.

- One of the most essential things you need to do for yourself is to choose a goal that is important to you. Perfection does not exist—you can always do better and you can always grow.

- When you face your fear, most of the time you will discover that it was not really such a big threat after all. We all need some form of deeply rooted, powerful motivation—it empowers us to overcome obstacles so we can live our dreams.

- Your goals are the road maps that guide you and show you what is possible for your life.

❑ *The Best Way to Get Started with Les Brown*

When I think of Les Brown, I think of his speaking ability and the manner in which he empowers people. Les is a master communicator and motivator, and the best way to experience him is to listen to him speak. I would recommend that you get started with the *Choosing Your Future* audio set (available on CD or cassette) or the *Live Your Dreams* audio cassette.

If you're a reader, start with the *Live Your Dreams* book. Through his "Nine Principles of Life Enrichment," he stresses that anyone can succeed by "stoking the fires of hunger for a dream."

TO READ ADDITIONAL BOOK EXCERPTS or ARTICLES or to LISTEN TO LES BROWN RIGHT NOW, VISIT
http://www.selfgrowth.com/experts

❑ *Books*

- Live Your Dreams
- It's Not Over Until You Win! How to Become the Person You Always Wanted to Be-No Matter What the Obstacle
- Up Thoughts For Down Times: Encouraging Words For Getting Through Life

❑ *Audio and Video Programs*

- Choosing Your Future: Creating Your Best Tomorrow
- The Courage to Live Your Dreams
- Sell Your Way to Greatness: Keys to Exceptional Sales

❑ *Other Programs and Highlights*

Les was selected as one of the World's Top Five Speakers for 1992 by Toastmasters International. He is also the recipient of the Golden Gavel Award. In 1990, Les recorded his first in a series of speech presentations called *You Deserve*, which was awarded a Chicago-area Emmy. It became the leading fundraising program of its kind for pledges to PBS stations nationwide.

❏ *Contact Information*

ADDRESS: Les Brown Enterprises
                8700 N. Second Street, Suite 205
                Brighton, MI 48116
PHONE: 1-800-733-4226
EMAIL: speak@lesbrown.com
WEBSITE: www.lesbrown.com

LOUISE HAY
(Expert #21)

LOUISE HAY QUICK FACTS	
Main Areas:	Spiritual Development; Healing; Publishing
NY Times Best-Seller:	"You Can Heal Your Life" (over 30 million copies sold)
Profile:	Author; Lecturer; Workshop and Support Group Leader
Affiliations:	Hay House, Inc.; Hay Foundation; Louise L. Hay Charitable Fund

❏ *Louise Hay Biography*

Louise Hay is known as one of the founders of the Self Help movement and is the head of Hay House, a successful publishing company. After an unstable and impoverished childhood, she started what would become her life's work in New York City in 1970. She attended meetings at the Church of Religious Science and began training in the Ministerial Program. She became a popular speaker at the church and soon found herself counseling clients.

After several years, Louise compiled a reference guide detailing the mental causes of physical ailments and positive thought patterns for reversing illness and creating health. This compilation was the basis for her best-selling book, *Heal Your Body*, which was introduced to people in 30 different countries. She began traveling throughout the United States, lecturing and facilitating work-shops on loving ourselves and healing our lives.

Louise put her philosophies into practice when she was diagnosed with cancer. After developing an intensive program of affirmations, visualization, nutritional cleansing, and psychotherapy, she was completely healed of cancer within six months. In 1985, Louise began her famous support group, "The Hayride," with six men diagnosed with AIDS. By 1988, the group had grown to a weekly gathering of 800 people.

❏ *David Riklan's Favorite Louise Hay Quotes and Thoughts*

• See God in every person, place, and thing, and all will be well in your world.

• Love is the great miracle cure. Loving ourselves works miracles in our lives.

- We may not know how to forgive, and we may not want to forgive; but the very fact we say we are willing to forgive begins the healing practice.

- Most people are doing the best they can, given what they know and understand. Including you. If they knew more and were aware of more, they would do things differently

- Remember, you are the only person who thinks in your mind! You are the power and authority in your world.

❑ *The Best Way to Get Started with Louise Hay*

Louise's publishing company, Hay House, has been responsible for spreading Self Improvement and Self Help books far and wide. To fully appreciate Louise Hay, you must appreciate what she has accomplished with Hay House. But her personal contribution to the Self Improvement market is best illustrated by her book, *You Can Heal Your Life,* and this is the place I suggest you start.

You Can Heal Your Life has been a best-seller for many years and was recently republished with bright, beautiful illustrations. In the book, she says that "we don't have to feel impotent in the face of illness or troubles in our lives, for, by changing our thoughts, we can re-create our future." At the beginning, she provides some points of her philosophy, such as:

- Every thought we think is creating our future.
- The point of power is always in the present moment.
- The bottom line for everyone is, "I'm not good enough."
- Resentment, criticism, and guilt are the most damaging patterns.
- We must be willing to begin to learn to love ourselves.
- When we really love ourselves, everything in our life works.

You Can Heal Your Life contains insights, exercises, and information to help you grow. With the new illustrations, the book has an almost spiritual or heavenly feel about it. Toward the end, Louise shares her personal story, and after finishing, all I could think of is that I need to give this woman a hug. Hopefully, one day I'll be able to.

TO READ ADDITIONAL BOOK EXCERPTS or ARTICLES or to LISTEN TO LOUISE HAY RIGHT NOW, VISIT
http://www.selfgrowth.com/experts

❑ *Books*

- You Can Heal Your Life

- Heal Your Body: The Mental Causes for Physical Illness and the Metaphysical Way to Overcome Them
- Heal Your Body A-Z
- Inner Wisdom: Meditations for the Heart and Soul

❑ *Audio and Video Programs*

- Self-Esteem: Motivational Affirmations for Building Confidence and Recognizing Self-Worth
- 101 Power Thoughts

❑ *Other Programs and Highlights*

The Hay Foundation and the Louise L. Hay Charitable Fund are two non-profit organizations that support many diverse organizations. Louise's healing message has also been the subject of many newspapers and magazine articles. She has appeared on television around the world, and her monthly column, "Dear Louise," appears in over 50 publications in the United States and abroad.

❑ *Contact Information*

ADDRESS: Hay House, Inc.
                     P.O. Box 5100
                     Carlsbad, CA 92018-5100
PHONE: (800) 654-5126
EMAIL: info@hayhouse.com
WEBSITE: www.hayhouse.com

BRIAN TRACY
(Expert #22)

BRIAN TRACY QUICK FACTS

Main Areas:	Empowerment; Sales Training; Personal Achievement
Profile:	Author; Speaker; Trainer
Affiliation:	Brian Tracy International

❏ *Brian Tracy Biography*

Brian Tracy is an authority on the development of human potential and personal effectiveness. He is chairman and CEO of Brian Tracy International, a company specializing in the training and development of individuals and organizations. Brian addresses more than 250,000 people each year, to audiences as large as 20,000 people.

Prior to founding his company, Brian was the COO of a $265 million dollar development company. He has had successful careers in sales and marketing, investments, real estate development and syndication, importation, distribution, and management consulting. He has also conducted high level consulting assignments with several billion-dollar plus corporations in strategic planning and organizational development.

Brian speaks to corporate and public audiences on personal and professional development, discussing such topics as leadership, selling, and self-esteem. He is also a best-selling author. Brian has written more than 30 books, including *Eat That Frog!* and *Goals!*, and has written and produced more than 300 audio and video learning programs like *The Psychology of Achievement*, which has been translated into more than 20 languages.

❏ *David Riklan's Favorite Brian Tracy Quotes and Thoughts*

- All successful men and women are big dreamers. They imagine what their future could be, ideal in every respect, and then they work every day toward their distant vision, that goal or purpose.

- You have within you right now, everything you need to deal with whatever the world can throw at you.

- Successful people are always looking for opportunities to help others. Unsuccessful people are always asking, "What's in it for me?".

- Optimism is the one quality more associated with success and happiness than any other.

- I've found that luck is quite predictable. If you want more luck, take more chances. Be more active. Show up more often.

- Your incredible brain can take you from rags to riches, from loneliness to popularity, and from depression to happiness and joy—if you use it properly.

- In times of turbulence and rapid change, you must constantly be re-evaluating yourself relative to the new realities.

- Peak performance begins with your taking complete responsibility for your life and everything that happens to you.

- Every study of high-achieving men and women proves that greatness in life is only possible when you become outstanding at your chosen field.

- Personal development is your springboard to personal excellence. On-going, continuous, non-stop personal development literally assures you that there is no limit to what you can accomplish.

- No one lives long enough to learn everything they need to learn starting from scratch. To be successful, we absolutely, positively have to find people who have already paid the price to learn the things that we need to learn to achieve our goals.

- You cannot control what happens to you, but you can control your attitude toward what happens to you, and in that, you will be mastering change rather than allowing it to master you.

❑ *The Best Way to Get Started with Brian Tracy*

When I was a full-time sales rep for Hewlett Packard, I remember hearing Brian Tracy's program, *The Psychology of Selling*, and it provided me with great information in the early part of my career. Years later I came across *The Psychology of Achievement*. After listening to the first few tapes in the series, I became a true Brian Tracy fan.

If you are a salesperson, start with *The Psychology of Selling*. If you are not, I would recommend that you start with *The Psychology of Achievement*, which has sold over one million copies. It is a six-cassette or six-CD audio program with information covering a variety of areas, including effective time management and how to eliminate worry. The program will show you how to build your self-esteem, set goals, re-program your mind for success, and unlock your mental powers.

I see Brian as the consummate business professional, always thinking, always planning, and always ready to capitalize on new opportunities. When he speaks, he brings a lot of personal experience and personal success to the table. If you prefer to *read* what Brian has to say, I would suggest starting with one of his newer books, like *Goals: How to Get Everything You Want—Faster Than You Ever Thought Possible.*

TO READ ADDITIONAL BOOK EXCERPTS or ARTICLES or to LISTEN TO BRIAN TRACY RIGHT NOW, VISIT
http://www.selfgrowth.com/experts

❑ *Books*

- Goals: How to Get Everything You Want—Faster Than You Ever Thought Possible
- Eat That Frog! 21 Great Ways to Stop Procrastinating and Get More Done in Less Time
- Many Miles to Go: A Modern Parable for Business Success

❑ *Audio and Video Programs*

- The Psychology of Achievement: Develop the Top Achiever's Mindset
- The Psychology of Selling: The Art of Closing Sales
- Advanced Selling Techniques: The Proven System of Sales Ideas, Methods, and Techniques Used by Top Salespeople Everywhere

❑ *Other Programs and Highlights*

Originally from Canada, Brian started on his own "road to success" in his twenties, when he left Canada to travel across the world. His goal was to cross the Sahara Desert. Experiencing some of the most arduous conditions of his life, Brian successfully crossed the Sahara and for eight years, worked and traveled in over 80 countries on five continents. He speaks four languages.

❑ *Contact Information*

ADDRESS: Brian Tracy International
                462 Stevens Avenue, Suite 202
                Solana Beach, CA 92075
PHONE: 858-481-2977

EMAIL: briantracy@briantracy.com
mschiller@briantracy.com *(Contact Michelle for general
questions and information.)*
WEBSITE: www.briantracy.com

MITCH ALBOM
(Expert #23)

MITCH ALBOM QUICK FACTS	
Main Area:	Empowerment
NY Times Best-Seller:	"Tuesdays with Morrie" (over 5 million copies in print)
Profile:	Author; Columnist; Radio Host; Sports Commentator

❑ *Mitch Albom Biography*

Mitch Albom is a best-selling author, television commentator, newspaper columnist, and radio host. *The Mitch Albom Show*—nationally syndicated for ABC radio—combines wit, opinion, news, and music with big name interviews. A Philadelphia native, Mitch graduated from Brandeis University with a sociology degree and earned master's degrees in journalism and business administration from Columbia University.

Mitch has written several books, including *Tuesdays with Morrie*, which is not only a *New York Times* best-seller but also one in Japan, Australia, Brazil, and England. There are more than five million copies now in print. The book was made into an Emmy Award-winning television movie for ABC, produced by Oprah Winfrey and starring Jack Lemmon. The movie earned four Emmy Awards.

Mitch has also done hundreds of speaking engagements for various corporate, professional, and charitable organizations. He is a panelist on ESPN's *Sports Reporters* and for 12 years, has been named the #1 sports columnist in the nation by the Associated Press Sports Editors, the highest honor in his field. He has received more than 100 writing awards during his career.

❑ *David Riklan's Favorite Mitch Albom Quotes and Thoughts*

- The way you get meaning into your life is to devote yourself to loving others, devote yourself to your community around you, and devote yourself to creating something that gives you purpose and meaning.

- The most important thing in life is to learn how to give out love, and to let it come in.

- So many people walk around with a meaningless life. They seem half-asleep, even when they're busy doing things they think are important. This is because they're chasing the wrong things. The way you get meaning into your life is to devote yourself to loving others, devote yourself to your community around you, and devote yourself to creating something that gives you purpose and meaning.

- Here is how we are different from those wonderful plants and animals. As long as we can love each other and remember the feeling of love we had, we can die without ever really going away. All the love you created is still there. All the memories are still there. You live on in the hearts of everyone you have touched and nurtured while you were here. Death ends a life, not a relationship.

❏ *The Best Way to Get Started with Mitch Albom*

The best way to get started with Mitch Albom is to read his book, *Tuesday with Morrie*. The book is the true story about the connection between a spiritual mentor (Morrie Schwartz) and his student (Mitch). It begins by introducing an aging college professor and continues by recounting the last months of his life.

Mitch describes his old professor as a "cross between a biblical prophet and Christmas elf." Morrie was diagnosed with amyotrophic lateral sclerosis (ALS), Lou Gehrig's disease, an illness of the neurological system that had no cure. His days were numbered.

Mitch and Morrie's dialogue is the subject of this emotionally stirring book in which Morrie discusses life, regrets, aging, love, and death. He offers his wisdom through short truths that have great impact. It would be difficult not be touched by this book.

I have been asked if Mitch Albom is really a Self Improvement Expert. His wisdom and knowledge come from Morrie Schwartz. Shouldn't Morrie be the expert then? In a sense, the answer is yes, but Mitch is the one that we need to credit for spreading Morrie's wisdom. Even though Mitch is primarily a sports writer, he enabled Morrie's story and perceptions to be shared with the world.

TO READ ADDITIONAL BOOK EXCERPTS or ARTICLES or to LISTEN TO MITCH ALBOM RIGHT NOW, VISIT
http://www.selfgrowth.com/experts

❏ *Books*

- Tuesdays with Morrie: An Old Man, a Young Man, and Life's Greatest Lesson
- The Five People You Meet in Heaven
- Fab Five: Basketball, Trash Talk, and the American Dream
- Live Albom (I through IV)
- Bo

❑ *Audio and Video Programs*

- Tuesdays with Morrie (on audio cassette or audio CD)
- The Five People You Meet in Heaven (on audio cassette or audio CD)

❑ *Other Programs And Highlights*

Mitch has founded two charities in the metropolitan Detroit area: "The Dream Fund" and "A Time To Help." His sports columns appear 3-4 times per week in the *Detroit Free Press*, and his work has appeared in numerous other national and international publications, including *Sports Illustrated*, *GQ*, and *USA Today*. Mitch has been profiled by ABC, NBC, CBS, and ESPN and has twice served as a network Olympic commentator.

❑ *Contact Information*

EMAIL: Go to www.mitchalbom.com/contactus.asp
WEBSITE: www.mitchalbom.com

MARIANNE WILLIAMSON
(Expert #24)

MARIANNE WILLIAMSON QUICK FACTS

Main Areas:	Love; A Course in Miracles; Spirituality
NY Times Best-Sellers:	"A Return to Love" (over 1 million copies sold); "Everyday Grace"
Profile:	Author, Lecturer
Affiliations:	Project Angel Food; Global Renaissance Alliance

---

❏ *Marianne Williamson Biography*

Marianne Williamson is an author and lecturer of contemporary spiritual literature and philosophy. She has published eight books, four of which have been #1 *New York Times* best-sellers, including *A Return to Love*. The book reveals how you can become a miracle worker by accepting God and by the expression of love in your daily life.

Born in 1952, Williamson explored a number of careers before she started lecturing professionally in 1983. In the 1980s, she lectured on "A Course in Miracles" to small groups in Los Angeles. "A Course in Miracles" is a contemporary expression of New Thought, which she describes as "a self-study program of spiritual psychotherapy." Her talks became very popular and soon attracted a large following.

In 1989, Williamson founded Project Angel Food, a meals-on-wheels program that serves homebound people with AIDS in the L.A. area. Today, Project Angel Food serves over 1,000 people daily. She also co-founded the Global Renaissance Alliance (GRA), a worldwide network of peace activists. The mission of the GRA is to harness the power of non-violence as a social force for good.

❏ *David Riklan's Favorite Marianne Williamson Quotes and Thoughts*

- The practice of forgiveness is our most important contribution to the healing of the world.

- Miracles occur naturally as expressions of love. The real miracle is the love that inspires them. In this sense everything that comes from love is a miracle.

- Our deepest fear is not that we are inadequate. Our deepest fear is that we are powerful beyond measure.

- It is our light, not our darkness which most frightens us.

- We ask ourselves, "Who am I to be brilliant, gorgeous, talented, and fabulous?" Actually, who are you not to be?

- You are a child of God. Your playing small doesn't serve the world. There is nothing enlightened about shrinking so that other people won't feel insecure around you.

- We are born to make manifest the glory of God that is within us. It's not just in some of us; it's in everyone. And, as we let our light shine, we unconsciously give other people permission to do the same.

- As we are liberated from our own fear, our presence automatically liberates others.

❑ *The Best Way to Get Started with Marianne Williamson*

The best place to get started with Marianne Williamson is with her *New York Times* best-seller, *A Return to Love: Reflections on the Principles of "A Course in Miracles."* This book is based on the author's experiences as a teacher and lecturer on the study guide "A Course in Miracles" (Foundation for Inner Peace, 1975).

In order to understand what Marianne Williamson has done in her book, I feel it would be helpful to describe "A Course in Miracles" (ACIM). About 1.8 million copies of ACIM were sold worldwide between 1976 and 2002. The Foundation for Inner Peace describes "A Course in Miracles" as follows:

> A Course in Miracles is a complete self-study spiritual thought system. As a three-volume curriculum consisting of a text, workbook for students, and manual for teachers, it teaches that the way to universal love and peace—or remembering God— is by undoing guilt through forgiving others. The Course thus focuses on the healing of relationships and making them holy. A Course in Miracles also emphasizes that it is but one version of the universal curriculum, of which there are "many thousands." Consequently, even though the language of the Course is that of traditional Christianity, it expresses a non-sectarian, non-denominational spirituality. A Course in Miracles therefore is a universal spiritual teaching, not a religion.

Williamson writes about love, relationships, God, self-esteem, and more. In a clear and understandable manner, *A Return to Love* describes what "A Course in Miracles" is about, outlining its basic principles and ideas. *A Return to Love* has sold over a million copies and is also available in audio format.

People have said that the three-volume curriculum of "A Course in Miracles" can be difficult to get through. Williamson brings "A Course in Miracles" to a larger audience in a very readable way. According to her, the book "is about the practice of love, as a strength and not a weakness, as a daily answer to the problems that confront us. How is love a practical solution? This book is written as a guide to the miraculous application of love as a balm on every wound. Whether our psychic pain is in the area of relationships, health, career, or elsewhere, love is a potent force, the cure, the answer."

TO READ ADDITIONAL BOOK EXCERPTS or ARTICLES or to LISTEN TO MARIANNE WILLIAMSON RIGHT NOW, VISIT http://www.selfgrowth.com/experts

❑ *Books*

- A Return to Love: Reflections on the Principles of "A Course in Miracles"
- Everyday Grace: Having Hope, Finding Forgiveness, and Making Miracles
- A Woman's Worth
- Illuminata: A Return to Prayer
- Healing the Soul of America: Reclaiming Our Voices as Spiritual Citizens
- Imagine: What American Could Be in the 21st Century

❑ *Audio and Video Programs*

- Marianne Williamson Audio Collection: on Love/on Relationships/on Self-Esteem/on Success
- Marianne Williamson on Transforming Your Life
- Letting Go and Becoming: Talks on Spirituality and Modern Life

(Marianne Williamson has many other audio and video programs. To find out more, visit www.marianne.com.)

❑ *Other Programs and Highlights*

Marianne Williamson edited *Imagine: What American Could Be in the 21st Century*, a compilation of essays by some of America's most visionary thinkers. She speaks regularly at Renaissance Unity Church in Warren, Michigan, and has been a popular guest on numerous television programs such as *The Oprah Winfrey Show*, *Larry King Live*, *Good Morning America*, and *Charlie Rose*.

❏ **Contact Information**

PHONE: 313-882-9917
               313-882-9919 *(fax number)*
WEBSITE: www.marianne.com

ECKHART TOLLE
(Expert #25)

ECKHART TOLLE QUICK FACTS

Main Area: Spiritual Development
NY Times Best-Seller: "The Power of Now"
Profile: Author; Spiritual Teacher

❑ *Eckhart Tolle Biography*

Eckhart Tolle is an inspiring spiritual teacher, who travels and teaches through-out the world. He conveys a simple yet profound message that there is a way out of suffering and into peace. His practical teachings have helped thousands of people find greater fulfillment in their lives. Tolle is not aligned with any particular religion or tradition but does not exclude any.

Tolle was born in Germany and spent the first 13 years of his life there. After graduating from the University of London, he was a research scholar and super-visor at Cambridge University. When he was 29, a deep spiritual transformation virtually dissolved his old identity and radically changed the course of his life.

Tolle's next few years were devoted to integrating and understanding that trans-formation, which marked the beginning of an intense inward journey. He is the author of *The Power of Now*, a *New York Times* best-seller which has been widely recognized as one of the most influential spiritual books of our time. It has been translated into 28 languages.

❑ *David Riklan's Favorite Eckhart Tolle Quotes and Thoughts*

- You are here to enable the divine purpose of the universe to unfold. That is how important you are!

- When you are present, when your attention is fully and intensely in the Now, Being can be felt, but it can never be understood mentally. To regain awareness of Being and to abide in that state of "feeling-realization" is enlightenment.

- There's no need to seek out some other place or some other condition or situation and then do it there. Do it right here and now. Wherever you are is the place for surrender. Whatever the situation you're in, you can say "yes" to what is, and that is then the basis for all further action.

- To be identified with your mind is to be trapped in time—the compulsion to live almost exclusively through memory and anticipation. This creates an endless preoccupation with past and future and an unwillingness to honor and acknowledge the present moment and allow it to be. The compulsion arises because the past gives you an identity and the future holds the promise of salvation, of fulfillment in whatever form. Both are illusions.

❑   *The Best Way to Get Started with Eckhart Tolle*

Eckhart Tolle is known for his *New York Times* best-seller, *The Power of Now: A Guide to Spiritual Enlightenment*. His message is simple—living in the *now* is the truest path to happiness and enlightenment. *The Power of Now* is clearly the place to get started with Tolle. At first, I knew very little about him. I couldn't even pronounce his name. Then I started reading his book and was captivated after his first paragraph:

> A beggar had been sitting by the side of the road for over thirty years. One day a stranger walked by. "Spare some change?" mumbled the beggar, mechanically holding out his old baseball cap. "I have nothing to give you," said the stranger. Then he asked, "What's that you are sitting on?" "Nothing," replied the beggar. "Just an old box. I have been sitting on it for as long as I can remember." "Ever looked inside?" asked the stranger. "No," said the beggar. "What's the point? There's nothing in there." "Have a look inside," insisted the stranger. The beggar managed to pry open the lid. With astonishment, disbelief, and elation, he saw that the box was filled with gold.

> I am that stranger who has nothing to give you and who is telling you to look inside. Not inside any box, as in the parable, but somewhere even closer inside: inside yourself.

Tolle later writes: "Always say 'yes' to the present moment. What could be more futile, more insane, than to create inner resistance to something that already is? What could be more insane than to oppose life itself, which is now and always now? Surrender to what is. Say 'yes' to life—and see how life suddenly starts working for you rather than against you."

The Power of Now can be viewed as a spiritual guidebook that inspires and helps you change you life. The book's acceptance is tied into Tolle's ability to teach, clarify, and make you think. According to the author, "It's not a Buddhist book or a Christian book, but it conveys the essence of spirituality, not only conceptually, but also energetically." It is for anybody who ever wondered what it really means to "live in the now."

TO READ ADDITIONAL BOOK EXCERPTS or ARTICLES or to LISTEN
TO ECKHART TOLLE RIGHT NOW, VISIT
http://www.selfgrowth.com/experts

❑ *Books*

- The Power of Now: A Guide to Spiritual Enlightenment
- Practicing the Power of Now: Essential Teachings, Meditations, and Exercises from the Power of Now
- Stillness Speaks

❑ *Audio and Video Programs*

- Timeless Freedom
- A Guide for the Spiritual Teacher and Health Practitioner
- Touching the Eternal
- Living a Life of Inner Peace
- The Realization of Being

❑ *Other Programs and Highlights*

Eckhart Tolle is able to convey the deepest spiritual truth in clear and simple words. To view a list of his upcoming events, to find out information about attending a local group using Tolle's teachings, and to purchase any of the above audios, videos, and more, visit his website at www.eckharttolle.com.

❑ *Contact Information*

ADDRESS: Eckhart Teachings
P.O. Box 93661 Nelson Park RPO
Vancouver, B.C.
Canada V6E 4L7
PHONE: (604) 893-8500
EMAIL: eckhartteachings@telus.net
WEBSITE: www.eckharttolle.com

OG MANDINO
(Expert #26)

OG MANDINO QUICK FACTS

Main Areas:	Success; Motivation; Sales Training
NY Times Best-Seller:	"The Greatest Salesman in the World"
Profile:	Author; Speaker; Inspirational Writer; Salesman; Magazine Editor; 1923-1996
Affiliation:	The Greatest Salesman, Inc.

❑ *Og Mandino Biography*

Og Mandino was one of the most widely read inspirational and self-help authors in the world. His 14 books of wisdom, inspiration, and love have sold more than 36 million copies worldwide in 18 different languages. Og was the first recipient of the Napoleon Hill Gold Medal for literary achievement. He was also one of the most sought-after speakers in the country.

Og struggled as a life insurance salesman after World War II. Already in deep debt, his wife and daughter left him after he developed a drinking problem. Og started making visits to the public library, reading books on success and motivation. His drinking gradually subsided. Og was so impressed with the work and success philosophy of W. Clement Stone, that he got a job as a salesman at Stone's insurance company and was promoted within a year.

Og soon became editor of Stone's magazine, *Success Unlimited*. After writing a piece about golf for the magazine, a New York publisher sent him a letter about possibly publishing a book if he were to write one. *The Greatest Salesman in the World* was soon published and became a best-seller. Thousands of people have openly credited Og with saving or changing their lives.

❑ *David Riklan's Favorite Og Mandino Quotes and Thoughts*

- Always do your best. What you plant now, you will harvest later.

- All your problems, discouragements, and heartaches are, in truth, great opportunities in disguise.

- Every memorable act in the history of the world is a triumph of enthusiasm. Nothing great was ever achieved without it because it gives any challenge or any occupation, no mater how frightening or difficult, a new meaning. Without enthusiasm you are doomed to a life of mediocrity, but with it you can accomplish miracles.

www.SelfGrowth.com

- I will make love my greatest weapon and none on who I call can defend against its force. ...My love will melt all hearts liken to the sun whose rays soften the coldest day.

- Realize that true happiness lies within you. Waste no time and effort searching for peace and contentment and joy in the world outside. Remember that there is no happiness in having or in getting but only in giving. Reach out. Share. Smile. Hug. Happiness is a perfume you cannot pour on others without getting a few drops on yourself.

- Take the attitude of a student—never be too big to ask questions, never know too much to learn something new.

- Treasure the love you receive above all. It will survive long after your gold and good health have vanished.

- Work as though you would live forever, and live as though you would die today.

❑ *The Best Way to Get Started with Og Mandino*

The Greatest Salesman in the World is one of the most inspiring appealing books that I have ever read, and it is not only for salespeople. Reading this book is clearly the best way to get started with Og Mandino. First published in 1968, it remains an invaluable guide to a philosophy of salesmanship.

The Greatest Salesman in the World is written as a parable set in the time just prior to Christianity, and it integrates mythology with spirituality into a valuable message of inspiration. At the heart of the book is the story of 10 Scrolls that can empower each of us to be more successful. The title of the 10 Scrolls are listed below, but the power comes in the story and the details of the scrolls.

Scroll I.	Today I begin a new life.
Scroll II.	I will greet this day with love in my heart.
Scroll III.	I will persist until I succeed.
Scroll IV.	I am nature's greatest miracle.
Scroll V.	I will live this day as if it is my last.
Scroll VI.	Today I will be master of my emotions.
Scroll VII.	I will laugh at the world.
Scroll VIII.	Today I will multiply my value a hundredfold.
Scroll IX.	I will act now.
Scroll X.	I will seek guidance.

The Greatest Salesman in the World can be read in a day and is a great introduction to the works of Og Mandino.

[117]

TO READ ADDITIONAL BOOK EXCERPTS or ARTICLES or to LISTEN TO OG MANDINO RIGHT NOW, VISIT
http://www.selfgrowth.com/experts

❑ **Books**

- The Greatest Salesman in the World
- The Greatest Miracle in the World
- A Better Way to Live

❑ **Audio and Video Programs**

- The Greatest Secrets of Success
- Target: Success!
- Og Mandino's Keys to Success CD

❑ **Other Programs and Highlights**

As an officer in World War II, Og flew 30 bombing missions over Germany in a B-24 Liberator. In 1976, at the age of 52, he shocked the publishing industry by resigning his presidency of *Success Unlimited* magazine to devote all his time to writing and lecturing.

❑ **Contact Information**

ADDRESS: The Greatest Salesman, Inc.
                 249 W. 700 S.
                 Salt Lake City, UT 84101
PHONE: (800) 701-2394
EMAIL: info@ogmandino.com
WEBSITE: www.ogmandino.com

KEN BLANCHARD
(Expert #27)

KEN BLANCHARD QUICK FACTS

Main Area:	Business Management Training
Best-Seller:	"The One Minute Manager®"
Profile:	Author; Speaker; Business Consultant
Affiliation:	The Ken Blanchard Companies®

❏ *Ken Blanchard Biography*

Ken Blanchard is a global business consultant and sought-after author and speaker. He is characterized by friends, colleagues, and clients as one of the most powerful and insightful individuals in business today. When Ken speaks to an audience, he speaks from the heart with warmth and humor and communicates with each person as if they were alone together.

Ken is a polished storyteller with a knack for making the seemingly complex easy to understand. His best-selling book, *The One Minute Manager*, co-authored with Spencer Johnson, has sold more than 9 million copies worldwide and has been translated into more than 25 languages. The story, which demonstrates practical management techniques, is about a young man in search of world-class management skills.

Ken earned his bachelor's degree and Ph.D. from Cornell University, where he is a visiting lecturer and trustee emeritus of the board of trustees. He earned his master's degree from Colgate University. Ken is Co-Chairman and Chief Spiritual Officer of The Ken Blanchard Companies®, which energizes organizations around the world with customized training and bottom-line business strategies. Situational Leadership® II, co-developed by Ken, is the company's core management training program and is among the world's most practical, effective, and widely used leadership programs on the market today.

❏ *David Riklan's Favorite Ken Blanchard Quotes and Thoughts*

- Catch people doing things right.

- Don't wait until people do things exactly right before you praise them.

- If God had wanted us to talk more than listen, He would have given us two mouths rather than two ears.

- The fastest way to drive an employee insane is to give him or her new responsibilities and fail to provide the necessary instruction and training to do the job.

- Leadership is not something you do *to* people. It's something you do *with* people.

- The most important habit is solitude, quiet time. People who enter their day by taking 45 minutes or an hour for themselves—meditation, prayer, inspirational reading, taking a walk—before they go for it in the real world do best. Research shows that those who take care of themselves first are better listeners and can be with others in a more constructive way.

- As a manager the important thing is not what happens when you are there, but what happens when you are *not* there.

- Leaders help ordinary people achieve extraordinary results.

- The first principle of ethical power is Purpose. By purpose, I don't mean your objective or intention—something toward which you are always striving. Purpose is something bigger. It is the picture you have of yourself—the kind of person you want to be or the kind of life you want to lead.

❏ *The Best Way to Get Started with Ken Blanchard*

The quickest way to get started with Ken Blanchard is to read *The One Minute Manager*, a #1 national best-selling phenomenon. It is an easily read story that demonstrates three practical management techniques for improving management effectiveness and employee productivity. The book is short, the language is simple, and the system works.

The One Minute Manager is valuable for both employees and employers. Employees look to their bosses for praise and for the message that their work is meaningful. Bosses are concerned with performance, the work process, or any number of issues that stem from leading a team. This book helps guide everyone through the critical process of communicating objectives.

When you follow the advice in the book, you'll be able to give praise or reprimands, set goals, and do much of the work that successful management requires. *The One Minute Manager* has inspired thousands of leaders and ranks as one of the most successful management books ever published.

TO READ ADDITIONAL BOOK EXCERPTS or ARTICLES or to LISTEN TO KEN BLANCHARD RIGHT NOW, VISIT
http://www.selfgrowth.com/experts

❑ *Books*

- The One Minute Manager (co-authored with Spencer Johnson)
- Whale Done!™ The Power of Positive Relationships (co-authored with Thad Lacinak, Chuck Tompkins, and Jim Ballard)
- Raving Fans: A Revolutionary Approach to Customer Service (co-authored with Sheldon Bowles)
- The Leadership Pill (co-authored with Mark Muchnick)
- Full Steam Ahead!™
- The Servant Leader™
- The One Minute Apology™
- The Generosity Factor™
- Zap the Gaps!™

❑ *Audio and Video Programs*

- Big Bucks! How to Make Serious Money for Both You and Your Company (co-authored with Sheldon Bowles) (book or audio cassette or audio CD)
- Gung Ho! Turn on the People in Any Organization (co-authored with Sheldon Bowles) (book or audio cassette or audio CD)
- High Five! The Magic of Working Together (co-authored with Sheldon Bowles) (book or audio cassette or audio CD)

❑ *Other Programs and Highlights*

The Ken Blanchard Companies® has offices in San Diego, London, and Toronto, as well as affiliates in 21 countries to offer classroom and virtual solutions to business needs around the globe.

Ken's awards and honors for his contributions in the field of management and leadership include the Council of Peers Award of Excellence from the National Speakers Association and the Toastmaster International's Golden Gavel Award. He has been a guest on numerous national television programs, including *Good Morning America* and the *Today Show*, and has been featured in many popular publications such as *Time* and *People*.

❑ *Contact Information*

ADDRESS: The Ken Blanchard Companies
125 State Place
Escondido, CA 92029

PHONE: 800-728-6000 or 760-489-5005
EMAIL: Go to www.kenblanchard.com/contact/contact.cfm
WEBSITE: www.kenblanchard.com

L. RON HUBBARD
(Expert #28)

❏ *L. Ron Hubbard Biography*

L. Ron Hubbard is a well-known author and founder of the religion of Scientology. The Scientology philosophy is that man is an immortal spiritual being with unlimited capabilities. Scientology missions and churches have been established on six continents. After more than half a century of research into methods to better the human condition, Hubbard left a legacy that improves people's lives in numerous ways.

Hubbard's interest in education and the problems associated with it began early. Born in Tilden, Nebraska in 1911, he taught Chamorro children in Guam at age 15, utilizing unique methods he came up with. Then, while in the U.S. Navy during World War II, he trained ship crews and developed some of the techniques of pre-battle conditioning still used today.

Hubbard received worldwide attention with the publication of his book, *Dianetics: The Modern Science of Mental Health*, in 1950. The book, which marked a turning point in history, provided the first workable approach to solving the problems of the mind. It also provided the first hope that something could be done about the causes of irrational behavior—war, crime, and insanity.

❏ *David Riklan's Favorite L. Ron Hubbard Quotes and Thoughts*

- Look. See what you see, not what someone tells you that you see. What you observe is what *you* observe. Look at things and life and others directly, not through any cloud of prejudice, curtain of fear, or the interpretation of another.

- Instead of arguing with others, get them to look. The most flagrant lies can be punctured, the greatest pretenses can be exposed, the most intricate puzzles can be resolved, and the most remarkable revelations can occur, simply by gently insisting that someone look.

- There is a condition worse than blindness, and that is thinking you see something that isn't there.

- A person is either the effect of his environment or is able to have an effect upon his environment.

- Being competent means the ability to control and operate the things in the environment and the environment itself.

- A culture is only as great as its dreams, and its dreams are dreamed by artists.

❑ *The Best Way to Get Started with L. Ron Hubbard*

L. Ron Hubbard is best known for Dianetics and the Church of Scientology. The Church of Scientology has 3,700 churches, missions, and groups all over the world, and it all started with the book, *Dianetics: The Modern Science of Mental Health*. This book was first published in 1950, has sold over 20 million copies, and is clearly the place to get started.

According to L. Ron Hubbard and the book, there is a *single source* of all your problems, such as stress, unhappiness, and self-doubt. It is called the reactive mind—the hidden part of your mind that stores all painful experiences and then uses them against you. Dianetics teaches you how to get rid of the reactive mind.

In the book, Hubbard writes that the "mind is more accurately called your reactive mind, since it reacts illogically and irrationally, giving you feelings you don't understand and making you react in ways that are not you. The reactive mind is also the source of psychosomatic ills—which means illnesses which are caused by the mind. Feelings of unhappiness, uncontrollable emotions and the like are no more than the 'memory' of past painful experience being replayed by your reactive mind."

According to the book, Dianetics can tell you:

- The real reason for unexplained pains, negative emotions, and unhappy relationships in your life.

- Exactly what is destroying your belief in yourself and how Dianetics helps you get rid of it so you become more you.

Dianetics and Scientology get frequent endorsements from a variety of well-known actors, including John Travolta, Tom Cruise, and Isaac Hayes. According to Travolta, "Dianetics put me into the big time. I always had the ability to be somewhat successful, but Dianetics freed me up to the point where something really big could happen, without interference."

TO READ ADDITIONAL BOOK EXCERPTS or ARTICLES or to LISTEN TO L. RON HUBBARD RIGHT NOW, VISIT
http://www.selfgrowth.com/experts

❏ *Books*

- Dianetics: The Modern Science of Mental Health
- Dianetics: The Evolution of a Science
- Self Analysis
- Scientology: The Fundamentals of Thought
- Clear Body, Clear Mind: The Effective Purification Program
- What is Scientology?

❏ *Audio and Video Programs*

- How to Use Dianetics: A Visual Guidebook to the Human Mind
- An Introduction to Scientology

❏ *Other Programs and Highlights*

Hubbard studied engineering, mathematics, and nuclear physics at George Washington University, all disciplines that would serve him well through later philosophic inquiry. He was the first to rigorously employ Western scientific methods to the study of spiritual matters. Hubbard has described his philosophy in more than 5,000 writings, including dozens of books, and in 3,000 tape-recorded lectures.

❏ *Contact Information*

ADDRESS: Church of Scientology International
Public Affairs Information Officer
6331 Hollywood Boulevard, Suite 1200
Los Angeles, CA 90028
PHONE: (323) 960-3500
EMAIL: info@scientology.net
WEBSITE: www.lronhubbard.org
www.scientology.org

NORMAN VINCENT PEALE
(Expert #29)

NORMAN VINCENT PEALE QUICK FACTS	
Main Area:	Spirituality; Inspiration
NY Times Best-Seller:	"The Power of Positive Thinking" (over 20 million copies sold)
Profile:	Author; Pastor; Christian Psychology Pioneer; 1898-1993
Affiliation:	Guideposts magazine

❑ *Norman Vincent Peale Biography*

Dr. Norman Vincent Peale became one of the most influential clergymen in the United States during the 20th century. Ordained in the Methodist Episcopal Church in 1922, Peale served as pastor at a succession of churches before changing his affiliation to the Reformed Church in America. This enabled him to become pastor of the Marble Collegiate Church in New York City. There he gained fame for his sermons on a positive approach to modern living.

Born in 1898, Peale confessed that as a youth he had an inferiority complex and developed his philosophy of positive thinking just to help himself. In 1937, Peale established a clinic with Freudian psychiatrist Dr. Smiley Blanton in the basement of the Marble Collegiate Church, which grew to an operation with more than 20 psychiatric doctors and psychologically-trained ministers. In 1972, it became the Institute of Religion and Health (IRH).

Peale remained affiliated with the IRH as board president and chief fund raiser until his death in 1993. He was awarded the Presidential Medal of Freedom by Ronald Reagan in 1984 and has also published several best-selling books, including *The Power of Positive Thinking*, which has sold more than 20 million copies. Peale pioneered Christian Psychology and in 1945, founded the Foundation for Christian Living with his wife, Ruth.

❑ *David Riklan's Favorite Norman Vincent Peale Quotes and Thoughts*

- Become a possibilitarian. No matter how dark things seem to be or actually are, raise your sights and see possibilities—always see them, for they're always there.

- Believe it is possible to solve your problem. Tremendous things happen to the believer. So believe the answer will come. It will.

- Formulate and stamp indelibly on your mind a mental picture of yourself as succeeding. Hold this picture tenaciously. Never permit it to fade. Your mind will seek to develop the picture...Do not build up obstacles in your imagination.

- People become really quite remarkable when they start thinking that they can do things. When they believe in themselves they have the first secret of success.

- There is a real magic in enthusiasm. It spells the difference between mediocrity and accomplishment.

- Your enthusiasm will be infectious, stimulating, and attractive to others. They will love you for it. They will go for you and with you.

- Part of the happiness of life consists not in fighting battles but in avoiding them. A masterly retreat is in itself a victory.

- Action is a great restorer and builder of confidence. Inaction is not only the result, but the cause, of fear. Perhaps the action you take will be successful; perhaps different action or adjustments will have to follow. But any action is better than no action at all.

- Empty pockets never held anyone back. Only empty heads and empty hearts can do that.

❑ *The Best Way to Get Started with Norman Vincent Peale*

Dr. Norman Vincent Peale's book, *The Power of Positive Thinking*, still has a tremendous impact on millions of people's lives and is clearly the place to get started. Peale says:

> "The purpose of this book is a very direct and simple one. It makes no pretense to literary excellence nor does it seek to demonstrate any unusual scholarship on my part. This is simply a practical, direct-action, personal-improvement manual. It is written with the sole objective of helping the reader achieve a happy, satisfying, and worthwhile life."

Was Peale successful in satisfying the book's purpose? My answer is an enthusiastic yes.

In the first chapter, he outlines ten simple rules for overcoming inadequacy attitudes. To give you a sense of what Peale has to say, I have included Rule # 1 below:

Formulate and stamp indelibly on your mind a mental picture of yourself as succeeding. Hold this picture tenaciously. Never permit it to fade. Your mind will seek to develop this picture. Never think of yourself as failing; never doubt the reality of the mental image. That is most dangerous, for the mind always tries to complete what it pictures. So always picture "success," no matter how badly things seem to be going at the moment.

I have been asked if *The Power of Positive Thinking* is only for Christians. Though Christianity and the Bible are important parts of this book, I believe that almost anybody can benefit from reading it.

TO READ ADDITIONAL BOOK EXCERPTS or ARTICLES or to LISTEN TO NORMAN VINCENT PEALE RIGHT NOW, VISIT
http://www.selfgrowth.com/experts

❏ *Books*

- The Power of Positive Thinking
- Guide to Confident Living
- Positive Imaging
- The Tough-Minded Optimist
- Stay Alive All Your Life
- The Amazing Results of Positive Thinking
- The True Joy of Positive Living
- The New Art of Living

❏ *Audio and Video Programs*

- Positive Thinking: The Norman Vincent Peale Story
- The Power of Positive Thinking (on audio cassette or audio CD)
- www.guideposts.org/PositiveThinking *(web-based audio, video, and text)*

❏ *Other Programs And Highlights*

For 54 years, Peale's weekly radio program, *The Art of Living*, was broadcast on NBC. His sermons were mailed to 750,000 people a month, and his life was the subject of a 1964 movie called *One Man's Way*. Peale and his wife started *Guideposts* magazine in 1945. Its circulation now tops three million, the largest of any inspirational magazine in America.

❏ *Contact Information*

ADDRESS:	Peale Center
	66 East Main Street
	Pawling, NY 12564
PHONE:	845-855-5000
WEBSITE:	www.guideposts.org

DAVE PELZER
(Expert #30)

DAVE PELZER QUICK FACTS

Main Areas:	Empowerment; Survival
NY Times Best-Sellers:	"A Child Called 'It'"; "Help Yourself,"; "A Man Named Dave,"; "The Lost Boy"
Profile:	Author; Speaker

❑ *Dave Pelzer Biography*

Dave Pelzer is a best-selling author and presenter who helps others to help themselves. As a child, he was severely abused, mentally and physically tortured, and at the point of starvation. At age 12, his teachers notified the authorities and saved his life. Dave was placed in foster care until he enlisted in the U.S. Air Force at age 18. He was determined to better himself.

Today, Dave pays homage to those who make a difference in children's lives, such as educators, social services, and law enforcement. He travels over 250 days of the year and offers programs for youth-at-risk, corporate groups, and human services. His wit and unique outlook on life encourage people to overcome any obstacle. Dave's life is proof that it can be done.

Two of his books, *A Child Called "It"* and *Help Yourself*, have been nominated for the Pulitzer Prize. Four of his books have appeared simultaneously on the *New York Times* best-sellers list. Dave has also received personal commendations from Presidents Ronald Reagan, George H.W. Bush, Bill Clinton, and George W. Bush. He was the recipient of J.C. Penney Golden Rule Award in 1990, making him the California Volunteer of the Year.

❑ *David Riklan's Favorite Dave Pelzer Quotes and Thoughts*

- All those years you tried your best to break me, and I'm still here. I make mistakes, I screw up, but I learn. I don't blame others for my problems. I stand on my own. And you'll see. I'm going to make something of myself.

- Hate is a cancer that spreads one cell at a time.

- I believe it is important for people to know that no matter what lies in their past, they can overcome the dark side and press on to a brighter world.

- Childhood should be carefree, playing in the sun, not living a nightmare in the darkness of the soul.

- It is perhaps a paradox that without the abuse of my past, I might not be what I am today. Because of the darkness in my childhood, I have a deep appreciation for life. I was fortunate enough to turn tragedy into triumph.

- I'm so blessed. The challenges of my past have made me immensely strong inside. I adapted quickly, learning how to survive from a bad situation. I learned the secret of internal motivation. My experience gave me a different outlook on life, that others may never know. I have a vast appreciation for things that others may take for granted.

❑ *The Best Way to Get Started with Dave Pelzer*

The best way to get started with Dave Pelzer is to read *A Child Called "It*," the first in a trilogy about Dave's life. Dave grew up with horrific abuse and torment; his mother was an alcoholic and emotionally unstable. The book begins by recounting his life of desperation and then goes on to explain how he overcame such great obstacles. *A Child Called "It"* has been described as the story of the triumph of the human spirit.

Dave was involved in "one of the most severe child abuse cases in California history." In *A Child Called "It,"* you experience the atrocities of his upbringing, but you also get to experience the strength of his inner desire to survive. This book has touched millions of people, and after reading only a few pages, it is easy to see why. The subsequent books in the trilogy are *The Lost Boy* and *A Man Name Dave*.

TO READ ADDITIONAL BOOK EXCERPTS or ARTICLES or to LISTEN TO DAVE PELZER RIGHT NOW, VISIT
http://www.selfgrowth.com/experts

❑ *Books*

- A Child Called "It": One Child's Courage to Survive
- The Lost Boy: A Foster Child's Search for the Love of a Family
- A Man Named Dave: A Story of Triumph and Forgiveness
- Help Yourself: Finding Hope, Courage, and Happiness
- Privilege of Youth *(due out in January 2004)*

❑ *Audio and Video Programs*

- A Child Called "It"; The Lost Boy; A Man Named Dave; Help Yourself (each on audio cassette)

- Most Important Person (Video) *(Jr. High to High School Age)*

❑ *Other Programs and Highlights*

Dave's life story has been featured on such TV shows as *The Oprah Winfrey Show* and *The Montel Williams Show*. In 1993, he was honored as one of the Ten Outstanding Young Americans, and one year later, he was the only American to be honored as one of the Outstanding Young Persons of the World. As a member of the armed forces, Dave was hand-picked to mid-air refuel the highly secretive SR-71 Blackbird and the F-117 Stealth Fighter.

❑ *Contact Information*

ADDRESS: P.O. Box 1846
                      Rancho Mirage, CA 92270
PHONE: 760-321-4452
WEBSITE: davepelzer.com

NAPOLEON HILL
(Expert #31)

<table>
<tr><td colspan="2">NAPOLEON HILL QUICK FACTS</td></tr>
<tr><td>Main Area:</td><td>Success</td></tr>
<tr><td>NY Times Best-Seller:</td><td>"Think and Grow Rich"</td></tr>
<tr><td>Profile:</td><td>Author; Speaker; Motivational Writer; Teacher;
Lecturer; Journalist; 1883-1970</td></tr>
</table>

❏ Napoleon Hill Biography

Napoleon Hill was one of the most influential people in the area of personal success. Born into poverty in 1883 in Wise County, Virginia, he became a beloved motivational author, teacher, and lecturer. Hill dedicated more than 25 years of his life to define the reasons by which so many people fail to achieve true financial success and happiness in their lives.

Hill began his writing career at age 13 as a mountain reporter for small town newspapers and later achieved great success as an author and journalist. His early career as a reporter helped Hill to finance his higher education. In this position, he was given an assignment to write a series of success stories of famous men and was asked to interview steel-magnate Andrew Carnegie.

Carnegie challenged Hill to interview over 500 millionaires to find a success formula that could be understood and used by the average person. Hill accepted the challenge and formulated a philosophy of success, drawing on the thoughts and experiences of a multitude of rags-to-riches tycoons. The book, *Think and Grow Rich,* took over 20 years to produce but has sold over 26 million copies internationally.

❏ David Riklan's Favorite Napoleon Hill Quotes and Thoughts

- Every adversity, every failure, and every heartache carries with it the Seed of an equivalent or a greater Benefit.

- Desire is the starting point of all achievement, not a hope, not a wish, but a keen pulsating desire which transcends everything.

- There are no limitations to the mind except those we acknowledge

- Both poverty and riches are the offspring of thought.

- A positive mental attitude is an irresistible force that knows no such thing as an immovable body.

- Success in highest and noblest form calls for peace of mind and enjoyment and happiness which comes only to the man who has found the work he likes best.

- What the mind of man can conceive and believe, it can achieve.

- When defeat comes, accept it as a signal that your plans are not sound, rebuild those plans, and set sail once more toward your coveted goal.

- Self-discipline begins with the mastery of your thoughts. If you don't control what you think, you can't control what you do. Simply, self-discipline enables you to think first and act afterward.

- No man ever achieved worthwhile success, who did not at one time or another find himself with at least one foot hanging well over the brink of failure.

- Victory is always possible for the person who refuses to stop fighting.

- Until you have learned to be tolerant with those who do not always agree with you; until you have cultivated the habit of saying some kind word of those whom you do not admire; until you have formed the habit of looking for the good instead of the bad there is in others, you will be neither successful nor happy.

- The starting point of all achievement is desire. Keep this constantly in mind. Weak desire brings weak results, just as a small amount of fire makes a small amount of heat.

- Patience, persistence, and perspiration make an unbeatable combination for success.

- If the winds of fortune are temporarily blowing against you, remember that you can harness them and make them carry you toward your definite purpose, through the use of your imagination.

- Cherish your visions and your dreams as they are the children of your soul, the blueprints of your ultimate achievements.

- There is one quality which one must possess to win, and that is definiteness of purpose, the knowledge of what one wants, and a burning desire to possess it.

- Do not wait; the time will never be "just right." Start where you stand, and work with whatever tools you may have at your command, and better tools will be found as you go along.

❏ *The Best Way to Get Started with Napoleon Hill*

The best place to get started with Napoleon Hill is to read *Think and Grow Rich*. The story for the creation of the book is almost as interesting as the book itself. In 1908, Hill had the opportunity to interview the American industrialist, Andrew Carnegie. According to the story, Hill had arranged for a three-hour interview, which turned into three days during which Carnegie sold Hill on organizing what would become *Think and Grow Rich*.

Throughout the book, Hill provides insights into some of the most successful people of his time, including Alexander Graham Bell, Thomas Edison, George Eastman, John D. Rockefeller, Charles Schwab, and Woodrow Wilson. He also provides insight into the principles of success that they used. One example of these principles can be found in Dr. Hill's "Six Steps of Desire":

1. Fix in your mind the exact amount of money you desire. It is not sufficient to say "I want plenty of money." Be definite as to the amount.

2. Determine exactly what you intend to give in return for the money you desire (there is no such thing as "something for nothing").

3. Establish a definite date when you intend to possess the money you desire.

4. Create a definite plan for carrying out your desire, and begin at once, whether you are ready or not, to put this plan into action.

5. Write out a clear, concise statement of the amount of money you intend to acquire, name the time limit for its acquisition, state what you intend to give in return for the money, and describe clearly the plan through which you intend to accumulate it.

6. Read your written statement aloud, twice daily, once just before retiring at night, and once after arising in the morning. As you read—see and feel and believe yourself already in the possession of the money.

The above six steps are a small part of the countless ideas in this book, which is not only a best-seller but also a classic in the Self Improvement and Success arena.

TO READ ADDITIONAL BOOK EXCERPTS or ARTICLES or to LISTEN
TO NAPOLEON HILL RIGHT NOW, VISIT
http://www.selfgrowth.com/experts

❏ **Books**

- Law of Success
- The Magic Ladder of Success
- Think and Grow Rich
- How to Sell Your Way Through Life
- Mental Dynamite
- The Master Key to Riches
- How to Raise Your Own Salary
- Success through A Positive Mental Attitude
- PMA Science of Success Course
- Grow Rich! With Peace of Mind
- Succeed and Grow Rich Through Persuasion
- You Can Work Your Own Miracles
- Believe and Achieve with W. Clement Stone
- The Success System That Never Fails (by W. Clement Stone)

❏ **Audio and Video Programs**

- Selling You! A Practical Guide to Achieving the Most by Becoming Your Best
- The Principles of Self-Mastery
- Master Key to Success (video series)
- Think and Grow Rich (on audio cassette and audio CD)

❏ **Other Programs and Highlights**

In recent years, the Napoleon Hill Foundation has published Hill's best-selling writings. It is the Foundation's goal to have new editions of all of Dr. Hill's works in print by 2005. Dr. Hill established the Foundation as a non-profit educational institution whose mission is to perpetuate his philosophy of leadership, self-motivation, and individual achievement worldwide. The Foundation's mission includes both educational programs and correctional programs. Corporate seminars are conducted for groups as well. The Napoleon Hill Foundation is dedicated to making this world a better place in which to live.

The Napoleon Hill World Learning Center is the educational component of the Napoleon Hill Foundation. Located just minutes from downtown Chicago in Hammond, Indiana, the Napoleon Hill World Learning Center provides educational opportunities for students of Napoleon Hill's Philosophy of Success. Established with a $1 million grant from the Foundation, the Learning Center's mission parallels the mission of the Foundation.

❏ *Contact Information*

ADDRESS: *Judith Williamson, Director* *Don Green, Executive Director*
Napoleon Hill® World The Napoleon Hill®
Learning Center Foundation
2300 173rd Street P.O. Box 1277
Hammond, IN 46323 Wise, VA 24293

PHONE: 219-989-3173 or 219-989-3166
EMAIL: nhf@calumet.purdue.edu
WEBSITE: www.naphill.org

CAROLINE MYSS
(Expert #32)

CAROLINE MYSS QUICK FACTS	
Main Areas:	Spirituality; Healing; Personal Power
NY Times Best-Sellers:	"Anatomy of the Spirit"; "Why People Don't Heal and How They Can"; "Sacred Contracts"
Profile:	Author; Lecturer; Teacher; Theologian
Affiliations:	Caroline Myss Education Institute; Caroline's Shop/Myss.com

❑ *Caroline Myss Biography*

Caroline Myss, Ph.D., is a sought-after speaker on spirituality and personal power. She is recognized for her work in teaching intuitive diagnosis and is a pioneer in the field of energy medicine. Raised Catholic in the Chicago area, she graduated from St. Mary of the Woods College in Indiana and then pursued a career in journalism.

As a freelance writer, Dr. Myss attended a seminar of Elisabeth Kubler-Ross and was thrown into a "crisis of meaning." This inspired her to attend Mundelein College and receive her master's degree in theology. Dr. Myss started the Stillpoint Publishing Company in New Hampshire, where, for the first time, she acknowledged her medical intuitive abilities.

Dr. Myss began working with holistic doctors and co-wrote the book, *The Creation of Health*, with C. Norman Shealy, M.D. She also started creating audiotapes and lecturing around the world. In 1996, her book, *Anatomy of the Spirit* was published and became a *New York Times* best-seller. She has written other best-sellers since.

❑ *David Riklan's Favorite Caroline Myss Quotes and Thoughts*

- I firmly believe that intuitive or symbolic sight is not a gift but a skill— a skill based in self-esteem.

- By far the strongest poison to the human spirit is the inability to forgive oneself or another person. Forgiveness is no longer an option but a necessity for healing.

- Do you really want to look back on your life and see how wonderful it could have been had you not been afraid to live it?

- Intuition is neither the ability to engage prophecy nor a means of avoiding financial loss or painful relationships. It is actually the ability to use energy data to make decisions in the immediate moment.

- The forgiving heart is capable of anything. I believe that deeply. And that's where in terms of becoming an empowered individual...when you get to the point where you realize you can look at someone and say "I love myself enough—not in a schmaltzy garbage sense, Hallmark stuff, I'm talking respect myself—I respect my life-force enough to no longer waste it."

- We grow primarily through our challenges, especially those life-changing moments when we begin to recognize aspects of our nature that make us different from the family and culture in which we have been raised.

- When I look at someone's face, I look beyond that face and into the cellular memory in my heart that says, "Finally you and I have met again. And now we must find out why."

❑ *The Best Way to Get Started with Caroline Myss*

Anatomy of the Spirit was Caroline Myss's first best-seller, and it is the best place to get started. Her book shows the direct link between our emotional/spiritual stresses and specific illnesses in our bodies. Her system of energy medicine teaches you the specific psychological, physical, and emotional factors that lie at the root of illness.

In her book, Dr. Myss presents a complete program for spiritual growth. She says that as you begin to understand the "anatomy of your spirit," you will not only discover the spiritual causes of illness but also how to sense and correct an energy imbalance before it expresses itself as illness. *Anatomy of the Spirit* will also show you how to recover, both physically and emotionally, from an illness you may already have.

The book presents Dr. Myss's model of the body's seven centers of spiritual and physical power. In her model, she has integrated ancient wisdom of three spiritual traditions—the Hindu chakras, the Christian sacraments, and the Kabbalah's Tree of Life. In the excerpt below, she describes Energy Medicine and The Human Energy Field:

> Energy Medicine and Intuition
> I disappoint some people when I discuss intuition because I
> firmly believe that intuitive or symbolic sight is not a gift but
> a skill, a skill based in self-esteem. Developing this skill and
> a healthy sense of self becomes easier when you can think in

the words, concepts, and principles of energy medicine. So as you read this chapter, think of learning to use intuition as learning to interpret the language of energy.

The Human Energy Field
Everything that is alive pulsates with energy, and all of this energy contains information. While it is not surprising that practitioners of alternative or complementary medicine accept this concept, even some quantum physicists acknowledge the existence of an electromagnetic field generated by the body's biological processes. Scientists accept that the human body generates electricity because living tissue generates energy.

The best way to get a sense of Caroline's beliefs is directly from her book. *Anatomy of the Spirit* is certainly a valuable contribution to the ongoing exploration of spirituality and health.

TO READ ADDITIONAL BOOK EXCERPTS or ARTICLES or to LISTEN TO CAROLINE MYSS RIGHT NOW, VISIT
http://www.selfgrowth.com/experts

❑ *Books*

- Anatomy of the Spirit: The Seven Stages of Power and Healing
- Why People Don't Heal and How They Can
- Sacred Contacts: Awakening Your Divine Potential
- The Creation of Health: The Emotional, Psychological, and Spiritual Responses That Promote Health and Healing (co-authored with C. Norman Shealy, M.D.)

❑ *Audio and Video Programs*

- Self-Esteem: Your Fundamental Power
- Finding Your Sacred Contract: Live Workshop
- The Call to Live a Symbolic Life

❑ *Other Programs and Highlights*

Caroline Myss has appeared on *The Oprah Winfrey Show* and was formerly a columnist at *New Age Journal* and *Healthy Living Magazine*. She had a show on the Oxygen Network called *The Journey with Caroline Myss*. She is the founder and director of the Caroline Myss Education Institute and also co-founder and director of The Language of Intuition Program and the Institute for the Science of Medical Intuition.

❏ *Contact Information*

(Contact David Smith, online business manager, for questions, comments, or information on the Caroline Myss Education Institute.)

ADDRESS:	Caroline's Shop/Myss.com 141 Gooding Street La Salle, IL 61301	David Smith Online Office of Caroline Myss 1004 Brittany Road Highland Park, IL 60035
PHONE:	877-507-MYSS	847-266-8630
EMAIL:	customerservice@myss.com	info@myss.com
WEBSITE:	www.myss.com	

THICH NHAT HANH
(Expert #33)

THICH NHAT HANH QUICK FACTS	
Main Areas:	Spirituality; Mindfulness
Best-Sellers:	"Living Buddha, Living Christ"; "Being Peace"; "Anger"
Profile:	Author; Speaker; Buddhist Monk; Scholar; Retreat Leader
Affiliation:	Unified Buddhist Church

❏ *Thich Nhat Hanh Biography*

Thich Nhat Hanh has been a Buddhist monk since age 16. He has been living in exile from his native Vietnam since 1966. That year the South Vietnamese government did not allow him to return home because of his role in working to stop the violence he saw affecting his people. Known as Thây (pronounced "tie") to his followers, he championed a movement known as "engaged Buddhism," which combined traditional meditative practices with non-violent social action.

When Thây left Vietnam, he set out on a mission around the world to work for peace in Vietnam. When he came to the United States for the first of many visits, the territory was not completely new to him because he had experienced American culture as a student at Princeton and professor at Columbia. He offered an enlightened view on ways to end the Vietnam conflict. Dr. Martin Luther King, Jr. nominated him for the Nobel Peace Prize.

Even after the unification of Vietnam under Communist rule, Thây is still seen as a threat by the Vietnamese government. A respected writer, scholar, and leader, he now lives in southwestern France, where he founded a retreat center. The center, Plum Village, houses about 200 monks, nuns, and laypeople, but thousands from around the globe call it home. Thây has written more than 75 books of prose, poetry, and meditations; his teachings appeal to a wide audience.

❏ *David Riklan's Favorite Thich Nhat Hanh Quotes and Thoughts*

- People have a hard time letting go of their suffering. Out of a fear of the unknown, they prefer suffering that is familiar.

- People usually consider walking on water or in thin air a miracle. But I think the real miracle is not to walk either on water or in thin air but to walk on Earth. Every day we are engaged in a miracle which we don't even recognize: a blue sky, white clouds, green leaves, the black, curious eyes of a child—our own two eyes. All is a miracle.

• Feelings, whether of compassion or irritation, should be welcomed, recognized, and treated on an absolutely equal basis because both are ourselves. The tangerine I am eating is me. The mustard greens I am planting are me. I plant with all my heart and mind. I clean this teapot with the kind of attention I would have were I giving the baby Buddha or Jesus a bath. Nothing should be treated more carefully than anything else. In mindfulness, compassion, irritation, mustard green plant, and teapot are all sacred."

• If we are too busy, if we are carried away every day by our projects, our uncertainty, our craving, how can we have the time to stop and look deeply into the situation—our own situation, the situation of our beloved one, the situation of our family and of our community, and the situation of our nation and of the other nations?

• Do not be idolatrous about or bound to any doctrine, theory, or ideology, even Buddhist ones. All systems of thought are guiding means; they are not absolute truth.

❑ *The Best Way to Get Started with Thich Nhat Hanh*

Thich Nhat Hanh (Thây) is a prolific writer with a wide variety of starting points. The ideal starting point varies depending on your vantage point, but I would recommend beginning with his national best-seller, *Living Buddha, Living Christ.*

Buddha and Christ are arguably two of the most important figures in the history of humankind. Each of them left behind a legacy of teachings and practices that have shaped the lives of billions of people in the East and in the West. During Thây's life and now in this book, he tries to identify parallels between these two traditions and see how these two religions can co-exist.

In Thây's book, he quotes Professor Hans Kung: "Until there is peace between religions, there can be no peace in the world." According to Thây, "When we believe that our faith is the only faith that contains the truth, then violence and suffering will surely be the result." The challenge, of course, is how to reconcile these two religions.

In Thây's life, he has been part of a decades-long dialogue between these two traditions. Thây starts with his Buddhist background and works to incorporate Christian beliefs into his thoughts. He says, "On the altar in my hermitage are images of Buddha and Jesus, and I touch both of them as my spiritual ancestors."

In Christianity, he "finds mindfulness in the Holy Spirit as an agent of healing." In Buddhism, he "finds unqualified love in the form of compassion for all living things. And in both he finds an emphasis on living practice and community spirit."

In *Living Buddha, Living Christ*, Thây uses anecdotes, scripture references, and teachings from both traditions and points out that mindfulness is an integral part of all religious practice and teaches us how to cultivate it in our own lives. Thây does not want to downplay the theological and ritual teachings that distinguish Buddhism and Christianity, but he does cause one to consider that beyond the letter of doctrine lies a unity of truth.

If you want to get a sense of how respected Thây is, all you need to do is look at the back cover of his book and read the quotes by Martin Luther King and the Dalai Lama.

TO READ ADDITIONAL BOOK EXCERPTS or ARTICLES or to LISTEN TO THICH NHAT HANH RIGHT NOW, VISIT
http://www.selfgrowth.com/experts

❑ *Books*

- Living Buddha, Living Christ
- Anger: Wisdom for Cooling the Flames
- Going Home: Jesus and Buddha as Brothers
- Being Peace
- The Miracle of Mindfulness
- Peace is Every Step: The Path of Mindfulness is Everyday Life

❑ *Audio and Video Programs*

- No Death, No Fear: Comforting Wisdom for Life (book, audio cassette, or audio CD)
- Living Buddha, Living Christ; Anger; Being Peace (each on audio cassette or audio CD)

❑ *Other Programs and Highlights*

Thây speaks to the individual's desire for wholeness and inner calm. In 1993, he drew a crowd of 1,200 people at the National Cathedral in Washington D.C., led a retreat of 500 people in upstate New York, and assembled 300 people in West Virginia. The Unified Buddhist Church, Inc., a non-profit corporation, officially represents Thich Nhat Hanh and his sangha (community of practice) in the United States.

❏ *Contact Information*

(For addresses and phone numbers for Unified Buddhist Church Monasteries and Practice Centers around the world, go to www.plumvillage.com, click on "Plum Village, France," and then click on "Contact Plum Village.")

EMAIL: info@plumvillage.org
WEBSITE: www.plumvillage.org

TOM HOPKINS
(Expert #34)

TOM HOPKINS QUICK FACTS	
Main Area:	Sales Skills
Best-Seller:	"How to Master the Art of Selling" (over 1.4 million copies sold)
Profile:	Author; Speaker; Sales Trainer
Affiliation:	Tom Hopkins International

❑ *Tom Hopkins Biography*

Tom Hopkins is an authority on the subject of selling. He is known as the nation's #1 sales trainer and developed many successful selling techniques from his own experiences in sales. Yet Tom is quick to admit that his early sales career was not successful. In fact, he failed miserably during his first six months of selling. He learned that the secret to high level productivity is combining a desire to sincerely help others make decisions that are good for them with "how to" training.

Tom's sales leadership has changed the lives and careers of millions of salespeople. By utilizing the skills he teaches today, he became a millionaire at age 27. Tom, the author of 12 books, has reached a wide variety of businesses by providing sales training in several mediums. His first book, *How to Master the Art of Selling*, has sold over 1.4 million copies and is required reading for new salespeople in many different industries.

Tom Hopkins International, incorporated in 1976, is dedicated to teaching others through seminars, books, and audio and video training systems. Tom was a pioneer in bringing broadcast-quality video training to the marketplace, and over 16,000 of his video sales training systems are utilized in-house by companies around the world. Tom firmly believes that everyone can benefit from utilizing his techniques, concepts, and ideas.

❑ *David Riklan's Favorite Tom Hopkins Quotes and Thoughts*

- I am not judged by the number of times I fail but by the number of times I succeed, and the number of times I succeed is in direct proportion to the number of times I can fail and keep trying.

- Getting in touch with your true self must be your first priority.

- Read something positive every night and listen to something helpful every morning.

- Successful people begin where failures leave off. Never settle for "just getting the job done." Excel!

- Every evening, write down the six most important things that you must do the next day. Then while you sleep, your subconscious will work on the best ways for you to accomplish them. Your next day will go much more smoothly.

- The human body has two ears and one mouth. To be good at persuading or selling, you must learn to use those natural devices in proportion. Listen twice as much as you talk, and you'll succeed in persuading others nearly every time.

❑ *The Best Way to Get Started with Tom Hopkins*

Tom Hopkins offers sales training programs, has developed many sales training videos, and has written a number of new books. But the best way to get started is to read Tom's classic book, *How to Master the Art of Selling*, which he wrote over 20 years ago and which is still a popular guide to selling.

For those of you who are not sales people and think that sales skills aren't important for you, I humbly disagree. We are all, at different times of our lives, selling something. We might be selling our ideas to our colleagues or selling ourselves to prospective employers, but in the end, we are always trying to make a sale in some area.

Tom's book is a soup-to-nuts sales guide. It covers a wide variety of topics including:

- What the Profession of Selling Really Is.
- Asking Questions.
- Creating the Selling Climate.
- Referral and Non-Referral Prospecting.
- Using the Phone.
- Putting Champion Selling Power in Your Presentations and Demonstrations.
- Qualification.
- Handling Objections.
- Closing.
- How to Sell Your Way Out of a Sales Slump.

If you want to know about selling products or services or selling yourself, then *How to Master the Art of Selling* is the book for you.

TO READ ADDITIONAL BOOK EXCERPTS or ARTICLES or to LISTEN TO TOM HOPKINS RIGHT NOW, VISIT
http://www.selfgrowth.com/experts

❑ Books

- How to Master the Art of Selling
- Selling for Dummies
- Sell It Today, Sell It Now: Mastering the Art of the One-Call Close

❑ Audio and Video Programs

- The Gentle Art of Persuasion
- How to Gain, Train, and Maintain a Dynamic Sales Force
- Achieving Sales Excellence

❑ Other Programs and Highlights

Tom has personally trained over three million students on five continents. He has shared the stage with some of the great leaders of our times, including Ret. Gen. Norman Schwartzkopf, former President George H.W. Bush and First Lady Barbara Bush, Secretary of State Colin Powell, and Lady Margaret Thatcher.

❑ Contact Information

ADDRESS: Tom Hopkins International
7531 East Second Street
Scottsdale, AZ 85251
PHONE: 1-800-528-0446
EMAIL: info@tomhopkins.com
WEBSITE: www.tomhopkins.com

ALBERT ELLIS
(Expert #35)

ALBERT ELLIS QUICK FACTS	
Main Areas:	Rational Emotive Behavioral Therapy; Clinical Psychology
Best-Seller:	"A Guide to Rational Living" (over 1.5 million copies sold)
Profile:	Author; Psychologist; Counselor; College Professor; Creator of REBT
Affiliation:	The Albert Ellis Institute

❑ *Albert Ellis Biography*

Albert Ellis, Ph.D., is an author and psychologist who developed Rational Emotive Behavioral Therapy (REBT), a therapeutic approach that stimulates emotional growth and teaches people to replace self-defeating thoughts and actions with more effective ones. REBT gives individuals the power to change the unhealthy behaviors that interfere with their ability to enjoy life. The Albert Ellis Institute is a world center for research, training, and practice of REBT.

Born in 1913, Dr. Ellis established his interest in counseling while promoting what he called the "sex-family revolution." As he was collecting materials for a treatise called "The Case for Sexual Liberty," his friends, considering him an expert on the subject, started to ask him for advice. In 1942, he entered the clinical psychology program at Columbia University and started a part-time private practice in family and sex counseling soon after receiving his master's degree.

Dr. Ellis, who earned his Ph.D. from Columbia as well, began to practice classical psychoanalysis and became a college professor and clinical psychologist. By 1955, he gave up psychoanalysis entirely and instead concentrated on changing people's behavior by persuading them to confront their irrational beliefs and adopt rational ones. He has written approximately 800 articles and 75 books on REBT, sex, and marriage, including *A Guide to Rational Living*.

❑ *David Riklan's Favorite Albert Ellis Quotes and Thoughts*

- The best years of your life are the ones in which you decide your problems are your own. You do not blame them on your mother, the ecology, or the president. You realize that you partly control your own destiny.

- Studies have shown that having an optimistic attitude tends to appreciably help people to be productive, to eventually live healthier and happier lives."

- The more sinful and guilty a person tends to feel, the less chance there is that he will be a happy, healthy, or law-abiding citizen. He will often become a compulsive wrong-doer. This is because he does not nearly blame his behavior—but also blames his total self, his entire being.

- U.S.A. or Unconditional Self-Acceptance means that you can accept yourself 100 percent even when faced with failure or rejection by others. U.S.A. is a very healthy state to be in.

- Irrational Beliefs/Rational Beliefs (IB's and RB's):
  IB's are very disrupting and harmful for a person to have. They will often think worse of themselves and what others think of them then is really reality. Phrases such as "I must" or "I have too" are IB's. RB's are constructive and helpful beliefs to have. They enable a person to realize what is important and what is reality. They breed healthy life styles and patterns of thought.

❑ *The Best Way to Get Started with Albert Ellis*

Albert Ellis developed Rational Emotive Behavioral Therapy (REBT), which is the foundation for the cognitive therapy approaches that are used today by many therapists. He has written many articles for therapists and psychologists, describing in detail the workings of and benefits of REBT. One of his most important books targeted individuals (the layman) to enable them to apply the principles of REBT themselves. It is *A Guide to Rational Living*, co-written with Robert A. Harper, and it is the best place to get started.

In the "Albert Ellis Biography" section above, we provided a basic definition of REBT. This book takes you to the next step. In it, Dr. Ellis provides many examples and very specific instructions on how to change negative, irrational, and destructive feelings, behaviors, and thoughts. He gives us a method for disputing these thoughts and brings us closer to "rational living."

The title of the first chapter in *A Guide to Rational Living* is "How Far Can You Go With Self Therapy?". Here are some other chapters that effectively deal with a wide range of irrational thoughts and behavior:

- Overcoming the influences of your past.
- Refusing to be desperately unhappy.
- Tackling dire needs for approval.
- Eradicating dire fears of failure.

- How to feel undepressed though frustrated.
- Conquering anxiety.

Will self therapy work for everybody? Absolutely not. Can self therapy help many people? Definitely. How do we determine if we need to work with a trained therapist or can apply self therapy? The best way to find out is by trying.

TO READ ADDITIONAL BOOK EXCERPTS or ARTICLES or to LISTEN TO ALBERT ELLIS RIGHT NOW, VISIT
http://www.selfgrowth.com/experts

❑ *Books*

- A Guide to Rational Living (co-authored with Robert A. Harper, Ph.D)
- How to Stubbornly Refuse to Make Yourself Miserable about Anything…Yes Anything!
- Rational Emotive Behavior Therapy: A Therapist's Guide (co-authored with Catharine MacLaren, M.S.W.)
- How to Make Yourself Happy and Remarkably Less Disturbable
- Feeling Better, Getting Better, Staying Better

❑ *Audio and Video Programs*

- How to Control Your Anxiety Before It Controls You (book or audio cassette)
- How to Control Your Anger Before It Controls You (book or audio cassette)

❑ *Other Programs and Highlights*

Currently the president of The Albert Ellis Institute, Dr. Ellis remains one of the most influential psychologists of our time. His Friday Night Workshop offers the opportunity to see REBT in action through two lively problem-solving sessions with audience volunteers. A devoted writer, playwright, and novelist, Dr. Ellis finished almost two dozen full-length manuscripts by age 28.

❑ *Contact Information*

ADDRESS: The Albert Ellis Institute
             45 East 65th Street
             New York, NY 10021
PHONE: (800) 323-4738 or (212) 535-0822
EMAIL: info@rebt.org
WEBSITE: www.rebt.org

LEO BUSCAGLIA
(Expert #36)

LEO BUSCAGLIA QUICK FACTS	
Main Areas:	Love; Relationships
Best-Seller:	"Love" (over 1 million copies sold)
Profile:	College Professor; Author; Lecturer; 1924-1998

❑ *Leo Buscaglia Biography*

Leo Buscaglia, known as "Dr. Hug," was the author of a series of best-selling books on loving and human relationships. Born in 1924, he was the son of Italian immigrants in Los Angeles. He earned a bachelor's degree in English and speech, a master's degree in language and speech pathology, and a Ph.D. in language and speech pathology.

Dr. Buscaglia was a supervisor of special education in Pasadena City schools from 1960 to 1965 and then taught special education and counseling as a faculty member at the University of Southern California School of Education. In the 1970s he started a class titled Love 1A, combining sociology, psychology, and everyday wisdom.

His first book, *Love*, came out in 1972 and examined the phenomenon of human love as the one unifying force in life. Overall, Dr. Buscaglia wrote more than a dozen books and sold more than 11 million copies in 20 languages. After retiring from teaching, Dr. Buscaglia served on the USC School of Education's Board of Councilors.

❑ *David Riklan's Favorite Leo Buscaglia Quotes and Thoughts*

- Don't smother each other. No one can grow in shade.

- Too often we underestimate the power of touch, a smile, a kind word, a listening ear, an honest compliment, or the smallest act of caring, all of which have the potential to turn a life around.

- Hold on to your dreams for they are, in a sense, the stuff of which reality is made. It is through our dreams that we maintain the possibility of a better, more meaningful life.

- A wonderful realization will be the day you realize that you are unique in all the world. There is nothing that is an accident. You are a special combination for a purpose—and don't let them tell you otherwise, even if they tell you that purpose is an illusion. (Live an illusion if you have to.) You are that combination so that you can do what is essential for you to do. Don't ever believe that you have nothing to contribute. The world is an incredible unfulfilled tapestry. And only you can fulfill that tiny space that is yours.

- A single rose can be my garden...a single friend, my world.

- Change is the end result of all true learning.

- Don't hold to anger, hurt, or pain. They steal your energy and keep you from love.

- Never idealize others. They will never live up to your expectations.

- What we call the secret of happiness is no more a secret than our willingness to choose life.

- Your talent is God's gift to you. What you do with it is your gift back to God.

❏ *The Best Way to Get Started with Leo Buscaglia*

In 1969, one of Leo Buscaglia's students committed suicide, and her death led him to begin an experimental class on personal growth at his university. He called it the "Love Class." Buscaglia's role was more of a facilitator than a teacher, with hopes that he and the students would guide "each other closer to an understanding of the delicate phenomenon of human love." His book, *Love*, is an outgrowth of this class, and this is where I recommend that you get started.

Love is a wonderful, easy-to-read book with the capability to enlighten you about what love really is. The book is for anybody who has ever reached out to touch the heart of another. In the book, Dr. Buscaglia reminds us that:

- Real love always creates, it never destroys. In this, lies man's only promise.
- One cannot give what he does not possess. To give love you must possess love.
- Love is open arms. If you close your arms about love you will find that you are left holding only yourself.

This book, which started his writing career, is the first of many gifts that Leo Buscaglia gave to the world.

TO READ ADDITIONAL BOOK EXCERPTS or ARTICLES or to LISTEN
TO LEO BUSCAGLIA RIGHT NOW, VISIT
http://www.selfgrowth.com/experts

❑ **Books**

- Love
- Living, Loving and Learning
- Loving Each Other: The Challenge of Human Relationships
- The Fall of Freddie the Leaf

❑ **Audio and Video Programs**

- Seven Stories of Christmas Love (book or audio cassette)
- Born for Love: Reflections on Loving (book or audio cassette)
- The Art of Being Fully Human (audio cassette)

❑ **Other Programs and Highlights**

In 1984, Dr. Buscaglia founded the Felice Foundation. He established the
Foundation to give special aid and attention to those who have dedicated themselves to helping one another. The Felice Foundation is structured around the
dynamics of sharing and giving and influencing others to do the same. Felice is
an Italian word for peace and joy.

❑ **Contact Information**

ADDRESS: Slack, Inc. [publisher]
6900 Grove Road
Thorofare, NJ 08086
EMAIL: info@leobuscaglia.com
jbond@slackinc.com
WEBSITE: www.buscaglia.com
www.leobuscaglia.com

JIM ROHN
(Expert #37)

JIM ROHN QUICK FACTS

Main Areas:	Business Coaching; Motivation
Profile:	Author; Speaker; Counselor; Seminar Leader
Affiliation:	Jim Rohn International

❑ *Jim Rohn Biography*

Jim Rohn is one of the most influential thinkers of our time. His profound business philosophy, creative insight, and inspirational messages have made him a popular speaker, writer, and counselor. His seminars have spanned over 39 years, and he has addressed over 6,000 audiences and 4 million people worldwide.

As a motivational speaker, Jim addresses such topics as sales and entrepreneurial skills, leadership, sales and marketing, and personal development. He always approaches the subjects of personal and business success by asking four questions: Why?, Why not?, Why not you?, and Why not now?. He answers these questions and reveals practical secrets for productivity. Jim's anecdotes and witty style fascinate listeners, igniting their enthusiasm and "can-do" spirit.

Jim is the recipient of the 1985 National Speakers Association CPAE Award, and he is the author of various books, such as *The Five Major Pieces to the Life Puzzle*. He also has assorted audio and video programs, like *The Art of Exceptional Living*, which provides the ideas and inspiration that lead to unstoppable daily progress.

❑ *David Riklan's Favorite Jim Rohn Quotes and Thoughts*

- If you keep doing what you've always done, you'll keep getting what you've always gotten.

- Success is neither magical nor mysterious. Success is the natural consequence of consistently applying the basic fundamentals.

- Whoever renders service to many puts himself in line for greatness— great wealth, great return, great satisfaction, great reputation, and great joy.

- Formal education will make you a living; self education will make you a fortune.

- Success is not to be pursued; it is to be attracted by the person you become.

- Disgust and resolve are two of the great emotions that lead to change.

- Don't wish it was easier; wish you were better. Don't wish for less problems; wish for more skills. Don't wish for less challenges; wish for more wisdom.

- You cannot change your destination overnight, but you can change your direction overnight.

- Discipline is the foundation upon which all success is built. Lack of discipline inevitably leads to failure.

❑ *The Best Way to Get Started with Jim Rohn*

Jim Rohn is the quintessential business philosopher. He tells it to you straight with honest, informative, and useful ideas. A good way to get started with Jim Rohn is to read some of his quotes or articles, but the best way is to listen to him speak. Jim has a wide variety of audio programs to choose from, and the audio program that I recommend to get started is *The Art of Exceptional Living*.

There are two versions of this audio program—the abridged version or the complete program that you can buy through his company. Jim has been described as the "Socrates of the Modern era," and *The Art of Exceptional Living* will give you an understanding of this description.

In the program, Jim covers four major lessons you must master to become successful and how to overcome self-imposed restrictions. He goes through a detailed step-by-step goal-setting workshop that will enable you to design exactly what you want the next ten years to bring. Jim also describes the five abilities for true success and how the cultivation of lifestyle molds your life into a successful masterpiece.

Here are the subjects that Jim Rohn covers:

- The Fundamentals of Exceptional Living.
- Developing a Powerful Personal Philosophy.
- Filling Your Reservoir of Knowledge.
- The Miracle of Personal Development.
- The Five Abilities for True Success.
- Achieving Financial Independence.
- The Principal of Association.
- The Art of Setting Goals.
- Designing the Next 10 Years.

- The Cultivation of Lifestyle.
- The Day That Turns Your Life Around.

In *The Art of Exceptional Living*, Jim relates his 39-plus years of experience and personal investigation into success. If you follow his advice, you'll be on your way to a happier, more prosperous life.

TO READ ADDITIONAL BOOK EXCERPTS or ARTICLES or to LISTEN TO JIM ROHN RIGHT NOW, VISIT
http://www.selfgrowth.com/experts

❑ *Books*

- The Five Major Pieces to the Life Puzzle
- The Seasons of Life
- The Treasury of Quotes
- Leading an Inspired Life

❑ *Audio and Video Programs*

- The Art of Exceptional Living
- Take Charge of Your Life
- The Power of Ambition
- The Challenge to Succeed
- Cultivating an Unshakable Character
- The Weekend Seminar
- The Jim Rohn New Millennium Package *(training package with 20 cd's and 21 hours on DVD)*

❑ *Other Programs and Highlights*

Jim Rohn has been the mentor to the mentors. A wide variety of experts have learned from him, including Les Brown and Tony Robbins, who specifically credits Jim for the positive impact in his life when he was first forming the philosophies that guide him today. To view Jim Rohn's updated schedule, his free weekly online newsletter, and his e-zine archives, visit www.jimrohn.com.

❑ *Contact Information*

ADDRESS: Jim Rohn International
2835 Exchange Blvd., Suite 200
Southlake, TX 76092
PHONE: (800) 929-0434
EMAIL: info@jimrohn.com
WEBSITE: www.jimrohn.com

DANIEL GOLEMAN
(Expert #38)

DANIEL GOLEMAN QUICK FACTS

Main Area:	Emotional Intelligence
Best-Seller:	"Emotional Intelligence"
Profile:	Author; Lecturer; Psychologist; Consultant
Affiliation:	The Consortium for Research on Emotional Intelligence in Organizations (at Rutgers University)

❑ *Daniel Goleman Biography*

Daniel Goleman, Ph.D., is a psychologist, lecturer, and international consultant. His best-selling book, *Emotional Intelligence*, has more than 5 million copies in print and has been translated into nearly 30 languages. Dr. Goleman was previously a visiting faculty member at Harvard University and for many years, reported on the brain and behavioral sciences for *The New York Times*.

Born in Stockton, California, Dr. Goleman has been nominated twice for the Pulitzer Prize and has received the Career Achievement Award for journalism from the American Psychological Association. He graduated magna cum laude from Amherst College and received his M.A. and Ph.D. in clinical psychology and personality development from Harvard.

Dr. Goleman was a co-founder of the Collaborative for Academic, Social and Emotional Learning at the Yale University Child Studies Center with the goal to help schools introduce emotional literacy courses. He is also co-chairman of The Consortium for Research on Emotional Intelligence in Organizations, based at Rutgers University, which seeks to recommend best practices for developing emotional competence.

❑ *David Riklan's Favorite Daniel Goleman Quotes and Thoughts*

- Emotional intelligence consists of five skills: knowing what you're thinking as you're thinking it; handling your feelings so that distracting emotions don't interfere with your ability to concentrate and learn; motivating yourself, including maintaining optimism and hope; having empathy; and social skills.

- Emotional intelligence is the capacity for recognizing our own feelings and those of others, for motivating ourselves, and for managing emotions well in ourselves and in our relationships.

- In a study of skills that distinguish star performers in every field from entry-level jobs to executive positions, the single most important factor was not I.Q., advanced degrees, or technical experience; it was E.Q.

- I.Q. and academic skills are entry-level requirements for jobs of all kinds...but have little to do with how you'll succeed once you get there. Emotional intelligence accounts for 90 percent of what's required for leadership.

- People who are optimistic see a failure as due to something that can be changed so that they can succeed next time around, while pessimists take the blame for the failure, ascribing it to some characteristic they are helpless to change.

- Who does not recall school at least in part as endless dreary hours of boredom punctuated by moments of high anxiety?

- Women, on average, tend to be more aware of their emotions, show more empathy, and are more adept interpersonally. Men on the other hand, are more self-confident and optimistic, adapt more easily, and handle stress better.

- What counts in making a happy relationship is not so much how compatible you are but how you deal with incompatibility.

❑ *The Best Way to Get Started with Daniel Goleman*

Are you trapped with the I.Q. that you were born with? Does your I.Q. define your destiny? Is there something that will have a greater impact on your success? Daniel Goleman's book *Emotional Intelligence* takes on these questions and more and is surely the best place to get started. This fascinating book will show you how to develop your emotional intelligence in ways that can improve success at work, in relationships, and in parenting.

Dr. Goleman argues that an I.Q.-only view is far too narrow and that a person's emotional intelligence is a critical part of defining his/her success. He makes the case for emotional intelligence being the strongest indicator of human success and defines it with attributes that include self-awareness, empathy, personal motivation, altruism, and the ability to love and be loved by friends, partners, and family members.

Dr. Goleman uses discoveries from psychology and neuroscience to provide insight into your rational and emotional sides. He bases many of his conclusions on empirical data and scientific research and covers a wide variety of other topics, such as learned optimism and the theory of multiple intelligences. Dr.

Goleman's vivid examples demonstrate the crucial skills of emotional intelligence.

TO READ ADDITIONAL BOOK EXCERPTS or ARTICLES or to LISTEN
TO DANIEL GOLEMAN RIGHT NOW, VISIT
http://www.selfgrowth.com/experts

❑ *Books*

- Emotional Intelligence
- Primal Leadership: Realizing the Power of Emotional Intelligence
- Working with Emotional Intelligence
- Destructive Emotions: A Scientific Dialogue with the Dalai Lama

❑ *Audio and Video Programs*

- The Art of Meditation
- Future Medicine

❑ *Other Programs and Highlights*

Dr. Goleman was elected a Fellow of the American Association for the Advancement of Science, in recognition of his efforts to communicate the behavioral sciences to the public. He is also a member of the board of directors of the Mind & Life Institute and in 2003, published *Destructive Emotions*, an account of a scientific dialogue between the Dalai Lama and a group of psychologists, neuroscientists, and philosophers.

❑ *Contact Information*

EMAIL: Go to www.eiconsortium.org/form.html
WEBSITE: www.eiconsortium.org

KEVIN TRUDEAU
(Expert #39)

KEVIN TRUDEAU QUICK FACTS

Main Area:	Memory Training
Profile:	Author; Speaker; Memory Trainer
Affiliations:	Trudeau Online; American Memory Institute

❑ *Kevin Trudeau Biography*

Kevin Trudeau is one of the world's foremost authorities on memory improvement training. As founder of the American Memory Institute, he has helped a vast number of people to improve their memory. Over one million people have benefited from his home study system, making his *Mega Memory* series the most utilized Self Improvement series of all time.

Trudeau says that there is no such thing as a good or bad memory—only a trained or untrained memory. He says you can access the area of your mind that never forgets, called the knowledge bank, which stores information like your name and the alphabet. The techniques in *Mega Memory* teach you to file new information in the knowledge bank permanently.

At an early age, Trudeau was labeled with a learning disability and was convinced it was due to his inability to recall information. *Mega Memory* is based on methods first discovered while working with blind and retarded children. He adapted these techniques so that anyone could release their own instant-recall memory ability. Kevin is also an author and speaks before thousands of people each year.

❑ *David Riklan's Favorite Kevin Trudeau Quotes and Thoughts*

- Your mind thinks in pictures. Pictures are its vocabulary, what it understands best. It's like an instant camera, clicking away, taking pictures, and reproducing them in all sorts of combinations.

❑ *The Best Way to Get Started with Kevin Trudeau*

The best way to get started with Kevin Trudeau is to read his book, *Kevin Trudeau's Mega Memory: How to Release Your Superpower Memory in 30 Minutes or Less a Day*. Each *Mega Memory* lesson in this book takes less than 30 minutes per day and uses pictures to activate our inborn photographic memory.

Trudeau's book contains an easy-to-follow system that will enable you to instantly remember names, phone numbers, addresses, financial data, speeches, and schoolwork. His system ensures instant recall and long-term mega memory. The book has been expanded into a complete home study system that includes six instructional audio CDs (or eight audio cassettes), a pocket guide, and an interactive workbook. If you want to get a more complete learning experience of Trudeau's system, I would recommend the CD program after reading his book.

TO READ ADDITIONAL BOOK EXCERPTS or ARTICLES or to LISTEN TO KEVIN TRUDEAU RIGHT NOW, VISIT
http://www.selfgrowth.com/experts

❏ *Books*

- Kevin Trudeau's Mega Memory: How to Release Your Superpower Memory in 30 Minutes or Less a Day

❏ *Audio and Video Programs*

- Mega Memory
- Advanced Mega Memory
- Mega Speed Reading
- Mega Math
- 5 Minutes a Day to Perfect Spelling

❏ *Other Programs and Highlights*

Kevin Trudeau is seen each week on his popular *Mega Memory* television show. His techniques have been demonstrated on *The Tonight Show with Johnny Carson*, *20/20*, *Donahue*, and many others. He has also shared the platform with such notable personalities as President Ronald Reagan, Zig Ziglar, General Norman Schwarzkopf, Mikhail Gorbachev, Brian Tracy, and Pat Boone.

❏ *Contact Information*

ADDRESS:	Trudeau Online
	P.O. Box 6192
	Bloomingdale, IL 60108
PHONE:	805-646-2947
EMAIL:	info@trudeau.com
WEBSITE:	www.trudeau.com

ROBERT FULGHUM
(Expert #40)

ROBERT FULGHUM QUICK FACTS	
Main Area:	Life Wisdom
NY Times Best-Seller:	"All I Really Need to Know I Learned in Kindergarten" (over 7 million copies sold)
Profile:	Author; Minister; Philosopher

❑ *Robert Fulghum Biography*

Robert Fulghum is a best-selling author, even though he never intended to be. In 1985, his short essay won the International Refrigerator Award, the Office Bulletin Board Sweepstakes, the Send-A-Copy-To-Your-Mom Trophy, and even the My-Rabbi-Read-It-In-His-Sermon Prize. He turned the essay into a book, *All I Really Need to Know I Learned in Kindergarten*, which has sold seven million copies in at least 39 countries.

Fulghum says that what we learn in kindergarten will come up repeatedly in our lives, and we will be tested over the years to see if we understand what we have learned. He says that we will wrestle with questions of right and wrong and good and bad across the course of our lives. And it will all come back to when we were very young in kindergarten.

When asked what he does for a living, Fulghum replies that he is a philosopher. In his life, he has been a working cowboy, folksinger, IBM salesman, professional artist, parish minister, bartender, teacher of drawing and painting, and father. He has written seven books and in October 2003, published a revised 15th anniversary edition of *All I Really Need To Know I Learned in Kindergarten* with 25 new stories. There are currently more than 15 million copies of Fulghum's books in print, published in 27 languages in 93 countries.

❑ *David Riklan's Favorite Robert Fulghum Quotes and Thoughts*

- Be aware of wonder. Live a balanced life—learn some and think some and draw and paint and sing and dance and play and work every day some.

- Don't worry that children never listen to you. Worry that they are always watching you.

- I believe that imagination is stronger than knowledge—that myth is more potent than history. I believe that dreams are more powerful than facts—that hope always triumphs over experience—that laughter is the only cure for grief. And I believe that love is stronger than death.

- If you break your neck, if you have nothing to eat, if your house is on fire, then you got a problem. Everything else is inconvenience.

- If you want an interesting party sometime, combine cocktails and a fresh box of Crayolas for everybody.

- The grass is not always greener on the other side of the fence. Fences have nothing to do with it. The grass is greenest where it is watered. When crossing over fences, carry water with you and tend the grass wherever you may be.

- The world does not need tourists who ride by in a bus clucking their tongues. The world as it is needs those who will love it enough to change it, with what they have, where they are.

- It will be a great day when our schools have all the money they need, and our air force has to have a bake-sale to buy a bomber.

❏ *The Best Way to Get Started with Robert Fulghum*

There is only one place to start with Robert Fulghum, and that is with his book, *All I Really Need to Know I Learned in Kindergarten*, a wonderful adventure in reading and insight. I would best describe Fulghum as a modern day Buddha. The premise of the book is defined by its title. Fulghum takes the wisdom we were taught when we were little children—"Play fair. Don't hit people. Say you're sorry when you hurt somebody."—and expands on it, showing us how he himself applied these principles during his life.

Fulghum is part philosopher, part teacher, part minister, and part student. An example of this can be found in one of the passages and recommendations from his book. Fulghum writes:

> Maybe we should develop a Crayola bomb as our next secret weapon. A happiness weapon. A Beauty Bomb. And every time a crisis developed, we would launch one first—before we tried anything else. It would explode high in the air—explode softly—and send thousands, millions, of little parachutes into the air. Floating down to earth—boxes of Crayolas. And we wouldn't go cheap, either—not little boxes of eight. Boxes of sixty-four, with the sharpener built right in. With silver and gold and copper, magenta and peach and lime, amber and umber and all the rest. And people would smile and get a little funny look on their faces and cover the world with imagina-

tion instead of death. A child who touched one wouldn't have his hand blown off.

All in all, *All I Really Need to Know I Learned in Kindergarten* lets you relive parts of your life and see it again from a simpler perspective. Try to pick up the new and revised 15th anniversary edition.

TO READ ADDITIONAL BOOK EXCERPTS or ARTICLES or to LISTEN TO ROBERT FULGHUM RIGHT NOW, VISIT
http://www.selfgrowth.com/experts

❑ *Books*

- All I Really Need to Know I Learned in Kindergarten: Uncommon Thoughts on Common Things
- 15th Anniversary Edition: All I Really Need to Know I Learned in Kindergarten
- It Was On Fire When I Lay Down On It
- Uh-Oh: Some Observations From Both Sides of the Refrigerator Door
- Maybe (Maybe Not) Second Thoughts From a Secret Life
- From Beginning to End: The Rituals of Our Lives
- True Love
- Words I Wish I Wrote: A Collection of Writing that Inspired My Ideas

❑ *Audio Programs*

- 15th Anniversary Edition: All I Really Need to Know I Learned in Kindergarten (on audio cassette)

(All of Robert Fulghum's books were published in audio format as well as in print.)

❑ *Other Programs and Highlights*

There are currently two stage productions based on Robert Fulghum's books. These original works were adapted by Ernest Zulia with original scores by David Caldwell. Entitled *All I Really Need to Know I Learned in Kindergarten* and *Uh-Oh, Here Comes Christmas*, they are available for licensing through Dramatic Publishing (www.dramaticpublishing.com).

❑ *Contact Information*

(The address, phone, and email are for speaking engagements.)

ADDRESS:	The Leigh Bureau
PHONE:	(908) 253-8600
	(908) 253-8601 *(fax number)*
EMAIL:	Info@leighbureau.com
WEBSITE:	www.robertfulghum.com

GARY ZUKAV
(Expert #41)

GARY ZUKAV QUICK FACTS

Main Areas:	Spirituality; The Soul
Best-Sellers:	"The Seat of the Soul"; "Soul Stories"; "The Heart of the Soul: Emotional Awareness"
Profile:	Author; U.S. Army Special Forces Officer; Degree in International Relations
Affiliation:	Seat of the Soul Foundation

❑ *Gary Zukav Biography*

Gary Zukav is a best-selling author, dedicated to the birth of a new humanity. He calls himself a student of life who has made the journey away from an angry man with no regard for life. He still feels that the best contribution he can make to the world is to live a conscious life, challenge and heal the frightened parts of himself, and be a good neighbor.

Many of Zukav's books are *New York Times* best-sellers, including *The Seat of the Soul*, which spent three years on the list (31 times in the #1 position), *Soul Stories*, and *The Heart of the Soul: Emotional Awareness*. Together they have sold 5 million copies and have been translated into 24 languages. *The Dancing Wu Li Masters: An Overview of the New Physics*, which he wrote in 1979, won The American Book Award for Science. It has become the bible for those who are interested in learning about quantum physics but are not drawn to mathematics or science.

A Harvard University graduate, Zukav was a U.S. Army Special Forces (Green Beret) officer in Vietnam and co-founded the Seat of the Soul Foundation with Linda Francis. The Foundation assists people in the creation of authentic power—the alignment of the personality with the soul—as outlined in *The Seat of the Soul*. Its vision is a world of harmony, cooperation, sharing, and reverence for Life.

❑ *David Riklan's Favorite Gary Zukav Quotes and Thoughts*

- An authentically empowered person is humble. This does not mean the false humility of one who stoops to be with those who are below him or her. It is the inclusiveness of one who responds to the beauty of each soul. ...It is the harmlessness of one who treasures, honors, and reveres life in all its forms.

- Eventually you will come to understand that love heals everything, and love is all there is.

- The purpose of our journey on this precious Earth is now to align our personalities with our souls. It is to create harmony, cooperation, sharing, and reverence for Life. It is to grow spiritually. This is our new evolutionary pathway. The old pathway –pursuing the ability to manipulate and control—no longer works. It now produces only violence and destruction.

- Try to realize that what stands between you and a different life are matters of responsible choice.

- We are evolving form a species that pursues external power into a species that pursues authentic power... Authentic power has its roots in the deepest source of our being. An authentically empowered person is incapable of making anyone or anything a victim. An authentically empowered person is one who is so strong, so empowered, that the idea of using force against another is not a part of his or her consciousness.

- If you wish the world to become loving and compassionate, become loving and compassionate yourself. If you wish to diminish fear in the world, diminish your own. These are the gifts that you can give.

- Emotions reflect intentions. Therefore, awareness of emotions leads to awareness of intentions. Every discrepancy between a conscious intention and the emotions that accompany it, points directly to a splintered aspect of the self that requires healing.

- When you interact with another, an illusion is part of this dynamic. This illusion allows each soul to perceive what it needs to understand in order to heal.

- Reality is what we take to be true. What we take to be true is what we believe. What we believe is based upon our perceptions. What we perceive depends upon what we look for. What we look for depends upon what we think. What we think depends upon what we perceive. What we perceive determines what we believe. What we believe determines what we take to be true. What we take to be true is our reality.

❑ *The Best Way to Get Started with Gary Zukav*

The best way to get started with Gary Zukav is to read *The Seat of the Soul*. Zukav alleges that the human species is in the midst of a great transformation of consciousness, evolving from a species that is limited in its perception to the five senses and understands power as the ability to manipulate and control—"external power"—to one that is not limited to the perceptions of the five senses and understands power as the alignment of the personality with the soul — "authentic power."

In the book, Zukav discusses the transformation of human consciousness from five-sensory to "multisensory" and provides the tools to create "authentic power," the alignment of the personality with the soul. *The Seat of the Soul* is valuable and thought-provoking because it tries to describe the evolution of human consciousness through the expansion of our senses into the realm of intuition, spiritual guidance, and self-responsibility.

Zukav believes that humans are immortal souls first, physical beings second, and that we grow spiritually by using emotional awareness, responsible choice, intuition, and trust to create a life of meaning and joy. His book, *Soul Stories*, is an excellent follow-up to *The Seat of the Soul*, and I recommend it as the second place to go. *Soul Stories* includes 52 short stories of how intuition and spirit are part of people's lives.

TO READ ADDITIONAL BOOK EXCERPTS or ARTICLES or to LISTEN TO GARY ZUKAV RIGHT NOW, VISIT
http://www.selfgrowth.com/experts

❑ *Books*

- The Seat of the Soul
- Soul Stories
- The Dancing Wu Li Masters: An Overview of the New Physics
- The Heart of the Soul: Emotional Awareness (co-authored with Linda Francis)

❑ *Video Programs*

- The Heart of the Soul: The PBS Special *(taped at a five-day intensive)*

❑ *Other Programs and Highlights*

Gary Zukav is a member of numerous organizations and activities including Native American Earth Ambassadors, CoCreate with the Earth Foundation, EarthSave, and the World Business Academy. He has offered spiritual insights and guidance to many viewers of *The Oprah Winfrey Show*.

❑ *Contact Information*

ADDRESS:	Gary Zukav	Seat of the Soul Foundation
	P.O. Box 339	P.O. Box 339
	Ashland, OR 97520	Ashland, OR 97520
PHONE:		888-440-7685
EMAIL:	Gary@zukav.com	welcome@seatofthesoul.org
WEBSITE:	www.zukav.com	www.seatofthesoul.org

JULIA CAMERON
(Expert #42)

JULIA CAMERON QUICK FACTS

Main Area:	Creativity
NY Times Best-Seller:	"The Artist's Way" (over 1 million copies sold)
Profile:	Author; Poet; Playwright; Novelist; Filmmaker; Songwriter; Teacher

---

❑ *Julia Cameron Biography*

Julia Cameron is an award-winning poet, playwright, filmmaker, and author of 15 books, including *The Artist's Way*. Her works range from fiction to beloved volumes of prayers and children's poems. A writer since the age of 18, she has written for most major national publications, including *Rolling Stone* and *The New York Times*.

Cameron is internationally known for her work on creativity. Her teaching and workshops on unlocking creativity inspired the international best-seller, *The Artist's Way*, which has sold nearly a million and a half copies worldwide. The book links creativity to spirituality by showing how to connect with the creative energies of the universe. Her follow-up best-sellers include *The Vein of Gold* and *The Right to Write*.

Cameron is credited with having founded a new human potential movement, which has enabled millions of people to realize their creative dreams. Yet she prefers to describe herself simply as an "artist." Cameron has taught *The Artist's Way* workshops to such places as the Smithsonian and *The New York Times*, and her work is frequently taught in theological degree programs as well as in the arts.

❑ *David Riklan's Favorite Julia Cameron Quotes and Thoughts*

- Creativity is our true nature; blocks are an unnatural thwarting of a process at once as normal and as miraculous as the blossoming of a flower at the end of a slender green stem.

- As artists, we must learn to be self-nourishing. We must become alert enough to consciously replenish our creative resources as we draw on them.

- Over any extended period of time, being an artist requires enthusiasm more than discipline. Enthusiasm is not an emotional state. It is spiritual commitment, a loving surrender to our creative process, a loving recognition of all the creativity around us.

- In order to have a real relationship with our creativity, we must take the time and care to cultivate it.

- I have said before that creativity is a spiritual issue. Any progress is made by leaps of faith, some small and some large.

- I have learned, as a rule of thumb, never to ask whether you can do something. Say, instead, that you are doing it. Then fasten your seat belt. The most remarkable things follow.

- Growth is an erratic forward movement: two steps forward, one step back. Remember that and be very gentle with yourself.

- The grace to be a beginner is always the best prayer for an artist. The beginner's humility and openness lead to exploration. Exploration leads to accomplishment. All of it begins at the beginning, with the first small and scary step.

❑ *The Best Way to Get Started with Julia Cameron*

When I think of Julia Cameron, one thing comes to mind: her book, *The Artist's Way*, which has been described as the "seminal book on the subject of creativity." When I first started to read it, I had the misconception that the book, her workshops, and her exercises were for "artists." Artists, in my mind, were painters, musicians, writers, anybody whose main focus in life is their creativity.

Shortly into the book, it became clear that Julia Cameron's popularity comes from the fact that she can help any of us use our creativity in dealing with our careers, family, or personal interests, regardless of our primary interest in life. We are all creative beings.

In the first chapter, Cameron outlines ten basic principles. I want to share with you the first three to get a sense of where she is coming from:

1. Creativity is the natural order of life. Life is energy. Pure creative energy.
2. There is an underlying, in-dwelling creative force infusing all of life—including ourselves.
3. When we open ourselves to our creativity, we open ourselves to the creator's creativity within us and our lives.

All of Julia Cameron's work comes back to *The Artists Way*. This book provides a 12-week program with specific exercises to unlock ideas and expand your creativity. It is a guide to living the artist's life, but in truth, it is a guide to a creative life. I have one suggestion: plan on doing at least some of the exercises. It's all about "Living the Artist's Life," not about *reading about* the Artist's Life.

TO READ ADDITIONAL BOOK EXCERPTS or ARTICLES or to LISTEN TO JULIA CAMERON RIGHT NOW, VISIT
http://www.selfgrowth.com/experts

❑ *Books*

- The Artist's Way: A Spiritual Path to Higher Creativity
- The Vein of Gold: A Journey to Your Creative Heart
- The Right to Write: An Invitation and Initiation into the Writing Life
- God is No Laughing Matter: Observations and Objections on the Spiritual Path
- The Artist's Way Morning Pages Journal: A Companion Volume to *The Artist's Way*
- The Artist's Date Book: A Companion Volume to *The Artist's Way* (illustrated by Elizabeth "Libby" Cameron)
- Supplies: A Pilot's Manual for Creative Flight (illustrated by Elizabeth "Libby" Cameron)
- God is Dog Spelled Backwards
- Heart Steps: Prayers and Declarations for a Creative Life
- Blessings: Prayers and Declarations for a Heartful Life
- Transitions: Prayers and Declarations for a Changing Life
- The Artist's Way at Work: Riding the Dragon: Twelve Weeks to Creative Freedom (co-authored with Mark Bryan and Catherine Allen)
- Money Drunk, Money Sober: 90 Days to Financial Freedom (co-authored with Mark Bryan)
- Walking in *This* World: The Practical Art of Creativity

❑ *Audio and Video Programs*

- The Artist's Way; The Vein of Gold; Blessings; Transitions; Heart Steps; Walking in *This* World (each on audio cassette)

❑ *Other Programs and Highlights*

As a playwright, Julia Cameron's work has graced such stages as Princeton's McCarter Theater, The Denver Center of the Performing Arts, and the tiny Taos Community Auditorium in her hometown. It was there that she first workshopped her musical *Avalon*, under the guidance of legendary director John

Newland. Cameron serves as a composer on her musicals, as well as a libretto-writer and lyricist. This musical aspect of her career began in her mid-40s.

❑ *Contact Information*

(Any correspondence not directly related to booking a workshop—fan mail, etc.—should be sent to Julia Cameron at the address listed below.)

ADDRESS: Penguin Group USA
                    Fourth Floor
                    375 Hudson Street
                    New York, NY 10014
WEBSITE: www.theartistsway.com

JOHN ELDREDGE
(Expert #43)

JOHN ELDREDGE QUICK FACTS

Main Areas:	Masculinity; Christian Masculinity; Relationships
Best-Seller:	"Wild at Heart"
Profile:	Author; Lecturer; Counselor
Affiliation:	Ransomed Heart Ministries

❑ *John Eldredge Biography*

John Eldredge is the founder and director of Ransomed Heart Ministries in Colorado Springs, Colorado. The Ransomed Heart Ministries is a fellowship devoted to helping people live from their deep heart. Those at the ministry believe that from the heart, a person finds intimacy with God and others and discovers life's purpose and calling.

Eldredge is also a best-selling author, counselor, and lecturer. For more than 12 years, he was a writer and speaker for Focus on the Family. Eldredge received his undergraduate degree in theater from Cal Poly and worked as an actor and director in Los Angeles for ten years. He received his M.A. in counseling from Colorado Christian University.

Eldredge has written several books, including *Wild at Heart*, in which he urges men to recover their masculine heart and helps women understand the implications of masculinity in their romantic relationships. Eldredge also co-authored *The Sacred Romance*, which inspires readers to enter into a romance with God. The book was followed up by *The Journey of Desire*.

❑ *David Riklan's Favorite John Eldredge Quotes and Thoughts*

- ...in the heart of every man is a desperate desire for a battle to fight, an adventure to live, and a beauty to rescue.

- Most messages for men ultimately fail. The reason is simple. They ignore what is deep and true to a man's *heart*, his real passions, and simply try to shape him up through various forms of pressure.

- If a man is ever to find out who he is and what he is here for, he has got to take that journey for himself. He has got to get his heart back.

- Even if he can't put it into words, every man is haunted by the question, "Am I really a man? Have I got what it takes...when it counts?"

- Don't ask yourself what the world needs. Ask yourself what makes you come alive and go do that because what the world needs is people who have come alive.

❑ *The Best Way to Get Started with John Eldredge*

The best way to get started with John Eldredge is to read his book, *Wild at Heart: Discovering the Secret of a Man's Soul.* Eldredge's major focus is enabling Christian men to return to their true masculinity, yet his principles, beliefs, and stories can apply to Christian and non-Christians alike. He wants men to live life the way God designed it to be—dangerous, passionate, alive, and free.

The premise of the book is that contemporary men are bored; they fear risk, and they refuse to pay attention to their deepest desires. Eldredge believes that if Christian men are going to change from a wimpy bunch of "really nice guys" to men who are made in the image of God, they must re-examine their preconceptions about who God is and recover their true "wild" hearts.

Eldredge claims that men often seek validation in venues like work or in the conquest of women. He urges men to take time out and come to grips with the "secret longings" of their hearts. Although *Wild at Heart* is written for men, it also helps women to understand men while in relationships.

Eldridge uses the backdrop of his personal outdoor experiences with his family to communicate the ideas associated with men searching for their true wildness of heart. Eldridge believes, "The only way to live in this adventure…with all its danger and unpredictability and immensely high stakes…is in an ongoing, intimate relationship with God."

TO READ ADDITIONAL BOOK EXCERPTS or ARTICLES or to LISTEN TO JOHN ELDREDGE RIGHT NOW, VISIT
http://www.selfgrowth.com/experts

❑ *Books*

- Wild at Heart: Discovering the Secret of a Man's Soul
- The Sacred Romance: Drawing Closer to the Heart of God (co-authored with Brent Curtis)
- The Journey of Desire: Searching for the Life We Only Dreamed Of
- Waking the Dead: The Glory of a Ransomed Heart

❑ *Audio and Video Programs*

- Wild at Heart (on audio cassette or audio CD)
- Waking the Dead (on audio cassette or audio CD)

❏ *Other Programs and Highlights*

Ransomed Heart Ministries hosts several conferences and retreats in the United States and abroad that have been the point of connection on a deeper level with God. For more information, visit www.ransomedheart.com.

❏ *Contact Information*

ADDRESS: Ransomed Heart Ministries
ATTN: John Eldredge
P.O. Box 51065
Colorado Springs, CO 80949-1065
WEBSITE: www.ransomedheart.com

JIM COLLINS
(Expert #44)

JIM COLLINS QUICK FACTS	
Main Area:	Business
NY Times Best-Seller:	"Good to Great"
Profile:	Author; Researcher; Teacher

❑ *Jim Collins Biography*

Jim Collins is a student of enduring great companies—how they grow, how they attain superior performance, and how good companies can become great companies. Having invested more than a decade of research into the topic, Jim has co-authored four books, including the classic *Built to Last*, a fixture on the *Business Week* best-seller list for more than six years, and *The New York Times* best-seller, *Good to Great*.

Driven by a relentless curiosity, Jim began his research and teaching career on the faculty of Stanford's Graduate School of Business, where he received the Distinguished Teaching Award. After seven years at Stanford, Jim returned to his hometown of Boulder, Colorado to found his management research laboratory.

Jim set up his research lab in the same building where he attended grammar school. Still a place of learning, Jim uses the laboratory to conduct large-scale research projects to develop fundamental insights and then translate those findings into books, articles, and lectures. Jim continues to conduct rigorous research while maintaining an active teaching schedule with leaders in the corporate and social sectors.

❑ *David Riklan's Favorite Jim Collins Quotes and Thoughts*

- Start a "stop-doing" list. …"Stop-doing" lists are more important than "to-do" lists.

- The real path to greatness, it turns out, requires simplicity and diligence. It requires clarity, not instant illumination.

- Good-to-great leaders…know how to simplify a complex world into a single, organizing idea—the kind of basic principle that unifies, organizes, and guides all decisions.

❑ *The Best Way to Get Started with Jim Collins*

The best way to get started with Jim Collins is to read his book *Good to Great: Why Some Companies Make the Leap...and Others Don't.* Even though Jim Collins is known more for his "Business Improvement" than for his "Self Improvement," I feel the impact he has made on people and business justifies his being considered one of the Top 101 Self Improvement Experts.

Good to Great primarily discusses what goes into a company's transformation from mediocre to excellent, but his book can also give us insights into how we can help ourselves transform from good to great.

Two issues for companies that easily transition into "Self Improvement" include:

1. Discover your core values and purpose beyond simply making money.
2. Greatness is not a function of circumstance; it is clearly a matter of conscious choice.

Jim Collins' book is unquestionably a business classic, but I believe it is also an important book for anybody looking to improve their lives.

TO READ ADDITIONAL BOOK EXCERPTS or ARTICLES or to LISTEN TO JIM COLLINS RIGHT NOW, VISIT
http://www.selfgrowth.com/experts

❑ *Books*

- Good to Great: Why Some Companies Make the Leap...and Others Don't
- Built to Last: Successful Habits of Visionary Companies
- Managing the Small to Mid-Sized Company: Concepts and Cases
- Beyond Entrepreneurship: Turning Your Business into an Enduring Great Company

❑ *Other Programs and Highlights*

Jim's work has been featured in *Fortune, The Economist, Fast Company, USA Today, Industry Week, Business Week, Newsweek, Inc.,* and *Harvard Business Review.* In addition to his day job, he is an avid rock climber and has made free ascents of the West Face of El Capitan and the East Face of Washington Column in Yosemite Valley. To listen to Jim's thoughts, go to the Lecture Hall section of his website at www.jimcollins.com.

❑ *Contact Information*

(Contact Stefanie Judd, the chair of the council that handles all inquiries and requests for Jim Collins.)

ADDRESS: P.O. Box 1699
                      Boulder, CO 80306
PHONE: (303) 316-7283
                      (303) 322-0375 *(fax number)*
EMAIL: SJwithJimCollins@aol.com
WEBSITE: www.jimcollins.com

ORIAH MOUNTAIN DREAMER
(Expert #45)

ORIAH MOUNTAIN DREAMER QUICK FACTS

Main Area:	Spirituality
Best-Seller:	"The Invitation"
Profile:	Author; Speaker; Poet; Counselor; Workshop/Retreat Leader

---

❏ *Oriah Mountain Dreamer Biography*

Oriah Mountain Dreamer is a facilitator of spiritual retreats, workshops, and ceremonies throughout the United States and Canada. She is a student of philosophy, seeking to understand how we can all be who we truly are. Her name was given to her by the elders with whom she apprenticed. It means one who likes to push the edge and can help others do the same.

Oriah grew up in a small town in northern Ontario. When she was 19, she went to Toronto and trained as a social worker. There she worked with teens on the street, abused women, and families in crisis. Oriah inspires and challenges people to live a full life by mixing ruthless honesty with humor and compassion for human struggle.

As an accomplished speaker and author, Oriah shares stories of her personal life and years of training in an inter-tribal tradition of shamanic medicine. Her debut book, *The Invitation*, was a best-seller. It is based on a prose poem of the same name that she wrote after returning home from a party one night. She wrote the poem as an expression of all the things she really wanted to know about and share with others.

❏ *David Riklan's Favorite Oriah Mountain Dreamer Quotes and Thoughts*

From her book, *The Invitation:*

- It doesn't interest me what you do for a living. I want to know what you ache for, and if you dare to dream of meeting your heart's longing.

  It doesn't interest me how old you are. I want to know if you will risk looking like a fool for love, for your dream, for the adventure of being alive.

It doesn't interest me what planets are squaring your moon. I want to know if you have touched the center of your own sorrow, if you have been opened by life's betrayals or have become shriveled and closed from fear of further pain! I want to know if you can sit with pain, mine or your own, without moving to hide it or fade it, or fix it.

(To read the rest of this poem, visit www.oriahmountaindreamer.com)

❑ *The Best Way to Get Started with Oriah Mountain Dreamer*

Oriah wrote the start of her poem, *The Invitation*, after an unsatisfying evening at a party. She says the poem "took on a life of its own" and that "people copied it and shared it with friends and colleagues around the world." The poem became the basis for her book, *The Invitation*, which is the best place to start with Oriah Mountain Dreamer.

According to Oriah, *The Invitation* "is a declaration of intent, a map into the longing of the soul, the desire to live passionately, face-to-face with ourselves and skin-to-skin with the world around us, to settle for nothing less than what is real." In the book, she offers inspiration on experiencing the beauty and sacredness of life.

Each chapter of the book uses passages from her poem to lead you to a more passionate and fulfilling life, one with greater truth and integrity. Each chapter ends with a guided meditation related to what was written. All sections of the book contain personal experiences to help guide you, and the power of Oriah's words will take you on a journey to the inner depths of your soul.

TO READ ADDITIONAL BOOK EXCERPTS or ARTICLES or to LISTEN TO ORIAH MOUNTAIN DREAMER RIGHT NOW, VISIT
http://www.selfgrowth.com/experts

❑ *Books*

- The Invitation
- The Dance: Moving to the Rhythms of Your True Self
- The Call: Discovering Why You Are Here

❑ *Audio and Video Programs*

- Your Heart's Prayer
- The Invitation; The Dance; The Call (each on audio cassette or audio CD)

❏ ***Other Programs and Highlights***

Oriah has shared her stories with audiences throughout the world. She has made TV and radio appearances for *The Oprah Winfrey Show*, National Public Radio, PBS, and others.   To view her current calendar, visit her website at www.oriahmountaindreamer.com.

❏ ***Contact Information***

ADDRESS: Mountain Dreaming
                         300 Coxwell Avenue, Box 22546
                         Toronto, ON,
                         Canada, M4L 2A0
EMAIL: mail@oriahmountaindreamer.com
WEBSITE: www.oriahmountaindreamer.com

BOB PROCTOR
(Expert #46)

BOB PROCTOR QUICK FACTS	
Main Areas:	Coaching; Inspiration
Best-Seller:	"You Were Born Rich"
Profile:	Lecturer; Counselor; Business Consultant
Affiliation:	LifeSuccess Productions, L.L.C.

❏ *Bob Proctor Biography*

Bob Proctor is a lecturer, counselor, business consultant, and teacher, who explains how people can recognize their potential and achieve their goals in life. For 40 years, he has helped create lives of prosperity, rewarding relationships, and spiritual awareness. Born in northern Ontario, Bob stresses the ideas of positive thinking and self-motivation.

In 1960, Bob was a high school dropout with a resume of dead-end jobs and a future clouded in debt. But by using Napoleon Hill's *Think and Grow Rich*, he found the initiative to start an office cleaning business, which he grew to international scope in his first year of operation. He was making more than $100,000, and soon his salary topped $1 million.

Bob then moved to Chicago to work at Nightingale-Conant, where he became vice president of sales. In the mid-1970s, he established his own seminar company. Bob now teaches thousands of people how to believe in and act upon the greatness of their own minds. He has earned praise for his teaching from places around the world. Bob is also the author of a number of books, including the international best-seller, *You Were Born Rich*.

❏ *David Riklan's Favorite Bob Proctor Quotes and Thoughts*

- All of the great achievers of the past have been visionary figures; they were men and women who projected into the future. They thought of what could be, rather than what already was, and then they moved themselves into action, to bring these things into fruition.

- The only competition you will ever face is with your own ignorance.

- Persistence is a unique mental strength; a strength that is essential to combat the fierce power of the repeated rejections and numerous other obstacles that sit in waiting and are all part of winning in a fast-moving, ever-changing world.

❏ *The Best Way to Get Started with Bob Proctor*

Bob Proctor's special skill is mentoring and coaching people. He has demonstrated an ability to assist others with reaching their goals and attaining a life of prosperity. There is no one way to get started with Bob Proctor; the choice is too closely aligned with your specific needs. Yet here are some suggestions:

His coaching programs, The Freedom Series and the 3% Club, are both excellent ways to work with Bob Proctor and his company. The Freedom Series will help you tap your inner power and realize that you are capable of doing something incredible with your life. The 3% Club—based on the fact that 3 percent of the population earns 97 percent of the money in the world—will help you learn how to earn wealth by sharing the secrets of building a financial empire.

Before paying for tapes in The Freedom Series or becoming a member of the 3% Club, I suggest you first visit each program's website to get more information. Each site (www.thefreedomseries.com & www.3percentclubonline.com) offers its own contact information if you have additional questions.

Another way to get started with Bob Proctor is to read his book *You Were Born Rich*. It gives you a very good sense of his methods and beliefs, providing motivation, inspiration, and practical advice on how to improve your life. For an example on Bob's message in writing, here is a small excerpt from one of his articles about persistence:

> Let me give you four relatively simple steps that will help you to turn persistence into a habit. These steps can be followed by virtually anyone.
>
> 1. Have a clearly defined goal. The goal must be something you are emotionally involved with, something you want very much. (In the beginning, you may not even believe that you can accomplish it—the belief will come.)
> 2. Have a clearly established plan that you can begin working on immediately. (Your plan will very likely only cover the first and possibly the second stage of the journey to your goal. As you begin executing your plan, other steps required to complete your journey will be revealed at the right time.)
> 3. Make an irrevocable decision to reject any and all negative suggestions that come from friends, relatives, or neighbors. Do not give any conscious attention to conditions or circumstances that appear to indicate the goal cannot be accomplished.

4. Establish a mastermind group of one or more people who will encourage, support, and assist you wherever possible.

All of the aforementioned products and services can be accessed or purchased through Bob Proctor's main website at www.bobproctor.com.

TO READ ADDITIONAL BOOK EXCERPTS or ARTICLES or to LISTEN TO BOB PROCTOR RIGHT NOW, VISIT
http://www.selfgrowth.com/experts

❑ *Books*

- You Were Born Rich
- The Goal Achiever
- Mission in Commission

❑ *Audio and Video Programs*

- The Freedom Series
- Born Rich Learning System
- Your Winner's Image
- Success Series CD

❑ *Other Programs and Highlights*

During Bob's first seminar with agents from Prudential Life Insurance Company of America in Chicago, he suggested that any agent could write $5 million in business that year if he/she made a decision to do so. The suggestion seemed implausible because the year was already half-over, and no agent in that region had ever written so much business in the company's history. But once one agent actually reached this mark, Bob established himself as a reputable motivator.

❑ *Contact Information*

ADDRESS: LifeSuccess Productions, L.L.C.
8900 E Pinnacle Peak Rd. Suite D240
Scottsdale, AZ 85255
PHONE: 1-800-871-9715
EMAIL: ContactUs@bobproctor.com
WEBSITE: www.bobproctor.com

RAM DASS
(Expert #47)

❑ *Ram Dass Biography*

Ram Dass is a beloved spiritual figure, who teaches and promotes service in ecology, socially-conscious business practices, and care for the dying. Born in 1931, he studied psychology in school, specializing in human motivation and personality development. After receiving an M.A. from Wesleyan and a Ph.D. from Stanford, Dass served on the psychology faculties at Stanford and the University of California.

From 1958 to 1963, Dass taught and did research at Harvard University's Graduate School of Education, as well as in Harvard's Department of Social Relations. In 1961, he explored human consciousness and collaborated with professionals like Timothy Leary to research psilocybin, LSD-25, and other psychedelic chemicals. Because of the controversial nature of this research, Dass was dismissed from Harvard in 1963.

Four years later, Dass traveled to India, where he studied yoga and meditation. There he met his Guru, Neem Karoli Baba, and received the name Ram Dass, which means "servant of God." Since 1968, he has pursued a variety of spiritual practices, including guru kripa, devotional yoga focused on the Hindu spiritual figure Hanuman, karma yoga, and Sufi and Jewish studies. His book, *Be Here Now*, is a great spiritual classic of the 20th century.

❑ *David Riklan's Favorite Ram Dass Quotes and Thoughts*

• You work on yourself, spiritually, as an offering to your fellow beings. Because, until you have cultivated that quality of peace, love, joy, presence, honesty, and truth, all of your acts are colored by your attachments.

• It is important to expect nothing, to take every experience, including the negative ones, as merely steps on the path, and to proceed.

- Learn to watch your drama unfold while at the same time knowing you are more than your drama.

- The intellect is a beautiful servant but a terrible master. Intellect is the power tool of our separateness. The intuitive, compassionate heart is the doorway to our unity.

- You must come to see every human being including yourself, as an incarnation in the body or personality, going through a certain life experience which is functional.

- Being conscious is cutting through your own melodrama and being right here. Exist in no mind, be empty, here now, and trust that as a situation arises, out of you will come what is necessary to deal with that situation, including the use of your intellect when appropriate.

- Your intellect need not be constantly held on to to keep reassuring you that you know where you're at, out of fear of loss of control.

- If you think you're free, there's no escape possible.

- Ultimately, when you stop identifying so much with your physical body and with your psychological entity, that anxiety starts to disintegrate.

❏ *The Best Way to Get Started with Ram Dass*

The best place to get started with Ram Dass is to read his first book, *Be Here Now*, which has become a classic spiritual guide after being published in 1971. *Be Here Now* is the book that introduced a generation of Westerners to the teachings of the East. In it, he describes how he went from Harvard professor Richard Alpert (his original name) to Ram Dass, a devotee of Neem Caroli Baba.

Dass takes us on his personal journey that includes the mind-expanding powers of LSD, his trip to India, and his experiences with Neem Caroli Baba. The book is broken up into several sections including "Journey: The Transformation: Dr. Richard Alpert, Ph.D. Into Baba Ram Dass," "From Bindu to Ojas: The Core Book," and "The Cookbook for a Sacred Life: A Manual for Conscious Being."

In "The Cookbook for a Sacred Life," Dass introduces you to the basics of Hindu religion, in which he presents information on a whole range of concepts and practices having to do with yoga postures, meditation, renunciation, dying, and sexual energy. As for Dass's other works, I recommend his most up-to-date book, *Still Here*, in which he shares the new wisdom he has gained through his own aging.

TO READ ADDITIONAL BOOK EXCERPTS or ARTICLES or to LISTEN
TO RAM DASS RIGHT NOW, VISIT
http://www.selfgrowth.com/experts

❑ *Books*

- Be Here Now
- Still Here: Embracing Changing, Aging and Dying
- Journey of Awakening: A Meditator's Guidebook

❑ *Audio and Video Programs*

- The Listening Heart
- Ego and Soul
- Facing Death

❑ *Other Programs and Highlights*

The Ram Dass Tape Library contains about 1,200 audiotapes of Ram Dass's
lectures, workshops, and retreats recorded over the last four decades. The Ram
Dass Tape Library Foundation ensures that his ongoing teachings are recorded
and preserved.

❑ *Contact Information*

ADDRESS: The Ram Dass Tape Library
               524 San Anselmo Avenue, #203
               San Anselmo, CA 94960
PHONE: (415) 499-8587
EMAIL: RDTapes@aol.com
WEBSITE: www.ramdasstapes.org

BARBARA SHER
(Expert #48)

BARBARA SHER QUICK FACTS

Main Areas:	Career Transitions; Goal Achievement; Team Building
NY Times Best-Seller:	"I Could Do Anything if I Only Knew What It Was"
Profile:	Author; Career Counselor; Workshop Presenter; Webradio Talk Show Host; Host of Three Public Television Pledge Specials

---

❑ *Barbara Sher Biography*

Barbara Sher is a business owner, career counselor, and best-selling author on goal achievement and teamwork. She has presented her seminars and workshops to people throughout the world for professional organizations, colleges, corporations, and government agencies. She also consults with clients in her New York office.

In 1972, Sher invented Success Teams—small groups in which members help each other make their dreams come true. Today, Sher's teams are operating across the globe. She is also the author of four books, including *Wishcraft: How to Get What You Really Want*, which has sold over one million copies. Readers of the book will learn effective strategies for making real change in their lives.

Sher discovered that many people didn't know what they would really love to do. She began hosting problem-solving sessions and developing dozens of powerful techniques that freed people from "goal-paralysis." Her innovative techniques for overcoming resistance have been widely accepted by psychologists and career counselors and made her second book, *I Could Do Anything if I Only Knew What It Was*, a *New York Times* best-seller.

❑ *David Riklan's Favorite Barbara Sher Quotes and Thoughts*

- You can learn new things at any time in your life if you're willing to be a beginner. If you actually learn to like being a beginner, the whole world opens up to you.

- There is always a realistic way to fulfill any dream. There has never been a dream that you can't have—at least, not the heart of it, not the part you love the most.

- Real obstacles don't take you in circles. They can be overcome. Invented ones are like a maze.

- If you truly feared failure, you'd be very successful.

- Every single one of us can do things that no one else can do, can love things that no one else can love. We are like violins. We can be used for doorstops or we can make music. You know what to do.

- Doing is a quantum leap from imagining. Thinking about swimming isn't much like actually getting in the water.

- What will determine the course of your life more than any other thing is whether or not you're willing to tolerate necessary discomfort.

❑ *The Best Way to Get Started with Barbara Sher*

Barbara Sher has written several wonderful books, and it was a challenge for me to determine the best way to get started. Two books stand out in my mind: *Wishcraft: How to Get What You Really Want* and *I Could Do Anything if I Only Knew What It Was*. You will benefit from reading either work.

Wishcraft raised Sher's standing to that of a renowned expert in the Self Improvement community. The book's exercises and games show you how to brainstorm and turn your ideas into action. "This book is designed to help you find the good life," Sher says, and to "crave work that will spark you into excitement and energy."

Her follow-up to *Wishcraft* was *I Could Do Anything If I Only Knew What It Was*. First off, it's a great title. It includes information like "How to get off the fast track—and on to the right track," "First aid techniques for paralyzing chronic negativity," and "How to regroup when you've lost your big dream." Sher provides a practical approach for finding the career for you.

TO READ ADDITIONAL BOOK EXCERPTS or ARTICLES or to LISTEN TO BARBARA SHER RIGHT NOW, VISIT
http://www.selfgrowth.com/experts

❑ *Books*

- Wishcraft: How to Get What You Really Want
- I Could Do Anything if I Only Knew What It Was: How to Discover What You Really Want and How to Get It
- Live the Life You Love in Ten Easy Step-by-Step Lessons
- It's Only Too Late If You Don't Start Now: How to Create Your Second Life at Any Age

❑ *Audio and Video Programs*

- Dare to Live Your Dream (*a 12-cassette audio course based on* Live the Life You Love, *read by the author*)
- I Could Do Anything if I Only Knew What It Was; It's Only Too Late If You Don't Start Now *(an 8-cassette audiobook set read by the author)*
- How to Create Your Second Life After 40 *(an 80-minute video TV special)*
- Live the Life You Love/Map to Success *(a two-hour video TV special)*
- Barbara Sher's Idea Party *(a 67-minute video TV special)*

❑ *Other Programs and Highlights*

Barbara Sher's third book, *Live the Life You Love*, guides readers to a 10-step program which identifies goals and achieves them. It won the first-place award for motivational book by the Books for a Better Life Commission.

Her most recent book, *It's Only Too Late If You Don't Start Now: How to Create Your Second Life At Any Age*, was made into an Emmy-nominated public television pledge special of the same name. She has since made two additional record-breaking pledge specials for public television: "Live the Life You Love" and "Barbara Sher's Idea Party."

Sher has appeared on local and national radio and television shows, including *The Oprah Winfrey Show*, *CNN*, the *Today Show*, *60 Minutes*, and *Good Morning America*, and has been featured in *The New York Times*, *The Wall Street Journal*, and many other newspapers and magazines. In 2002, she was a monthly columnist for *Real Simple Magazine*. Sher maintains a free bulletin board where people help each other attain their goals at www.barbarasher.com.

❑ *Contact Information*

ADDRESS: Box 20052
            Park West Station
            New York, NY 10025
EMAIL: Go to www.barbarasher.com/ask.htm
WEBSITE: www.barbarasher.com
            www.shersuccessteams.com

ANTHONY DE MELLO
(Expert #49)

ANTHONY DE MELLO QUICK FACTS	
Main Areas:	Spirituality; Christianity; Awareness
Best-Sellers:	"Awareness"; "The Way to Love"; "Sadhana: A Way to God"
Profile:	Author; Jesuit Priest; Workshop/Seminar Leader; 1931-1987

❑ *Anthony de Mello Biography*

Anthony de Mello was a Jesuit priest from India, known for his writings and spiritual conferences. He was the director of the Sadhana Institute of Pastoral Counseling in Poona, India, as well as a member of the Jesuit province of Bombay. De Mello challenged people to encounter the God behind all words, concepts, and religious formulas.

De Mello taught meditation techniques that are a blend of Eastern religious thought, modern psychology, and the spiritual exercises of Ignatius of Loyola, founder of the Jesuit religious order. De Mello claimed that most people are asleep and need to wake up, open up their eyes, and see what is real—both inside and outside of themselves. He insisted that the greatest human gift is to be aware and be in touch with your body and mind.

De Mello was the author five best-selling books, including *Awareness*, which combines Christian spirituality, Buddhist parables, Hindu breathing exercises, and psychological insight. In it, he insists that to become aware, we must realize the needs and potential of others. Today, his retreats, workshops, seminars on prayer, and therapy courses are still widely known in many English-speaking and Spanish-speaking countries.

❑ *David Riklan's Favorite Anthony de Mello Quotes and Thoughts*

- As soon as you look at the world through an ideology you are finished. No reality fits an ideology. Life is beyond that. That is why people are always searching for a meaning to life...Meaning is only found when you go beyond meaning. Life only makes sense when you perceive it as mystery and it makes no sense to the conceptualizing mind.

- Obedience keeps the rules. Love knows when to break them.

- People mistakenly assume that their thinking is done by their head; it is actually done by the heart which first dictates the conclusion, then commands the head to provide the reasoning that will defend it...

- Problems only exist in the human mind.

- These things will destroy the human race: politics without principle, progress without compassion, wealth without work, learning without silence, religion without fearlessness, and worship without awareness.

❏ *The Best Way to Get Started with Anthony De Mello*

The best way to get started with Anthony de Mello is to read his book, *Awareness: The Perils and Opportunities of Reality*. *Awareness* is a short but very influential book. In it, de Mello uses humor and compassion to teach you to welcome the challenge of knowing yourself and living the "aware" life.

In the first chapter, de Mello had me thinking, laughing, and hungry for more. Here is the beginning, Chapter 1 titled "On Waking Up":

> Spirituality means waking up. Most people, even though they don't know it are asleep. They're born asleep, they live asleep, they marry in their sleep, they breed children in their sleep, they die in their sleep without ever waking up. They never understand the loveliness and beauty of this thing that we call human existence. You know, all mystics—Catholic, Christian, non-Christian, no matter what their theology—are unanimous on one thing: that all is well, all is well. Though everything is a mess, all is well. Strange paradox to be sure. But, tragically, most people never get to see all is well because they are asleep. They are having a nightmare.

De Mello incorporates elements of Buddhist and Hindu traditions (i.e.— emphasis on awareness, mindfulness) and combines them with elements of Christianity (i.e.—emphasis on love). His book has been described as one that "provokes a revolution in outlook and attitude that can only be pondered over a lifetime." So wake up and get *Awareness*!

TO READ ADDITIONAL BOOK EXCERPTS or ARTICLES or to LISTEN TO ANTHONY DE MELLO RIGHT NOW, VISIT
http://www.selfgrowth.com/experts

❏ *Books*

- Awareness: The Perils and Opportunities of Reality
- The Way to Love: The Last Meditations of Anthony de Mello

- Sadhana: A Way to God: Christian Exercises in Eastern Form
- The Song of the Bird
- Wellsprings: A Book of Spiritual Exercises

❑ *Audio and Video Programs*

- Wake Up to Life
- A Way to God for Today
- Rediscovery of Life

❑ *Other Programs and Highlights*

Rev. J. Francis Stroud, S.J. is the executive director of the De Mello Spirituality Center, also called The Center for Spiritual Exchange. His teaching course consists of applying Anthony de Mello's spiritual principles to students' experiences of film and television.

❑ *Contact Information*

ADDRESS: Rev. J. Francis Stroud, S.J., De Mello Spirituality Center
PHONE: 718-817-4508
EMAIL: stroud@fordham.edu
WEBSITE: www.demello.org

LAUREL MELLIN
(Expert #50)

LAUREL MELLIN QUICK FACTS	
Main Areas:	Personal Growth; Happiness; Weight Loss
Profile:	Author; Medical School Professor; Obesity Expert.
Affiliations:	The Institute for Health Solutions; University of California, San Francisco

❏ *Laurel Mellin Biography*

Laurel Mellin developed The Solution, a scientifically proven method for adults to turn off their drive for all the common excesses and experience more emotional balance, relationship intimacy, and spiritual connection. This new method, described in her book *The Pathway*, goes to the roots of not just one of the common excesses but all of them: overeating, overspending, overworking, drinking too much, and smoking, as well as the softer excesses like people-pleasing, rescuing others, putting up walls, and thinking too much. Mellin, who first applied this method to weight loss, is an associate clinical professor of family and community medicine and pediatrics at the University of California, San Francisco School of Medicine.

The Solution method is based on the scientific literature that since 1940 has shown that at the roots of excessive behaviors, other than genetics, is the need for two very basic internal skills: self-nurturing and effective limits. Mastering these skills changes nearly every aspect of life. The first time that most people use the skills, they immediately shift their emotional state from imbalance to balance and their drive for another cookie, drink, or spending spree fades. However, the state of balance does not last. For emotional balance is a product of the feeling brain and the feeling brain only chances with practice. However, as people stay on the "pathway" of using these skills, their personal balance becomes spontaneous and lasting. They typically experience a Solution, that is, freedom from all the excessive appetites and an abundance of all the rewards of a happy, healthy life (balance, integration, sanctuary, intimacy, vibrancy and spirituality).

The method is so simple that Mellin first taught it to children and so powerful that *Health* magazine named it as one of the top ten medical advances of 2000. Researchers at the University of California, San Francisco and the University of Illinois, Chicago have shown that users of The Solution, on average, feel healthier and happier right away, and these changes last years later without ongoing medications, diets, or support. More than 200,000 people have used this method. Mellin, the director of the Institute for Health Solutions, lectures extensively to health professionals and self-help groups.

❏ *David Riklan's Favorite Laurel Mellin Quotes and Thoughts*

- Self-nurturing is the skill of checking our feelings and needs throughout the day, so we know and honor ourselves and meet our needs more often.

- Effective limits is the skill of having reasonable expectations—not too harsh or too easy –and following through with them, so we can take action and have more power and greater safety in our lives.

- If you have a truckload of insight and nickel, you only have five cents.

- Traditional interventions—insight, knowledge, planning and deciding—are processed primarily by the thinking brain. Unfortunately, there is no significant relationship between what is processed by the thinking brain our most primitive human drives. That's why you can have a Ph.D. in nutrition and an eating disorder. True transformation comes from revising the feeling brain.

- On the day that you were born, you had all the inherent strength, goodness and wisdom you would ever need. All that you required were the tools to access it. These two skills –nurturing and limits—are those tools.

❏ *The Best Way to Get Started with Laurel Mellin*

Before jumping right into The Solution, I suggest you start by going to The Solution website at www.thepathway.org. You will have the opportunity to learn more about the program, get the answers to frequently asked questions, and take a self-test to determine your reason for using The Solution. The Solution was based on research that started over 20 years ago and is proven to work in many areas of your life.

Once you become familiar with The Solution, you should then read Laurel Mellin's book, *The Pathway*, to get a better understanding of it, so you can put it into action. If you want the skills to become spontaneous and lasting, consider participating in the training. It's based on her course, which involves completing six Solution Kits (workbooks and CDs). You can use them on your own, with support from The Solution Internet community, through local self-help Solution Circle or professionally-conducted Solution Groups.

Another of Mellin's books, *The Solution: 6 Winning Ways to Permanent Weight Loss*, will help those who particularly want to end their overeating. If this is the case for you, Mellin recommends that you read this book in addition to *The Pathway*.

This approach can also be used to resolve child obesity. Mellin's SHAPEDOWN Program, a family-based approach to child and adolescent obesity, is based on The Solution. The program targets nutrition and activity in both children and their parents and teaches the skills of nurturing and limits to parents and children alike. Again, before starting it right away, it would be best to read more about it. Visit www.shapedown.com to learn if SHAPEDOWN is right for your family. If so, look into ordering the SHAPEDOWN Getting Started Family Pack, which is described on the website.

TO READ ADDITIONAL BOOK EXCERPTS or ARTICLES or to LISTEN
TO LAUREL MELLIN RIGHT NOW, VISIT
http://www.selfgrowth.com/experts

❑ *Books*

- The Pathway: Follow the Road to Health and Happiness
- The Solution: 6 Winning Ways to Permanent Weight Loss
- The SHAPEDOWN Program *(for weight problems in children)*

❑ *Audio and Video Programs*

- The Solution Kits #1 through #6
- The Solution (on audio cassette)

❑ *Other Programs and Highlights*

Laurel Mellin has appeared on *The Oprah Winfrey Show,* the *Today Show, Good Morning America,* and the *CBS Evening News*. Her work has been featured in *Time, Life, Newsweek, Fortune, Shape, U.S. News & World Report,* and every major women's magazines. It has outstanding endorsements, including C. Everett Koop, former surgeon general.

The SHAPEDOWN Program has been selected by the American Medical Association at its national congress as an exemplary health promotion program. It has also received an award for excellence in consumer education from the National Food and Drug Administration.

❑ *Contact Information*

ADDRESS:	The Institute for Health Solutions	SHAPEDOWN
	1623A Fifth Avenue	1323 San Anselmo Ave.
	San Rafael, CA 94901	San Anselmo, CA 94960
PHONE:	415-457-3331	415-453-8886

EMAIL: support@sweetestfruit.org   shapedown@aol.com
WEBSITE: www.thepathway.org   www.shapedown.com

BRUCE WILKINSON
(Expert #51)

<table>
<tr><td colspan="2" align="center">**BRUCE WILKINSON QUICK FACTS**</td></tr>
<tr><td>*Main Areas:*</td><td>Prayer; Religious Beliefs; Spirituality</td></tr>
<tr><td>*NY Times Best-Sellers:*</td><td>"The Prayer of Jabez" (over 12 million copies sold);
"Secrets of the Vine"; "A Life God Rewards"</td></tr>
<tr><td>*Profile:*</td><td>Author; Speaker</td></tr>
<tr><td>*Affiliation:*</td><td>Global Vision Resources</td></tr>
</table>

❏ *Bruce Wilkinson Biography*

Dr. Bruce Wilkinson has based his life on making himself available to God to do things far beyond his own ability. His work, *The Prayer of Jabez*, has been named "the fastest-selling book of all time" by *Publishers Weekly*. Through the story of a little-known Biblical hero named Jabez, Dr. Wilkinson shows how one daily prayer can help you break through to the life you were meant to live. His books have sold over 15 million copies combined.

Dr. Wilkinson graduated from Northeastern Bible College and Dallas Theological Seminary and was awarded a doctorate of divinity by Western Conservative Baptist Seminary. In 1972, he devised a unique method for teaching the big picture of the content of Scripture book by book. Four years later, he founded Walk Thru the Bible Ministries, which is now the largest Christian seminar organization in the United States.

In 1998, Dr. Wilkinson founded Walk Thru the Bible International, a global initiative to develop a Bible teacher for every 50,000 people in every nation of the world. He also founded Global Vision Resources (GVR) in 2001, a private, non-profit operating foundation. GVR produces, markets, and distributes video and curriculum products to retail outlets, businesses, schools, and ministries across the globe

❏ *David Riklan's Favorite Bruce Wilkinson Quotes and Thoughts*

- Communion with God is a relationship, not a sensation.

- Dependence upon God makes heroes of ordinary people like you and me!

- God's power under us, in us, surging through us, is exactly what turns dependence into unforgettable experiences of completeness.

- How would your day unfold if you believed that God wants your borders expanded at all times with every person and if you were confident that God's powerful hand is directing you even as you minister?

- Neither is repentance a one-time act. It is a lifestyle, an ongoing commitment to keep putting aside our rebellion and receive God's forgiveness.

- What if your very best friend were about to move away? What if you had only a few hours left to spend together? How valuable would that time be? Now imagine that your friend had something really important to say to you. "Listen carefully," he might say. Would you pay better attention then? "I have to tell you something," he might add. "I waited until now...but I can't wait any longer." Would you cling to his words, hoping to remember them forever? Now what if that person about to speak were Jesus? How closely would you listen to Him?

❑ *The Best Way to Get Started with Bruce Wilkinson*

Bruce Wilkinson's international best-seller, *The Prayer of Jabez: Breaking Through to the Blessed Life*, is clearly the place to get started. The book's main character is named Jabez, a man from the Bible who is virtually unknown. In Chronicles 1, Chapter 4:

> Jabez called on the God of Israel saying, "Oh, that You would bless me indeed, and enlarge my territory, that Your hand would be with me, and that You would keep me from evil, that I may not cause pain." So God granted him what he requested.

Jabez's simple petition to God is the cornerstone of the book and has become a call to live a more "blessed life" for millions of readers. Dr. Wilkinson says he has recited this prayer every day for more than 30 years, and he testifies enthusiastically to the changes it has wrought in his own life.

Dr. Wilkinson writes in a very personal, conversational style and challenges readers to recite the Jabez prayer every morning and keep a record of the changes that occur. He says the power is not in the prayer itself, but "rather, the power is in what you believe will happen as a result of the prayer and the action you take."

TO READ ADDITIONAL BOOK EXCERPTS or ARTICLES or to LISTEN TO BRUCE WILKINSON RIGHT NOW, VISIT
http://www.selfgrowth.com/experts

❑ **Books**

- The Prayer of Jabez: Breaking Through to the Blessed Life
- A Life God Rewards: Why Everything You Do Today Matters For-ever
- Secrets of the Vine: Breaking Through to Abundance
- The Seven Laws of the Learner: How to Teach Almost Anything to Practically Anyone

❑ **Audio and Video Programs**

- The Prayer of Jabez (on audio cassette or audio CD)
- A Life God Rewards (on audio cassette or audio CD)
- Secrets of the Vine (on audio cassette or audio CD)

❑ **Other Programs and Highlights**

A sought-after speaker, Dr. Wilkinson has been a featured guest on programs like the *Today Show Weekend Edition*, *Larry King Live*, and CNN's *TalkBack Live*. His books have been featured on *Good Morning America* and National Public Radio, as well as in *The New York Times*, *USA Today*, *The Los Angeles Times*, *The Chicago Tribune*, and *Time*.

❑ **Contact Information**

ADDRESS: Multnomah Publishers Publicity
PHONE: 541-549-1144
EMAIL: information@multnomahbooks.com
WEBSITE: www.thebreakthroughseries.com
                       www.brucewilkinson.com
                       www.multnomahbooks.com

TONY BUZAN
(Expert #52)

TONY BUZAN QUICK FACTS	
Main Areas:	Learning; Brain Improvement; Mind Mapping
Best-Seller:	"Use Both Sides of Your Brain" (over 2 million copies sold)
Profile:	Author; Psychologist; Poet; Teacher; Editor; Television Host; Creator of Mind Maps®
Affiliation:	Buzan Centres Ltd.

❏ *Tony Buzan Biography*

Tony Buzan is the creator of Mind Maps and the originator of the concept of Mental Literacy. Mind Maps is a graphic technique that provides a universal key to unlock the potential of the brain. In 1968, Tony was working in London as a teacher and editor of the Mensa International Journal, when the BBC asked him to host a ten-part educational series called *Use Your Head*. This program started a successful 25-year collaboration.

Tony is the holder of the world record for Creative I.Q. and is head of an international network of brain clubs. He established the Brain Foundation, which organizes the World Memory Championships, and is co-founder of the International Mind Sports Olympiad. In addition, much of his work is devoted to helping those with learning disabilities.

Tony is an elected member of the International Council of Psychologists and a Fellow of the Institute of Training and Development. He is also a prize-winning poet and author of over 20 best-sellers on the brain and learning. His classic, *Use Both Sides of Your Brain*, has sold more than two million copies worldwide. His books have been published in 50 countries and translated into 20 languages.

❏ *David Riklan's Favorite Tony Buzan Quotes and Thoughts*

- Modern research has shown that your eye-brain system is thousands of times more complex and powerful than had previously been estimated, and that with proper training you can quickly reap the benefits of this enormous potential.

- Learning how to learn is life's most important skill.

- The early development of speed reading can be traced to the beginning of (the 20th) century, when the publication explosion swamped readers with more than they could possibly handle at normal reading rates.

- Your brain is like a sleeping giant.

❑ *The Best Way to Get Started with Tony Buzan*

To understand Tony Buzan is to understand his mission. He says, "My goal and the goal of the Buzan Centres is the creation of a Mentally Literate planet, one in which every human being is fully aware of the physical and behavioral alphabets of that remarkable organ, the human brain."

One of the ways that Tony has accomplished this inspiring mission is through his book, *Use Both Sides of Your Brain*, and this is the best place to get started. In the book, Tony uses the latest research on the workings of the human brain to teach us how to unleash its power. His book provides step-by-step exercises for using the left and right side of our brain to learn more effectively, and by reading it, we can learn a variety of things like:

- How to read faster and more effectively.
- How to study more efficiently and increase overall memory.
- How language and imagery can be used for recording, organizing, remembering, creative thinking, and problem solving.

Use Both Sides of Your Brain provides the tools to reach our full potential. Tony Buzan is also world renowned for the concept of Mind Mapping, which he defines as "a powerful graphic technique which provides a universal key to unlock the potential of the brain." The best place to find out about Mind Mapping is through his work, *The Mind Map Book*.

TO READ ADDITIONAL BOOK EXCERPTS or ARTICLES or to LISTEN TO TONY BUZAN RIGHT NOW, VISIT
http://www.selfgrowth.com/experts

❑ *Books*

- Use Both Sides of Your Brain
- The Mind Map Book:
- Use Your Perfect Memory
- Head Strong
- Head First

❑ *Audio and Video Programs*

- Buzan on…audio series

- MindPower
- Developing Family Genius
- Learning with Lana
- If at First…

❑ *Other Programs and Highlights*

Tony Buzan has been featured in, presented, or co-produced various satellite broadcasts and television, radio, or video programs. He is an advisor to international Olympic coaches and athletes and also to the British Olympic Rowing Squad and the British Olympic Chess Squads.

❑ *Contact Information*

ADDRESS: *(USA)* Buzan Centres Inc.   *(UK)* Buzan Centres Ltd.
                 P.O. Box 4   54 Parkstone Road
                 Palm Beach, FL 33480   Poole, Dorset BH15 2PG.
PHONE: 1-561-881-0188   44 (0) 1202 674676
EMAIL: buzan@buzancentres.com
WEBSITE: www.buzancentres.com

JAMES REDFIELD
(Expert #53)

JAMES REDFIELD QUICK FACTS

Main Area: Spiritual Development
NY Times Best-Seller: "The Celestine Prophecy"
Profile: Author; Former Therapist

❑ *James Redfield Biography*

James Redfield is a former therapist and the author of *The Celestine Prophecy*, a *New York Times* best-seller and one of the most successful self-published books of all time. The book is an adventure parable about a spiritual journey to Peru. It tells readers how to make connections among the events in their lives—at the present moment and in the years to come. The sequel, *The Tenth Insight*, also became a best-seller.

Redfield has been interested in human spirituality all his life. Born in 1950, he grew up in a rural area near Birmingham, Alabama and early on, was motivated by a need for clarity about spiritual matters. He was brought up in a Methodist Church that was loving and community-oriented, yet he was frustrated by a lack of answers to his questions about the true nature of spiritual experience.

Redfield studied Eastern philosophies, including Taoism and Zen, while majoring in sociology at Auburn University. He later received a master's degree in counseling and spent more than 15 years as a therapist to abused adolescents. During this time, he was drawn into the human potential movement and turned to it for theories about intuitions that would help his troubled clients. In 1989, he left his job to write full-time.

❑ *David Riklan's Favorite James Redfield Quotes and Thoughts*

- Life is really about a spiritual unfolding that is personal and enchanting—an unfolding that no science or philosophy or religion has yet fully clarified.

- Knowing our personal mission further enhances the flow of mysterious coincidences as we are guided toward our destinies. First we have a question, then dreams, daydreams, and intuitions lead us toward the answers, which usually are synchronistically provided by the wisdom of another human being.

- Together we are going somewhere, each generation building upon the accomplishments of the previous one, destined for an end we can only dimly remember. We're all in the process of awakening and opening up to who we really are, and what we came here to do, which is often a very difficult task.

- I don't mean to minimize the formidable problems still facing humanity, only to suggest that each of us in our own way is involved in the solution. If we stay aware and acknowledge the great mystery that is this life, we will see that we have been perfectly placed, in exactly the right position…to make all the difference in the world.

- The awareness begins with a feeling of restlessness—an inner urging to find more meaning in life. As we respond to this inner prompting we begin to notice the "chance coincidences"—strange synchronistic events in our life. We begin to realize that some underlying process is operating our life.

❑ *The Best Way to Get Started with James Redfield*

I started with James Redfield by reading his best-selling book, *The Celestine Prophecy*, and this is where I recommend you start as well. It is a story of the discovery of an ancient Peruvian manuscript, which contains nine insights for spiritual living that will help humanity move toward a completely spiritual culture on Earth.

The first three insights are as follows:

- A Critical Mass
  A new spiritual awakening is occurring in human culture, an awakening brought about by a critical mass of individuals who experience their lives as a spiritual unfolding, a journey in which we are led forward by mysterious coincidences.

- The Longer Now
  This awakening represents the creation of a new, more complete worldview, which replaces a five-hundred-year-old preoccupation with secular survival and comfort. While this technological preoccupation was an important step, our awakening to life's coincidences is opening us up to the real purpose of human life on this planet, and the real nature of our universe.

- A Matter of Energy
  We now experience that we live not in a material universe, but in a universe of dynamic energy. Everything extant is a field of sacred energy that we can sense and intuit. Moreover, we humans can project

our energy by focusing our attention in the desired direction...where attention goes, energy flows...influencing other energy systems and increasing the pace of coincidences in our lives.

Originally self-published, *The Celestine Prophecy*'s strong selling was sparked mostly by word of mouth. This is because you can view the book in two ways: as an exceptionally written work of fiction, or as an insightful spiritual worldview of the past, present, and future. Either way, it is an interesting and compelling read.

TO READ ADDITIONAL BOOK EXCERPTS or ARTICLES or to LISTEN TO JAMES REDFIELD RIGHT NOW, VISIT
http://www.selfgrowth.com/experts

❑ *Books*

- The Celestine Prophecy: An Adventure
- The Tenth Insight: Holding the Vision
- The Secret of Shambhala: In Search of the Eleventh Insight

❑ *Audio and Video Programs*

- The Celestine Meditations: A Guide to Meditating Based on the Celestine Prophecy
- The Celestine Vision: Living the New Spiritual Awareness (book or audio cassette)
- God and the Evolving Universe: The Next Step in Personal Evolution (co-authored with Michael Murphy and Sylvia Timbers) (book or audio cassette)

❑ *Other Programs and Highlights*

In 1997, Redfield was awarded the highly prestigious Medal of the Presidency of the Italian Senate at the XXIII Pio Manzu International Conference in Rimini, Italy. In 2000, he was one of only two recipients of Humanitarian of the Year honors from his alma mater, Auburn University. He was given the same honor by the International New Thought Alliance.

❑ *Contact Information*

EMAIL: jamesredfield@celestinevision.com
WEBSITE: www.celestinevision.com

M. SCOTT PECK
(Expert #54)

M. SCOTT PECK QUICK FACTS

Main Area:	Personal Growth
NY Times Best-Seller:	"The Road Less Traveled" (over 6 million copies sold)
Profile:	Author; Psychiatrist
Affiliation:	The Foundation for Community Encouragement

❏ *M. Scott Peck Biography*

Dr. M. Scott Peck is a nationally recognized authority on the relationship between religion and science. In 1980, at age 43, Dr. Peck was nondenominationally baptized by a Methodist minister in an Episcopalian convent, where he has frequently gone on retreat. In 1992, he was selected by the American Psychiatric Association as a distinguished psychiatrist lecturer.

Dr. Peck is the author of several books, including *The Road Less Traveled*, which has sold over six million copies to date in North America alone. He received his B.A. degree magna cum laude from Harvard College in 1958 and his M.D. degree from the Case Western Reserve University School of Medicine in 1963.

In 1984, Dr. Peck and his wife met with nine others to establish The Foundation for Community Encouragement, a non-profit, public educational foundation, whose mission is to promote and teach the principles of community. As a result of his work with community-building, Dr. Peck has received a number of awards, including the 1984 Kaleidoscope Award for Peacemaking and the 1994 Temple International Peace Prize.

❏ *David Riklan's Favorite M. Scott Peck Quotes and Thoughts*

- Life is difficult. This is a great truth, one of the greatest truths. It is a great truth because once we truly see this truth, we transcend it. Once we truly know that life is difficult—once we truly understand and accept it—then life is no longer difficult. Because once it is accepted, the fact that life is difficult no longer matters.

- Most do not fully see this truth that life is difficult. Instead they moan more or less incessantly, noisily or subtly, about the enormity of their problems, their burdens, and their difficulties as if life were generally easy, as if life should be easy. They voice their belief, noisily or subtly, that their difficulties represent a unique kind of affliction that should not be and that has somehow been especially visited upon them, or else upon their families, their tribe, their class, their nation, their race, or even their species, and not upon others.

- An essential part of true listening is the discipline of bracketing—the temporary giving up or setting aside of one's own prejudices, frames of reference, and desires so as to experience as far as possible the speaker's world from the inside, step in inside his or her shoes.

- Nirvana or lasting enlightenment or true spiritual growth can be achieved only through persistent exercise of real love.

- Until you value yourself you will not value your time. Until you value your time, you will not do anything with it.

- You cannot truly listen to anyone and do anything else at the same time.

- Problems do not go away. They must be worked through or else they remain, forever a barrier to the growth and development of the spirit.

❑ *The Best Way to Get Started with M. Scott Peck*

Dr. M. Scott Peck is best known for his book, *The Road Less Traveled*, and this is the best place to start. The book was first published in 1978 but didn't become a best-seller until 1983. It has had a tremendous impact on a wide range of people and is still an important part of any Self Improvement library. *The Road Less Traveled* was one of the first books dealing with the psychology of spirituality and set the groundwork for other authors to write their works.

The Road Less Traveled can be seen as a primer on personal growth, trying to meld psychology, religion, love, and science into one book. It is not a fluffy, feel-good book or a quick inspirational manual. It delves deeply into ideas from psychoanalysis, philosophy, spirituality, and religion. The book starts out with the premise that "life is difficult" and personal growth is a "complex, arduous, and lifelong task."

Dr. Peck provides details from his own life combined with stories from anonymous therapy clients. He uses a variety of sources including traditional psychology, Gospel passages, and New Age spirituality and insists that problems must be overcome through suffering, discipline, and hard work.

TO READ ADDITIONAL BOOK EXCERPTS or ARTICLES or to LISTEN TO M. SCOTT PECK RIGHT NOW, VISIT
http://www.selfgrowth.com/experts

❑ *Books*

- The Road Less Traveled: A New Psychology of Love, Traditional Values and Spiritual Growth
- People of the Lie: The Hope for Healing Human Evil
- A World Waiting to be Born: Civility Rediscovered

❑ *Audio and Video Programs*

- Golf and the Spirit: Lessons for the Journey (book or audio cassette or audio CD)
- The Road Less Traveled (on audio cassette)
- People of the Lie (on audio cassette)

❑ *Other Programs and Highlights*

Dr. Peck served in the United States Army from 1963 until 1972, resigning from the position of Assistant Chief Psychiatry and Neurology Consultant to the Surgeon General of the Army with the rank of Lieutenant Colonel. From 1972 to 1983, Dr. Peck was engaged in the private practice of psychiatry in Litchfield County, Connecticut.

❑ *Contact Information*

WEBSITE: www.mscottpeck.com
www.fce-community.org

NEALE DONALD WALSCH
(Expert #55)

NEALE DONALD WALSCH QUICK FACTS	
Main Area:	Spirituality
NY Times Best-Seller:	"Conversations with God: An Uncommon Dialogue, Book 1"
Profile:	Author; Spiritual Messenger
Affiliation:	Conversations with God Foundation

❑ *Neale Donald Walsch Biography*

Neale Donald Walsch is a modern day spiritual messenger whose words continue to touch the world. Early on, Neale was interested in religion and had a deeply felt connection to spirituality. After dropping out of college and suffering turmoil in his health, income, and relationship life, he eventually worked his way into full time employment and a spot on a syndicated radio talk show host. Yet he felt emptiness in his life.

In 1992, following a period of deep despair, Neale awoke in the middle of a February night and wrote an anguished letter to God. He angrily scratched across a yellow legal pad, "What does it take to make life work?" Neale says that he heard a "voiceless voice" that gave him an answer. As more questions came, more answers came in the same fashion.

Neale continued this first "conversation" for hours and had many more in the weeks that followed. He always awoke in the middle of the night and was drawn to his legal pad. Neale's handwritten notes would later become the best-selling *Conversations with God* books, which have been translated into 27 languages. *Conversations with God, Book 1* occupied *The New York Times* best-seller list for over two and half years.

❑ *David Riklan's Favorite Neale Donald Walsch Quotes and Thoughts*

- If the whole world followed you, would you be pleased with where you took it?

- Whatever you choose for yourself, give to another. If you choose to be happy, cause another to be happy. If you choose to be prosperous, cause another to prosper. If you choose more love in your life, cause another to have more love in theirs.

- Enlightenment is understanding that there is nowhere to go, nothing to do, and nobody you have to be except exactly who you're being right now.

- Decisions will be made in the next few years, which will set our course and direction for decades to come. The choices now being placed before the human community are enormous, and tomorrow's choices will be even more momentous as our options become increasingly limited.

- All of us will play a role in the making of these decisions. They will not be left to someone else. We are the *someone else*. The decisions I am talking about cannot, or will not, be made by any political power structure, the influential elite, or corporate giants. They will be made in the hearts and in the homes of individuals and families around the world.

❑ *The Best Way to Get Started with Neale Donald Walsch*

There is only one place to start, and that's with his book *Conversations with God: An Uncommon Dialogue, Book 1*. Neale says that he had been in "the habit for years of writing my thoughts down in letters," and one time, "rather than another letter to another person I imagined to be victimizing me, I thought I'd go straight to the source; straight to the greatest victimizer of them all. I decided to write a letter to God." His thoughts were primarily a series of questions for God.

Neale adds, "To my surprise, as I scribbled out the last of my bitter, unanswerable questions and prepared to toss my pen aside, my hand remained poised over the paper, as if held there by some invisible force. Abruptly, the pen began moving on its own. I had no idea what I was about to write, but an idea seemed to be coming, so I decided to flow with it."

The entire book is a dialogue between Neale and God. Neale was able to ask any question to God, with answers that begin to unravel every mystery in the universe. Whether or not you believe that the answers came from an "invisible force," the book remains fascinating, inspiring and compelling.

These are some of the questions that Neale asked God in the book. This is only a small subset of the questions contained in the book.

- Why is there so much suffering and pain in the world? If God were truly loving, why does God allow it?
- What is the purpose for all of life?
- What does it take to achieve success? When will our lives finally take off? Can the struggle ever end?
- Is there such thing as hell?

- Is there a way to be happy in relationships? Must they be constantly challenging?
- How can we solve the health problems we face?
- Is sex okay? Is sex purely for procreation, as some religions say?
- How can we attract enough money in our lives?
- Is there such thing as reincarnation? Have we had past lives?
- Is there such thing as being psychic? Are people who claim to be psychic "trafficking with the devil"?
- Is it O.K. to take money for doing good? Or are the two mutually exclusive?
- Why can't I do what I really want to do with my life and still make a living?

A specific example of the "conversation" from the book follows:

How does God talk, and to whom? When I asked this question, here's the answer I received:

"I talk to everyone. All the time. The question is not to whom do I talk, but who listens."

Intrigued, I asked God to expand on this subject. Here's what God said:

"First, let's exchange the word talk with the word communicate. It's a much better word, a much fuller, more accurate one. When we try to speak to each other—Me to you, you to Me, we are immediately constricted by the unbelievable limitation of words. For this reason, I do not communicate by words alone. In fact, rarely do I do so. My most common form of communication is through feeling.

"Feeling is the language of the soul.

"If you want to know what's true for you about something, look to how you're feeling about it.

"Feelings are sometimes difficult to discover—and often even more difficult to acknowledge. Yet hidden in your deepest feelings is your highest truth."

The dialogue continues and provides one of the most powerful new spiritual books written in a long time. If you finish this first book, Neale provides ample room to continue with *Conversations with God, Book 2* and *Book 3*.

TO READ ADDITIONAL BOOK EXCERPTS or ARTICLES or to LISTEN
TO NEALE DONALD WALSCH RIGHT NOW, VISIT
http://www.selfgrowth.com/experts

❑ *Books*

- Conversations with God: An Uncommon Dialogue (Books 1, 2, & 3)
- Bringers of the Light
- Recreating Yourself
- The Little Soul and the Sun: A Children's Parable Adapted from Conversations with God
- Moments of Grace
- The New Revelations

❑ *Audio and Video Programs*

- Friendship with God: An Uncommon Dialogue (book or audio cassette)
- Conversations with God for Teens (book or audio cassette or audio CD)
- Communion with God (book or audio cassette or audio CD)
- Conversations with God, The Journey

❑ *Other Programs and Highlights*

In order to deal with the enormous response to his writings, Neale created the Conversations with God Foundation. The Foundation is a non-profit educational organization dedicated to inspiring the world to help itself move from violence to peace, confusion to clarity, and anger to love.

❑ *Contact Information*

ADDRESS: Conversations with God Foundation
PMB #1150
1257 Siskiyou Blvd.
Ashland, OR 97520
PHONE: 541-482-8806
EMAIL: foundation@cwg.info
WEBSITE: www.cwg.org

ROLLO MAY
(Expert #56)

ROLLO MAY QUICK FACTS	
Main Area:	Existential Psychology
Best-Seller:	"Love and Will"
Profile:	Author; Psychologist

❑ *Rollo May Biography*

Rollo May was the one of the leading American existential psychologists of the 20th century. His work focused on the positive aspects of human potential and on the will of individuals toward self-fulfillment. After graduating from Oberlin College in Ohio, he traveled across Europe, where he taught English and spent time as an itinerant artist.

When May returned to the United States, he entered Union Theological Seminary and became friends with one of his teachers, Paul Tillich, an existentialist theologian, who would have a profound effect on his thinking. May's existential psychology examines reality as created by man himself. Man is ultimately responsible for the quality of his own existence, which takes precedence over simply living in the world.

May's life changed when he contracted tuberculosis and had to spend three years in a sanatorium. In 1949, he received his Ph.D. in clinical psychology from Columbia University, and in 1958, he edited the book, *Existence*, which introduced existential psychology to the United States. May's many other writings include *The Courage to Create* and *Love and Will*.

❑ *David Riklan's Favorite Rollo May Quotes and Thoughts*

- Creativity arises out of the tension between spontaneity and limitations, the latter (like the river banks) forcing the spontaneity into the various forms which are essential to the work of art or poem.

- Creativity is not merely the innocent spontaneity of our youth and childhood; it must also be married to the passion of the adult human being, which is a passion to live beyond one's death.

- Courage is not a virtue of value among other personal values like love or fidelity. It is the foundation that underlies and gives reality to all other virtues and personal values. Without courage our love pales into mere dependency. Without courage our fidelity becomes conformism.

- Freedom is man's capacity to take a hand in his own development. It is our capacity to mold ourselves.

- If you do not express your own original ideas, if you do not listen to your own being, you will have betrayed yourself.

❏ *The Best Way to Get Started with Rollo May*

The best way to get started with Rollo May is to read *The Courage to Create*. May, throughout his books, writes from the perspective of an existential psychologist. In order to appreciate what he has done for Self Improvement, it helps to have a base understanding of existential psychology. Spark Notes from Barnes and Nobles provides some insight:

> Why are existential psychology and philosophy called "existential?" The reason is that they focus on existence in the here and now. At each moment, a person is free to choose what he or she will do and be. The most important aspect of a person is not what she has genetically inherited, or how her parents treated her when she was an infant, but how she interprets and responds to the world around her at each given instant, and the kinds of choices she makes about what to do next. Thus, existential and humanistic psychologies reject Freud's claim that the most important factor in understanding a person is early life experience. It also rejects the idea that biological or inherited factors are the most important aspect of a person (though only the most radical and misguided existentialist would claim that such factors have *no* influence on behavior). Furthermore, conscious choice and responsibility are central to existential psychology, and the unconscious is given little or no role to play.

In *The Courage to Create*, May shows us how we can break out of old patterns in our lives. He offers a way to help deal with our fears enabling us to become our fully realized selves. He also explains that existential philosophers such as Kierkegaard, Nietzsche, Camus, and Sartre all concurred that courage didn't mean the absence of despair; rather it meant "the capacity to move ahead in spite of despair."

In his book, May asks, "What if imagination and art are not frosting at all but the fountainhead of human experience? What if our logic and science derive from art forms and are fundamentally dependent on them rather than art being merely a decoration for our work when science and logic have produced it?"

Throughout *The Courage to Create*, Rollo May helps us find those creative impulses that offer new possibilities for achievement.

TO READ ADDITIONAL BOOK EXCERPTS or ARTICLES or to LISTEN
TO ROLLO MAY RIGHT NOW, VISIT
http://www.selfgrowth.com/experts

❑ **Books**

- The Courage to Create
- Love and Will
- Existence
- Art of Counseling

❑ **Audio and Video Programs**

- Creativity and the Diamonic
- Violence and the Diamonic

❑ **Other Programs and Highlights**

While in the sanatorium, May filled the hours and solitude by reading and
theorizing about man's ultimate responsibility for his own existence. Among
the literature he read were the writings of Soren Kierkegaard, the Danish religious writer who inspired much of the existential movement. After receiving
his doctorate, May went on to teach at a variety of top schools.

❑ **Contact Information**

(This information is for the publisher of May's The Courage to Create.*)*

ADDRESS: W. W. Norton & Company, Inc.
500 Fifth Avenue
New York, NY 10110
PHONE: 212-354-5500
WEBSITE: www.wwnorton.com

DAVID R. HAWKINS
(Expert #57)

DAVID R. HAWKINS QUICK FACTS	
Main Area:	Research in Human Consciousness and Spiritual Realities
Best-Seller:	"Power vs. Force"
Profile:	Author; Lecturer; Psychiatrist; Researcher
Affiliation:	The Institute for Advanced Theoretical Research

❑ *David R. Hawkins Biography*

Dr. David R. Hawkins is a nationally renowned psychiatrist and physician, as well as a lecturer and expert on mental processes. He began work in psychiatry in 1952 and is a lifetime member of the American Psychiatric Association. Since relinquishing his extensive New York practice for a life of research, he continues spiritual teaching and attending to patients with special needs.

In his book, *Power vs. Force*, Dr. Hawkins proves how to instantly determine the truth or falsehood in any statement. He then demonstrates the application of this method in such areas as commerce, art, and sports. The research behind his work is based on quantum theory, nonlinear dynamics, advanced theoretical physics, and chaos theory.

Dr. Hawkins has written numerous scientific papers. In 1973, he co-authored *Orthomolecular Psychiatry* with Nobel Prize winner Linus Pauling. Currently the director of The Institute for Advanced Theoretical Research, Dr. Hawkins has a biographical listing in *Who's Who in the World*, which notes his background as a therapist and teacher.

❑ *David Riklan's Favorite David R. Hawkins Quotes and Thoughts*

- All human endeavor has the common goal of understanding or influencing human experience. To this end, man has developed numerous descriptive and analytical disciplines: morality, philosophy, psychology, and so on. …Regardless what branch of inquiry one starts from—philosophy, political theory, theology—all avenues of investigation eventually converge at a common meeting point: the quest for an organized understanding of the nature of pure consciousness.

- IMAGINE—what if you had access to a simple yes-or-no answer to any question you wished to ask? A demonstrably true answer…Any question.

- Spiritual evolution occurs as the result of removing obstacles and not actually acquiring anything new. Devotion enables surrender of the mind's vanities and cherished illusions so that it progressively becomes more free and more open to the light of Truth.

❑ *The Best Way to Get Started with David R. Hawkins*

The best way to get started with David R. Hawkins is read his book, *Power vs. Force*. Dr. Hawkins starts with the proposition that "...the human mind is like a computer terminal connected to a giant database. The database is human consciousness itself...with its roots in the common consciousness of all mankind. ...The unlimited information contained in the database has now been shown to be readily available to anyone in a few seconds, at any time and in any place."

Dr. Hawkins says this giant database of human consciousness can be accessed using the science of kinesiology, which includes a diagnostic tool called "muscle testing," a simple procedure for testing strength and evaluating how it varies in response to an outside stimulus. Dr. Hawkins uses kinesiological testing "as a tool for assessing value and motive, revealing the hidden determinants of human behavior."

Using these techniques, Dr. Hawkins has made a logarithmic scale ranking different levels of consciousness, from shame (20) to courage (200) to enlightenment (700 – 1,000). According to Dr. Hawkins, effectiveness of activity from the higher states of consciousness is based on power, the influence of good or leadership. The effectiveness of activity from the lower states of consciousness is based on force.

This section on "The Best Way to Get Started" doesn't provide adequate room to fully communicate the implications of Dr. Hawkins's ideas, but hopefully, it provides you with a beginning. *Power vs. Force* is not a quick or simple read, but it does provide some powerful ideas.

TO READ ADDITIONAL BOOK EXCERPTS or ARTICLES or to LISTEN TO DAVID R. HAWKINS RIGHT NOW, VISIT
http://www.selfgrowth.com/experts

❑ *Books*

- Power vs. Force: The Hidden Determinants of Human Behavior
- The Eye of the I: From Which Nothing is Hidden
- I: Reality and Subjectivity

❑ *Audio and Video Programs*

- Discovering the Truth about Anything
- Consciousness: The Way Out of Addiction
- Giving Up Illness

❑ *Other Programs and Highlights*

Dr. Hawkins has made national television appearances on such shows as *The MacNeil-Lehrer News Hour* and the *Today Show*. For more information on his book *Power vs. Force*, go to www.veritaspub.com, click on "Books" on the left side of the screen, and then choose "Power vs. Force."

❑ *Contact Information*

ADDRESS: Veritas Publishing
P.O Box 3516
W. Sedona, AZ 86340
PHONE: (928) 282-8722
(928) 282-4789 *(fax number)*
EMAIL: info@veritaspub.com
WEBSITE: www.veritaspub.com

ROBERT M. PIRSIG
(Expert #58)

ROBERT M. PIRSIG QUICK FACTS	
Main Areas:	Spirituality; Metaphysics; Zen Buddhism
Best-Seller:	"Zen and the Art of Motorcycle Maintenance"
Profile:	Author

❑ *Robert M. Pirsig Biography*

Robert M. Pirsig is the author of the best-selling book, *Zen and the Art of Motorcycle Maintenance*. It is an autobiographical novel, detailing a cross-country motorcycle trip by a man with his 11-year-old son, as well as his quest for truth. Pirsig says the study of the art of motorcycle maintenance is really a study of the art of rationality itself.

Pirsig was born in Minneapolis and studied chemistry, philosophy, and journalism at the University of Minnesota. He also attended Benares Hindu University in India, where he studied Oriental philosophy. Pirsig says the idea for the book was first conceived in 1968 as a short and light-hearted essay, following a motorcycle trip with his son and two friends.

In his other work, *LILA: An Inquiry into Morals*, Pirsig offers another lengthy investigation on how we can live well. The Metaphysics of Quality (MOQ) is explained in both of Pirsig's books. It is a philosophy and a theory about reality. The MOQ asks questions like "What is real?", "What is good?", and "What is moral?" and comes up with surprising conclusions about our lives and existence.

❑ *David Riklan's Favorite Robert M. Pirsig Quotes and Thoughts*

- Working on a motorcycle, working well, caring, is to become part of a process, to achieve an inner peace of mind. The motorcycle is primarily a mental phenomenon.

- The cycle you're working on is a cycle called "yourself."

- Metaphysics is a restaurant where they give you a thirty thousand page menu and no food.

- The solutions all are simple—after you have arrived at them. But they're simple only when you know already what they are.

❑ *The Best Way to Get Started with Robert M. Pirsig*

The best way to get started with Robert M. Pirsig is to read *Zen and the Art of Motorcycle Maintenance*. The first chapter sets up the scene for the motorcycle journey that he and his 11-year-old son embark on:

> You see things vacationing on a motorcycle in a way that is completely different from any other. In a car you're always in a compartment and because you're used to it you don't realize that through that car window everything you see is just more TV. You're a passive observer, and it is all moving by you boringly in a frame.

> On a cycle the frame is gone. You're completely in contact with it all. You're *in* the scene, not just watching it anymore, and the sense of presence is overwhelming. That concrete whizzing by five inches below your foot is the real thing, the same stuff you walk on; it's right there, so blurred you can't focus on it, yet you can put your foot down and touch it anytime, and the whole thing, the whole experience, is never removed from immediate consciousness.

This book can best be described as "a personal and philosophical odyssey into fundamental questions of how to live. The narrator's relationship with his son leads to a powerful self-reckoning; the craft of motorcycle maintenance leads to an austerely beautiful process for reconciling science, religion, and humanism."

In the preface to his book, Pirsig notes that it "should in no way be associated with that great body of factual information relating to orthodox Zen Buddhism." He goes on to add that "it's not very factual on motorcycles, either."

Zen and the Art of Motorcycle Maintenance has sold millions of copies and has profoundly affected many people. The book, first published in 1974, continues to be a major source of debate and inquiry for its many readers. An ongoing discussion of the meaning of Pirsig's writings and philosophy can be found on the web at www.moq.org.

TO READ ADDITIONAL BOOK EXCERPTS or ARTICLES or to LISTEN TO ROBERT M. PIRSIG RIGHT NOW, VISIT
http://www.selfgrowth.com/experts

❑ *Books*

- Zen and the Art of Motorcycle Maintenance: An Inquiry into Values
- LILA: An Inquiry into Morals

❑ *Audio and Video Programs*

- Zen and the Art of Motorcycle Maintenance (on audio cassette and audio CD)
- LILA: An Inquiry into Morals (on audio cassette)

❑ *Other Programs and Highlights*

Much of the MOQ has to do with a non-intellectual Zen-like view of the universe. Pirsig departs from Eastern thinking by arguing that reason and logic are important in seeking understanding. For more on the Metaphysics of Quality, visit www.moq.org.

❑ *Contact Information*

(Get in touch with Robert M. Pirsig through his publisher.)

ADDRESS: William Morrow
1350 Avenue of the Americas
New York, NY 10019
WEBSITE: www.moq.org

JOHN BRADSHAW
(Expert #59)

JOHN BRADSHAW QUICK FACTS	
Main Areas:	Inner Child; Dysfunctional Families
NY Times Best-Sellers:	"Homecoming"; "Healing the Shame That Binds You"; "Bradshaw On: The Family"; "Creating Love"; "Family Secrets"
Profile:	Author; Lecturer; Counselor; Theologian, Management Consultant
Affiliation:	The Meadows, Wickenberg, AZ

❑ *John Bradshaw Biography*

John Bradshaw is one of America's leading personal growth experts. He pioneered the concept of the "inner child" and brought the term "dysfunctional family" into the mainstream. Bradshaw is the author of five *New York Times* best-sellers, including *Homecoming*, which shows readers how to reclaim and nurture their inner child. His books have sold over four million copies in North America.

Bradshaw has lived everything he writes about. Born in Houston into a troubled family, he was abandoned by his alcoholic father and became a high academic achiever who was also an out-of-control teenager. He completed his education in Canada, where he studied for the Roman Catholic priesthood, earning three degrees from the University of Toronto.

During the past 25 years, Bradshaw has worked as a counselor, theologian, management consultant, and public speaker. He created and hosted four nationally broadcast PBS television series based on his best-selling books. He also lectures and holds workshops throughout the country, touching millions of lives.

❑ *David Riklan's Favorite John Bradshaw Quotes and Thoughts*

- It's okay to make mistakes. Mistakes are our teachers—they help us to learn.

- Children are curious and are risk takers. They have lots of courage. They venture out into a world that is immense and dangerous. A child initially trusts life and the processes of life.

- Recovery begins with embracing our pain and taking the risk to share it with others. We do this by joining a group and talking about our pain.

- The more we know about how we lost our spontaneous wonder and creativity, the more we can find ways to get them back.

- Children are natural Zen masters; their world is brand new in each and every moment.

❑ *The Best Way to Get Started with John Bradshaw*

John Bradshaw is best known for his book, *Homecoming: Reclaiming and Championing Your Inner Child*, and the PBS special of the same title. These are the places to the get started. If you don't have access to the PBS special, start with the book. Bradshaw believes that we all have an "inner child," and for many of us, it was damaged or wounded during our childhood from living in a dysfunctional family. In *Homecoming*, Bradshaw offers a guide to understanding and mourning our wounded inner child.

The book, his therapy, and his programs are about healing yourself. He draws on techniques used in his workshops to help put readers in touch with painful childhood memories and experiences. He believes that only after confronting and re-experiencing these past hurts can we break the family cycle of dysfunction and move ahead with our lives.

Bradshaw uses practical techniques, case histories, and questionnaires to demonstrate how your wounded inner child may be causing you pain. You'll learn to gradually and safely go back to reclaim and nurture that inner child—and literally help yourself grow up again. *Homecoming* shows you how to:

- Validate your inner child through meditations and affirmations.
- Give your child permission to break destructive family roles and rules.
- Adopt new rules allowing pleasure and honest self-expression.
- Deal with anger and difficult relationships.
- Pay attention to your innermost purpose and desires...and find new joy and energy in living.

To give you a sense of the type of material he provides, here is an excerpt from John Bradshaw:

> I like mnemonic formulas, so I'll describe some of the ways the wounded inner child contaminates our lives using the word contaminate. Each letter stands for a significant way in which the inner child sabotages adult life. ...

Co-Dependence
Offender Behaviors
Narcissistic Disorders
Trust Issues
Acting Out/Acting In Behaviors
Magical Beliefs
Intimacy Dysfunctions
Non-disciplined Behaviors
Addictive/Compulsive Behaviors
Thought Distortions
Emptiness (Apathy, Depression)

John Bradshaw's books and ideas have impacted millions of people. If you feel that you were brought up in a dysfunctional family and want some help, *Homecomings* is for you.

TO READ ADDITIONAL BOOK EXCERPTS or ARTICLES or to LISTEN TO JOHN BRADSHAW RIGHT NOW, VISIT
http://www.selfgrowth.com/experts

❏ *Books*

- Homecoming: Reclaiming and Championing Your Inner Child
- Healing the Shame That Binds You
- Bradshaw On: The Family: A New Way of Creating Solid Self Esteem
- Creating Love: The Next Great Stage of Growth
- Family Secrets: The Path to Self-Acceptance and Reunion

❏ *Audio and Video Programs*

- The Price of Nice
- Family Secrets: What You Don't Know Can Hurt You
- Men & Women Are from Earth After All: Effective Ways to Deal with Ten Problems Inherent in All Relationships

❏ *Other Programs and Highlights*

John Bradshaw's video and audio cassette series highlight subjects such as family relationships, co-dependency, inner-child work, divorce, addictions, recovery, and spirituality. To view his catalog of titles, visit www.johnbradshaw.com.

❑ *Contact Information*

ADDRESS:	Bradshaw Cassettes
	P.O.Box 720947
	Houston,TX 77272
EMAIL:	bradshaw@bradshawcassettes.com
PHONE:	1-800-6-BRADSHAW *(Bradshaw Cassettes)*
	713-541-4254 *(Asst., Barbara Bradshaw)*
WEBSITE:	www.johnbradshaw.com

LORETTA LaROCHE
(Expert #60)

LORETTA LaROCHE QUICK FACTS

Main Area:	Stress Management; Humor
Best-Sellers:	"Relax—You May Only Have a Few Minutes Left"; "Life is Not a Stress Rehearsal"
Profile:	Author; Speaker; Lecturer; Workshop/Seminar Leader
Affiliation:	Loretta LaRoche & Company

❑ *Loretta LaRoche Biography*

Loretta LaRoche has helped people deal with everyday stress for over 30 years. She has made people see how needlessly complex and stressful our lives can become. As a keynote speaker and lecturer in the field of stress management, she inspires and motivates audiences with her wisdom and humor. She shows how humor can benefit the health of an organization and improve productivity in the workplace.

Every year, Loretta conducts over 100 lectures, seminars, and training workshops for healthcare professionals, hospitals, Fortune 500 companies, government agencies, and non-profit organizations. At the Kripalu Center for Yoga & Health, she teams up with Joan Borysenko—a mind-body scientist, clinician, and teacher—for a series of weekend conferences for women. Loretta is also an adjunct faculty member at The Mind/Body Medical Institute of Boston.

Loretta's latest book is *Life is Short—Wear Your Party Pants*; her other books include the best-sellers *Relax—You May Only Have a Few Minutes Left* and *Life is Not a Stress Rehearsal*. *Relax* helps you to put humor back in your life and take yourself less seriously. *Life is Not a Stress Rehearsal* helps you to slow down and separate the noise around you from the clarity within you.

❑ *David Riklan's Favorite Loretta LaRoche Quotes and Thoughts*

- Don't get drawn into the trap of doing what everyone else does. If you spend your life trying to do what everyone else does, you're going to be a mightily unhappy, boring person.

- I'm always reminding people that the one constant you can count on is that things happen—and usually when you're not in the mood for them.

- Buy something silly and wear it. A Groucho Marx nose, mustache, and glasses are my favorite. When the stress seems unbearable, when you've really reached the limits of your endurance, go into a bathroom, look into the mirror, put on your glasses, and ask yourself, "How serious is this?"

- Most of us don't realize what an impact we have on the world around us. A positive energy field is going to affect others in a beneficial way, even if you don't notice it at first. Why not ask for a standing ovation once in a while? When you go in to work, say, "I came in—it wasn't easy. I could have gone somewhere else. I'd like a standing ovation."

❑ *The Best Way to Get Started with Loretta LaRoche*

Loretta LaRoche has the uncanny ability to use humor to help us relieve the stress of our everyday lives. She has done it through her books, her PBS specials, and her live performances. If you have access to one of her six award-winning PBS specials, I would recommend it as the place to start. If not, I would suggest reading or listening to *Life is Not a Stress Rehearsal: Bringing Yesterday's Sane Wisdom into Today's Insane World*.

LaRoche believes that, for most of us, life has become a pressure cooker of unrealistic expectations. *Life Is Not a Stress Rehearsal* takes an amusing and stress-reducing look at the gizmos, self-help regimens, and the talking heads that are designed to make our lives better but in truth frequently contribute to making us feel powerless, stressed out, overwhelmed, and inferior.

In her book, LaRoche shares her view of self-help books and her refreshing brand of humor:

> There seems to be no limit to the stuff that people will write books about. Something like three thousand new self-help books get published every year. Who would have guessed that we could have so many things wrong with us? The subjects just get more and more narrow. Books for adults with depression. Books for women on running with the wolves. Books for people with borderline personality disorder. I really saw a book the other day that promised to cure people of attention deficit disorder. Excuse me, but how are you going to get someone who has attention deficit disorder to SIT STILL LONG ENOUGH TO READ A BOOK?

Loretta shows us how to step back and see the insanity for what it is, hopefully laughing our way to become calmer, saner people. Some chapters include:

- Listening to the Inner Grandmother

- A Three Dollar Bottle of Water!: On Consumerism and Common Sense
- Who Cares? You're Gonna Die Anyway: On Status and Power
- Who Wants to Be an Idiot?: On Mass Media and Choice

Life Is Not a Stress Rehearsal is a breath of fresh air for everyone who's suffocating in our crazy, stressed-out world. The book is also available in tape form for entertaining listening.

TO READ ADDITIONAL BOOK EXCERPTS or ARTICLES or to LISTEN TO LORETTA LaROCHE RIGHT NOW, VISIT
http://www.selfgrowth.com/experts

❑ Books

- Life is Not a Stress Rehearsal: Bringing Yesterday's Sane Wisdom into Today's Insane World
- Relax—You May Only Have a Few Minutes Left: Using the Power of Humor to Overcome Stress In Your Life and Work
- Life is Short—Wear Your Party Pants: Ten Simple Truths that Lead to an Amazing Life
- How Serious Is This? Seeing Humor in Daily Stress

❑ Audio and Video Programs

- Love, Laughter and Lasagna: A Recipe for a Positive Outlook
- Life is Not a Stress Rehearsal (on audio cassette)
- Relax—You May Only Have a Few Minutes Left (on audio cassette)

❑ Other Programs and Highlights

Loretta LaRoche has been published in many magazines and newspapers, including *USA Today*, *The Boston Globe*, *First*, *Woman's Day*, and *Self*. Her weekly column, "Get a Life," is published every Monday in *The Patriot Ledger's* Lifestyle section. Her latest PBS special is *Life is Short—Wear Your Party Pants*, which is the title of her newest book. Loretta has also appeared as a guest expert on CNN, ABC, NBC, and CBS.

❑ Contact Information

ADDRESS: Loretta LaRoche & Company Corporate Offices
50 Court Street
Plymouth, MA 02360
PHONE: 1-800-99-TADAH or 508-746-3998

EMAIL: loretta@lorettalaroche.com *(for Loretta LaRoche)*
inquiries@lorettalaroche.com *(for general questions/inquires)*
WEBSITE: www.lorettalaroche.com

CHERYL RICHARDSON
(Expert #61)

CHERYL RICHARDSON QUICK FACTS

Main Area:	Career and Life Change
NY Times Best-Sellers:	"Life Makeovers"; "Take Time for Your Life"
Profile:	Author; Speaker; Master Certified Coach

❑ *Cheryl Richardson Biography*

Cheryl Richardson is a lifestyle expert who supports busy people in achieving personal success without compromising their quality of life. She was the first president of the International Coach Federation and holds one of their first Master Certified Coach credentials. She is the author of *The New York Times* best-sellers *Life Makeovers* and *Take Time for Your Life.*

Cheryl received the 2000 Motivational Book Award for Life Makeovers from Books for a Better Life, which honors the year's most outstanding books and magazines in the Self Improvement genre. She is also a professional speaker. Cheryl was the team leader for the Lifestyle Makeover Series on *The Oprah Winfrey Show* and accompanied Oprah on the "Live Your Best Life" nationwide tour in 2001.

Cheryl has designed and presented programs to universities, Fortune 500 companies, educational conferences, and professional associations. She served as the co-executive producer and host of *The Life Makeover Project with Cheryl Richardson* on the Oxygen Network and is also the co-executive producer and host of two public television specials. *Stand Up for Your Life* and *Create an Abundant Life* premiered in 2002.

❑ *David Riklan's Favorite Cheryl Richardson Quotes and Thoughts*

- A high-quality life starts with a high-quality you! Don't rush into this new year frantically trying to catch up or make up for what you didn't do in the past. This kind of frenetic rushing and hopeless browbeating keeps you tied to the past and feeling bad about yourself. Get a fresh start on this process by being gentle with yourself. Set aside some time to reflect on all you've done right over the last year by considering the following questions:

  - What qualities of character have you strengthened? Are you more honest with others about how you feel? Have you learned to set boundaries with those people who drain your energy? Maybe you've improved your communication skills or become more sensitive to the needs of others?

- Have you shared an act of kindness or supported others in some way? Did you help a friend who is going through a divorce or care for an elderly parent? Maybe you coached your kid's sports team or volunteered for a non-profit organization?

- What special memories have you created with those you love? Did you take a vacation that was particularly memorable? Did you organize an event that brought people closer together? Were there any special moments that stand out?

- What have you achieved or accomplished? Consider both your personal and professional life. Did you meet your business goals or get a promotion at work? Maybe you finished an important project, like writing a book or developing a workshop, or channeled your creative energy into painting or cooking?

❏ *The Best Way to Get Started with Cheryl Richardson*

Cheryl Richardson is first and foremost a life coach, helping countless clients make substantial changes in their lives. She has taken her personal coaching knowledge and distilled it down into a year-long program that will absolutely help you improve your life. This program can be found in her book, *Life Makeovers*, and it is where I suggest that you begin.

In her book, Cheryl provides countless exercises along with very specific advice on how to grow and change your life. The book is very readable and is designed like a workbook for life enhancement. She has developed a wide range of exercises and ideas to help you, including:

- Identify your most important accomplishments.
- Identify the quality that you would most like to develop and the actions necessary to develop them.
- Keep a journal.
- Manage your time.
- Identify and eliminate energy drains.
- Stay focused.

This list goes on and on. Cheryl borrows ideas liberally from a variety of other Self Improvement Experts and puts them into a cohesive 52-week package. She also provides information about a wide range of resources that you can contact for further studies. If you participate in her book, you'll no doubt be at the start to a better life.

TO READ ADDITIONAL BOOK EXCERPTS or ARTICLES or to LISTEN TO CHERYL RICHARDSON RIGHT NOW, VISIT http://www.selfgrowth.com/experts

❑ *Books*

- Life Makeovers
- Take Time for Your Life: A Personal Coach's Seven-Step Program for Creating the Life You Want
- Stand Up for Your Life: A Practical Step-by-Step Plan to Build Inner Confidence and Personal Power

❑ *Audio and Video Programs*

- Tuning In: Listening to the Voice of Your Soul
- Finding Your Passion
- Life Makeovers; Take Time for Your Life; Stand Up for Your Life (each on audio cassette or audio CD)

❑ *Other Programs and Highlights*

Cheryl was voted one of the top ten coaches in America in 1997 by readers of *The Professional Coach* magazine. Her work has been covered widely in the media, including *Good Morning America*, the *Today Show*, *CBS This Morning*, *The New York Times*, *USA Today*, and *Good Housekeeping*.

❑ *Contact Information*

ADDRESS: Cheryl Richardson
                 P.O. Box 13
                 Newburyport, MA 01950
PHONE: (978) 462-2204
EMAIL: jan@cherylrichardson.com *(Contact Jan Silva.)*
WEBSITE: www.cherylrichardson.com

STUART WILDE
(Expert #62)

STUART WILDE QUICK FACTS

Main Areas:	Metaphysics; Spirituality
Profile:	Author; Lecturer; Teacher
Affiliation:	Stuart Wilde Publishing

❑ *Stuart Wilde Biography*

Stuart Wilde is an author, lecturer, and one of the most knowledgeable metaphysical teachers in the world. He started writing in the early 1980s and has written 15 books on consciousness and awareness, including *Affirmations* and *The Quickening*. His quirky yet perceptive way of writing has won him a loyal readership over the years. His books have been translated into a dozen languages.

Over 20 years, Stuart came to be known as "the teacher's teacher" because of the impact he has had on other writers and thinkers. When he makes predictions, he goes into a trance and tells you what will happen later. He writes that the majority of his adult life has been driven by visions, most of which are personal, showing things about his life or those around him.

Stuart rarely appears in public anymore but instead teaches advanced metaphysics to small groups via his Transcendental Tours. Stuart is often described as a mystical man with a mysterious persona, but those who train with him realize that he is a caring teacher whose purpose is to help people recognize their own truth.

❑ *David Riklan's Favorite Stuart Wilde Quotes and Thoughts*

- Our life's journey of self-discovery is not a straight-line rise from one level of consciousness to another. Instead, it is a series of steep climbs and flat plateaus, then further climbs. Even though we all approach the journey from different directions, certain of the journey's characteristics are common to all of us.

- It is pointless to get your knickers in a twist if a certain person fails to react the way you want. It is best to avoid people and situations that you know drive you crazy. Remember to vote with your feet. If a situation is untenable or unchangeable, walk away.

- The person who said money is the root of all evil just flat out didn't have any.

- Life was never meant to be a struggle, just a gentle progression from one point to another, much like walking through a valley on a sunny day.

- I don't know about you but I like my Spiritual Enlightenment on the hurry-up. I don't have time to read 60 volumes of this or that. If you can't explain it to me in 30 seconds, it can't be the Godforce in my view anyway.

❏ *The Best Way to Get Started with Stuart Wilde*

Stuart Wilde has written many books and has developed a variety of audio programs. I recommend that you get started with *Infinite Self: 33 Steps to Reclaiming Your Inner Power*, which is available in book or audio form.

If you want to experience the realm of consciousness beyond your everyday, business-as-usual life—to "transcend"—then Stuart Wilde is the person for you. In his book and six-CD audio program, Stuart helps you tap into your eternal nature and pass through the doorway of perception that leads beyond your physical senses.

Some examples of his 33 steps are:

- Step 2:   Expanding Your Awareness.
- Step 4:   The Courage to Accept Spirit as Your Inner Guide.
- Step 9:   Power Comes from Discipline.
- Step 18:   Respect All Living Things; Observe the Beauty in All Things.
- Step 22:   Understanding That Inspiration and Creativity Come from Within.
- Step 23:   Always Maintain Freshness; Watch Nature, Align to Nature.

Infinite Self contains exercises that help you feel more wonder, less fear, definitely less seriousness, and greater positive energy in every moment of your life.

Stuart Wilde believes that spiritual power is everyone's birthright, and you need only to free yourself to reclaim it. Once you've experienced the "infinite self," you'll feel a deeper love and gratitude for your life in every way.

TO READ ADDITIONAL BOOK EXCERPTS or ARTICLES or to LISTEN TO STUART WILDE RIGHT NOW, VISIT
http://www.selfgrowth.com/experts

❏ *Books*

- Affirmations
- The Quickening
- Infinite Self: 33 Steps to Reclaiming Your Inner Power
- The Trick to Money is Having Some!
- Silent Power
- The Force
- Miracles

❏ *Audio and Video Programs*

- Affirmations; Silent Power; The Force; Miracles (each on audio cassette)

❏ *Other Programs and Highlights*

Stuart Wilde used to be a stage hand with the English Stage Company at Sloan Square in London. He also trained as a spirit medium at the College of Psychic Studies. To read excerpts of Stuart Wilde's work, learn source material, or listen to audio clips, visit www.stuartwilde.com.

❏ *Contact Information*

(The phone and email are for Stuart's agent, Johann Euringer.)

PHONE: +49 8052 957121
EMAIL: johann.euringer@t-online.de
WEBSITE: www.stuartwilde.com

MARK VICTOR HANSEN
(Expert #63)

MARK VICTOR HANSEN QUICK FACTS

Main Areas:	Inspiration; Motivation; Entrepreneurship
NY Times Best-Sellers:	"Chicken Soup for the Soul"; "The One Minute Millionaire"; "The Power of Focus" (over 80 million books in print from all his books)
Profile:	Author; Speaker; Coach; Seminar Leader
Affiliations:	Mark Victor Hansen & Associates, Inc.; One Minute Millionaire, LLC; Chicken Soup for the Soul Enterprises, Inc.

❏ *Mark Victor Hansen Biography*

Mark Victor Hansen has been empowering people to live lives filled with purpose and resounding success since 1974. As a professional speaker, he has made over 4,000 presentations to more than 2 million people in 32 countries. He helps people and organizations reshape their personal vision of what's possible. Mark and his business partner, Jack Canfield, created the *Chicken Soup for the Soul* series, what *Time* magazine calls "the publishing phenomenon of the decade."

Mark is the founder of MEGA Book Marketing University and Building Your MEGA Speaking Empire. Both are annual conferences where Mark coaches and teaches new and aspiring authors, speakers, and experts on building lucrative publishing and speaking careers. Mark presents 50 to 75 seminars each year. He also serves as chairman of Mark Victor Hansen & Associates, Inc. and president of One Minute Millionaire, LLC.

Mark has had entrepreneurial success, in addition to an extensive academic background. In 2002, the University of Toledo presented him with an honorary Ph.D. in business administration and established the Mark Victor Hansen Entrepreneurial Excellence Fund. The Fund will help shape the minds of future business leaders and assist in the development of the faculty who will teach them.

❏ *David Riklan's Favorite Mark Victor Hansen Quotes and Thoughts*

- It's time to stop tiptoeing around the pool and jump into the deep end, head first. It's time to think big, want more, and achieve it all!

- Don't wait until everything is just right. It will never be perfect. There will always be challenges, obstacles, and less than perfect conditions. So what. Get started now. With each step you take, you will grow stronger and stronger, more and more skilled, more and more self-confident, and more and more successful.

- You control your future, your destiny. What you think about comes about. By recording your dreams and goals on paper, you set in motion the process of becoming the person you most want to be. Put your future in good hands—your own.

- Great people are great because they solve countless, seemingly unsolvable problems—you can too if you choose to.

- To realize a dream, you must have a dream to realize.

- Lack of forgiveness causes almost all of our self-sabotaging behavior.

- It matters only that you manifest your genius; it doesn't matter when. It's never too late or too early.

- Each of us must do massive right thinking, take massive right action, and get massive right results, right here, right now.

- Predetermine the objectives you want to accomplish. Think big, act big, and set out to accomplish big results.

- End your day by privately looking directly into your eyes in the mirror and saying, "I love you!" Do this for thirty days and watch how you transform.

- Now is the only time there is. Make your now wow, your minutes miracles, and your days pay. Your life will have been magnificently lived and invested, and when you die you will have made a difference.

- The majority of people meet with failure because they lack the persistence to create new plans to take the place of failed plans.

- You don't become enormously successful without encountering some really interesting problems.

❑ *The Best Way to Get Started with Mark Victor Hansen*

Mark Victor Hansen is best known as co-author of the *Chicken Soup of the Soul* series. Ten years ago, I read the original *Chicken Soup* book, *Chicken Soup for the Soul: 101 Stories to Open the Heart and Rekindle the Spirit*, and I would highly recommend it as the place to begin. It is one of my inspirations for the title of this book.

When my wife got pregnant, she read *Chicken Soup for the Expectant Mother's Soul*, and I read *Chicken Soup for the Father's Soul*. The list of *Chicken Soup* books fits an endless variety of occupations, characteristics, and interests. The series is truly a phenomenon.

For those looking to increase their wealth, I would recommend one of Mark's newer projects, a book called *The One Minute Millionaire*, which he co-wrote with Robert Allen. In this work, the authors combine forces to produce a step-by-step guide for becoming a millionaire in a short period of time.

The unique format of the book actually provides two books for the price of one. On the right-hand pages, you can read the fictional story of Michelle, a waitress and mother of two, and her struggle to come up with $1 million to get her children back from her in-laws. On the left-hand pages are short, inspirational stories and lessons for becoming an "enlightened millionaire."

I would also highly recommend subscribing to Mark Victor Hansen's e-zine, *Rich Results*. It is a fabulous newsletter packed with information designed specifically for people who want to create a better life for themselves. And the best part…it's free!

TO READ ADDITIONAL BOOK EXCERPTS or ARTICLES or to LISTEN TO MARK VICTOR HANSEN RIGHT NOW, VISIT
http://www.selfgrowth.com/experts

❑ *Books*

- Chicken Soup for the Soul series (co-authored with Jack Canfield)
- The One Minute Millionaire: The Enlightened Way to Wealth (co-authored with Robert Allen)
- The Power of Focus (co-authored with Jack Canfield and Les Hewitt)
- The Aladdin Factor (co-authored with Jack Canfield)

❑ *Audio and Video Programs*

- Dreams Don't Have Deadlines
- Sell Yourself Rich

❑ *Other Programs and Highlights*

In 2000, Mark was honored with the prestigious Horatio Alger Award, and Northwood University honored him as the Outstanding Business Leader of the Year. He has been featured on television and radio on such shows as *The*

Oprah Winfrey Show and the *Today Show*, as well as in magazines and newspapers like *U.S. News & World Report* and *USA Today*.

❑ **Contact Information**

ADDRESS: Mark Victor Hansen & Associates, Inc.
                 P.O. Box 7665
                 Newport Beach, CA 92658-7665
PHONE: 949-764-2640
                 949-722-6912 *(fax number)*
EMAIL: service@markvictorhansen.com
WEBSITE: www.markvictorhansen.com

PO BRONSON
(Expert #64)

❑ *Po Bronson Biography*

Po Bronson is a novelist and writer of op-eds, performance monologues, book reviews, screenplays, and radio scripts. He believes that anything that gets people to read is meaningful, and when someone reads a whole book, his/her close attention is like a gift to the author. He is on the board of directors of Consortium Book Sales & Distribution and the editorial board of *Zoetrope: All Story* magazine.

Po, who grew up in Seattle, received an M.F.A. in creative writing from San Francisco State University and a B.A. in economics from Stanford University. Since high school, he has had many different jobs. At age 24, he was offered a position as a full-time bond salesman with projected first-year commissions of $300,000. But he turned it down.

Po began work on his book, *What Should I Do With My Life?,* because he was asking himself the same question. He found ordinary people across America who had discovered their true calling or at least were trying to find it. He then compiled profiles of those who had actually confronted and gotten past their psychological stumbling blocks. Po's first novel, *Bombardiers,* became an international best-seller

❑ *David Riklan's Favorite Po Bronson Quotes and Thoughts*

- Addressing the question, "What should I do with my life?," isn't just a productivity issue. It's a moral imperative.

- Failure's hard, but success is far more dangerous.

- The tougher the times, the more clarity you gain about the difference between what really matters and what you only pretend to care about.

- As I get older, I've learned to listen to people rather than accuse them of things.

- It's a real disconnect to assume that the way to a better life is something that happens only in good times.

- Holding onto fear and other assorted emotional baggage is much like holding onto a 20-pound watermelon; you can't get close enough to someone to give them a good hug.

- The things we really want to do are usually the ones that scare us the most.

❏ *The Best Way to Get Started with Po Bronson*

According to Po Bronson, the fundamental question for most people is "What should I do with my life?". He felt it was so important that he spent two years asking hundreds of people how they answered it. He conducted interviews with 50 people, which he used as the backbone for his best-selling book, *What Should I Do With My Life?*. I recommend it as the place to get started.

The book is an interesting set of stories, interspersed with Po's thoughts and analysis. Each chapter contains a profile of a person searching for their "their soft spot—their true calling." He talks about the idea that "nothing is braver than people facing up to their own identity" and uses the backdrop of these people's lives to help us figure out what we, ourselves, should do with our lives.

Po Bronson is a very successful writer, and this book is his primary venture into the Self Help and Self Improvement genre. The book was on *The New York Times* best-seller list for 22 weeks and was #1 twice during that time period. *What Should I Do With My Life?* is compelling because it gives you a glimpse into the lives of real people whose thoughts, hopes, dreams, and plans often parallel our own.

TO READ ADDITIONAL BOOK EXCERPTS or ARTICLES or to LISTEN TO PO BRONSON RIGHT NOW, VISIT
http://www.selfgrowth.com/experts

❏ *Books*

- What Should I Do With My Life?
- Bombardiers
- The First $20 Million is Always the Hardest: A Novel
- The Nudist on the Late Shift
- Men Seeking Women: Love and Sex Online

❑ *Audio and Video Programs*

- What Should I Do With My Life? (on audio cassette or audio CD)

❑ *Other Programs and Highlights*

Po Bronson has written for such publications as *The Wall Street Journal* and *Fast Company* and has appeared on *The Oprah Winfrey Show*. His novel, *The First $20 Million Is Always the Hardest,* was derived from interviews and experiences conducted while writing about Silicon Valley for *Wired, The New York Times Magazine*, and *Forbes ASAP*.

❑ *Contact Information*

(The phone number is for Brian McLendon, Po's publicist.)

PHONE: 212-572-2681
EMAIL: pobronson@pobronson.com
WEBSITE: www.pobronson.com

RICHARD BANDLER
(Expert #65)

RICHARD BANDLER QUICK FACTS	
Main Areas:	Behavior; Language; The Brain
Profile:	Author; Psychologist; Workshop/Seminar Leader; Co-Founder of Neuro-Linguistic Programming
Affiliation:	NLP Seminars Group International

❑ *Richard Bandler Biography*

Richard Bandler is the co-founder of Neuro-Linguistic Programming (NLP) with John Grinder. NLP is predicated upon the belief that all behavior has structure. It was created to develop new ways of understanding how verbal and non-verbal communication affect the human brain. NLP helps us to not only communicate better, but also learn how to gain control over the automatic functions of own neurology.

Richard Bandler met John Grinder, a linguistics professor, as a student at the University of California at Santa Cruz. In 1974, they began to make a model of the language patterns used by therapists Fritz Perls, Virginia Satir, and Milton Erickson, which they published in books such as *The Structure of Magic, Volumes I & II*. Richard Bandler has authored and co-authored many other books on NLP and its applications, including *Using Your Brain For a Change*, *Time For a Change*, and *Persuasion Engineering™*, co-authored with John La Valle.

Richard Bandler continually develops new human change technologies and conducts workshops and training seminars internationally for NLP. These workshops and seminars include Neuro-Hypnotic Repatterning™, Design Human Engineering™, Persuasion Engineering™, Personal Enhancement™, Charisma Enhancement™, and Hypnosis.

❑ *David Riklan's Favorite Richard Bandler Quotes and Thoughts*

- Do you want to know a good way to fall in love? Just associate all your pleasant experiences with someone and disassociate from all the unpleasant ones.

- The good thing about the past is it's over.

- Why be yourself when you can be someone so much better?

- There are no such things as learning disabilities, only teaching disabilities.

- The question you must ask yourself is…just how much pleasure and success can you stand?

- If it's worth feeling bad about, it's worthy of amnesia.

❑ *The Best Way to Get Started with Richard Bandler*

Neuro-Linguistic Programming has become a very important part of the Self Improvement Industry. In essence, NLP is a set of models of how communication impacts and is impacted by subjective experience. Tony Robbins, for one, teaches NLP-like techniques, and there has been a significant development in Self Improvement based on its concepts. To get started, I recommend that you first go to the NLP website (www.neurolinguisticprogramming.com) and read in full what it is all about. To see if it is right for you, I would take a look at the frequently-asked-questions section.

If you are serious about understanding the basis for NLP, you should then read *The Structure of Magic: A Book About Language and Therapy*, which is Volume I of II. I wouldn't describe it as a typical Self Help book, though. Written by Richard Bandler and John Grinder, their work was based on finding a theoretical base for describing human interaction. The book requires a lot of mental work to understand, but it will help you gain insight into the origin and implementation of NLP.

TO READ ADDITIONAL BOOK EXCERPTS or ARTICLES or to LISTEN
TO RICHARD BANDLER RIGHT NOW, VISIT
http://www.selfgrowth.com/experts

❑ *Books*

- The Structure of Magic: A Book About Language and Therapy (Volume I of II) (co-authored with John Grinder)
- The Structure of Magic: A Book About Communication and Change (Volume II of II) (co-authored with John Grinder)
- Patterns of the Hypnotic Techniques of Milton H. Erickson, Volumes I and II (co-authored with John Grinder)
- Magic in Action
- Using Your Brain for a Change
- Persuasion Engineering (co-authored with John La Valle)

❑ *Audio and Video Programs*

- Stepping Through Anxiety (with Denver Clay) (on audio cassette or audio CD)
- Ferocious Resolve (with Denver Clay) (on audio cassette or audio CD)
- Melting Phobias (with Denver Clay) (on audio cassette or audio CD)

❑ *Other Programs and Highlights*

Richard Bandler has a background as a musician. His interest in sound theory and the neurological impact of sound led him to develop the area of Neuro-Sonics, which utilizes qualities of music and sound to create specific internal states. Richard Bandler is also the founder of Design Human Engineering™.

❑ *Contact Information*

ADDRESS: NLP Seminars Group International
P.O. Box 424
Hopatcong, NJ 07843
PHONE: 973-770-3600
WEBSITE: www.richardbandler.com
www.neurolinguisticprogramming.com

DAN MILLMAN
(Expert #66)

DAN MILLMAN QUICK FACTS

Main Area:	Spiritual Development
Best-Seller:	"Way of the Peaceful Warrior"
Profile:	Author; Speaker; World Trampoline Champion

❑ *Dan Millman Biography*

Dan Millman is an author and speaker who shares his message that we are all peaceful warriors in training. He has written a dozen books, including the best-seller, *Way of the Peaceful Warrior*, which has inspired men and women of all ages in 29 languages worldwide. It is a beloved spiritual saga that has helped readers rediscover life's larger meaning and purpose.

Dan is a former world trampoline champion, Stanford gymnastics coach, and Oberlin College professor. His interests changed from developing talent for sports to developing talent for living. Dan offers fresh perspectives that reveal a clear path to deeper fulfillment, so people can enjoy a spiritual life in the material world and live with a peaceful heart and warrior's spirit.

As an international speaker, Dan has influenced people from all walks of life, including leaders of business and finance, heath, psychology, education, politics, entertainment, sports, and the arts. For more than two decades, he has presented talks and seminars to professional organizations across the world. He discusses such topics as "The Twelve Gateways to Human Potential," "Laws of Business, Laws of Life," and "Living on Purpose."

❑ *David Riklan's Favorite Dan Millman Quotes and Thoughts*

- Act happy, feel happy, be happy, without a reason in the world. Then you can love and do what you will.

- All the peoples of the world are trapped within the cave of their minds. Only those few warriors, who see the light, who cut free, surrendering everything, can laugh into eternity.

- Embrace this moment, put one foot in front of the other, and handle what's in front of you. Because no matter where your mind may roam, your body always remains here and now.

- When in haste, rest in the present. Take a deep breath and come back to here and now.

- Everything you'll ever need to know is within you; the secrets of the universe are imprinted on the cells of your body. But you haven't learned how to read the wisdom of the body.

- If you want a kinder world, then behave with kindness; if you want a peaceful world, make peace within.

- Inside you is untapped strength of will, of spirit, of heart. The kind of strength that will not flinch in the face of adversity. You have only to remember your purpose, the vision that brought you to Earth—the vision that will take you to the stars—and to the depths of the oceans and up the stairway of the soul. Great strength of will resides within you, waiting for expression.

- Wake up! If you knew for certain you had a terminal illness—if you had little time left to live—you would waste precious little of it! Well, I'm telling you...you do have a terminal illness. It's called birth. You don't have more than a few years left. No one does! So be happy now, without reason—or you will never be at all.

- We are both burdened and blessed by the great responsibility of free will—the power of choice. Our future is determined, in large part, by the choices we make now. We cannot always control our circumstances, but we can and do choose our response to whatever arises. Reclaiming the power of choice, we find the courage to live fully in the world.

❏ *The Best Way to Get Started with Dan Millman*

Dan Millman is first and foremost known for his best-selling book, *Way of the Peaceful Warrior*, and this is the ideal place to get started. In the book, Dan takes you on a first-hand spiritual odyssey, or quest, for happiness. In his journey, he meets a 94-year-old mentor nicknamed Socrates.

Socrates warns him, "To survive the lessons ahead, you're going to need far more energy than ever before. ...You must cleanse your body of tension, free your mind of stagnant knowledge, and open your heart to the energy of true emotion." Socrates then proceeds to teach Dan the "way of the peaceful warrior."

If you are looking for spiritual understanding of the human condition, *The Way of the Peaceful Warrior* is a quick read. Socrates shatters every preconceived notion that Dan has about academics, athletics, and achievement. Dan eventually stops resisting the lessons and begins to try on a whole new ideology—one that values being conscious over being smart, and strength in spirit over strength in body.

TO READ ADDITIONAL BOOK EXCERPTS or ARTICLES or to LISTEN TO DAN MILLMAN RIGHT NOW, VISIT
http://www.selfgrowth.com/experts

❑ Books

- Way of the Peaceful Warrior: A Book That Changes Lives
- The Life You Were Born to Live: A Guide to Finding Your Life Purpose
- Sacred Journey of the Peaceful Warrior

❑ Audio and Video Programs

- The Laws of Spirit: A Tale of Transformation: Powerful Truths for Making Life Work (book or audio cassette)
- Everyday Enlightenment: The Twelve Gateways to Personal Growth (book or audio cassette)
- Body Mind Mastery: Creating Success in Sport and Life (book or audio cassette)

❑ Other Programs and Highlights

Dan Millman has spoken at national and international conferences, such as Apple University, United Bank of Switzerland, Unity Churches, The Center for Professional Development, and the International Conference on Business and Consciousness. He has also lectured at institutions like Luton University in England and the University of California, Berkeley.

❑ Contact Information

ADDRESS: Box 6148
                 San Rafael, CA 94903
EMAIL: pw@danmillman.com *(Contact Mary Brandon,*
                                    Dan's assistant.)
WEBSITE: www.danmillman.com

EVELYN WOOD
(Expert #67)

EVELYN WOOD QUICK FACTS	
Main Area:	Speed Reading
Profile:	Teacher; Speed Reader; Writer; 1909-1995
Affiliations:	The Literacy Company; Reading Dynamics International

❏ *Evelyn Wood Biography*

Evelyn Wood was well-known for developing a system to teach speed reading and comprehension. Her discovery began when she watched her college professor read her 80-page term paper in less than ten minutes. Her professor could not explain how he did it. Wood wondered if she could do the same thing and if there were others with similar skills.

Wood learned that people have been reading rapidly for centuries. After a two-year search, she analyzed 50 people who could read between 1,500 and 6,000 words per minute. She found that they read more than one word at a time and saw words in meaningful patterns. They moved their eyes quickly and easily down the page, adjusted their speed to the type of material they were reading, and did not vocalize words as they read.

Wood started to teach herself these principles and soon was able to read several thousand words per minute, while still understanding and remembering everything she read. She then developed a system for teaching others. Taught and proven at the University of Utah, the first Evelyn Wood Institute opened in Washington, D.C. in 1959.

❏ *David Riklan's Favorite Evelyn Wood Quotes and Thoughts*

- So many people are dubious about trying my method because they think they're liable to miss a lot. I say which would you rather do—eat a dish of rice, kernel by kernel, or take a spoonful to get a good taste? My reading technique is actually comprehension by accumulation.

❏ *The Best Way to Get Started with Evelyn Wood*

Obviously, Evelyn Wood is best-known for teaching speed-reading techniques. Yet I'm sure you have questions as to the need and effectiveness of learning to speed-read. First off, I've used her Reading Dynamics system, and it works. I was able to read about three times as fast as I did at the beginning, and with the amount of reading material I go through as a Self Improvement aficionado, it has helped me learn and get through more in a shorter period of time.

Reading Dynamics, which made Evelyn Wood world-famous, has been taught to millions of people. The best way to get to know her program is to join the ranks of these millions. But before you do, I recommend that you go to the Reading Dynamics website (www.readingdynamicsusa.com) to read more about it. You should look at the frequently-asked-questions section and take the reading speed test to see if you are in need of this kind of system. It is still taught in a classroom environment and is also available as a home study course.

TO READ ADDITIONAL BOOK EXCERPTS or ARTICLES or to LISTEN TO EVELYN WOOD RIGHT NOW, VISIT
http://www.selfgrowth.com/experts

❑ *Books*

- Remember Everything You Read: The Evelyn Wood 7-Day Speed Reading and Learning Program (by Stanley D. Frank)
- How to Read Faster and Better, (by Franklin J. Agardy)
- Reading Skills (by Evelyn Nielsen Wood and Margorie W. Barrows)

❑ *Audio and Video Programs*

- Evelyn Wood Reading Dynamics
- The Reader's Edge® Fluent Reading Software

❑ *Other Programs and Highlights*

Prominent people who have used Evelyn Wood Reading Dynamics include CEOs of Fortune 500 companies, college professors, and United States presidents, such as President John F. Kennedy, who took the course along with his staff. There are over 2 million Evelyn Wood graduates.

❑ *Contact Information*

(Reading Dynamics International will only reply to email, not to post office mail.)

ADDRESS: The Literacy Company   Reading Dynamics International
P.O. Box 12757   7419 Beacon Hill Lane, #3
Scottsdale, AZ 85267   Charlotte, NC 28270

PHONE: 866-READFAST   704-366-0866
480-998-4889 *(corporate offices)*

EMAIL: Info@readfaster.com Info@ReadingDynamicsUSA.com
WEBSITE: www.evelynwood.com www.readingdynamicsusa.com

SPENCER JOHNSON
(Expert #68)

SPENCER JOHNSON QUICK FACTS

Main Areas:	Dealing with Change; Empowerment
NY Times Best-Sellers:	"Who Moved My Cheese?" (over 15 million copies sold); "The One Minute Manager" (over 12 million copies sold); "The Present"
Profile:	Author; M.D.
Affiliation:	Who Moved My Cheese? LLC—Learning Programs

❑ *Spencer Johnson Biography*

Spencer Johnson, M.D., is one of the most respected and beloved authors in the world. He has helped tens of millions of people discover how they can enjoy better lives by using simple truths that lead to fulfillment and success at work and at home. Inspiring and entertaining people with his insightful stories that speak directly to the heart and soul, he is often referred to as the best there is at taking complex subjects and presenting simple solutions that work.

Dr. Johnson is the author or co-author of numerous *New York Times* best-selling books, including #1 international best-sellers like *The One Minute Manager* and *Who Moved My Cheese?* Many years ago, Dr. Johnson was having a difficult time dealing with a major change in his life, so he made up the story of *Who Moved My Cheese?* to get him to laugh at himself. He wanted the book to encourage him to change, move on, and realize something better. The story is a simple parable that can be interpreted as you like, depending on where you feel you are—at work or in your life. His books are available around the world in 41 languages.

Dr. Johnson's education includes a B.A. in psychology from the University of Southern California, an M.D. degree from the Royal College of Surgeons, and medical clerkships at Harvard Medical School and the Mayo Clinic. He was medical director of communications for Medtronic, research physician at The Institute for Inter-Disciplinary Studies, consultant to the Center for the Study of the Person, and Leadership Fellow at the Harvard Business School.

❑ *David Riklan's Favorite Spencer Johnson Quotes and Thoughts*

- Yesterday is history. Tomorrow is a mystery. Today is a gift. That's why it's called The Present. Cherish it.

From *Who Moved My Cheese?:*

- The more important your cheese is to you, the more you want to hold on to it.

- Integrity is telling myself the truth. And honesty is telling the truth to other people.

- THE HANDWRITING ON THE WALL
    Change Happens
    Anticipate Change
    Monitor Change
    Adapt to Change
    Enjoy Change
    Be Ready to Quickly Change Again and Again

❑ *The Best Way to Get Started with Spencer Johnson*

The best way to get started with Spencer Johnson is to read his books— *The Present, The One Minute Manager, Who Moved My Cheese?*—depending on your preference. Here are descriptions of all three:

- *The Present* is a story of a young man's journey to adulthood and his search for The Present, a mysterious and elusive gift he first hears about from a great old man. This Present, according to the old man, is "the best present a person can receive."

    Later, when the young man, disillusioned with his work and his life, returns to ask the old man to help him once again find The Present, the old man responds, "Only you have the power to find The Present for yourself." So the young man embarks on a tireless search for this magical gift that holds the secret to his personal happiness and business success.

    It is only after the young man has searched high and low and given up his relentless pursuit that he relaxes and discovers The Present—and all the promises it offers.

    The Present will help you focus on what will make you happy and successful in your work and in your personal life. You may find, like the young man, that The Present is the best gift you can give yourself.

- *The One Minute Manager* is the book that started it all. Written in 1982, the story became the first small-book business parable to become an international best-seller. It has gone on to become a popular personal self growth book as millions of individuals apply its three One-Minute Secrets to their lives as well as their work.

The first step is to use One-Minute Goals, goals written on a single sheet of paper that can be read and re-read in one minute. One-Minute Praisings are used to catch people (including yourself) doing something right. These praisings build confidence. One-Minute Reprimands are used when people's behavior does not help them achieve their goals. The person is reminded that they are better than the ineffective behavior.

In the parable, a young man discovers how to use the three secrets and why they work so well (based on studies in medicine and the behavioral sciences).

- *Who Moved My Cheese?* opens with a casual conversation between several former classmates that are meeting for lunch the day after their high school reunion. During the conversation, one of them offers to share a story called "Who Moved My Cheese?," which is a parable that takes place in a maze. This is where the essence of the book begins.

There are four characters that live in the maze. Their main focus in life involves finding and eating cheese. Two characters are mice, Sniff and Scurry, who are non-analytical and non-judgmental. They just want cheese and are willing to do whatever it takes to get it. The other two characters are Hem and Haw, who are actually "little people," mouse-size humans who have an entirely different relationship with cheese. It is not just sustenance to them; it is their self-image. Their lives and belief systems are built around the cheese they find.

At the onset of the story, all four characters are in search of and then find their cheese. Change is suddenly introduced into the story. The cheese is moved, and the heart of the parable is how the four characters react to this change. Will the change be seen as a blessing or a curse? The message of the book is that change can be seen as a blessing if you understand the nature of cheese (i.e.—change) and the role it plays in our lives.

While reading *Who Moved My Cheese?*, we can see the story of the cheese as a symbol for something related to our jobs or our career paths. But it can stand for anything that involves change, from our health to our relationships. The point of the story is that we have to be alert to changes in our lives (i.e.—when cheese is moved), and we need to be prepared to deal with this change. The book is simple, the message is clear, and the lesson learned is quite valuable.

TO READ ADDITIONAL BOOK EXCERPTS or ARTICLES or to LISTEN TO SPENCER JOHNSON RIGHT NOW, VISIT
http://www.selfgrowth.com/experts

❑ *Books*

- The Present: The Gift That Makes You Happy and Successful at Work and In Life
- Who Moved My Cheese? An A-Mazing Way To Deal With Change In Your Work And In Your Life
- The One Minute Manager: The World's Most Popular Management Method (co-authored with Kenneth Blanchard, Ph.D.)
- The Precious Present: The Gift That Makes You Happy Forever
- The One Minute Mother
- The One Minute Father
- The One Minute Sales Person
- "Yes" or "No": The Guide to Better Decisions

❑ *Audio and Video Programs*

- Who Moved My Cheese? Change Program: Part 1—Changing the Way You Look at Change
  (This program is an effective way to experience more success with less stress in times of change—and have fun in the process. It is designed for a 30-90 minute video presentation combined with facilitator-led discussions on looking at change differently. The video contains the new Who Moved My Cheese? animated movie in VHS and DVD format.)

- Who Moved My Cheese? Change Program: Part 2—The Cheese Experience
  (This program is a 4-6 hour certified trainer-led learning program based on Dr. Johnson's best-selling book, Who Moved My Cheese?. Among other things, this program explores the participants change readiness and helps individuals and organizations embrace change as an opportunity rather than an obstacle to be feared.)

  (For more, view the online catalog and services at www.WhoMovedMyCheese.com.)

❑ *Other Programs and Highlights*

Dr. Johnson's work has captured the attention of major media, like CNN, the *Today Show*, *Time*, the BBC, *Business Week*, *The New York Times*, *Reader's Digest*, *The Wall Street Journal*, *Fortune*, *USA Today*, and the Associated Press.

❑ *Contact Information*

ADDRESS: Who Moved My Cheese? LLC
                     1775 West 2300 South Suite B
                     Salt Lake City, UT 84119,
PHONE: 800-851-9311 or 801-924-0260
EMAIL: Go to www.whomovedmycheese.com/contact
WEBSITE: www.whomovedmycheese.com

KRISHNA DAS
(Expert #69)

KRISHNA DAS QUICK FACTS	
Main Areas:	Chanting; Music; Yoga
Profile:	Recording Artist; Chanter; Seminar/Workshop Leader
Affiliation:	Karuna Music/Triloka Records

❑ *Krishna Das Biography*

Krishna Das is an internationally acclaimed recording artist and co-founder of Karuna Music/Triloka Records, which has become a leading distributor of world music recordings. Krishna Das shares the path of the heart through music and chanting. He has made numerous pilgrimages throughout India, meeting teachers and saints of many spiritual traditions.

In 1968, he met Ram Dass, who had just returned from his first trip to India. After living and traveling with him and hearing his stories about Maharaj-ji Neem Karoli Baba, Krishna Das traveled to India, where he was blessed to meet and stay with this guru. His heart was drawn to the practice of Bhakti Yoga, the yoga of devotion, and Maharaj-ji led him into the practice of Kirtan-chanting the Names of God.

On his audio cassette, *Pilgrim of the Heart*, Krishna Das tells his life story and introduces people to the path of devotion. He continues to conduct seminars, workshops, and chanting sessions and also continues to teach with Ram Dass. He has sung for many saints and yogis of all traditions and leads Kirtans in yoga centers all over the world.

❑ *David Riklan's Favorite Krishna Das Quotes and Thoughts*

- Caught in the storm,
  The ship of my life is battered by waves
  And blown around by the winds of desire.

  Where can I find rest?

  The Breath rises in me,
  The sweet Breath, the Breath of the heart.
  The sacred breath leads me in.

  The winds begin to die down

And the waters calm.
I am released into refuge
in the Harbour of the Name.

- We become free by interacting with beings who are already free. A true guru knows himself to be no different than who we really are.

❑ **The Best Way to Get Started with Krishna Das**

Krishna Das is known for his spiritual chanting music. To know more about his path, I would recommend starting with *Pilgrim of the Heart: Stories of Neem Karoli Baba, Hanuman, and the Devotional Tradition of India*. To get started chanting, I would recommend his second CD, *Pilgrim Heart*.

What is chanting music exactly? Chanting with Krishna Das consists of:

- Chanting with musical accompaniment.
- Meditation instruction.
- Readings from different spiritual traditions.
- Teachings and discussions about the spiritual path.

In *Pilgrim of the Heart*, Krishna Das shares the story of his life. But it is as much metaphorical and meaningful as it is biographical. As it says in the book description on Amazon.com, this audio program is an "invitation into the infinite yoga of faith, compassion, and surrender." In *Pilgrim of the Heart*, Krishna Das shares his heart through music and chanting; we would all surely benefit from listening.

TO READ ADDITIONAL BOOK EXCERPTS or ARTICLES or to LISTEN TO KRISHNA DAS RIGHT NOW, VISIT
http://www.selfgrowth.com/experts

❑ **Audio and Video Programs**

- Pilgrim of the Heart: Stories of Neem Karoli Baba, Hanuman, and the Devotional Tradition of India
- Door of Faith
- Breathe of the Heart
- LIVE…on Earth *(for limited time only)*
- Pilgrim Heart
- One Track Heart
- The Yoga of Chant video/DVD

❑ *Other Programs and Highlights*

During his almost three years in India, Krishna Das was an appointed pujari (priest) for the Durga temple in Maharaj-ji's ashram in the foothills of the Himalayas. He has studied Buddhist meditation practices with Anagarika Munindra and S.N. Goenka and has been initiated into Tibetan Buddhist practices by lamas from various lineages.

❑ *Contact Information*

ADDRESS:	Karuna Music/Triloka Records
	23852 Pacific Coast Highway #745
	Malibu, CA 90265
EMAIL:	kd@krishnadas.com
	info@karunamusic.com
WEBSITE:	www.krishnadas.com
	www.karunamusic.com

ERNEST HOLMES
(Expert #70)

ERNEST HOLMES QUICK FACTS

Main Areas:	Metaphysics; International Religious Science
Best-Seller:	"Science of the Mind"
Profile:	Author; Speaker; Minister; Founder of the Religious Science Movement; 1887-1960
Affiliation:	United Church of Religious Science

❑ *Ernest Holmes Biography*

Ernest Holmes founded the International Religious Science movement. His Science of Mind teaching is recognized today as one of the leading viewpoints in modern metaphysics. It is a spiritual philosophy that has brought to people around the world a positive approach to daily living and a sense of their relationship to God and their place in the Universe.

Holmes left school at age 18 and set out on his lifelong course of independent thinking. In 1914, at age 25, he discovered the writings of Thomas Troward, which increased his interest from earlier studies of metaphysics. He began speaking on Troward's writings to small groups. His ministry had begun. As his audiences grew, he was ordained as a minister of the Divine Science Church.

Holmes wrote *The Science of Mind*, published in 1926, and many other books on metaphysics. His many students urged him to set up an incorporated organization. The Institute of Religious Science and the School of Philosophy was formed in 1927, which is known today as the United Church of Religious Science.

❑ *David Riklan's Favorite Ernest Holmes Quotes and Thoughts*

- Never limit your view of life by any past experience.

- Life is a mirror and will reflect back to the thinker what he thinks into it.

- All limitations are self-imposed.

- There is a power for good in the Universe, greater than we are, available to everyone, and we can use it.

- Your thoughts are tools that you use in affirming the Creative Power into your experience.

- We cannot lead a choiceless life. Every day, every moment, every second, there is a choice. If it were not so, we would not be individuals.

- Faith is a mental attitude which is so convinced of its own idea, which so completely accepts it, that any contradiction is unthinkable and impossible.

❏ **The Best Way to Get Started with Ernest Holmes**

The best place to start with Ernest Holmes is with his book *The Science of Mind: A Philosophy, A Faith, A Way of Life*. In the opening sentence of the book, Holmes says that "we all look forward to the day when science and religion shall walk hand in hand through the visible to the invisible."

Later, Holmes begins to define the study of Science of the Mind. He writes, "The study of Science of the Mind is the study of First Cause, Spirit, Mind, or that Invisible Essence, that ultimate Stuff and Intelligence from which everything comes, the Power Back of Creation, the Thing Itself."

This book contains the fundamentals of Holmes's teachings. He has combined the teachings of great philosophers, knowledge of Eastern and Western traditions, and the nature of science to create a philosophy of religion and psychology that emphasizes the limitless potential of the human mind.

The principles are designed to apply to people of all religious and spiritual backgrounds, and Holmes provides us with the steps necessary to master the powers of the mind to find purpose in life. *The Science of Mind* is considered by many to be a spiritual classic that belongs on every Self Improvement bookshelf.

TO READ ADDITIONAL BOOK EXCERPTS or ARTICLES or to LISTEN TO ERNEST HOLMES RIGHT NOW, VISIT
http://www.selfgrowth.com/experts

❏ **Books**

- The Science of Mind: A Philosophy, A Faith, A Way of Life
- Creative Mind
- This Thing Called Life
- How to Use the Science of Mind
- Can We Talk to God?

❑ *Audio and Video Programs*

- The Science of Mind (on audio cassette)

❑ *Other Programs and Highlights*

Holmes Institute, formerly Ernest Holmes College, has been preparing individuals to enter the ministry for over 30 years. Ernest Holmes originated the international magazine *Science of Mind*, which has been in continuous publication since 1927.

❑ *Contact Information*

ADDRESS: Science of Mind Editorial   Holmes Institute Home Office
Offices   3251 West Sixth Street
3251 West Sixth Street   P.O. Box 75127
Los Angeles, CA 90020-5096 Los Angeles, CA 90075-0127

PHONE: (213) 388-2181 *(offices)*
(800) 247-6463 *(for subscription information)*

WEBSITE: www.scienceofmind.com   www.holmesinstitute.org

DON MIGUEL RUIZ
(Expert #71)

DON MIGUEL RUIZ QUICK FACTS

Main Areas:	Empowerment; Healing; Toltec Wisdom
NY Times Best-Seller:	"The Four Agreements"
Profile:	Author; Teacher of Toltec Knowledge

❏ *Don Miguel Ruiz Biography*

Don Miguel Ruiz is a teacher who shares his knowledge of the ancient Toltec wisdom. Born into a family of healers, his parents anticipated that he would embrace their legacy of healing and teaching and carry forward the esoteric Toltec knowledge. Instead, distracted by modern life, don Miguel chose to attend medical school and later teach and practice as a surgeon.

In the late 1970s, don Miguel was involved in a car accident and had a near-death experience. He saw that he existed separately from his body. His survival allowed him to begin an intensive practice of self-inquiry, and he devoted himself to the mastery of the ancestral wisdom by studying intensely with his mother. Don Miguel then completed an apprenticeship with a powerful shaman in the Mexican desert.

In the tradition of the Toltecs, a *nagual* guides an individual to personal freedom. Don Miguel is a *nagual* from the Eagle Knight lineage. He is the author of *The Four Agreements*, a *New York Times* best-seller, which reveals the source of self-limiting beliefs that create needless suffering. The book helps to transform people's lives, so they can experience freedom, love, and true happiness.

❏ *David Riklan's Favorite Don Miguel Ruiz Quotes and Thoughts*

"From the book The Four Agreements © 1997, don Miguel Ruiz. Reprinted by permission of Amber-Allen Publishing, Inc. P.O. Box 6657, San Rafael, CA 94903. All rights reserved."

- *The Four Agreements:*
  Be impeccable with your word.
  Don't take anything personally.
  Don't make assumptions.
  Always do your best.

- "Be Impeccable With Your Word":

Speak with integrity. Say only what you mean. Avoid using the word to speak against yourself or to gossip about others. Use the power of your word in the direction of truth and love.

- "Don't Take Anything Personally":
  Nothing others do is because of you. What others say and do is a projection of their own reality, their own dream. When you are immune to the opinions and actions of others, you won't be the victim of needless suffering.

- "Don't Make Assumptions":
  Find the courage to ask questions and to express what you really want. Communicate with others as clearly as you can to avoid misunderstandings, sadness, and drama. With just this one agreement, you can completely transform your life.

- "Always Do Your Best":
  Your best is going to change from moment to moment; it will be different when you are healthy as opposed to sick. Under any circumstance, simply do your best, and you will avoid self-judgement, self-abuse, and regret.

"From the book The Four Agreements © 1997, don Miguel Ruiz. Reprinted by permission of Amber-Allen Publishing, Inc. P.O. Box 6657, San Rafael, CA 94903. All rights reserved."

❑ **The Best Way to Get Started with Don Miguel Ruiz**

The Four Agreements: A Practical Guide to Personal Freedom is unquestionably the place to get started with Don Miguel Ruiz. The book is short, inspiring, and thought-provoking. In it, you get the opportunity to learn the great wisdom that was passed down from his Toltec ancestors.

The four agreements are listed above under "Quotes and Thoughts." They are simple, but it's the how and why that makes *The Four Agreements* such a valuable book.

In his work, Don Miguel Ruiz writes:

There are thousands of agreements you have made with yourself, with other people, with your dream of life, with God, with society, with your parents, with your spouse, with your children. But the most important agreements are the ones you made with yourself. In these agreements you tell yourself who you are, what you feel, what you believe, and how to behave. The result is what you call your personality. In these agreements you say, "This is what I am. This is what I believe. I can do certain things, and some things I cannot do. This is reality, that is fantasy; this is possible, that is impossible."

One single agreement is not such a problem, but we have many agreements that make us suffer, that make us fail in life. If you want to live a life of joy and fulfillment, you have to find the courage to break those agreements that are fear-based and claim your personal power. The agreements that come from fear require us to expend a lot of energy, but the agreements that come from love help us to conserve energy and even gain extra energy.

Don Miguel Ruiz's book only took a day to read, yet after I was finished, I immediately understood the power of The Four Agreements.

TO READ ADDITIONAL BOOK EXCERPTS or ARTICLES or to LISTEN TO DON MIGUEL RUIZ RIGHT NOW, VISIT
http://www.selfgrowth.com/experts

"From the book The Four Agreements © 1997, don Miguel Ruiz. Reprinted by permission of Amber-Allen Publishing, Inc. P.O. Box 6657, San Rafael, CA 94903. All rights reserved."

❑ *Books*

- The Four Agreements: A Practical Guide to Personal Freedom
- The Mastery of Love: A Practical Guide to the Art of Relationship
- The Four Agreements Companion Book: Using the Four Agreements to Master the Dream of Your Life
- Prayers: A Communion with our Creator: Inspiration and Guided Meditations for Living in Love and Happiness
- The Voice of Knowledge: A Practical Guide to Inner Peace

❑ *Audio and Video Programs*

- The Four Agreements (on audio cassette or audio CD)
- The Mastery of Love (on audio cassette)

❑ *Other Programs and Highlights*

Don Miguel Ruiz allowed his many teachings to be formulated into classes and training seminars that will be offered to the public at the University of Transformation. TransformU was assembled on don Miguel's behalf to ensure that his message of truth and love will be preserved for generations to come.

❑ *Contact Information*

ADDRESS: Don Miguel Ruiz
                 P.O. Box 1846
                 Carlsbad, CA 92018-1846
EMAIL: info@miguelruiz.com
WEBSITE: www.miguelruiz.com

BYRON KATIE
(Expert #72)

BYRON KATIE QUICK FACTS

Main Areas:	Self-Inquiry; Self Awakening
Best-Seller:	"Loving What Is"
Profile:	Author; Program Leader; Creator of The Work
Affiliation:	Byron Katie International

❑ *Byron Katie Biography*

Byron Katie developed the powerful method of inquiry known as The Work, which helps people see their problems from an entirely different perspective. Katie became severely depressed while in her thirties and spent almost ten years in deep depression—rarely leaving her bed for the last two. Then one morning, in a sudden flash of insight, she realized that her problem was not the world around her but her *beliefs* about the world. "What I understood," she says, "was that when I believed my thoughts, I suffered, but when I questioned my thoughts, I didn't suffer."

Katie developed The Work without any knowledge of religion or psychology. It is based on her direct experience of how suffering is created and ended. Since 1986, she has introduced The Work to hundreds of thousands of people in over 30 countries around the world. She has brought The Work into corporations, universities, schools, churches, prisons, and hospitals.

Since 1998, Katie has directed The School for The Work, a nine-day curriculum of exercises offered several times a year in America and Europe. She also hosts an annual New Year's Mental Cleanse—a five-day program of continuous inquiry that takes place in Southern California—and weekend intensives in major cities around the world. Katie's book, *Loving What Is*, written with her husband Stephen Mitchell, has been translated into 16 languages and has been on best-seller lists at bookstores across the United States.

❑ *David Riklan's Favorite Byron Katie Quotes and Thoughts*

- A teacher of fear can't bring peace on Earth. We have been trying to do it that way for thousands of years. The person who turns inner violence around, the person who finds peace inside and lives it, is the one who teaches what true peace is. We are waiting for just one teacher. You're the one.

- I am a lover of what is. When I argue with reality, I lose—but only 100 percent of the time.

- If you want reality to be different than it is, you might as well try to teach a cat to bark. You can try and try, and in the end the cat will look up at you and say, "Meow." Wanting reality to be different than it is is hopeless.

- An uncomfortable feeling is not an enemy. It's a gift that says, "Get honest; inquire." We reach out for alcohol or television or credit cards, so we can focus out there and not have to look at the feeling. And that's as it should be because in our innocence we haven't known how. So now what we can do is reach out for a paper and a pencil, write our thoughts down, and investigate them.

❑ *The Best Way to Get Started with Byron Katie*

The best way to get started with Byron Katie and The Work is to read her book, *Loving What Is*. I had heard of The Work, but I wasn't particularly familiar with the specifics of it. Then one day, I got a package in the mail that included a copy of her book, an audiobook sampler CD, and a letter from Stephen Mitchell, the book's co-author.

I sat down and then started reading, listening, and learning about her unique process of self-inquiry. Katie has been traveling around the world by invitation, sharing The Work, a technique that has you challenge your stressful beliefs about the world around you (i.e.—your relationships with family, friends, employers, employees, etc.).

Katie's system is very straightforward. It is really broken down into two parts—writing down your thoughts and then investigating them. You begin your work by writing down who angers, saddens, or disappoints you, including follow-up information connected to your feelings. For example, "How do you want them to change? What it is that they should or shouldn't be?"

After you write down your thoughts, it's time to start with the four questions, which make up the heart of The Work. These questions are:

1. Is it true?
2. Can you absolutely know that it's true?
3. How do you react when you think that thought?
4. Who would you be without the thought?

After the four questions, you do what is called "turning the thought around," which is a way of experiencing the opposite of what you believe is true. This turnaround might at first seem like simply blaming yourself instead of blaming the other person, but go deeper into it and you'll find an acceptance of reality that is independent of fault and blame.   Byron Katie's process of self-examination can lead directly to freedom, the feeling that a burden is almost magically lifted from your shoulders.

Loving What Is is filled with examples of people applying The Work to a variety of situations, from everyday frustrations all the way to rape, incest, and cancer. The Work is amazingly simple, and the rewards can lead to lasting peace, clarity, and greater intimacy with the people in your life.

TO READ ADDITIONAL BOOK EXCERPTS or ARTICLES or to LISTEN TO BYRON KATIE RIGHT NOW, VISIT
http://www.selfgrowth.com/experts

❑ *Books*

- Loving What Is: Four Questions that Can Change Your Life
- A Brief Anthology of Katie's Words *(available on Katie's website)*

❑ *Audio and Video Programs*

Several dozen audio and video titles are available on Katie's website, with more released each quarter. Titles include:

- Cancer Meets Inquiry
- The Work on Racism
- Weight, Sex, and Adultery
- This Body
- Sex & Relationships

❑ *Other Programs and Highlights*

Time magazine called Katie "a visionary for the new millennium," and she has recently been approached by several television producers who hope to make The Work available to millions. Katie maintains a busy schedule of public events that attract between 400 and 1,200 people. She is committed to sharing this process with anyone truly interested in living a life of freedom and joy.

❑ *Contact Information*

ADDRESS: Byron Katie International
P.O. Box 2110
Manhattan Beach, CA 90267
PHONE: (310) 760-9000
EMAIL: info@thework.org
WEBSITE: www.thework.org

JAMES ALLEN
(Expert #73)

JAMES ALLEN QUICK FACTS

Main Areas:	Success; Empowerment
Best-Seller:	"As a Man Thinketh"
Profile:	Author; Essayist; 1864-1912

❑ *James Allen Biography*

James Allen was a 19th century English writer, best known for his classic work, *As a Man Thinketh*. For nearly a century, the book has motivated readers to lead more peaceful and successful lives. It was his most successful book and has been translated into at least five major languages. Yet Allen was dissatisfied with it and felt it was a minor work. His wife, Lily, had to persuade him to publish it.

Allen's writings focus on teaching personal responsibility and finding the cause of personal problems within our own selves. He never gained fame or fortune and rarely made enough money from his writings to cover expenses. Born in Leicester, England in 1864, he spent his later years in Ilfracombe, where he wrote over 20 books.

After the murder of his father, a financial crisis at home forced Allen to leave school at age 15. He eventually became a private secretary and worked for several British manufacturers until 1902, when he decided to devote all his time to writing. Allen's literary career lasted only nine years, until his death in 1912. He was an advocate of ethics in all the areas of life and believed in the power of thought to bring fame, fortune, and happiness.

❑ *David Riklan's Favorite James Allen Quotes and Thoughts*

- You are today where your thoughts have brought you; you will be tomorrow where your thoughts take you.

- Above all be of single aim; have a legitimate and useful purpose and devote yourself unreservedly to it.

- Dream lofty dreams, and as you dream, so shall you become.

- Men are anxious to improve their circumstances but are unwilling to improve themselves; they therefore remain bound.

- To begin to think with purpose is to enter the ranks of those strong ones who only recognize failure as one of the pathways to attainment.

- The more tranquil a man becomes, the greater is his success, his influence, his power for good. Calmness of mind is one of the beautiful jewels of wisdom.

- Cherish your visions; cherish your ideals; cherish the music that stirs in your heart, the beauty that forms in your mind, the loveliness that drapes your purest thoughts, for out of them will grow delightful conditions, all heavenly environment; of these if you but remain true to them, your world will at last be built.

- Circumstances do not make the man; they reveal him.

- The law of harvest is to reap more than you sow. Sow an act, and you reap a habit. Sow a habit, and you reap a character. Sow a character, and you reap a destiny.

- You will never do anything in this world without courage. It is the greatest quality of the mind next to honor.

❏ *The Best Way to Get Started with James Allen*

James Allen passed away over 90 years ago, yet he is still an important part of the Self Improvement Industry. The reason for it is very simple—his book *As A Man Thinketh*. It contains timeless material. Allen's practical philosophy of successful living has awakened millions to the discovery and perception of the truth that "they themselves are makers of themselves."

Building on the Bible verse, "As a man thinketh, so he is," Allen insists that it is within the power of each person to form his own character and create his own happiness. This first paragraph describes the importance of and power of thought:

> "As you think, so you are." This not only embraces the whole
> of your being but also everything that ever happens to you in
> life. You are, literally, what you think, and your character is
> the complete sum of all your thoughts.

James Allen wrote 20 other books on Self Improvement, empowerment, and creating your own destiny, but *As A Man Thinketh* is the best way to start. You can get a free copy of the book by going to www.asamanthinketh.net.

TO READ ADDITIONAL BOOK EXCERPTS or ARTICLES or to LISTEN
TO JAMES ALLEN RIGHT NOW, VISIT
http://www.selfgrowth.com/experts

❑ *Books*

- As a Man Thinketh (free eBook)
- Above Life's Turmoil
- Byways of Blessedness
- Day by Day with James Allen
- The Path to Prosperity
- The Mastery of Destiny
- The Way of Peace
- Entering the Kingdom.

❑ *Audio and Video Programs*

- As a Man Thinketh *(on mp3 audio)*
- As A Man Thinketh Study Program

❑ *Other Programs and Highlights*

James Allen is something of an enigma in that he remains almost unknown
today. None of his books give much of a clue to his life other than to mention
his place of residence. His name cannot be found in a major reference work.
Even the Library of Congress and the British Museum have little information
about him.

❑ *Contact Information*

WEBSITE: www.asamanthinketh.net

*(There is no specific company to contact about James Allen's material. The
print version of* As A Man Thinketh *is published by DeVorss & Company.
Their website is www.devorss.com, and they can be reached at 800-843-5743 or
805-322-9010.)*

HARVILLE HENDRIX
(Expert #74)

HARVILLE HENDRIX QUICK FACTS	
Main Areas:	Marriage; Relationships
NY Times Best-Seller:	"Getting the Love You Want" (nearly 2 million copies sold)
Profile:	Author; Lecturer; Workshop Leader; Pastoral Counselor
Affiliation:	Imago Relationships International

❑ *Harville Hendrix Biography*

Harville Hendrix, Ph.D., is a pastoral counselor whose specialty is marriage and other intimate relationships. He has spent more than 35 years as a therapist, educator, workshop leader, and public lecturer. He has specialized in studying intimate partnerships and couples therapy for the past 15 years.

Dr. Hendrix and his wife, Helen LaKelly Hunt, are the collaborators in the creation of Imago Relationship Therapy and the concepts of "conscious marriage" and "conscious parenting." He is the co-founder for Imago Relationships International. More than 2,000 therapists practice Imago Therapy in 21 countries, and over 160 certified Imago presenters offer workshops and seminars each year.

Dr. Hendrix is a graduate of Mercer University, which awarded him an Honorary Doctorate of Humane Letters. He has a theology degree from the Union Theological Seminary in New York and an M.A. and Ph.D. in religion and psychology from the University of Chicago Divinity School. Dr. Hendrix is also an author, whose best-sellers include *Getting the Love You Want* and *Keeping the Love You Find*. His books are published in more than 50 languages.

❑ *David Riklan's Favorite Harville Hendrix Quotes and Thoughts*

- Psychologists say that "chemistry" is really our unconscious attraction to someone who we imagine will meet our particular emotional needs. What we unconsciously want is to get what we didn't get in childhood from someone who is like the people who didn't give us what we needed in the first place.

- Love and anger are two sides of the same coin.

- Most marriages fail because of the persistence of the unconscious aspects of the relationship. Any unfinished business we had with our caretakers becomes a compelling agenda with our partners. All too commonly, however, the partners never become aware of the hidden needs that drive their relationship and never learn the skills they need to successfully address those needs.

❑ *The Best Way to Get Started with Harville Hendrix*

The best place to get started with Harville Hendrix is to read his best-selling book, *Getting the Love You Want: A Guide for Couples*. The book is a valuable and effective guide to achieving a more loving and satisfying relationship. Dr. Hendrix says he wrote it "to share with you what [he has] learned about the psychology of love relationships and to help you transform your relationship into a lasting source of love and companionship."

Dr. Hendrix believes that when we choose partners for our relationships, we often choose people we hope will help us heal our childhood wounds. We unconsciously seek out people who possess both the positive and negative traits of our original caretakers. *Getting the Love You Want* is designed to help us overcome these challenges. The book has helped a countless number of couples improve their relationships.

Getting the Love You Want is divided into three sections. The first covers the "The Unconscious Marriage," which shows how the remaining desires and behavior of childhood interfere with the current relationship. The next section, "The Conscious Marriage," shows a marriage that fulfills those childhood needs in a positive manner. Finally, Dr. Hendrix provides a 10-week course in relationship therapy, which gives step-by-step exercises to help you and your partner learn how to "replace confrontation and criticism…with a healing process of mutual growth and support."

TO READ ADDITIONAL BOOK EXCERPTS or ARTICLES or to LISTEN TO HARVILLE HENDRIX RIGHT NOW, VISIT
http://www.selfgrowth.com/experts

❑ *Books*

- Getting the Love You Want: A Guide for Couples
- Keeping the Love You Find: A Personal Guide
- Giving the Love that Heals: A Guide for Parents (co-authored with wife Helen LaKelly Hunt)
- The Couples Companion: Meditations and Exercises for Getting the Love You Want (co-authored with wife Helen LaKelly Hunt)
- The Parent's Companion: Meditations and Exercises for Giving the Love that Heals (co-authored with wife Helen LaKelly Hunt)

- Personal Guide: Meditations and Exercises for Keeping the Love You Find (co-authored with wife Helen LaKelly Hunt)

❏ *Audio and Video Programs*

- Staying Together
- Marriage as a Path to Wholeness
- Love's Trilogy *(three cassettes)*
- Getting The Love You Want—Safety & Passion
- Conscious Communication
- Getting The Love You Want: A Video Workshop for Couples *(seven hours)*

❏ *Other Programs and Highlights*

Dr. Hendrix has appeared on *The Oprah Winfrey* many times and speaks regularly on local and national radio shows. He has also been written up in numerous magazines and newspapers internationally. Dr. Hendrix is the recipient of several honors, including the 1995 Outstanding Pastoral Counselor of the Year Award from the American Baptist's Churches and the 1995 Distinguished Contribution Award from the American Association of Pastoral Counselors.

❏ *Contact Information*

ADDRESS: Imago Relationships International
335 North Knowles Avenue
Winter Park, FL 32789
PHONE: 1-800-729-1121 or 407-644-4937
EMAIL: info@ImagoRelationships.org
WEBSITE: www.imagorelationships.org

JOHN GOTTMAN
(Expert #75)

JOHN GOTTMAN QUICK FACTS

Main Areas: Marriage; Relationships; Emotional Development
NY Times Best-Seller: "The Seven Principles for Making Marriage Work"
Profile: Author; Lecturer; Executive Director of the Relationship Research Institute; Co-Founder of the Gottman Institute
Affiliations: The Gottman Institute; Relationship Research Institute; University of Washington

---

❑ *John Gottman Biography*

John Gottman, Ph.D., is recognized for his work on marital stability and divorce prediction, involving the study of emotions, physiology, and communication. He is Professor Emeritus of Psychology at the University of Washington, where he founded the Family Research Lab, also known as "The Love Lab." He has earned several awards for his research on marriage and parenting, including four National Institute of Mental Health Research Scientist Awards.

Dr. Gottman has authored or co-authored 119 published academic articles and 37 books, including the *New York Times* best-seller, *The Seven Principles for Making Marriage Work*. In it, he says there is more to a solid marriage than communicating and sharing every feeling and thought. The book is the definitive guide for anyone who wants their relationship to attain its highest potential.

He and his wife, Dr. Julie Schwartz Gottman, founded the Gottman Institute, which helps couples directly and provides training to mental health professionals and health care providers. He is also the executive director of the non-profit Relationship Research Institute. The Gottmans present couples workshops throughout the country.

❑ *David Riklan's Favorite John Gottman Quotes and Thoughts*

- In the last decade or so, science has discovered a tremendous amount about the role emotions play in our lives. Researchers have found that even more than I.Q., your emotional awareness and abilities to handle feelings will determine your success and happiness in all walks of life, including family relationships.

- I liken an affair to the shattering of a Waterford crystal vase. You can glue it back together, but it will never be the same again.

- We have a group of very passionate, romantic couples. They sort of enjoy the bickering and the arguing…to them, it symbolizes real involvement and connection.

❏ *The Best Way to Get Started with John Gottman*

According to many relationship books, the key to a solid marriage is communication. Phooey, says John Gottman. He says there is much more to a solid, emotionally intelligent marriage than sharing every feeling and thought, though most therapists ineffectively and expensively harp on these concepts. In his book, *The Seven Principles for Making Marriage Work*, Dr. Gottman discusses his view on how to make for a successful marriage. I recommend it as the best place to start.

Dr. Gottman studied marriage by using rigorous scientific procedures to observe the habits of married couples. In the book, he shares the four not-so-obvious signs of a troubled relationship and includes a series of in-depth quizzes, checklists, and exercises similar to the ones found in his workshops. These are his seven principles for making marriage work:

- Maintain awareness of your partner's world.
- Foster fondness and admiration.
- Turn toward instead of away.
- Accept your partner's influence.
- Solve solvable conflicts.
- Cope with unresolvable conflicts.
- Create shared meaning.

The Seven Principles for Making Marriage Work is a great book if you want to improve your marriage. Dr. Gottman also has an audio and video program for it.

TO READ ADDITIONAL BOOK EXCERPTS or ARTICLES or to LISTEN TO JOHN GOTTMAN RIGHT NOW, VISIT
http://www.selfgrowth.com/experts

❏ *Books*

- The Seven Principles for Making Marriage Work: A Practical Guide from the Country's Foremost Relationship Expert
- Why Marriages Succeed or Fail…and How You Can Make Yours Last
- Raising an Emotionally Intelligent Child: The Heart of Parenting
- The Mathematics of Marriage: Dynamic Non-Linear Models
- The Relationship Cure: A 5 Step Guide for Building Better Connections with Family, Friends, and Lovers

❑ *Audio and Video Programs*

- Relationship Exercise—For Effective and Loving Marital Communication
- The Seven Principles for Making Marriage Work; Raising an Emotionally Intelligent Child; The Relationship Cure (each on audio cassette)

❑ *Other Programs and Highlights*

John Gottman has appeared on a number of TV programs, including *The Oprah Winfrey Show*, *Good Morning America*, and the *Today Show*. He has also been featured in articles from such publications as *The New York Times*, *Ladies Home Journal*, *Redbook*, and *Reader's Digest*.

❑ *Contact Information*

ADDRESS: Relationship Research Institute
4000 NE 41st Street, Building G
Seattle, WA 98105
PHONE: 206-832-0300
EMAIL: jgottman@gottman.com
johng@gottmanresearch.com
WEBSITE: www.gottman.com

JOY BROWNE
(Expert #76)

JOY BROWNE QUICK FACTS

Main Areas:	Clinical Psychology; Relationships; Empowerment
Best-Seller:	"Dating for Dummies"
Profile:	Author; Radio Host; Licensed Clinical Psychologist; Volunteer
Affiliations:	WOR Radio 710; Dr. Joy to the World

❑ *Joy Browne Biography*

Dr. Joy Browne is a licensed clinical psychologist and host of her own nationally syndicated radio show. Every day, millions of listeners on more than 300 stations in the United States and Canada hear her give advice on a variety of subjects. Before starting her radio career, she was a teacher, archeologist, and engineer on the space program.

Dr. Browne has won a number of awards for her work, including the American Psychological Association's President's Award and the Talker's Magazine Award for Best Female Talk Show Host—two years in a row. She has also written several books, including the best-seller *Dating for Dummies*. In it, she shows that dating and relationships do not have to be intimidating.

In addition to her professional career, Dr. Browne is an active volunteer. She has spent many years working with The Herbert G. Birch Summer Project, a summer camp for children and families of children living with HIV and AIDS. She most recently worked with the Salvation Army following the World Trade Center attack in New York City and has started Dr. Joy to the World, her own charitable foundation. She is currently serving on the advisory board of the Mayor's Commission to combat domestic violence.

❑ *David Riklan's Favorite Joy Browne Quotes and Thoughts*

- Adulthood was invented to sort out what we feel was done to us in childhood.

- If we give up the notion that everybody's life is perfect but ours, we would be a lot happier. Nobody's life is perfect.

- Charity always feels better to the donor than to the recipient.

- Just doing something—being there, showing up—is how we get braver. Self-esteem is about doing.

- We've turned into a nation of mothers to our men. I think it's a dreadful mistake that doesn't benefit anybody.

❏ *The Best Way to Get Started with Joy Browne*

Dr. Browne is an accomplished writer, has been on many talk shows, hosted her own nationally syndicated TV show, and is involved in many charities, yet there is only way to know and understand her. You have to listen to her radio show. A few minutes of listening to Dr. Browne will demonstrate why she has been described as "classy, feisty, and consistently sensible all at the same time." She is straight forward but not brazen, sensitive but not maudlin.

For those of you who cannot access her radio show live, you can listen to it on the Internet through www.wor710.com. If you are still unable to hear her show, I would suggest starting with one of her books, either *The Nine Fantasies That Will Ruin Your Life (and the eight realities that will save you)* or *Getting Unstuck: 8 Simple Steps to Solving Any Problem.*

The following brief excerpt from *The Nine Fantasies That Will Ruin Your Life* will give you a taste of her attitudes:

> I want you to get real! I want you to be willing to look at these nine fantasies that can ruin your life until you are willing to examine, adjust, and discard them. These fantasies are causing you to spend time and energy living in an imaginary world that will not allow you to be effective. These assumptions are pervasive, ubiquitous, and dangerous. The big ugly nine fantasies concern...
>
> - Home: Functional families exist.
> - Perfection: Describes everybody...except me.
> - Money: Winning the lottery would free me.
> - Truth: It will set you free.
> - Sex: Men and women are from different planets.
> - Innocence: Ignorance is bliss.
> - Righteousness: Stick to your guns.
> - Fairness: Good always triumphs.
> - Love: Somewhere I have a soul mate.

Dr. Browne has developed a reputation for her straight talk and levelheaded advice, and she is definitely worth listening to.

TO READ ADDITIONAL BOOK EXCERPTS or ARTICLES or to LISTEN
TO JOY BROWNE RIGHT NOW, VISIT
http://www.selfgrowth.com/experts

❏ **Books**

- Dating for Dummies
- It's a Jungle Out There, Jane: Understanding the Male Animal
- The Nine Fantasies That Will Ruin Your Life (and the eight realities that will save you)
- Getting Unstuck: 8 Simple Steps to Solving Any Problem

❏ **Audio and Video Programs**

- Dating for Dummies; It's a Jungle Out There, Jane; The Nine Fantasies That Will Ruin Your Life (each on audio cassette)

❏ **Other Programs and Highlights**

The Dr. Joy Browne Show was syndicated on television by CBS Eyemark Enter-tainment in the 1999-2000 season. Dr. Browne can be seen on television as a guest on shows like *The Oprah Winfrey Show* and *Larry King Live*. For more about her radio show, visit www.drjoy.com.

❏ **Contact Information**

ADDRESS: Dr. Joy Browne Show
                 c/o WOR Radio
                 1440 Broadway
                 New York, NY 10018

PHONE: 800-544-7070 *(The call-in number for the* Dr. Joy
                               Browne Show *on the radio.)*
                 212-642-4495 *(Dr. Joy Browne's office)*

EMAIL: Go to www.drjoy.com/contact/index.html
WEBSITE: www.drjoy.com

PARAMAHANSA YOGANANDA
(Expert #77)

PARAMAHANSA YOGANANDA QUICK FACTS

Main Areas:	Spirituality; Eastern Religion
Best-Seller:	"Autobiography of a Yogi"
Profile:	Author; Lecturer; Philosopher; Yogi; 1893-1952
Affiliation:	Self-Realization Fellowship

❏ *Paramahansa Yogananda Biography*

Paramahansa Yogananda was a world teacher and one of the greatest emissaries to the West of India's ancient wisdom. His mission in the West was to spread the knowledge of Yoga practices, by which man can enter into union with God. In 1917, Yogananda began his life's work with the founding of a school for boys, where modern educational methods were combined with yoga training and instruction in spiritual ideals.

In 1920, Yogananda was invited to serve as India's delegate at a meeting with the International Congress of Religions in Boston. His address to the Congress on "The Science of Religion" was well-received. As a lecturer, Yogananda emphasized the underlying unity of the world's great religions and taught methods for attaining direct personal experience with God.

Yogananda founded Self-Realization Fellowship in 1920 to make available the universal teachings of Kriya Yoga, a sacred spiritual science originating millenniums ago in India. Today, the Self-Realization Fellowship has hundreds of centers throughout the world. Yogananda is also a best-selling author. His life story, *Autobiography of a Yogi*, is widely regarded as a modern spiritual classic.

❏ *David Riklan's Favorite Paramahansa Yogananda Quotes and Thoughts*

- We are all part of the One Spirit. When you experience the true meaning of religion, which is to know God, you will realize that He is your Self, and that He exists equally and impartially in all beings. *(Man's Eternal Quest)*

- Only those who partake of the harmony within their souls know the harmony that runs through nature. *(Journey to Self-Realization)*

- The season of failure is the best time for sowing the seeds of success. *(The Law of Success)*

- Do not take life's experiences too seriously. Above all, do not let them hurt you, for in reality they are nothing but dream experiences. ...If circumstances are bad and you have to bear them, do not make them a part of yourself. Play your part in life, but never forget it is only a role. What you lose in the world will not be a loss to your soul. Trust in God and destroy fear, which paralyzes all efforts to succeed and attracts the very things you fear. *(Spiritual Diary)*

- This life is a master novel, written by God, and man would go crazy if he tries to understand it by reason alone. That is why I tell you to meditate more. Enlarge the magic cup of your intuition and then you will be able to hold the ocean of infinite wisdom. *(Sayings of Paramahansa Yogananda)*

- To have any color prejudice is to discriminate against God, who is sitting in the hearts of all the red, white, yellow, olive, and black peoples of the world. *(Man's Eternal Quest)*

- True friends want nothing from you except the joy of your presence. ...No matter what you do, they will always be your friend. *(Journey to Self-Realization)*

❏ *The Best Way to Get Started with Paramahansa Yogananda*

Paramahansa Yogananda's book, *Autobiography of a Yogi*, continues to attract countless readers seeking authoritative insight into metaphysical truths and Eastern Religion. Clearly it is the place to get started. Originally introduced in book form, it is now also available as an audio collection narrated by Ben Kingsley.

The book is popular because it has introduced millions of readers to Eastern spiritual thought. The yogi begins by sharing information on his childhood and continues with information on his training. The book concludes with details about his time living and teaching in the United States. Yogananda describes and interprets his spiritual evolution and provides an insightful look at the ultimate mysteries of human existence. An example of his clear writing style can be found below:

> The science of Kriya Yoga, mentioned so often in these pages, became widely known in modern India through the instrumentality of Lahiri Mahasaya, my guru's guru. The Sanskrit root of Kriya is kri, to do, to act and react; the same root is found in the word karma, the natural principle of cause and effect. Kriya Yoga is thus "union (yoga) with the Infinite through a certain action or rite." A yogi who faithfully follows its tech-

nique is gradually freed from karma or the universal chain of causation.

Kriya Yoga is a simple, psychophysiological method by which the human blood is decarbonized and recharged with oxygen. The atoms of this extra oxygen are transmuted into life current to rejuvenate the brain and spinal centers. By stopping the accumulation of venous blood, the yogi is able to lessen or prevent the decay of tissues; the advanced yogi transmutes his cells into pure energy. Elijah, Jesus, Kabir, and other prophets were past masters in the use of Kriya or a similar technique, by which they caused their bodies to dematerialize at will.

When *Autobiography of a Yogi* was originally published in 1946, *Newsweek* called it "fascinating." *The New York Times* described it as a "rare account." The book is still popular 50 years after its publication because of the value that it provides.

TO READ ADDITIONAL BOOK EXCERPTS or ARTICLES or to LISTEN TO PARAMAHANSA YOGANANDA RIGHT NOW, VISIT
http://www.selfgrowth.com/experts

❑ *Books*

- Autobiography of a Yogi
- Why God Permits Evil and How to Rise Above It
- Scientific Healing Affirmations
- God Talks With Arjuna: The Bhagavad Gita

❑ *Audio and Video Programs*

- Awake in the Cosmic Dream
- Songs of My Heart
- Be a Smile Millionaire

❑ *Other Programs and Highlights*

In 1924, Yogananda began a decade-long series of lecture tours in which he spoke to capacity audiences and met with such notable figures of the time as President Calvin Coolidge, horticulturist Luther Burbank, symphony conductor Leopold Stokowski, and Kodak camera inventor George Eastman.

In 1935, Yogananda began an 18-month tour of Europe and India, where he spoke and met with Mahatma Gandhi, Nobel-prize-winning physicist Sir C. V. Raman, and some of India's renowned spiritual figures. During this time,

Swami Sri Yukteswar bestowed on Yogananda India's highest spiritual title—
"Paramahansa"—which signifies one who manifests the supreme state of un-
broken communion with God.

In 1977, on the 25th anniversary of the passing of Paramahansa Yogananda, the
Government of India issued a commemorative stamp in his honor.

❏ *Contact Information*

ADDRESS: Self-Realization Fellowship
                 3880 San Rafael Avenue
                 Los Angeles, CA 90065-3298
PHONE: (323) 225-2471
WEBSITE: www.yogananda-srf.org

BARBARA DE ANGELIS
(Expert #78)

BARBARA DE ANGELIS QUICK FACTS	
Main Area:	Relationships; Personal Growth
Best-Sellers:	"How to Make Love All The Time"; "Secrets About Men Every Woman Should Know"; "Are You The One for Me?"; "Real Moments"
Profile:	Author; Speaker; TV Relationship Personality; "Making Love Work" Infomercial Producer
Affiliation:	Shakti Communications, Inc.

❏ *Barbara De Angelis Biography*

Barbara De Angelis, Ph.D. is one of America's most renowned experts on relationships and is a highly respected leader in the field of personal growth. As a best-selling author, popular television personality, and sought-after motivational speaker, she has reached millions of people with her positive messages about love, happiness, and the search for meaning in our lives.

Dr. De Angelis is the author of 13 best-selling books, which have sold over seven million copies and have been published in 20 languages. Her first book, *How to Make Love All The Time,* was a national best-seller. Her next two books, *Secrets About Men Every Woman Should Know* and *Are You The One For Me?* were #1 on *The New York Times* best-seller list for months. Her fourth book, *Real Moments*, also became an overnight *New York Times* best-seller.

Dr. De Angelis' first television infomercial, *Making Love Work,* which she wrote and produced, won numerous awards including Best Infomercial of the Year. It has aired on hundreds of channels throughout the United States and Canada and is the most successful relationship program of its kind. Dr. De Angelis also appeared weekly for two years on CNN as their *NewsNight* relationship expert dispensing advice via satellite all over the world. For 12 years, she was the founder and Executive Director of the Los Angeles Personal Growth Center. She is President of Shakti Communications, Inc., which provides production and consulting services.

❑ *David Riklan's Favorite Barbara De Angelis Quotes and Thoughts*

- The more connections you and your lover make, not just between your bodies, but between your minds, your hearts, and your souls, the more you will strengthen the fabric of your relationship, and the more real moments you will experience together.

- Love is a force more formidable than any other. It is invisible—it cannot be seen or measured, yet it is powerful enough to transform you in a moment and offer you more joy than any material possession could.

- At the end of our time on earth, if we have lived fully, we will not be able to say, "I was always happy." Hopefully, we will be able to say, "I have experienced a lifetime of real moments, and many of them were happy moments."

- The journey in between what you once were and who you are now becoming is where the dance of Life really takes place.

- You never lose by loving. You always lose by holding back.

- You don't develop courage by being happy in your relationships every day. You develop it by surviving difficult times and challenging adversity.

- The more anger towards the past you carry in your heart, the less capable you are of loving in the present.

- Love and kindness are never wasted. They always make a difference. They bless the one who receives them, and they bless you, the giver.

❑ *The Best Way to Get Started with Barbara De Angelis*

Barbara De Angelis, Ph.D., has developed a wide range of programs for couples, singles, and parents that help create fulfilling relationships. The one product that really put Barbara on the map is the home seminar called *Making Love Work*, and that's where I'd start. It is a dynamic program that guides you step-by-step through an emotional personal workshop on communication, love, and healing the heart.

Making Love Work includes two videos, five audio tapes, and a 94-page personal guidebook. It gives you a wealth of techniques you can use immediately to create more happiness and harmony with your mate, children, and friends. Some of the areas covered in this course include "The Secret Dynamics of Your

Relationship," "Live Demonstrations of How to Use the Love Techniques," and "The Wrong and Right Way to Communicate."

Over half a million people have used this award-winning relationship program, and her popular infomercial was responsible for its success. If you don't invest in the program, though, her book *How To Make Love All The Time* is also a great place to start. It will teach you how to build a successful relationship, no matter if you're currently in one or looking for one.

If you are in a relationship, the best two books are "Secrets About Men Every Woman Should Know" and "What Women Want Men to Know." For singles, I recommend, "Are You The One for Me?" and "Real Rules." For general inspiration and keys to successful living, two great books are "Secrets About Life Every Woman Should Know" and "Real Moments."

TO READ ADDITIONAL BOOK EXCERPTS or ARTICLES or to LISTEN TO BARBARA DE ANGELIS RIGHT NOW, VISIT
http://www.selfgrowth.com/experts

❏ *Books*

- How to Make Love all the Time: Make Lost Last a Lifetime!
- Secrets About Men Every Woman Should Know: Find Out How They *Really* Feel About Women, Relationships, Love, and Sex
- Are You The One For Me? Knowing Who's Right & Avoiding Who's Wrong
- Real Moments: Discover the Secret for True Happiness
- Real Moments for Lovers
- Confidence
- Inspirations About Love
- Ask Barbara: The 100 Most Asked Questions About Love, Sex, and Relationships
- Real Rules
- Passion
- Chicken Soup for the Couple's Soul
- Secrets About Life Every Woman Should Know: Ten Principles for Total Emotional and Spiritual Fulfillment
- What Women Want Men to Know
- Chicken Soup for the Romantic Soul

❏ *Audio and Video Programs*

- Making Love Work
- Finding Love
- Making Relationships Work
- The Lover's Guide to Sex, Passion & Romance

- Living with Purpose, Loving with Passion

❑ *Other Programs and Highlights*

Dr. De Angelis has been a frequent guest on such shows as *The Oprah Winfrey Show*, the *Today Show*, and *The View*. She also produced and starred in a one-hour TV special for PBS called *Love Secrets*, which aired nationwide in 2001. Dr. De Angelis contributes regularly to *Entertainment Tonight* and to magazines like *Cosmopolitan*, *Ladies Home Journal*, and *Redbook*.

Dr. De Angelis has hosted her own daily television show for CBS-TV and her own popular radio talk show in Los Angeles. Over the past 20 years, she has been in demand as a motivational speaker in North America, giving hundreds of presentations to groups including AT&T, Proctor & Gamble, Crystal Cruise Lines, and Young Presidents Organization. She has resumed her personal consultations.

❑ *Contact Information*

ADDRESS: Barbara De Angelis, Ph.D.
12021 Wilshire Blvd. #607
Los Angeles, CA 90025
PHONE: 310-535-0988
EMAIL: AskBarbaraD@aol.com
WEBSITE: www.barbaradeangelis.com

DAVID BURNS
(Expert #79)

DAVID BURNS QUICK FACTS

Main Areas:	Depression; Anxiety
Best-Seller:	"Feeling Good" (over 3 million copies sold)
Profile:	Author; Psychiatrist; Teacher; Researcher
Affiliation:	Stanford University School of Medicine

❑ *David Burns Biography*

David D. Burns, M.D., is a psychiatrist and author on mood and relationship problems. His books include the best-seller, *Feeling Good*, which has sold over three million copies in the United States. Surveys indicate that American mental health professionals rate it as the top self-help book on depression. In the book, Dr. Burns shows how you can lift your spirits and develop greater self-esteem and a positive outlook on life.

Dr. Burns graduated magna cum laude from Amherst College, received his M.D. from Stanford University School of Medicine, and completed his psychiatry residency at the University of Pennsylvania School of Medicine. He has served as acting chief of psychiatry at the Presbyterian/University of Pennsylvania Medical Center and as visiting scholar at the Harvard Medical School. Dr. Burns is certified by the National Board of Psychiatry and Neurology.

Dr. Burns is currently adjunct clinical associate professor of psychiatry and behavioral sciences at his alma mater, the Stanford University School of Medicine. In 1998, 2000, and 2001, he received the Teacher of the Year award from the class of graduating residents there. When he is not teaching or actively doing research at Stanford, he lectures to civic and professional groups throughout the United States and Canada.

❑ *David Riklan's Favorite David Burns Quotes and Thoughts*

- Depression is an illness and not a necessary part of healthy living. What's more important—you can overcome it by learning some simple methods for mood elevation.

- The first principle of cognitive therapy is that all your moods are created by your "cognitions," or thoughts. A cognition refers to the way you look at thing—your perceptions, mental attitudes, and beliefs. It includes the way you interpret things—what you say about something or someone to yourself. You feel the way you do right now because of the thoughts you are thinking at this moment.

❑ *The Best Way to Get Started with David Burns*

Dr. David Burns's primary focus is helping people to deal effectively with depression, anxiety, and low self-esteem. Is depression a major issue? Absolutely. The World Health Organization reported that major depression is the #1 cause of disability in the world. In the United States, 17 percent of adults experience at least one episode of major depression during their lives (Kessler et al., 1994).

In years past, depression was treated either chemically, through traditional psychotherapy, or through some combination of the two. Yet during the past 30 years, a new revolutionary treatment was developed, known as cognitive therapy. Cognitive therapy has been described as "a fast acting technology of mood modification that you can learn to apply on your own." Dr. Burns's book, *Feeling Good: The New Mood Therapy*, shows you how.

At 736 pages, *Feeling Good* was the first and most comprehensive book designed to describe these methods to the general public. It is Dr. Burns's most successful work. In the book, he explains what the simple mood-control techniques of cognitive therapy provide:

1. Rapid Symptomatic Improvement: Research indicates that two-thirds of patients with major depressive episodes have recovered in just four weeks after receiving a copy of Dr. Burns's book, *Feeling Good: The New Mood Therapy*, even though these patients received no other treatment during that period of time.

2. Understanding: A clear explanation of why you get moody and what you can do to change your moods. You will learn what causes negative feelings, how to distinguish "normal" from "abnormal" emotions, and how to diagnose and assess the severity of your problems.

3. Self-control: You will learn how to apply safe and effective coping strategies that will help you break out of bad mood. You will learn to develop a practical, realistic, step-by-step self-help plan. As you apply it, your moods can come under greater voluntary control.

4. Prevention and Personal Growth: You will learn to prevent future mood swings by changing the self-defeating attitudes (like perfectionism) that make you vulnerable to painful mood swings. You will learn how to challenge your assumptions about the basis for human worth.

If you or someone you know suffers from depression, *Feeling Good* is the book to start with. It gives you the details behind the scientifically proven techniques that can lift your spirits and help you develop a positive outlook on life.

TO READ ADDITIONAL BOOK EXCERPTS or ARTICLES or to LISTEN TO DAVID BURNS RIGHT NOW, VISIT
http://www.selfgrowth.com/experts

❏ *Books*

- Feeling Good: The New Mood Therapy
- Intimate Connections: The Clinically Proven Program for Making Close Friends and Finding a Loving Partner
- The Feeling Good Handbook
- Ten Days to Self-Esteem
- Ten Days to Self-Esteem: The Leader's Manual
- Worried Sick *(due out by the second quarter of 2004)*

❏ *Audio and Video Programs*

- Feeling Good with Dr. Burns
  (This is a multi-media version of Feeling Good *published by Time-Life in 2002. It includes three new books plus audio and video tapes that illustrate the techniques. This product is available at www.timelife.com/feelinggood.)*

❏ *Other Programs and Highlights*

Dr. Burns has received a number of awards, including the A. E. Bennett Award in 1975 from the Society for Biological Psychiatry for his research on brain chemistry and the Distinguished Contribution to Psychology through the Media Award in 1995 from the Association of Applied and Preventive Psychology.

❏ *Contact Information*

EMAIL: feedback@feelinggood.com
WEBSITE: www.feelinggood.com

SARK
(Expert #80)

SARK QUICK FACTS	
Main Areas:	Women's and Men's Empowerment; Self-Acceptance; Succulence; Creativity
Best-Sellers:	"Succulent Wild Woman"; "Transformation Soup"; "Eat Mangoes Naked"
Profile:	Author; Artist, Speaker; Teacher
Affiliation:	Camp SARK

❑ *SARK Biography*

SARK (Susan Ariel Rainbow Kennedy) is the best-selling author and artist of 11 books, with a twelfth being released in 2004. Her work encourages your most playful and uninhibited self. There are over two million of SARK's books in print, including the national best-seller, *Succulent Wild Woman*. She is founder and president of Camp SARK, a company offering products and services to inspire creative living, such as cards, posters, and calendars.

Born in Minneapolis, SARK's first and favorite job was as Wake-Up Fairy in kindergarten. She studied at the Minneapolis Art Institute, University of Tampa, and the University of Minnesota before her parents begged her to graduate from something. SARK graduated from the School of Communication Arts in radio/TV production.

SARK was one of ten women featured in the PBS series *Women of Wisdom and Power*. She was also one of the facilitators on *Cheryl Richardson's Life Makeover Series* on the Oxygen network. SARK is a recovering procrastinator and perfectionist who practices what she teaches. She lives in a Magic Cottage in San Francisco with her "fur husband" cat, Jupiter.

❑ *David Riklan's Favorite SARK Quotes and Thoughts*

Excerpted from SARK's poster "How To Be An Artist:

- Plant impossible gardens.
  Look forward to dreams. Cry during movies.
  Swing as high as you can on a swingset, by moonlight.
  Cultivate moods.
  Do it for love. Take lots of naps.
  Take moonbaths.
  Giggle with children.

Listen to old people.
Drive away fear. Play with everything.
Entertain your inner child.
Build a fort with blankets.
Get wet. Hug trees. Write love letters.

- I send you radical self-acceptance, power-full healing, and the miracle of your heart speaking-and you listening.

- We are each a gift, exactly as we are in this moment, with no improvements!

- We are all free spirits. We must choose to practice freedom.

- It isn't easy for any of us to transcend the past, or pain we might have suffered. Yet there are gifts in those pains, and we can choose to let light into the dark places. We are not alone!

- We are each born creative—then we forget our purpose, or mission. We believe our doubts and fears, and slowly stop "being creative," as though it were a separate thing.

- Groups are a great way to dance with your wonder-full self in the company of others! They can be very spontaneous and informal, or more organized.

❑ *The Best Way to Get Started with SARK*

I came across SARK and *Succulent Wild Woman* while reading *Life Makeovers* by Cheryl Richardson. After starting to read SARK's book, I found her message to be highly refreshing. Her books and programs are designed to create an awakening for people, enabling them to embrace their true self.

Succulent Wild Woman will jump out at you and is definitely the place to start with SARK. In it, she equates "succulent" with ripe, juicy, whole, round, exuberant, wild, rich, wide, deep, firm, rare, and female. SARK says, "We have the right to live wild succulent lives. Right now. Open your window and yell at the top of your lungs. I'm Here. I'm Wild. I will live a daring and remarkable life."

I am obviously writing from a man's perspective, but if I were a woman, I'd want to be a Succulent Wild Woman. But as SARK herself told me, "David, you are a succulent wild man!"

[297]

TO READ ADDITIONAL BOOK EXCERPTS or ARTICLES or to LISTEN TO SARK RIGHT NOW, VISIT
http://www.selfgrowth.com/experts

❑ *Books*

- Succulent Wild Woman: Dancing with your Wonder-Full Self
- Make Your Creative Dreams REAL, Especially For Procrastinators, Perfectionists, Busy People, Avoiders, and People Who Would Rather Sleep All Day *(due out in spring 2004)*
- Prosperity Pie: How to Relax About Money and Everything Else
- The Bodacious Book of Succulence: Daring to Live Your Succulent Wild Life
- Eat Mangoes Naked: Finding Pleasure Everywhere and Dancing with the Pits!
- A Creative Companion: How to Free Your Creative Spirit
- Inspiration Sandwich: Stories to Inspire Our Creative Freedom
- Transformation Soup: Healing for the Splendidly Imperfect
- Change Your Life Without Getting Out of Bed: The Ultimate Nap Book
- Living Juicy: Daily Morsels for Your Creative Soul
- SARK's Journal and Play!Book: A Place to Dream While Awake
- The Magic Cottage Address Book by SARK

❑ *Other Programs and Highlights*

SARK wrote her first book at age 10. She held 250 jobs between 14 and 25 and got her professional start by hand-drawing 11,000 posters. She is a periodic guest on National Public Radio, and her own "Inspiration Line" has been inspiring people for ten years at 415-546-3742.

SARK's Juicy Living Cards are new ways of looking at subjects such as time, love, and money, as well as support for our "splendid imperfections." Published by Hay House, there are 50 simple ways to practice more self-love and "Juicy Living."

❑ *Contact Information*

PHONE: 415-397-7275 *(information line only)*
                415-546-3742 (EPIC) *(inspiration line)*
EMAIL: delicious_2003@campsark.com
WEBSITE: www.campsark.com

JACK CANFIELD
(Expert #81)

JACK CANFIELD QUICK FACTS

Main Areas:	Inspiration; Motivation; Self Esteem
NY Times Best-Seller:	"Chicken Soup for the Soul" (over 80 million books in print from all his books)
Profile:	Author; Speaker; Teacher; Workshop Leader; Trainer
Affiliations:	Chicken Soup for the Soul Enterprises, Inc.; Self-Esteem Seminars; The Foundation for Self Esteem; Souperspeakers.com

---

❑ *Jack Canfield Biography*

Jack Canfield is the founder and co-creator of the best-selling *Chicken Soup for the Soul* book series with Mark Victor Hansen, which currently has 71 titles and over 80 million copies in print in more than 39 languages. Jack is an understanding and empowering coach who speaks to companies and associations worldwide and has helped hundreds of thousands of people to achieve their dreams.

Jack's background includes a B.A. from Harvard University, a master's degree from the University of Massachusetts, and honorary doctorates from the University of Santa Monica, St. Ambrose University, and Parker College of Chiropractic. He has been a high school and university teacher, a workshop facilitator, a psychotherapist, and for the past 30 years, a leading authority in the area of self-esteem and personal development.

Jack founded Self Esteem Seminars in Santa Barbara, California and The Foundation for Self Esteem in Culver City, California. Self Esteem Seminars trains entrepreneurs, educators, corporate leaders, and employees how to accelerate the achievement of their personal and professional goals. The Foundation for Self Esteem provides self-esteem resources and trainings to social workers, welfare recipients, and human resource professionals.

❑ *David Riklan's Favorite Jack Canfield Quotes and Thoughts*

- Everything you want is out there waiting for you to ask. Everything you want also wants you. But you have to take action to get it.

- Kids don't care what you know until they know you care.

- Most fears cannot withstand the test of careful scrutiny and analysis. When we expose our fears to the light of thoughtful examination they usually just evaporate.

- People who say it cannot be done should not interrupt those who are doing it.

❑ *The Best Way to Get Started with Jack Canfield*

To get started with Jack Canfield, I would highly recommend the original *Chicken Soup* book, *Chicken Soup for the Soul: 101 Stories to Open the Heart and Rekindle the Spirit*. I first read this book ten years ago, and it has since spawned a highly successful series of books addressing an assortment of issues, hobbies, and positions for different groups of people. The *Chicken Soup* series is a phenomenon and an inspiration to many people, including myself.

For those looking for a more traditional Self Improvement book, I would suggest starting with *The Power of Focus*, co-written by Jack Canfield, Mark Victor Hansen, and Les Hewitt. The book is a practical guide showing you how to reach your business, personal, and financial goals. It covers a wide range of areas, including developing habits, seeing the big picture, creating optimum balance, building excellent relationships, taking decisive action, and living on purpose.

The Power of Focus contains many easy-to-follow, practical exercises that will lead you to success. One type of exercise comes in the chapter called "Action Steps—The Priority Focus Workshop." In it, the authors provide a six-step guide to maximize your time and productivity, and they have you identify the following information:

- List all of the business activities at work that use up your time.
- Describe three things that you are brilliant at doing at business.
- Name the three most important activities that produce income for your business.
- Name the three most important activities that you don't like to do or are weak at doing.
- Who could do these for you?
- What one time consuming activity are you going to say "no" to or delegate right away.

This is just a sample of the valuable exercises that this book provides. *The Power of Focus* is excellent for business people, entrepreneurs, and basically anyone who is serious about improving their overall lives.

TO READ ADDITIONAL BOOK EXCERPTS or ARTICLES or to LISTEN
TO JACK CANFIELD RIGHT NOW, VISIT
http://www.selfgrowth.com/experts

❑ **Books**

- Chicken Soup for the Soul series
- The Power of Focus
- The Aladdin Factor
- Dare to Win
- Heart at Work: Self-Esteem in the Workplace
- 100 Ways to Enhance Self-Concept in the Classroom

❑ **Audio and Video Programs**

- Maximum Confidence
- Self-Esteem and Peak Performance
- The Success Principles

❑ **Other Programs and Highlights**

Jack is the president of Souperspeakers.com, a speaking resource service providing incredible inspirational speakers for event planners worldwide. His long list of distinguished clients includes Virgin Records, Sony Pictures, Merrill Lynch, Society of Real Estate Professionals, Children's Miracle Network, and many others. Jack conducts a week-long seminar, Self-Esteem and Peak Performance Facilitating Skills, every summer to train Self Improvement trainers in his work.

❑ **Contact Information**

ADDRESS:	Chicken Soup for the Soul P.O. Box 30880 Santa Barbara, CA 93130	*(Souperspeakers.com)* Teresa Esparza P.O. Box 1840 Pismo Beach, CA 93442
PHONE:	(805) 563-2935	(805) 481-0327
EMAIL:	webmaster@chickensoupforthesoul.com	Teresa@souperspeakers.com
WEBSITE:	www.chickensoup.com www.jackcanfield.com	www.souperspeakers.com

MARTIN E.P. SELIGMAN
(Expert #82)

MARTIN E.P. SELIGMAN QUICK FACTS

Main Areas:	Positive Psychology; Learned Optimism
Profile:	Author; Lecturer; Columnist; Cognitive Psychologist; Former APA President; Psychology Professor
Affiliation:	University of Pennsylvania

❑ *Martin E.P. Seligman Biography*

Martin E.P. Seligman, Ph.D., works on positive psychology, learned helplessness, depression, and optimism and pessimism. He is currently The Fox Leadership Professor of Psychology at the University of Pennsylvania and Director of the Positive Psychology Network. In 1996, he was elected president of the American Psychological Association.

Since 2000, Dr. Seligman has been promoting the field of positive psychology—a discipline that includes the study of positive emotion, positive character traits, and positive institutions. He trains positive psychologists to make the world a happier place. Dr. Seligman's best-selling books, translated into 20 languages, include *Learned Optimism, Authentic Happiness, The Optimistic Child*, and *What You Can Change...And What You Can't.*

Dr. Seligman holds an A.B. degree in philosophy from Princeton University and a Ph.D. in psychology from the University of Pennsylvania. He also holds an honorary Ph.D. from Uppsala University in Sweden and a Doctorate of Humane Letters from the Massachusetts College of Professional Psychology. Dr. Seligman has received the American Psychological Society's William James Fellow Award for contribution to basic science, and the James McKeen Cattell Fellow Award for the application of psychological knowledge.

❑ *David Riklan's Favorite Martin E.P. Seligman Quotes and Thoughts*

- The defining characteristic of pessimists is that they tend to believe that bad events will last a long time, will undermine everything they do, and are their own fault. The optimists, who are confronted with the same hard knocks of this world, think about misfortune in the opposite way. They tend to believe that defeat is just a temporary setback or a challenge, that its causes are just confined to this one case.

- It's a matter of ABC. When we encounter ADVERSITY, we react by thinking about it. Our thoughts rapidly congeal into BELIEFS. These beliefs may become so habitual we don't even realize we have them unless we stop to focus on them. And they don't just sit there idly; they have CONSEQUENCES. The beliefs are the direct cause of what we feel and what we do next. They can spell the difference between dejection and giving up, on the one hand, and well-being and constructive action on the other. The first step is to see the connection between adversity, belief, and consequence. The second step is to see how the ABCs operate every day in your own life.

- The drive to resist compulsion is more important in wild animals than sex, food, or water. …The drive for competence or to resist compulsion is a drive to avoid helplessness.

❑ *The Best Way to Get Started with Martin E.P. Seligman*

Dr. Seligman's basic premise is tied into optimism and pessimism, and the core of his beliefs is that "pessimism is escapable." His book, *Learned Optimism*, is clearly the place to start. The idea of the book is very simple—you can learn to be optimistic, and optimism has great benefits.

Learned Optimism teaches readers how to choose optimism, enabling them to gain the freedom to build a life of real rewards and lasting fulfillment. This includes being able "to take charge, resist depression, and make [ourselves] feel better and accomplish more." All of Dr. Seligman's other books, 20 in total, build on the foundation of *Learned Optimism*.

I personally believe that optimism provides us with a power to achieve, and Dr. Seligman's books and his teachings teach us how to get this power. His theories are different from many others because it is based on hard scientific research.

TO READ ADDITIONAL BOOK EXCERPTS or ARTICLES or to LISTEN TO MARTIN E.P. SELIGMAN RIGHT NOW, VISIT
http://www.selfgrowth.com/experts

❑ *Books*

- Learned Optimism: How to Change Your Mind and Your Life
- Authentic Happiness: Using the New Positive Psychology to Realize Your Potential for Lasting Fulfillment
- The Optimistic Child: A Proven Program to Safeguard Children against Depression and Build Lifelong Resilience
- What You Can Change…And What You Can't* (* learning to accept who you are): The Complete Guide to Successful Self-Improvement

❑ *Audio and Video Programs*

- Authentic Happiness: Using the New Positive Psychology to Realize Your Potential for Lasting Fulfillment (on audio cassette or audio CD)
- Learned Optimism (on audio cassette)
- The Optimistic Child (on audio cassette)

❑ *Other Programs and Highlights*

Dr. Seligman has won several other awards for his research and writing and has served in many academic and clinical arenas. His work has been featured in such publications as *The New York Times*, *Time*, and *Newsweek*, and he has been on numerous TV and radio shows. Dr. Seligman has also written columns and lectured around the world.

❑ *Contact Information*

ADDRESS:	Dr. Martin E.P. Seligman, Ph.D.
	University of Pennsylvania
	Department of Psychology
	3815 Walnut Street
	Philadelphia, PA 19104-6196
PHONE:	215-898-7173
EMAIL:	SeligmanInfo@psych.upenn.edu
WEBSITE:	www.positivepsychology.org

LYNN GRABHORN
(Expert #83)

LYNN GRABHORN QUICK FACTS	
Main Areas:	Law of Attraction; Life Changes
NY Times Best-Seller:	"Excuse Me, Your Life is Waiting"
Profile:	Author; Lecturer; Seminar Leader

❑ *Lynn Grabhorn Biography*

Lynn Grabhorn is a student of the way in which thought and feelings format our lives. She is the author of the *New York Times* best-seller, *Excuse Me, Your Life is Waiting*. In the book, she introduces readers to the Law of Attraction and clarifies why most of our dreams have never materialized. With explanations, examples, and easy steps, she shows how to turn it all around.

Grabhorn increased her income 830 percent in just one year by following the principles in *Excuse Me*. She has written a number of other books to help people complete their understanding of our universe and figure out where they want to end up. Her first book, *Beyond the Twelve Steps*, has been highly praised. She also created a guide to the *Excuse Me* book, called *"Excuse Me, Your Life is Waiting" Playbook*.

Raised in Short Hills, New Jersey, Grabhorn moved to California in 1963, the same year she joined Alcoholics Anonymous. She continues to write and lecture, and she gives seminars in which she shows people how to make real changes in life by drawing from her own experiences.

❑ *David Riklan's Favorite Lynn Grabhorn Quotes and Thoughts*

- We create by feeling, not by thought. That's right. We get what we get by the way we feel, not by trying to slug things into place or control or minds.

- The Law of Attraction, like attracts like [like frequencies attract like frequencies]—is absolute (and has nothing to do with personalities). No one lives beyond this law because it is the law of the universe.

- The real reality is we have come here to thrive and prosper and live this grand human experience in lighthearted joy, not in struggle and pain…and to harvest our desires in the absolute knowledge that we can have it all once we learn how to handle our energies, meaning, our emotions.

- The truth is, in our everyday natural state, we have the sacred ability to maneuver this thing called "our life" to be any way we want it to be. Any way! Bar nothing!

❑ *The Best Way to Get Started with Lynn Grabhorn*

The best way to get started with Lynn Grabhorn is to read her book, *Excuse Me, Your Life is Waiting*. In it, she introduces us to the Law of Attraction and explains why most of our dreams have never materialized. In the opening chapter, she sets the tone of the book:

> We reach out anywhere and everywhere for relief from the tedium and struggle of daily living, yet the vast majority of us are still looking. How come? How come we've never learned the simple secret to living the good life, whatever that may represent to us? How come we continue to whack and scratch like frantic mad dogs to get what we want, when all along the key to obtaining our innermost desires has been as elemental as life itself?
>
> If you really think that things come to you by some stroke of good or bad luck, or by accident, or coincidence, or by knocking your brains out against some very unsympathetic stone walls, then get a grip. This book could be dangerous to your discontent.

Grabhorn shows us how to create the lives that we want. She says, "What comes to us has nothing to do with what we're doing physically, or how worthy we are, or how good we are, or what our non-existent destiny may be. It has only to do with how we are vibrating! Which means feeling, which means attracting. Period!"

In the book, Grabhorn defines four steps to help you bring into your life whatever is your passion:

Step 1:   Identify what you DON'T want.
Step 2:   From that, identify what you DO want.
Step 3:   Get into the feeling place of what you want.
Step 4:   Expect, listen, and allow it to happen.

The steps appear to be simple and counterintuitive to many things that we have learned in the past. But the system works. The book teaches us how to sense energy by checking in with the attached emotion around or behind a given situation. In *Excuse Me, Your Life is Waiting*, Grabhorn teaches us to use the steps and how to manifest what we want in our lives. In a nutshell, we get what we dwell on.

TO READ ADDITIONAL BOOK EXCERPTS or ARTICLES or to LISTEN
TO LYNN GRABHORN RIGHT NOW, VISIT
http://www.selfgrowth.com/experts

❑ *Books*

- Excuse Me, Your Life is Waiting: The Astonishing Power of Feelings
- "Excuse Me, Your Life is Waiting" Playbook with the 12 tenets of awakening
- Beyond the Twelve Steps: Roadmap to a New Life
- Dear God! What's Happening to Us? Halting Eons of Manipulation
- Planet Two...Are You Ready? *(due out in early 2004)*

❑ *Audio and Video Programs*

- Excuse Me, Your Life is Waiting (on audio cassette or audio CD)

❑ *Other Programs and Highlights*

Lynn Grabhorn began her working life in advertising in New York City and
then became the founder and manager of an audio-visual educational publishing
company in Los Angeles. To find the nearest study or support group to help
maintain the focus of her life-changing principles, visit her website at
www.lynngrabhorn.com.

❑ *Contact Information*

EMAIL: Go to www.lynngrabhorn.com/mail.htm
WEBSITE: www.lynngrabhorn.com

WERNER ERHARD
(Expert #84)

WERNER ERHARD QUICK FACTS	
Main Areas:	Transformation; Personal Growth
Profile:	Trainer; Volunteer; Company Leader; Founder of est
Affiliation:	The Werner Erhard Foundation

❏ *Werner Erhard Biography*

Werner Erhard introduced the breakthrough notion of "transformation" to the American public. His thinking gave rise to the idea that people could transform their lives in a short time, yielding powerful and long-lasting results. In 1971, he created The est Training and formed the company Erhard Seminars Training, Inc. Attended by approximately a million people, est was an extremely popular personal growth seminar.

With notoriety for tough honesty and skill, Erhard and his programs became the subject of various television, newspaper, magazine, and even movie attention. In 1981, he formed a new company, Werner Erhard and Associates. The est Training and Werner Erhard and Associates produced powerful results with hundreds of thousands of people worldwide. Erhard sold est during the 1980s.

Erhard and his work continued to be a source of influence yet also controversy due to misconceptions in the media. Still, he was committed to bettering the human condition through volunteerism and in 1988, was awarded the Mahatma Gandhi Humanitarian Award for his contribution to people and society. Werner Erhard closed his companies in 1991 and sold the rights to his technology so as to end a swirl of controversial media about him. It later came to light that all of the allegations about him were proven to be either untrue or recanted. However, Erhard chose to stay out of the spotlight.

❏ *David Riklan's Favorite Werner Erhard Quotes and Thoughts*

- Create your future from your future, not your past.

- You and I want our lives to matter. We want our lives to make a real difference—to be of genuine consequence in the world. We know that there is no satisfaction in merely going through the motions, even if those motions make us successful, or even if we have arranged to make those motions pleasant. We want to know we have made some impact on the world. In fact, you and I want to contribute to the quality of life. We want to make the world work.

- Life is a game. In order to have a game, something has to be more important than something else. If what already is, is more important than what isn't, the game is over. So, life is a game in which what isn't, is more important than what is. Let the good times roll.

- Happiness is a function of accepting what is. Love is a function of communication. Health is a function of participation. Self Expression is a function of responsibility.

- You don't have to go looking for love when it's where you come from.

❑ *The Best Way to Get Started with Werner Erhard*

Werner Erhard's legacy lives on in the contribution his work has made to millions of people, both directly and indirectly. Today, Landmark Education's programs are based on research and technology originally developed by Werner Erhard. However, Erhard himself has no ownership or management role in Landmark Education.

In 1991, Landmark Education purchased the intellectual properties of Werner Erhard, and from its inception, Landmark Education established a commitment to world-class innovation and creativity in the design of its program offerings. Since that time, the Research Design and Development Team of Landmark Education has created over two dozen new programs and products focused on a wide range of topics, including communication, productivity, ongoing adult learning, relationships, conflict resolution, cultural diversity, executive development, and corporate strategy. Currently, they are in the final phase of a three-year major redesign of all Landmark programs.

Landmark Education is hailed by *Time* magazine as "a global brand name" in the field of personal growth and development. HR.com, a company committed to helping people make smart human resources decisions, publishes the Buyer's Guide to Leadership and Development Training, where they distinguish the top Institutions and private organizations in the world of leadership training. Landmark Education is featured in the 2003 Buyer's Guide along with Harvard Business School, Kellogg Graduate School, The Niagara Institute, and FranklinCovey, as one of the top training and development institutions in the world.

Over 125,000 people participate in Landmark's programs annually at their 60 offices in 24 countries worldwide. To unofficially get started with Werner Erhard, I suggest you visit the Landmark Education website at www.landmarkeducation.com. Check out information on the Landmark Forum, a 3 ½ day seminar that is different from Erhard's est Training yet contains many of the concepts he originally developed.

TO READ ADDITIONAL BOOK EXCERPTS or ARTICLES or to LISTEN
TO WERNER ERHARD RIGHT NOW, VISIT
http://www.selfgrowth.com/experts

❑ *Other Programs and Highlights*

Erhard co-founded independent, non-profit charitable enterprises, including the
Breakthrough Foundation, the Hunger Project, the Holiday Project, the Werner
Erhard Foundation, and the Education Network. He lectured for a wide variety
of prestigious institutions and professional associations around the world, including Stanford University and the American Psychiatric Association.

❑ *Contact Information*

WEBSITE: www.wernererhard.com

JIDDU KRISHNAMURTI
(Expert #85)

<table>
<tr><td colspan="2" align="center">JIDDU KRISHNAMURTI QUICK FACTS</td></tr>
<tr><td>Main Areas:</td><td>Self-Awareness; Transformation</td></tr>
<tr><td>Profile:</td><td>Author; Speaker; Educator; Religious Philosopher; 1895-1986</td></tr>
<tr><td>Affiliation:</td><td>Krishnamurti Foundation of America</td></tr>
</table>

❑ *Jiddu Krishnamurti Biography*

Jiddu Krishnamurti was a religious philosopher, born in India, whose message centered on the need for maximum self-awareness and fundamental transformation. The core of his teaching is contained in the statement, "Truth is a pathless land." Early in his life, he was hailed as the messiah of the 20th century. The Theosophical Society was convinced that Krishnamurti was an incarnation of the Lord Maitreya who, the Theosophists believed, had earlier incarnated as Jesus.

During a speech in Holland in 1929, Krishnamurti dissolved the Order of the Star, of which he was the head, renouncing that position and all of its trappings in front of 3,000 surprised followers. From then on, he set out on a teaching mission of his own, as a secular philosopher of spirituality with no affiliation to sects or dogmas. He went on to have an active career as a public speaker, educator, and writer.

Krishnamurti traveled the world giving talks and interviews to millions of people, saying that peace in the world can come about only through a complete change in the hearts and minds of individuals. The Krishnamurti Foundation of America (KFA) began operations in 1969 to preserve and disseminate his teachings. Krishnamurti's many books include *The First and Last Freedom, Freedom from the Known, Think on These Things,* and *The Awakening of Intelligence.*

❑ *David Riklan's Favorite Jiddu Krishnamurti Quotes and Thoughts*

- So, it is not that one must be free from or resist fear but that one must understand the whole nature and structure of fear, *understand it;* that means, learn about it, watch it, come directly into contact with it. We are to learn about fear, not how to escape from it, not how to resist it… *(The Flight of the Eagle, p. 90)*

- You must understand the whole of life, not just one little part of it. That is why you must read, that is why you must look at the skies, that is why you must sing and dance, and write poems, and suffer, and understand, for all that is life. *(Think on These Things, p. 35)*

- The function of education, then, is to help you from childhood not to imitate anybody, but to be yourself all the time. *(Think on These Things, p. 20)*

- The moment you have in your heart this extraordinary thing called love and feel the depth, the delight, the ecstasy of it, you will discover that for you the world is transformed. *(ibid., p. 205)*

- In oneself lies the whole world, and if you know how to look and learn, then the door is there and the key is in your hand. Nobody on earth can give you either the key or the door to open, except yourself. *(You are the World, p. 135)*

❑ **The Best Way to Get Started with Jiddu Krishnamurti**

The best way to get started with Jiddu Krishnamurti is to read the statement below from the website www.jiddukrishnamurti.info. This statement, written by Krishnamurti on October 21, 1980, has been published under the title *The Core of the Teaching:*

> The core of Krishnamurti's teaching is contained in the statement he made in 1929 when he said, "Truth is a pathless land." Man cannot come to it through any organization, through any creed, through any dogma, priest or ritual, not through any philosophic knowledge or psychological technique. He has to find it through the mirror of relationship, through the understanding of the contents of his own mind, through observation and not through intellectual analysis or introspective dissection.
>
> Man has built in himself images as a fence of security— religious, political, personal. These manifest as symbols, ideas, beliefs. The burden of these images dominates man's thinking, his relationships, and his daily life. These images are the causes of our problems, for they divide man from man. His perception of life is shaped by the concepts already established in his mind.
>
> The content of his consciousness is his entire existence. This content is common to all humanity. The individuality is the name, the form and superficial culture he acquires from tradi-

tion and environment. The uniqueness of man does not lie in the superficial but in complete freedom from the content of his consciousness, which is common to all mankind. So he is not an individual.

Freedom is not a reaction; freedom is not a choice. It is man's pretence that because he has choice he is free. Freedom is pure observation without direction, without fear of punishment and reward. Freedom is without motive; freedom is not at the end of the evolution of man but lies in the first step of his existence. In observation one begins to discover the lack of freedom. Freedom is found in the choiceless awareness of our daily existence and activity.

Thought is time. Thought is born of experience and knowledge which are inseparable from time and the past. Time is the psychological enemy of man. Our action is based on knowledge and therefore time, so man is always a slave to the past. Thought is ever-limited and so we live in constant conflict and struggle. There is no psychological evolution.

When man becomes aware of the movement of his own thoughts, he will see the division between the thinker and thought, the observer and the observed, the experiencer and the experience. He will discover that this division is an illusion. Then only is there pure observation which is insight without any shadow of the past or of time. This timeless insight brings about a deep radical mutation in the mind.

Total negation is the essence of the positive. When there is negation of all those things that thought has brought about psychologically, only then is there love, which is compassion and intelligence.

If you are looking for more, I would suggest reading Krishnamurti's book *Freedom from the Known*. In it, he shows you how to free yourself from the "tyranny of the expected," no matter what your age. He says that by changing yourself first, you can change your relationship to society.

TO READ ADDITIONAL BOOK EXCERPTS or ARTICLES or to LISTEN TO JIDDU KRISHNAMURTI RIGHT NOW, VISIT http://www.selfgrowth.com/experts

❑ *Books*

- Freedom from the Known

- The First and Last Freedom
- Think on These Things
- The Awakening of Intelligence
- On Love and Loneliness
- Meeting Life: Writings and Talks on Finding Your Path Without Retreating from Society
- The Ending of Time (co-authored with David Bohm)
- To Be Human

❑ *Audio and Video Programs*

- The Transformation of Man *(the five-part series with David Bohm & David Shainberg)*
- Krishnamurti and Professor Allan W. Anderson *(the 18-part series of dialogues, also available in book form under the title* A Wholly Different Way of Living*)*

❑ *Other Programs and Highlights*

Throughout his lifetime, Krishnamurti insisted that he wanted no followers, and he authorized no one to become an interpreter of his work. The only thing he asked was that, after his death, those who shared his concerns maintain an authentic record of his talks, dialogues, and writings and make them widely available to the public.

❑ *Contact Information*

(For a complete list of Jiddu Krishnamurti's audio and video cassettes, apply to the address below.)

ADDRESS: Krishnamurti Foundation of America
P.O. Box 1560.
Ojai, CA 93024
PHONE: 805-646-2726
EMAIL: kfa@kfa.org
WEBSITE: www.jiddukrishnamurti.info
www.kfa.org

MARTHA BECK
(Expert #86)

MARTHA BECK QUICK FACTS	
Main Areas:	Life Design; Career Change; Listening to Your Heart
NY Times Best-Sellers:	"Expecting Adam"; "Finding Your Own North Star"
Profile:	Author; Life Coach; Magazine Columnist
Affiliation:	Martha Beck, Inc.

❑ Martha Beck Biography

Martha Beck, Ph.D., is an innovator in life design and a monthly columnist at *O: The Oprah Magazine*. She is the founder of Martha Beck, Inc., a life coaching firm that helps clients redirect their careers and lifestyles. Martha was a business consultant, a researcher at the Harvard Business School, and a professor at the International School of Business before becoming a life coach.

Martha left the academic environment and embraced change with the birth of her son Adam, who has Down's syndrome. This experience inspired her *New York Times* best-selling book, *Expecting Adam*. She also authored the *New York Times* best-seller *Finding Your Own North Star*. In her writing, Martha says that your heart is trying to tell you what you need, and listening makes a difference.

Martha earned a B.A., M.A., and Ph.D. in sociology from Harvard University. By the time Adam was born, aware of his disability, she says she "had to unlearn virtually everything Harvard taught [her] about what is precious and what is garbage." The mother of three children, Martha lectures and conducts seminars for a diverse clientele that includes medical professionals, magazine sales forces, boards of education, and business executives.

❑ David Riklan's Favorite Martha Beck Quotes and Thoughts

- Whoever said love is blind is dead wrong. Love is the only thing that lets us see each other with the remotest accuracy.

- Angels come in many shapes and sizes, and most of them are not invisible.

- You'll never be hurt as much by being open as you have been hurt by remaining closed.

❑ *The Best Way to Get Started with Martha Beck*

As far as Self Improvement goes, I recommend that you start with Martha Beck's book, *Finding Your Own North Star*. So what is a North Star? Martha writes, "Explorers depend on the North Star when there are no other landmarks in sight. The same relationship exists between you and your right life, the ultimate realization of your potential for happiness. I believe that a knowledge of that perfect life sits inside you just as the North Star sits in its unaltering spot."

Finding Your Own North Star is based on the premise that each of us has two sides: the essential self and the social self. The essential self contains several compasses that continuously point toward your North Star. The social self is the set of skills that actually carry you toward your goal. In the first chapter of her book, Martha illustrates this by sharing examples like: "Your essential self wants passionately to become a doctor; the social self struggles through organic chemistry and applies to medical school."

The system functions beautifully as long as the essential and social selves are communicating freely with each other and working in perfect synchrony. However, few people are lucky enough to experience such inner harmony. In *Finding Your Own North Star*, Martha will teach you how to read your internal compasses and move towards this inner harmony. She gives you a step by-step program to reach your own ideal life and includes exercises, questionnaires, and case studies to help you along the way.

TO READ ADDITIONAL BOOK EXCERPTS or ARTICLES or to LISTEN TO MARTHA BECK RIGHT NOW, VISIT
http://www.selfgrowth.com/experts

❑ *Books*

- Finding Your Own North Star: Claiming the Life You Were Meant to Live
- Expecting Adam: A True Story of Birth, Rebirth, and Everyday Magic
- The Joy Diet: Ten Daily Practices for a Happier Life

❑ *Audio and Video Programs*

- The Joy Diet (on audio cassette)

❑ *Other Programs and Highlights*

National Public Radio called Martha "the best-known life coach in America." According to Martha herself, she is learning to listen and is lucky enough to share that with millions of people via print, television, or in person. Her Polaris

Sessions (Claiming Your North Star) are focused, two-day sessions that help you claim the life you were meant to live. She directs them personally, each with a group of 5 to 8 people in a private yet comfortable setting.

❑ *Contact Information*

ADDRESS: P.O. Box 535
428 E. Thunderbird Rd.
Phoenix, AZ 85022
PHONE: 602-789-9367
EMAIL: martha@marthabeck.com
WEBSITE: www.marthabeck.com

DEBBIE FORD
(Expert #87)

DEBBIE FORD QUICK FACTS

Main Areas:	Transformation; Human Potential; Psychology
NY Times Best-Seller:	"The Dark Side of the Light Chasers"
Profile:	Author; Lecturer; Workshop Leader
Affiliations:	The Institute for Integrative Coaching; The Chopra Center for Well Being

---

❑ *Debbie Ford Biography*

Debbie Ford is a recognized expert in the field of personal transformation and human potential. Her four books, including the national best-seller *The Dark Side of the Light Chasers*, have been translated into 22 languages and are used as teaching tools in universities and institutions of learning worldwide. She also lectures and leads workshops across the nation.

Ford is an extended faculty member at The Chopra Center for Well Being in La Costa, California. She earned a degree in psychology with an emphasis in consciousness studies from JFK University, and in 2001, she received the Alumni of the Year Award for her outstanding contribution in the fields of psychology and spirituality.

Ford empowers people to design their lives in a way they desire. She is the founder of the Institute for Integrative Coaching, a personal development organization that provides professional training for individuals who wish to lead extraordinary lives. She also leads her acclaimed "Shadow Process Workshop," a three-day life-changing experience, several times each year.

❑ *David Riklan's Favorite Debbie Ford Quotes and Thoughts*

- Many of us are frightened to look within ourselves, and fear has us put up walls so thick we no longer remember who we really are.

- By choosing not to allow parts of ourselves to exist, we are forced to expend huge amounts of psychic energy to keep them beneath the surface.

- Whatever we refuse to recognize about ourselves has a way of rearing its head and making itself known when we least expect it.

- Our society nurtures the illusion that all the rewards go to the people who are perfect. But many of us are finding out that trying to be perfect is costly.

- Remember, all the answers you need are inside of you; you only have to become quiet enough to hear them.

- For when I can love all of me, I will love all of you.

❑ *The Best Way to Get Started with Debbie Ford*

The best place to get started with Debbie Ford is to read her book, *The Dark Side of the Light Chasers*. In the beginning of the book, she immediately defines its focus:

> Most of us set out on the path to personal growth because at some point the burden of our pain becomes too much to bear. *The Dark Side of the Light Chasers* is about unmasking that aspect of ourselves which destroys our relationships, kills our spirit, and keeps us from fulfilling our dreams. It is what the psychologist Carl Jung called the shadow. It contains all the parts of ourselves that we have tried to hide or deny. It contains those dark aspects that we believe are not acceptable to our family, friends, and most importantly, ourselves. The dark side is stuffed deeply within our consciousness, hidden from ourselves and others. The message we get from this hidden place is simple: there is something wrong with me. I'm not okay. I'm not lovable. I'm not deserving. I'm not worthy.

Simply put, we all have a dark side, and if deny our dark side, it will cast a "shadow" that will negatively impact our lives. In her book, Ford teaches us how to confront these "shadows." You can achieve harmony and "let your own light shine through" by owning every aspect of yourself. To Ford, "owning" means to "acknowledge that a quality belongs to us". She explains, "The purpose of doing shadow work is to become whole. To end our suffering. To stop hiding ourselves from ourselves. Once we do this we can stop hiding ourselves from the rest of the world."

According to Ford, "By facing these aspects of ourselves, we become free to experience our glorious totality: the good and the bad, the dark and the light. It is by embracing all of who we are that we earn the freedom to choose what we do in this world. As long as we keep hiding, masquerading, and projecting what is inside us, we have no freedom to be and no freedom to choose."

Ford's step-by-step guidebook is based on the course that she developed about embracing the shadow. Her advice frequently comes from experiences with friends and in workshops that she has taught or attended.

TO READ ADDITIONAL BOOK EXCERPTS or ARTICLES or to LISTEN TO DEBBIE FORD RIGHT NOW, VISIT
http://www.selfgrowth.com/experts

❑ **Books**

- The Dark Side of the Light Chasers: Reclaiming Your Power, Creativity, Brilliance, and Dreams
- The Right Questions: Ten Essential Questions to Guide You to an Extraordinary Life
- Spiritual Divorce: Divorce as a Catalyst for an Extraordinary Life
- The Secret of the Shadow: The Power of Owning Your Whole Story

❑ **Audio and Video Programs**

- The Answers are Within You *(produced by Nightingale-Conant)*
- The Dark Side of the Light Chasers; The Right Questions; Spiritual Divorce; The Secret of the Shadow (each on audio cassette)

❑ **Other Programs and Highlights**

Debbie Ford has appeared on such television programs as *The Oprah Winfrey Show*, *Good Morning America*, and *The Roseanne Show* and has been featured in publications like *O: The Oprah Magazine*, *USA Today*, and *Self*. Her Integrative Coaching Training Program challenges participants to reclaim their greatness in every aspect of their lives and equips them with the skills and distinctions to facilitate a unique form of coaching.

❑ **Contact Information**

ADDRESS: Debbie Ford's Institute for Integrative Coaching
P.O. Box 90848
San Diego, CA 92169
PHONE: (800) 655-4016
EMAIL: Debbie@Debbieford.com
WEBSITE: www.debbieford.com

SHAKTI GAWAIN
(Expert #88)

SHAKTI GAWAIN QUICK FACTS

Main Areas:	Visualization; Consciousness
Best-Seller:	"Creative Visualization" series
Profile:	Author; Workshop Leader
Affiliation:	Nataraj Publishing (a division of New World Library)

❏ *Shakti Gawain Biography*

Shakti Gawain is a pioneer in the field of personal growth and consciousness. She leads workshops internationally and has helped thousands of people to develop greater awareness, balance, and wholeness in their lives. Shakti, an only child, was brought up in a highly academic environment, and both her parents were atheists. When one of her love relationships broke up, she was left in a deep existential crisis and searched for the true purpose of life.

During a trip to India, Shakti became impressed with the culture and the religious beliefs she encountered. A self-proclaimed workaholic, she suddenly lost interest in material things and gave away all her possessions except those she could fit into a small canvass bag. She says she realized that, along the way, we will be given the things we truly need.

Shakti's many best-selling books have sold more than six million copies in 30 languages worldwide. *Creative Visualization* teaches personal growth methods that are easy to incorporate into daily life. *Living in the Light* introduces readers to a new way of life in which we listen to and rely on our intuition. Nataraj Publishing is a division of New World Library, which Shakti co-founded.

❏ *David Riklan's Favorite Shakti Gawain Quotes and Thoughts*

- Every moment of your life is infinitely creative and the universe is bountiful. Just put forth a clear enough request, and everything your heart desires must come to you.

- Every time you don't follow your inner guidance, you feel a loss of energy, loss of power, a sense of spiritual deadness.

- When I am trusting and being myself as fully as possible, everything in my life reflects this by falling into place easily, often miraculously.

- We avoid the things that we're afraid of because we think there will be dire consequences if we confront them. But the truly dire consequences in our lives come from avoiding things that we need to learn about or discover.

- We will discover the nature of our particular genius when we stop trying to conform to our own or to other people's models, learn to be ourselves, and allow our natural channel to open.

- The Universe will reward you for taking risks on its behalf.

- What I am actually saying is that we need to be willing to let our intuition guide us and then be willing to follow that guidance directly and fearlessly.

❏ *The Best Way to Get Started with Shakti Gawain*

Shakti Gawain has written several books and has created several audio programs. But her *Creative Visualization* series stands alone as her most important work, and it is the best way to get started. Available as a book or in audio form, it shows you how to harness the power of your imagination and creative mind to achieve your desires.

In *Creative Visualization*, Shakti covers a variety of areas, including "How to Visualize," "Affirmations," and "Creative Visualization Only Works for the Good." She then moves on to more challenging goals like "Contacting Your Higher Self," "Meeting Your Guide," "Setting Goals," and "Treasure Maps."

The program is full of exercises and practical suggestions that help you learn how to relax, heal yourself, send out more loving energy, meditate, and more. Here is one example:

> Make a point to express more appreciation to others in as many ways as you can think of. Sit down right now and make a list of people to whom you would like to outflow love and appreciation, and think of a way you can do so to each one within the next week. Outflow can take the form of words, touching, a gift, a phone call or letter, money, or any sharing of your talents that makes another person feel good. Choose something that makes you feel especially good too, even if it's a little more difficult for you.

> Practice speaking more words of thanks, appreciation, and admiration to people when you feel like it. "It was kind of you to help me." "I want you to know that I appreciate that."

Creative Visualization is a powerful and practical tool that illustrates the use of visualization. You cannot go wrong with either the book or audio tape.

TO READ ADDITIONAL BOOK EXCERPTS or ARTICLES or to LISTEN TO SHAKTI GAWAIN RIGHT NOW, VISIT
http://www.selfgrowth.com/experts

❑ *Books*

- Creative Visualization: Use the Power of Your Imagination to Create What You Want in Your Life
- Living in the Light: A Guide to Personal and Planetary Transformation
- Living in the Light Workbook
- Reflections in the Light: Daily Thoughts and Affirmations
- Developing Intuition: Practical Guidance for Daily Life
- Creating True Prosperity
- The Path of Transformation: How Healing Ourselves Can Change the World
- The Four Levels of Healing: A Guide to Balancing the Spiritual, Mental, Emotional, and Physical Aspects of Creative Visualization
- Meditations

❑ *Audio and Video Programs*

- Meditations for Creating True Prosperity
- Relationships as Mirrors
- Contacting Your Inner Guide
- Creative Visualization; Living in the Light; Developing Intuition; Creating True Prosperity; The Four Levels of Healing (each on audio cassette)

❑ *Other Programs and Highlights*

Shakti is the name of the female aspect of the Hindu God Shiva. She has appeared on such TV shows as *The Oprah Winfrey Show*, *Good Morning America*, and *Larry King Live*. She has also been featured in such publications as *Cosmopolitan*, *New Woman*, *New Age Journal*, and *Time*.

❑ *Contact Information*

ADDRESS: New World Library
14 Pamaron Way
Novato, CA 94949

PHONE: (800) 972-6657 Ext. 52 *(toll-free-ordering, New World Library)*

EMAIL: info@shaktigawain.com
                         or go to www.newworldlibrary.com/contact.html

WEBSITE: www.shaktigawain.com
                         www.newworldlibrary.com

NATHANIEL BRANDEN
(Expert #89)

NATHANIEL BRANDEN QUICK FACTS

Main Area:	Self-Esteem
Profile:	Author; Psychotherapist; Corporate Consultant; Workshop/Seminar Leader
Affiliation:	The Branden Institute for Self-Esteem

❑ *Nathaniel Branden Biography*

Nathaniel Branden, Ph.D., pioneered the psychology of self-esteem. He is a practicing psychotherapist in Los Angeles and also does corporate consulting. Dr. Branden offers workshops, seminars, and conferences on applying self-esteem principles to the problems of modern business. He addresses the relationship between self-esteem and such issues as leadership, effective communication, and managing change.

Dr. Branden has a Ph.D. in psychology and a background in philosophy. He has written 20 books, which have been translated into 18 languages. More than 3.5 million copies are in print, including the classic *The Psychology of Self-Esteem*, originally published in 1969. In it, he explains the need for self-esteem, the nature of that need, and how self-esteem—or lack of it—affects our values, responses, and goals.

Dr. Branden has done a great deal to help America realize the importance of self-esteem to human well-being. He is on the Advisory Board of the National Council for Self-Esteem and the Advisory Council for the International Academy of Behavioral Medicine, Counseling and Psychotherapy, Inc. He consults with clients around the world, not only in person but via telephone as well.

❑ *David Riklan's Favorite Nathaniel Branden Quotes and Thoughts*

- The first step toward change is awareness. The second step is acceptance.

- Of all the judgments we pass in life, none is more important than the judgment we pass on ourselves.

- If we do not believe in ourselves—neither in our efficacy nor in our goodness—the universe is a frightening place.

- Persons of high self-esteem are not driven to make themselves superior to others; they do not seek to prove their value by measuring themselves against a comparative standard. Their joy is being who they are, not in being better than someone else.

- Romantic love is a passionate spiritual-emotional-sexual attachment between a man and a woman that reflects a high regard for the value of each other's person.

- Self esteem is the reputation we acquire with ourselves.

- There is overwhelming evidence that the higher the level of self-esteem, the more likely one will treat others with respect, kindness, and generosity. People who do not experience self-love have little or no capacity to love others.

- To preserve an unclouded capacity for the enjoyment of life is an unusual moral and psychological achievement. Contrary to popular belief, it is not the prerogative of mindlessness but the exact opposite. It is the reward of self-esteem.

- Sometimes the subconscious mind manifests a wisdom several steps or even years ahead of the conscious mind, and has its own way of leading us toward our destiny.

❑ *The Best Way to Get Started with Nathaniel Branden*

Nathaniel Branden has a tremendous impact on self-esteem. His work, *The Psychology of Self-Esteem*, originally published in 1969, was a revolutionary book in the field of psychology, impacting our views of self-esteem for years to come. If you want to gain an understanding of the book that had a great impact on the self-esteem movement, read *The Psychology of Self-Esteem*. But if you want learn how to improve your own self-esteem, read Dr. Branden's *The Six Pillars of Self-Esteem*.

In *The Six Pillars of Self-Esteem*, Dr. Branden defines self-esteem by teaching us about six important areas or "pillars" of self-esteem. Here are the definitions:

Self-Esteem: Definitions[1]
Nathaniel Branden, Ph.D.

In discussing the relationship between self-esteem and professional effectiveness, I introduce certain key concepts. They
are defined as follows:

*Self-esteem is the experience of being competent to
cope with the basic challenges of life and of being worthy of
happiness.*[2]

Over three decades of study have led me to identify
six practices as the most essential to building self-esteem.

1. *The practice of living consciously:* respect for facts;
   being present to what we are doing while we are doing it (e.g., if our customer, supervisor, employee,
   supplier, colleague is talking to us, being present to
   the encounter); seeking and being eagerly open to
   any information, knowledge, or feedback that bears
   on our interests, values, goals, and projects; seeking
   to understand not only the world external to self but
   also our inner world as well, so that we do not act out
   of self-blindness. When asked to account for the extraordinary transformation he achieved at General
   Electric, Jack Welch spoke of "self-confidence, can-
   dor, and an *unflinching willingness to face reality,
   even when it's painful,*" which is essential to the
   practice of living consciously.

2. *The practice of self-acceptance*: the willingness to
   own, experience, and take responsibility for our
   thoughts, feelings, and actions, without evasion, de-
   nial, or disowning—and also without self-
   repudiation; giving oneself permission to think one's
   thoughts, experience one's emotions, and look at
   one's actions without necessarily liking, endorsing or
   condoning them. If we are self-accepting, we do not
   experience ourselves as always "on trial," and what
   this leads to is non-defensiveness and willingness to

---

[1] Copyright by Nathaniel Branden

[2] N. Branden, *The Six Pillars of Self-Esteem*, New York:
Bantam Books, 1994.

hear critical feedback or different ideas without becoming hostile and adversarial.

3. *The practice of self-responsibility:* realizing that we
    are the authors of our choices and actions; that each
    one of us is responsible for our life and well-being
    and for the attainment of our goals; that if we need
    the cooperation of other people to achieve our goals,
    we must offer values in exchange; and that the ques-
    tion is not "Who's to blame?" but always "What
    needs to be done?"

4. *The practice of self-assertiveness*: being authentic in
    our dealings with others; treating our values and per-
    sons with decent respect in social contexts; refusing
    to fake the reality of who we are or what we esteem
    in order to avoid someone's disapproval; the willing-
    ness to stand up for ourselves and our ideas in appro-
    priate ways in appropriate circumstances.

5. *The practice of living purposefully:* identifying our
    short-term and long-term goals or purposes and the
    actions needed to attain them, organizing behavior in
    the service of those goals, monitoring action to be
    sure we stay on track—and paying attention to out-
    come so as to recognize if and when we need to go
    back to the drawing-board.

6. *The practice of personal integrity:* living with con-
    gruence between what we know, what we profess,
    and what we do; telling the truth, honoring our com-
    mitments, exemplifying in action the values we pro-
    fess to admire; dealing with others fairly and
    benevolently. When we betray our values, we betray
    our mind, and self-esteem is an inevitable casualty.

I also recommend Dr. Branden's book *How to Raise Your Self-Esteem*. In it, he
shows us the importance of good self-esteem and then provides us with the tools
to improve our own. He teaches us how to work on many areas of our lives,
including how to:

- Break free of negative self concepts and self defeating behavior.
- Dissolve internal barriers to success in love and work.
- Overcome anxiety, depression, guilt, and anger.
- Conquer the fear of intimacy and success.

You can get started with Nathaniel Branden by reading any of the three books I
have already mentioned. Go ahead and feel better about yourself today!

TO READ ADDITIONAL BOOK EXCERPTS or ARTICLES or to LISTEN
TO NATHANIEL BRANDEN RIGHT NOW, VISIT
http://www.selfgrowth.com/experts

❏ *Books*

- The Psychology of Self-Esteem: A Revolutionary Approach to Self-Understanding That Launched a New Era in Modern Psychology
- Honoring the Self: Self-Esteem and Personal Transformation
- How to Raise Your Self-Esteem: The Proven, Action-Oriented Approach to Greater Self Respect and Self-Confidence
- The Six Pillars of Self-Esteem: The Definitive Work on Self-Esteem by the Leading Pioneer in the Field
- Taking Responsibility: Self-Reliance and the Accountable Life
- The Art of Living Consciously: The Power of Awareness to Transform Everyday Life
- The Power of Self-Esteem: An Inspiring Look At Our Most Important Psychological Resource

❏ *Audio and Video Programs*

- The Psychology of Self-Esteem (on audio cassette)
- The Six Pillars of Self-Esteem (on audio cassette)
- The Power of Self-Esteem (book or audio cassette)

❏ *Other Programs and Highlights*

Dr. Branden has been practicing phone therapy since 1985 and has found that consultations can be as effective on the telephone as in the office. To read Nathaniel Branden's essays and excerpts, view his upcoming events, and find out what's new, visit www.nathanielbranden.net.

❏ *Contact Information*

ADDRESS: Nathaniel Branden
P.O. Box 2609
Beverly Hills, CA 90213
PHONE: (310) 274-6361
EMAIL: N6666B@cs.com
WEBSITE: www.nathanielbranden.net

GANGAJI
(Expert #90)

GANGAJI QUICK FACTS

Main Areas:	Spirituality; Self-Inquiry
Profile:	Author; Spiritual Teacher
Affiliation:	The Gangaji Foundation

❑ *Gangaji Biography*

Gangaji is a spiritual teacher who shares the path of freedom through simple and direct self-inquiry. Born Antoinette Roberson in 1942, she searched for personal happiness and pursued many different things to change her life, including political activism and a career as an English teacher. However, her longing remained, and she made a prayer for help.

In 1990, her prayer was answered. Her husband, Eli Jaxon-Bear, went to India and discovered a teacher named Sri H.W.L. Poonja, also known as Papaji. Eli invited Gangaji to India to sit with this teacher, who was a disciple of Bhagavan Sri Ramana Maharshi. Gangaji's suffering ended upon meeting Papaji, and she discovered the source of true fulfillment.

Since that time, Gangaji has traveled the world, holding gatherings and retreats with spiritual seekers of all faiths. She tells her story in her autobiography, *Just Like You*. Gangaji has many video groups worldwide. The Gangaji Foundation offers many scholarships, and her teachings are available free of charge on public access television in various cities throughout the United States.

❑ *David Riklan's Favorite Gangaji Quotes and Thoughts*

- Recognize the power of mind, respect the power of mind. And also recognize the power behind the power, the ocean holding the wave. Recognize yourself as the ocean, with your stories, your feelings, as waves. Waves can be beautiful or terrifying, but always they return to the ocean. Every wave always is made up of the ocean. No wave can ever be separate from the ocean. Waves of thoughts, waves of emotions, waves of sensations, waves of events, are all made up of consciousness. And all return to consciousness, while never being separate from consciousness. And if this becomes another story, let this go, and see what is true.

- You are here. However you imagine yourself to be, you are here. Imagine yourself as a body, you are here. Imagine yourself as God, you are here. Imagine yourself as worthless, superior, nothing at all, you are still here. My suggestion is that you stop all imagining, here.

- Revelation is beyond doctrines and belief systems. It is beyond every-thing imaginable. It is beyond because it is so close. Revelation is more direct than every word, for it arises out of the truth of who you are. This truth is all you have ever longed for, all you have ever needed.

- Be still and know yourself as the Truth you have been searching for. Be still and let the inherent joy of that Truth capture your drama and destroy it in the bliss of consummation. Be still and let your life be lived by the purpose you were made for. Be still and receive the inher-ent truth of your heart.

- The most sublime truth of all has never been stated or written or sung, not because it is far away and can't be reached but because it is so in-timately close, closer than anything that can be spoken.

- I want to make sure you know you are not who you think you are.

- What I have to offer is very simple. It has nothing to do with acquiring any special powers or any state of mind. It is about recognizing what is already permanently here, in every moment, every situation, and every state of mind, and yet is ungraspable by the mind.

❑ *The Best Way to Get Started with Gangaji*

The best way to get started with Gangaji is by watching or listening to her. She offers a wide variety of video and audio programs on her website (www.gangaji.org), where you can listen to samples of her programs before you buy them. Go to the site, click on "Reading Room," and then choose "Listening Library."

The first program that I would recommend is titled *The Invitation*, which is available in either an audio or video version. This and many other of Gangaji's compilations can be purchased through the website by clicking on "Bookstore" and choosing "Compilations." *The Invitation* is best described in this section of the site. The description is as follows:

> Have you looked everywhere for fulfillment? In relationships, spirituality, health, self-image? Have you found what matters most? At the very heart of Gangaji's message is the simple yet radical invitation to stop looking outside yourself for reso-lution and simply be willing, just in this moment, to see what is already here. This compilation of crystalline monologues is

the encouragement, the support, and the inspiration to finally accept the invitation of your soul's deepest longing. Beyond any belief about yourself, closer than any joy or sorrow, more immediate than either sickness or health, is the endlessly fulfilling truth of who you are.

While at www.gangaji.org, also go to her "Reading Room" and check out her work in print. Gangaji offers an array of inspiring articles, poems, letters, and book excerpts.

TO READ ADDITIONAL BOOK EXCERPTS or ARTICLES or to LISTEN TO GANGAJI RIGHT NOW, VISIT
http://www.selfgrowth.com/experts

❑ *Books*

- Just Like You: An Autobiography
- You Are That! Satsang with Gangaji, Volumes I and II
- Freedom and Resolve: The Living Edge of Surrender

❑ *Audio and Video Programs*

- Who Are You? The Path of Self-Inquiry
- Unraveling the Knot of Suffering
- Open, Unprotected, and Free
- Revealing Strategies of Ego
- The Truth Alive in You

❑ *Other Programs and Highlights*

Gangaji first appeared on public access television in Hawaii. Today, she is on TV in over 70 communities. Her non-profit organization, The Gangaji Foundation, was established in 1993 to make her teaching available to anyone interested. It began with a small group in the basement of the first executive director's home, and today it is a worldwide network of volunteers.

❑ *Contact Information*

ADDRESS: The Gangaji Foundation
505A San Marin Drive, Suite 120
Novato, CA 94945
PHONE: 415-899-9855 or 800-267-9205
EMAIL: info@gangaji.org
WEBSITE: www.gangaji.org

EARL NIGHTINGALE
(Expert #91)

EARL NIGHTINGALE QUICK FACTS

Main Areas:	Success; Empowerment
Best-Sellers (Audio):	"The Strangest Secret"; "Lead the Field"
Profile:	Author; Radio Broadcaster; Co-Founder of Nightingale-Conant; 1921-1989
Affiliation:	Nightingale-Conant

❏ *Earl Nightingale Biography*

Earl Nightingale was one of the world's foremost experts on success and what makes people successful. A Depression-era child, Earl had a natural curiosity about the world and frequently visited the public library. From the time he was a young boy, Earl wondered how a person could reach his/her goals and make a major contribution to others.

Earl's early career began when, as a member of the Marine Corps, he volunteered to work as an announcer at a local radio station. He began his network radio career years later when he and his wife moved to Chicago. Eventually, Earl partnered with Lloyd Conant to create an "electronic publishing" company, Nightingale-Conant, which eventually grew to become a multi-million-dollar giant in the Self Improvement field.

When Earl bought his own insurance company, he spent a good number of hours motivating its sales force to greater accomplishments. His sales manager begged him to put his inspirational words on record. The recording, called *The Strangest Secret*, was the first spoken-word message to win a Gold Record by selling over a million copies. In *The Strangest Secret*, Earl found a way to leave a lasting legacy for others.

❏ *David Riklan's Favorite Earl Nightingale Quotes and Thoughts*

- Don't let the fear of the time it will take to accomplish something stand in the way of your doing it. The time will pass anyway; we might just as well put that passing time to the best possible use.

- We are at our very best, and we are happiest, when we are fully engaged in work we enjoy on the journey toward the goal we've established for ourselves. It gives meaning to our time off and comfort to our sleep. It makes everything else in life so wonderful, so worthwhile.

- The key that unlocks energy is "Desire." It's also the key to a long and interesting life. If we expect to create any drive, any real force within ourselves, we have to get excited.

- The biggest mistake that you can make is to believe that you are working for somebody else. Job security is gone. The driving force of a career must come from the individual. Remember, jobs are owned by the company; you own your career!

- Your life is controlled by your thoughts. Your thoughts are controlled by your goals.

- Success is the progressive realization of a worthy goal or ideal.

- Our attitude toward life determines life's attitude towards us.

❏ *The Best Way to Get Started with Earl Nightingale*

Earl Nightingale was a principal player in the Self Improvement Industry for years, leaving behind the legacy of Nightingale-Conant, one of the largest producers of motivational audio programs. If you want to see firsthand Earl's contribution to Self Improvement, visit the Nightingale.com website. But if you want to get a true sense of Earl Nightingale, start by listening to one of his audio programs.

I recommend that you start at the beginning of Earl's audio program career. His original tape, *The Strangest Secret*, was created many years ago and has been updated to include even more valuable information. Earl also created an audio program titled *Lead the Field*, which became a top seller for Nightingale-Conant. In the program, Earl teaches you how to do things like:

- Double your mental capability.
- Recognize and easily overcome the biggest stumbling block to high achievement.
- Dramatically improve your luck by changing one simple thing.
- Make success unavoidable with an easy three-minute-a-day exercise.

Lead the Field is a very professionally done audio program and is available on either six CDs or six cassettes with a corresponding workbook. You will get the best of Earl Nightingale if you start with either *The Strangest Secret* or *Lead the Field*.

TO READ ADDITIONAL BOOK EXCERPTS or ARTICLES or to LISTEN TO EARL NIGHTINGALE RIGHT NOW, VISIT
http://www.selfgrowth.com/experts

❑ *Books*

- Essence of Success: 163 Life Lessons from the Dean of Self Development
- Earl Nightingale's Greatest Discovery
- The Strangest Secret (Earl Nightingale's Library of Little Gems)

❑ *Audio and Video Programs*

- Earl Nightingale's The Strangest Secret
- Lead the Field
- Creative Thinking

❑ *Other Programs and Highlights*

As host of his own daily commentary program on WGN in Chicago, Earl arranged a deal that gave him a commission on his own advertising sales. By 1957, he was so successful that he decided to retire at the age of 35. Earl Nightingale and Lloyd Conant developed a syndicated, 5-minute daily radio program, *Our Changing World*, which became the longest-running, most widely syndicated show in radio. Earl was inducted into the Radio Hall of Fame in 1985.

❑ *Contact Information*

ADDRESS: Nightingale-Conant
6245 W. Howard St.
Niles, IL 60714
PHONE: 1-800-525-9000
EMAIL: support@nightingale.com
info@nightingaleproducts.com
WEBSITE: www.nightingale.com
www.nightingaleproducts.com

JULIE MORGENSTERN
(Expert #92)

JULIE MORGENSTERN QUICK FACTS	
Main Areas:	Organization; Time Management
Best-Sellers:	"Organizing from the Inside Out"; "Time Management from the Inside Out"
Profile:	Author; Speaker; Media Expert; Corporate Spokesperson
Affiliation:	Julie Morgenstern's Task Masters

❑ *Julie Morgenstern Biography*

Julie Morgenstern is the founder and owner of the organizing firm, Julie Morgenstern's Task Masters. The firm helps people get organized and helps companies do more in less time. Since 1989, Julie and her staff have organized the cluttered homes, offices, and schedules of numerous clients, such as American Express, The Miami Heat, and NBC television.

Julie is a speaker, media expert, and corporate spokesperson. The National Association of Professional Organizers (NAPO) honored her with its prestigious Founder's Award in 2002 for her significant contributions to the professional organizing industry. She has served actively on the board of directors for NAPO and is also a member of The National Speakers Association.

Julie is the author of such books as *The New York Times* best-seller, *Organizing from the Inside Out*, and the national best-seller, *Time Management from the Inside Out*. Her education includes a B.A. in theatre from Temple University and graduate studies in directing at the Goodman School of Drama. She believes that organizing requires the same set of skills as directing and producing—an appreciation of spatial design, the ability to see the big picture as well as the tiny details, and the talent to blend psychology and practical skills to guide people where they want to go.

❑ *David Riklan's Favorite Julie Morgenstern Quotes and Thoughts*

- Misconception: Organizing is a mysterious talent. Some lucky people are born with it, while others, like you, are left to suffer.

  Fact: Organizing is a skill. In fact, it's a remarkably simple skill that anyone can learn. How do I know? Because I was once a notoriously disorganized person myself. In fact, everyone who "knew me when" is amazed at the irony of how I make my living today.

- Misconception: Getting organized is an overwhelming, hopeless chore.

  Fact: No matter what you're organizing, no matter how daunting the task or how huge the backlog, getting organized boils down to the same very simple, predictable process.

- Misconception: It's impossible to stay organized.

  Fact: Organizing is sustainable, if your system is built around the way you think and designed to grow and adapt with you as your life and work change.

- Misconception: Organizing is a non-productive use of time.

  Fact: Life today moves more rapidly than it did fifty years ago and will continue accelerating in the years ahead, presenting us with more opportunities and ever-greater demands on our time and ability to make choices.

❏ *The Best Way to Get Started with Julie Morgenstern*

Do you feel overwhelmed by clutter and chaos in your life? Do you need better organization skills? Is your home or office a mess? If the answer to any of these questions is yes, than Julie Morgenstern's book, *Organizing from the Inside Out*, is for you, and I recommend it as the best place to get started.

In her book, Julie provides a wide range of strategies for organizing. Some of them include:

- Defining your goals and how your space can best help you achieve them.
- Identifying what obstacles are holding you back.
- Dividing the space into "zones" of activity.
- Organizing the space so that all the supplies for each activity are stored in the appropriate zone.

Julie Morgenstern has included many real-life client case studies to assist you along the way, and her book will definitely help you organize your space and your life. If you need help in the time management arena, I recommend starting with her book, *Time Management from the Inside Out*.

TO READ ADDITIONAL BOOK EXCERPTS or ARTICLES or to LISTEN TO JULIE MORGENSTERN RIGHT NOW, VISIT
http://www.selfgrowth.com/experts

❏ *Books*

- Organizing from the Inside Out: The Foolproof System for Organizing Your Home, Your Office, and Your Life
- Time Management from the Inside Out: The Foolproof System for Taking Control of Your Schedule—and Your Life
- Organizing from the Inside Out for Teens: The Foolproof System for Organizing Your Room, Your Time, and Your Life (co-authored with daughter Jessi)

❏ *Audio and Video Programs*

- "Julie, On…" Conversations on the Classic Hurdles to Getting Organized
- Organizing from the Inside Out (on audio cassette or audio CD)
- "Organizing From The Inside Out" PBS Home Video Special
- Time Management from the Inside Out (on audio cassette or audio CD)

❏ *Other Programs and Highlights*

Julie is a columnist for *O: The Oprah Magazine* where she solves readers' problems by helping to create order in their lives. She is a frequent guest on many TV and radio shows, including *The Oprah Winfrey Show* and the *Today Show*. She is also quoted and featured regularly in a variety of publications like *The New York Times* and *Cosmopolitan*.

❏ *Contact Information*

ADDRESS:	Julie Morgenstern
	Julie Morgenstern's Task Masters
	300 West 53rd Street, Suite 1L
	New York, NY 10019
PHONE:	1-86-ORGANISE or 1-212-544-8722
EMAIL:	organize@juliemorgenstern.com
WEBSITE:	www.juliemorgenstern.com

RICHARD CARLSON
(Expert #93)

❏ *Richard Carlson Biography*

Richard Carlson, Ph.D., is a leading expert on happiness and stress reduction. He is the author of 15 books, including the *New York Times* best-seller, *Don't Sweat The Small Stuff...and it's all small stuff*, which has sold over 10 million copies worldwide. The book shows you how to keep from letting the little things in life drive you crazy.

Don't Sweat The Small Stuff was named the country's #1 best-selling book in the United States for two consecutive years. Altogether, Dr. Carlson's books have appeared in over 100 countries and have become best-sellers worldwide in such places as Japan, Europe, and Latin America. Over 40 million people have read at least one book in the *Don't Sweat* series.

Dr. Carlson has been featured on his own PBS television special, which detailed the philosophy of his books. As a lecturer, he has spoken to audiences around the world and locally at such locations as the Smithsonian Institute in Washington, D.C. In 1997, he was chosen by *People* magazine as one of the most intriguing people to watch in the world.

❏ *David Riklan's Favorite Richard Carlson Quotes and Thoughts*

- Ask yourself this question: "Will this matter a year from now?"

- If someone throws you the ball, you don't have to catch it.

- Remember, when you die, there will still be unfinished business to take care of and you know what...someone else will do it for you! Don't waste anymore precious moments of your life regretting the inevitable.

- To a happy person, the formula for happiness is quite simple. Regardless of what happened early this morning, last week, or last year—or what may happen later this evening, tomorrow, or three years from now—now is where happiness lies.

- When we criticize another person, it says nothing about that person; it merely says something about our own need to be critical.

- Remind yourself that when you die, your IN-basket won't be empty.

❏ *The Best Way to Get Started with Richard Carlson*

There is only one place to get started with Richard Carlson. Get *Don't Sweat The Small Stuff... and it's all small stuff* and read it for ongoing inspiration. His book provides 100 chapters detailing how to live a happier life by not "sweating the small stuff" in life. His friendly, social style makes for a light and quick read.

Some of the chapter titles give you insight into this book: "Be the First One to Act Loving or Reach Out," "Choose Being Kind over Being Right," "Spend a Moment, Every Day, Thinking of Someone to Love," "Remember that You Become What You Practice Most," and "Remember, One Hundred Years From Now, All New People."

As for his additional books, people frequently asked Dr. Carlson about the "big stuff." In response to these questions, he wrote *What About the Big Stuff?*, which offers advice on how to deal with more important life issues, such as death, divorce, illness, difficulties at work, and family problems.

TO READ ADDITIONAL BOOK EXCERPTS or ARTICLES or to LISTEN TO RICHARD CARLSON RIGHT NOW, VISIT
http://www.selfgrowth.com/experts

❏ *Books*

- Don't Sweat the Small Stuff series
- You Can Feel Good Again: Common-Sense Therapy for Releasing Depression and Changing Your Life
- Shortcut Through Therapy: Ten Principles of Growth-Oriented, Contented Living
- What About the Big Stuff? Finding Strength and Moving Forward When the Stakes Are High

❏ *Audio and Video Programs*

- Don't Worry, Make Money: Spiritual and Practical Ways to Create Abundance and More Fun in Your Life.
- Don't Sweat It!: Richard Carlson's Low Stress Strategies for Success.
- Creating Miracles Every Day: How to Turn Ordinary Moments into Extraordinary Experiences

❏ *Other Programs and Highlights*

Dr. Carlson has been a popular guest on television programs like *The Oprah Winfrey Show*, *The View*, and the *Today Show*. To read his column and to view his thought of the week and weekly affirmation, visit his website at www.dontsweat.com.

❏ *Contact Information*

WEBSITE: www.dontsweat.com

JON KABAT-ZINN
(Expert #94)

JON KABAT-ZINN QUICK FACTS	
Main Areas:	Meditation; Mindfulness; Stress Reduction; Research
NY Times Best-Sellers:	"Full Catastrophe Living"; "Wherever You Go, There You Are"
Profile:	Author; Scientific Researcher; Mediation Teacher; College Professor; Retreat Leader
Affiliation:	University of Massachusetts Medical School

❑ *Jon Kabat-Zinn Biography*

Jon Kabat-Zinn, Ph.D., is a scientist, writer, and meditation teacher who brings mindfulness into the mainstream of medicine, healthcare, and society. He is professor of medicine emeritus at the University of Massachusetts Medical School, where he was founding executive director of the Center for Mindfulness in Medicine, Health Care, and Society. He is also the founder and former director of its world-renowned Stress Reduction Clinic.

Dr. Kabat-Zinn earned his Ph.D. in molecular biology from M.I.T. in 1971. His research has focused on mind-body interactions for healing, various clinical applications of mindfulness meditation training, and the effects of mindfulness-based stress reduction (MBSR) on the brain. The Center for Mindfulness offers a number of professional training opportunities in MBSR in which Dr. Kabat-Zinn continues to participate.

Dr. Kabat-Zinn is also a best-selling author of books like *Full Catastrophe Living* and *Wherever You Go, There You Are.* During his career, he has trained many people in mindfulness, including judges, business leaders, lawyers, clergy, and Olympic athletes. He conducts annual Power of Mindfulness retreats in various resort and retreat centers in the United States.

❑ *David Riklan's Favorite Jon Kabat-Zinn Quotes and Thoughts*

- If we are honest with ourselves, most of us will have to admit that we live out our lives in an ocean of fear.

- It is a commonly held view that meditation is a way to shut off the pressures of the world or of your own mind, but this is not an accurate impression. Meditation is neither shutting things out nor off. It is seeing clearly and deliberately positioning yourself differently in relationship to them.

- Meditation is simply about being yourself and knowing about who that is. It is about coming to realize that you are on a path whether you like it or not, namely the path that is your life.

- Stillness, insight, and wisdom arise only when we can settle into being complete in this moment, without having to seek or hold on to or reject anything.

- How we see and hold the full range of our experiences in our minds and in our hearts makes an enormous difference in the quality of this journey we are on and what it means to us. It can influence where we go, what happens, what we learn, and how we feel along the way.

❏ *The Best Way to Get Started with Jon Kabat-Zinn*

I recommend that you get started with Dr. Kabat-Zinn's book, *Wherever You Go, There You Are: Mindfulness Meditation in Everyday Life.* This is the follow-up book to *Full Catastrophe Living*, in which he presented basic meditation techniques as a way of reducing stress and healing from illness.

In *Wherever You Go, There You Are*, Dr. Kabat-Zinn outlines the Buddhist technique of "mindfulness," a method of living fully in the moment without judgment. This book is a great primer on meditation and mindfulness; you don't have to be a Buddhist or want to be a Buddhist to practice meditation or to read this book.

To Dr. Kabat-Zinn, meditation is important because it brings about a state of "mindfulness," a condition of "being" rather than "doing" during which you pay attention to the moment rather than the past, the future, or the multitudinous distractions of modern life. Meditation, he tells you, "is a Way of being, a Way of living, a Way of listening, a Way of walking along the path of life and being in harmony with things as they are. Mindfulness means paying attention in a particular way, on purpose, in the present moment, non-judgementally."

Wherever You Go, There You Are contains brief, clear chapters on different meditative practices and what they can do for you. Dr. Kabat-Zinn explains that the idea that meditation is "spiritual" is often confusing to people. He prefers to think of it as what you might call a workout for your consciousness.

TO READ ADDITIONAL BOOK EXCERPTS or ARTICLES or to LISTEN
TO JON KABAT-ZINN RIGHT NOW, VISIT
http://www.selfgrowth.com/experts

❑ **Books**

- Full Catastrophe Living: Using the Wisdom of Your Body and Mind to Face Stress, Pain, and Illness
- Wherever You Go, There You Are: Mindfulness Meditation in Everyday Life
- Everyday Blessings: The Inner Work of Mindful Parenting (co-authored with wife Myla)

❑ **Audio and Video Programs**

- Mindful Meditation Series 1 and 2
- Mindfulness Meditation: Cultivating the Wisdom of Your Body and Mind
- Meditation for Optimum Health: How to Use Mindfulness and Breathing to Heal Your Body and Refresh Your Mind (co-authored with Andrew Weil)

❑ **Other Programs and Highlights**

Dr. Kabat-Zinn's work was featured in Bill Moyers' PBS special, *Healing and the Mind*, and in the book of the same title. Dr. Kabat-Zinn has received a number of honors and awards, including the Interface Foundation Career Achievement Award and the New York Open Center's Tenth Year Anniversary Achievement in Medicine and Health Award in 1994.

❑ **Contact Information**

ADDRESS: 8-Week Stress Reduction Program   Stress Reduction Tapes
or Professional Training Information   P.O. Box 547
The Center for Mindfulness   Lexington, MA 02420
University of Massachusetts,
Medical School
419 Belmont Ave. 2nd floor
Worcester, MA 01604
PHONE: 580-856-2656
EMAIL: mindfulness@umassmed.edu
WEBSITE: www.umassmed.edu/cfm   www.mindfulnesstapes.com

ROBIN SHARMA
(Expert #95)

<table>
<tr><td colspan="2" align="center">ROBIN SHARMA QUICK FACTS</td></tr>
<tr><td>Main Areas:</td><td>Leadership; Personal Effectiveness; Life Management; Spirituality</td></tr>
<tr><td>Best-Sellers:</td><td>"The Monk Who Sold His Ferrari"; "Leadership Wisdom from The Monk Who Sold His Ferrari"</td></tr>
<tr><td>Profile:</td><td>Author; Speaker; Attorney</td></tr>
<tr><td>Affiliation:</td><td>Sharma Leadership International, Inc.</td></tr>
</table>

❑ Robin Sharma Biography

Robin Sharma is a sought-after professional speaker who shares insights on leadership, change, personal effectiveness, and life management. With his conferences and in-house seminars, he provides effective strategies to help people reach all-new levels of productivity and personal satisfaction. Each year, he travels more than 100,000 miles for speaking engagements.

Robin is the CEO and chief visionary officer of Sharma Leadership International, Inc., one of the world's most innovative leadership development firms. Its clients include some of the world's largest corporations, including Microsoft, General Motors, and IBM. Sharma Leadership International helps to develop employees so that they think, feel, and act as leaders in everything they do.

Robin holds two law degrees and had a distinguished legal career before entering the leadership arena. He is the international best-selling author of six books, including *The Monk Who Sold His Ferrari* and *Leadership Wisdom from The Monk Who Sold His Ferrari: The 8 Rituals of Visionary Leaders*.

❑ David Riklan's Favorite Robin Sharma Quotes and Thoughts

- The smallest of actions is always better than the noblest of intentions.

- To arrive at a place called Mastery, you must commit to daily and rigorous practice. Enjoy practicing your craft for its own sake without turning your attention to your ultimate destination. Understand, once and for all, that the journey is as important as the destination.

- The deeper your relationship with others, the more effective will be your leadership. People will not follow you if they do not trust you, and before someone will lend you a hand, you must first touch their heart.

- Mastery in work and in life is about committing yourself to being excellent in everything you do, no matter how small and no matter if no one is watching. Do you practice excellence in your most private moments?

- The first fifteen minutes of your day should be spent planning your day. Set specific goals as to what you will accomplish. These clear goals will give you focal points on which you can govern your actions and provide your with a template you can live your day from.

- I promise you this: at the end of your days, you will discover that the things you now perceive to be the big things in your life will be seen as little things, and all those things that you now believe to be the little things, you will realize were really the big things.

❑ *The Best Way to Get Started with Robin Sharma*

Robin Sharma has developed a reputation for his knowledge on leadership and spirituality. Part of his success is tied into the success of his best-selling book, *The Monk Who Sold His Ferrari*, and this is where I recommend that you begin. The book is a modern day fable that uses the life of a high-profile, high-powered, and highly stressed attorney to convey spiritual truths and wisdom to readers.

The book opens up with Julian Mantle, one of the "country's most distinguished trial lawyers," having an apparent heart attack. The near-fatal heart attack forces Julian to confront many of life's big questions. On his quest to find the secrets of true happiness, he undertakes an odyssey that leads him to the Himalayan sages, where he begins to discover the secrets.

I found a quote in *Time* magazine that I think nicely sums up the nature of *The Monk Who Sold His Ferrari*. Michelle Yeoh of *Crouching Tiger Hidden Dragon* says, "The book is about finding out what is truly important to your real spiritual self rather than being inundated with material possessions."

After reading this work from Robin Sharma, I also recommend that you continue with his follow-up book, *Leadership Wisdom from The Monk Who Sold His Ferrari*. The sequel details eight practical lessons that leaders and managers can apply to instill trust and commitment into their organizations.

TO READ ADDITIONAL BOOK EXCERPTS or ARTICLES or to LISTEN TO ROBIN SHARMA RIGHT NOW, VISIT
http://www.selfgrowth.com/experts

❑ *Books*

- The Monk Who Sold His Ferrari: A Fable About Fulfilling Your Dreams and Reaching Your Destiny
- Leadership Wisdom from The Monk Who Sold His Ferrari: The 8 Rituals of Visionary Leaders
- Who Will Cry When You Die? Life Lessons from The Monk Who Sold His Ferrari
- The Saint, The Surfer, and The CEO: A Remarkable Story About Living Your Heart's Desires

❑ *Audio and Video Programs*

- Meditation for Elite Performers
- Restoring Spirit at Work

❑ *Other Programs and Highlights*

Robin Sharma is a well-known media personality and has been featured in such publications as *USA Today*, *The National Post*, and *The Globe and Mail*. He has also appeared on over 700 radio and television programs. Robin frequently appears on programs with other top speakers, such as former President Bill Clinton, Stephen Covey, and Dr. Phil McGraw.

❑ *Contact Information*

ADDRESS: Sharma Leadership International
1 West Pearce Street, Suite 505,
Richmond Hill, Ontario, Canada L4B 3K3
PHONE: 1-888-RSHARMA
EMAIL: wisdom@robinsharma.com
WEBSITE: www.robinsharma.com

LYNN ANDREWS
(Expert #96)

LYNN ANDREWS QUICK FACTS	
Main Areas:	Native Spiritual Growth; Personal Development; Empowerment; Women's Health; Balancing Love and Power in One's Life and Work
NY Times Best-Seller:	"Jaguar Woman"
Profile:	Author; Shaman; Teacher; Retreat Leader
Affiliations:	Lynn Andrews Productions; Circle of Life

❑ *Lynn Andrews Biography*

Lynn Andrews is an internationally acclaimed author who has written 18 books, currently published in 12 languages. She has been on *The New York Times* best-seller list several times. Her books include *Medicine Woman* (now in its 40th printing), *Jaguar Woman*, *Woman at the Edge of Two Worlds: The Spiritual Journey Through Menopause*, and *Dark Sister: A Sorcerer's Love Story*. Andrews is also the author of *The Power Deck: The Cards of Wisdom*, a series of self-affirming meditation cards, and four workbooks, as well as over 20 meditation and teaching audio tapes.

Andrews has been appearing as a renowned guest speaker on national and international media for the past 20 years. She has also lectured for Whole Life Expos for the past 20 years and has done speakers tours with Warner Brothers, HarperCollins, and Jeremy P. Tarcher/Putnam, a member of Penguin Putnam, Inc. Considered a pre-eminent teacher in the field of personal development, Andrews is a 21st century shaman whose words reflect her path, a path of heart. For 15 years, women and men from all over the world have gathered with her for her annual Joshua Tree four-day retreat.

In 1994, The Lynn Andrews Center for Sacred Arts and Training (Mystery School) was created. This program is a unique mystery school designed to integrate the sacred into every aspect of life. The curriculum offers a four-year professional certification program, and bachelor's, master's, and doctorate degrees are available. The Center offers CEUs to nurses, medical practitioners, and therapists. Lynn Andrews also has a formal program for ordained ministers.

❑ *David Riklan's Favorite Lynn Andrews Quotes and Thoughts*

- You must never run from fear. You must face it. Fear is a tracker that will hunt you down.

- Shamanism is a subtle and alchemical process to transform and elevate the spirit beyond the constructs of the limits of reality. It is a space program for the soul and launches you out into the uncharted territory of the stars.

- Prayer is our heartsong to life and the great spirit.

- ...the Sisterhood is in all of us. It is every woman who is keeping the dream alive. And the oldest dreamkeepers, the Grandmothers, are in danger at this very moment. We must write and we must act to keep the knowledge and the powers of woman alive.

- The person who upsets you the most is your best teacher because they bring you face to face with who you are.

❏ *The Best Way to Get Started with Lynn Andrews*

The best place to gain a complete understanding of Lynn Andrews and her message is to attend her annual Joshua Tree four-day retreat in the California desert. Yet the best way to get started with Andrews is to read her book *Medicine Woman*. In the book, Andrews tells how she was guided to meet her Native American shaman teachers and how she is trained to gather and hold her female power.

Medicine Woman begins with Andrews seeing a photo of a Native American marriage basket in an art gallery during a show. She becomes obsessed with finding out about the basket and ends up meeting a Native American man named Hyemeyohsts Storm. Hyemeyohsts Storm sets her on her path to Canada to acquire this marriage basket.

During this journey, she meets two wise woman—Ruby Plenty Chiefs and Agnes Whistling Elk—and becomes an apprentice to Agnes. The book shares her experiences as a student of this Cree medicine woman in Manitoba, Canada. Through her training with Agnes, Andrews discovers a new aspect of herself, that of warrior and huntress. The message of *Medicine Woman* is that women can be powerful and strong, and the book provides this message through a very empowering story.

TO READ ADDITIONAL BOOK EXCERPTS or ARTICLES or to LISTEN TO LYNN ANDREWS RIGHT NOW, VISIT http://www.selfgrowth.com/experts

❏ *Books*

- Medicine Woman
- Flight of the Seventh Moon

- Jaguar Woman
- Star Woman
- Crystal Woman: The Sisters of the Dreamtime
- Windhorse Woman: A Marriage of Spirit
- Woman of Wyrrd: The Arousal of the Inner Fire
- Shakkai: Woman of the Sacred Garden
- Woman at the Edge of Two Worlds: The Spiritual Journey Through Menopause
- Dark Sister: A Sorcerer's Love Story
- Walk in Spirit: Prayers for the Seasons of Life
- Love and Power: The Fine Art of Mastery
- Tree of Dreams: A Spirit Woman's Vision of Transition and Change

❑ *Audio and Video Programs*

- Up the Mountain
- Power Animal in the Mask
- Parent Tree Book of the Child
- Act of Power
- Imagination
- Luminous Fibers
- Earth Wisdom, Death and Transition
- Sacred Dreams and Past Lifes
- Keeper of the Brain
- White Star Woman
- Spirit Retrieval
- Crystal Domain of the Sacred Masters
- Centering Meditation
- Practical Wisdom I & II
- Journey into the Dream-time
- Entering the Power Deck
- The Mask of Power tape set
- Woman at the Edge of Two Worlds tape set
- The Gatherings at Joshua Tree tape sets

❑ *Other Programs and Highlights*

The Lynn Andrews Center for Sacred Arts and Training has a non-profit organization called "Circle of Life" dedicated to the recording of legacies for elders.

The work of Lynn Andrews explores the ancient teachings taught by the Sisterhood of the Shields, which embrace the study of global shamanic cosmologies and sacred art technologies. It is her intention that through this work we understand how all that is sacred in life weaves together within our world. Throughout time, shamans have practiced the art of choreographing energy in a nonlinear field. Shamanic knowledge and practice is at the very heart of creation. As 21st century shamans, they learn to create a sacred circle in which they transform an ordinary life into a life of power.

Andrews' newest work, *Tree of Dreams*, is now available (in its 3rd printing). Her ability to teach people and show them how to live a life that is truly balanced, with one foot in the physical and one in the spiritual, is the foundation of this amazing new work.

❏ *Contact Information*

ADDRESS: *(To contact her directly)*
Lynn Andrews   Lynn Andrews
2934 1/2 Beverly Glen Circle   Productions (Retail)
Suite 378   P.O. Box 867
Los Angeles, CA 90077   Newburyport, MA 01950

PHONE: (310) 550-1873   (978) 352-5350
(To make a phone appointment with Lynn Andrews, call Patricia.)

EMAIL: orders@lynnandrews.com
WEBSITE: www.lynnandrews.com

ALAN COHEN
(Expert #97)

ALAN COHEN QUICK FACTS	
Main Areas:	Spiritual Growth; Empowerment
Best-Sellers:	"The Dragon Doesn't Live Here Anymore"; "Why Your Life Sucks…and What You Can Do About It"
Profile:	Author; Speaker; Columnist; Seminar Leader
Affiliation:	Alan Cohen Programs & Publications

❑ *Alan Cohen Biography*

Alan CohenF is the author of 20 popular inspirational books and tapes. He wrote the best-seller, *The Dragon Doesn't Live Here Anymore*, and the award-winner, *A Deep Breath of Life*. He is a contributing writer for the *New York Times* best-selling series *Chicken Soup for the Soul*, and his syndicated column, "From the Heart," appears in New Thought magazines internationally.

Alan lives in Maui, Hawaii, where he conducts retreats in spiritual growth and visionary living. One such retreat is the Mastery Training, which enables participants to reclaim passion and purpose in their lives. Alan also keynotes and presents workshops at many conferences and expos throughout the United States and abroad.

Alan brings a warm blend of wisdom, vision, humor, and intimacy to the spiritual path. He loves to extract spiritual lessons from the practical experiences of daily living. Many readers and participants in his seminars have reported that his teachings have brought them comfort, encouragement, and empowerment as they moved through a difficult or transitional phase in their lives.

❑ *David Riklan's Favorite Alan Cohen Quotes and Thoughts*

- It takes a lot of courage to release the familiar and seemingly secure, to embrace the new. But there is no real security in what is no longer meaningful. There is more security in the adventurous and exciting, for in movement there is life, and in change there is power.

- The point of life is not to be married or single—it is to be. We are human beings, or human being. It does not matter so much what life-style we choose –it's what we make of the opportunities to grow that counts.

- The world would have you agree with its dismal dream of limitation. But the light would have you soar like the eagle of your sacred visions.

- There are two kinds of people in the world: those who make excuses and those who get results. An excuse person will find any excuse for why a job was not done, and a results person will find any reason why it can be done.

- You are not a black hole that needs to be filled; you are a light that needs to be shined.

❑ *The Best Way to Get Started with Alan Cohen*

Alan Cohen has developed a variety of programs for empowerment and Self Improvement. His major best-selling book is *The Dragon Doesn't Live Here Anymore,* but to get a sense of who Alan is today, I would recommend that you start by reading *Why Your Life Sucks...And What You Can Do About It.*

Alan has distilled down hundreds of Self Improvement values and ideas and has created a simple solution to the challenge of the "sucky" life. His writing style is entertaining, straightforward, and non-judgmental. He takes us on a journey of self-discovery that reminds us that we have the ultimate power over our own lives.

Alan's book covers ten basic reasons your life may suck, such as "You Expect It To Suck," "You Keep Trying to Prove Yourself," "You Say Yes When You Mean No," and "You Think You Have to Do It All Yourself." He then explains exactly what you can do about it. *Why Your Life Sucks* includes great anec- dotes, personal experiences, and specific exercises to help us improve our lives. I also love the title.

TO READ ADDITIONAL BOOK EXCERPTS or ARTICLES or to LISTEN TO ALAN COHEN RIGHT NOW, VISIT
http://www.selfgrowth.com/experts

❑ *Books*

- The Dragon Doesn't Live Here Anymore: Living Fully, Living Freely
- A Deep Breath of Life: Daily Inspiration for Heart-Centered Living
- Why Your Life Sucks...And What You Can Do About It
- I Had It All the Time: When Self-Improvement Gives Way to Ecstasy
- Dare to Be Yourself: How to Quit Being an Extra in Other People's Movies and Become the Star of Your Own

❑ *Audio and Video Programs*

- Living from the Heart: Making Every Moment Count
- Deep Relaxation
- Peace
- Journey to the Center of the Heart

❑ *Other Programs and Highlights*

Alan Cohen has over 25 years of experience training a wide variety of clients in the medical, psychological, educational, corporate, and spiritual fields. He also offers a self-renewal training called Oxygen for healthcare professionals, and a one-year online course called The Year of Living Prosperously.

❑ *Contact Information*

ADDRESS:	Alan Cohen Programs & Publications
	P.O. Box 835
	Haiku, HI 96708
PHONE:	(800) 568-3079
EMAIL:	admin@alancohen.com
	acpubs@maui.net
WEBSITE:	www.alancohen.com

GARY CRAIG
(Expert #98)

GARY CRAIG QUICK FACTS

Main Areas:	Healing; Body Energy; Spirituality
Profile:	Stanford Engineer; Ordained Minister; Creator of EFT
Affiliation:	Emotional Freedom Techniques

❏ *Gary Craig Biography*

Gary Craig developed the Emotional Freedom Techniques (EFT), the core of which he learned as a student of Dr. Roger Callahan, a psychologist who devised Thought Field Therapy. Born in 1940, Gary has been interested in personal improvement via psychology since age 13. He recognized that the quality of his thoughts was mirrored in the quality of his life.

EFT is based on the natural flow of energy within our bodies. It is similar to Chinese acupuncture in that it allows the body to heal itself naturally. EFT strengthens and moves the body's energy, which helps restore the body to its naturally balanced state. It often provides relief for a very wide range of physical symptoms and is usually quite gentle.

Gary, an avid student of A Course in Miracles, is not a psychologist nor is he a licensed therapist. He is an engineering graduate of Stanford University and an ordained minister with the Universal Church of God in Southern California, which is non-denominational and embraces all religions. Although Gary approaches EFT from a distinctly spiritual perspective, people using it are not asked to follow any specific spiritual teaching.

❏ *David Riklan's Favorite Gary Craig Quotes and Thoughts*

- Based on impressive new discoveries involving the body's subtle energies, EFT (Emotional Freedom Techniques) has been clinically effective in thousands of cases for Trauma & Abuse, Stress & Anxiety, Fears & Phobias Depression, Addictive Cravings, Children's Issues, and hundreds of physical symptoms including headaches, body pains, and breathing difficulties. Properly applied, over 80 percent achieve either noticeable improvement or complete cessation of the problem. It is the missing piece to the healing puzzle.

- EFT (Emotional Freedom Techniques) is an emotional form of acupuncture except that we don't use needles. Instead, we tap with the fingertips to stimulate certain meridian energy points while the client is "tuned in" to the problem.

- The subtle energies that circulate throughout the body have been largely ignored (until recently) by Western scientists. As a result, our use of them for emotional and spiritual healing has been sparse at best. With EFT, however, we consider these subtle energies to be the front-running cause of emotional upsets.

❏ *The Best Way to Get Started with Gary Craig*

The best way to get started with Gary Craig and EFT is to go to his website (www.emofree.com) and starting looking around. He provides everything you need to know to begin using EFT, including the ability to download his EFT manual for free and purchase the entire EFT course. Make sure to check out the EFT tutorial and frequently-asked-questions sections.

Gary himself has recommended ways to get started. At www.emofree.com, click on "Newcomers's Message," and then choose "Getting around this content-rich site." Aside from downloading the EFT manual, you can order the EFT for Newcomers Video on CD.

Gary not only provides training for you to use EFT but also training to become an EFT practitioner. His website offers training videos and a list of EFT practitioners in over 25 countries around the world.

TO READ ADDITIONAL BOOK EXCERPTS or ARTICLES or to LISTEN TO GARY CRAIG RIGHT NOW, VISIT
http://www.selfgrowth.com/experts

❏ *Books*

- Emotional Freedom: Techniques Dealing with Emotional and Physical Distress (by Garry A. Flint, Ph.D., based on EFT by Gary Craig and Adrienne Fowlie; foreword by Gary Craig)

❏ *Audio and Video Programs*

- The EFT Course
- Steps toward Becoming the Ultimate Therapist
- From EFT to the Palace of Possibilities
- EFT Specialty Series 1

❑ *Other Programs and Highlights*

Gary Craig is a certified master practitioner in Neuro Linguistic Programming. His Emotional Freedom Techniques can be easily learned by anyone. It can heal you in a wide variety of areas, including common problems like headaches and allergies, emotions like anger and depression, and ailments like ulcers and digestive disorders.

❑ *Contact Information*

ADDRESS: Emotional Freedom Techniques
Gary H. Craig
P.O. Box 1393
Gualala, CA 95445
WEBSITE: www.emofree.com

ERIC BUTTERWORTH
(Expert #99)

ERIC BUTTERWORTH QUICK FACTS	
Main Areas:	Metaphysical Spirituality; Consciousness; New Thought Spiritual Movement
Best-Seller:	"Discover the Power Within You"
Profile:	Author; Lecturer; Theologian; Philosopher; Workshop Leader; 1916-2003
Affiliation:	The Unity Center of Practical Christianity

❏ *Eric Butterworth Biography*

Eric Butterworth was a theologian, philosopher, lecturer, and best-selling author on metaphysical spirituality. He inspired hundreds of thousands of people for over 50 years and began his daily radio broadcasts with the sentence, "You can change your life by altering your thoughts." At times, his radio broadcasts went around the world.

Butterworth established three powerful Unity ministries—in Pittsburgh, Detroit, and New York City. At the Detroit Unity Temple, more that 2,000 people attended his Sunday Services each week. His weekly attendance in New York City grew to several thousand. Butterworth also originated the Spiritual Therapy Workshops, which he conducted for over 35 years. His devotees included people from all walks of life.

Butterworth attended Fresno State University and Capital University in Ohio, where he studied music. He began training for the ministry at Unity Village in Missouri during World War II and after the war, graduated from Unity Ministerial School. In 1968, he wrote the best-seller, *Discover the Power Within You*, which is considered a classic in the New Thought Spiritual Movement.

❏ *David Riklan's Favorite Eric Butterworth Quotes and Thoughts*

- Attitudes are the forerunners of conditions.

- Believe that you are always in the presence of limitless substance which you form and shape and release through your faith. Keep the high watch of Truth by knowing that, wherever you are and whatever your experience, you are an inlet and may become an outlet for the flow of God-substance.

- Don't go through life, GROW through life.

- Fundamentalists believe Jesus was God becoming man. I believe that Jesus was man becoming God.

- Go within in a time of silence and get a renewed awareness of God as your resource, and then go about your business affairs in the strong consciousness of the omnipresence of substance.

- God is in us, not like a raisin in a bun but like the ocean in a wave.

- I am secure, for I know who I am: a richly endowed child of God. I am secure in all I do, for I know my oneness with the divine process. I am secure in all I have, for I know my treasure is in my mind, not in my things. I live my life from day to day as if God's supportive substance were as exhaustless and dependable as the air I breathe, which it most certainly is.

- I tell you and you forget. I show you and you remember. I involve you and you understand.

- More important than learning how to recall things is finding ways to forget things that are cluttering the mind.

- On human levels of consciousness, one may emphasize getting and having as the prime goals, in spiritual consciousness he seeks the way of giving and being.

- Our job is not to set things right but to see them right.

- Prosperity is a way of living and thinking and not just money or things. Poverty is a way of living and thinking and not just a lack of money or things.

- Where you are in consciousness has everything to do with what you see in experience.

- You are a rich and creative spiritual being. You can never be less than this. You may frustrate your potential. You may identify with that which is less than what you can be. But within you now and always is the unborn possibility of a limitless experience of inner stability and outer treasure, and yours is the privilege of giving birth to it. And you will, if you can believe.

- Nothing stops the man who desires to achieve. Every obstacle is simply a course to develop his achievement muscle. It's a strengthening of his powers of accomplishment.

- Prosperity is a way of living and thinking and not just money or things. Poverty is a way of living and thinking and not just a lack of money or things.

❑ *The Best Way to Get Started with Eric Butterworth*

Oprah Winfrey says that Eric Butterworth's book, *Discover the Power Within You*, "changed [her] perspective on life and religion." She adds, "Eric Butterworth teaches that God isn't up there. He exists inside each of us, and it's up to us to seek the divine within."

Who I am to argue with Oprah? We both agree that *Discover the Power Within You* is the best place to get started. The book opens with Chapter One, The Eternal Quest. According to Butterworth:

> The hope of mankind today lies in the great undiscovered depths within. The time is at hand when men everywhere must forsake the fruitless search of the world at the circumference of being and embark upon a courageous quest into inner space. It is a very real world, and its depths can be sounded, its potency released. It is not a conquest but a bequest. It is not as much something within man as it is the deeper level of man.

In this book, Butterworth reviews the lessons of Jesus with the underlying philosophy that we are all the sons and daughters of God and that within us lies the power and divinity necessary to achieve any dream we can conceive of.

Butterworth writes, "Not one person in a million is living up to the best within him. The great wisdom of the ages still lies locked in the depths of man's mental capacity; the great possibility of health and healing and eternal life still lies undiscovered in the depths of man's inner life, and the great key to success and opulence still lies within man's undiscovered potential."

Many consider *Discover the Power Within You* to be a classic. Butterworth sees the divine within us all to be a hidden and untapped resource of limitless abundance. Exploring this "depth potential," Butterworth outlines ways in which we can release the power locked within us and let our "light shine."

TO READ ADDITIONAL BOOK EXCERPTS or ARTICLES or to LISTEN TO ERIC BUTTERWORTH RIGHT NOW, VISIT
http://www.selfgrowth.com/experts

❏ *Books*

- Discover the Power Within You: A Guide to the Unexplored Depths Within
- The Universe is Calling: Opening to the Divine Through Prayer
- The Creative Life: 7 Keys to Your Inner Genius
- Unity: A Quest for Truth

❏ *Audio and Video Programs*

- Spiritual Economics: The Principles and Process of True Prosperity (book or audio cassette)

❏ *Other Programs and Highlights*

Eric Butterworth's books have been translated into several languages. Every Sunday, Butterworth lectured at Carnegie Hall, then Town Hall, and since 1976, Avery Fisher Hall in New York City.

❏ *Contact Information*

ADDRESS:	The Unity Center of Practical Christianity
	213 West 58th Street
	New York, NY 10019
PHONE:	(212) 582-1300
EMAIL:	unitycenter@worldnet.att.net
WEBSITE:	www.ericbutterworth.com

DENIS WAITLEY
(Expert #100)

DENIS WAITLEY QUICK FACTS	
Main Areas:	Winning; Success; Empowerment
Best-Seller:	"The Psychology of Winning" (over 10 million audio programs sold)
Profile:	Author; Speaker on High Performance Achievement
Affiliation:	The Waitley Institute

❑ *Denis Waitley Biography*

Denis Waitley, Ph.D., is an author, keynote lecturer, and productivity consultant on high performance human achievement. He inspires, informs, and entertains his audiences, which have included corporate board rooms, athletic locker rooms, and NASA control rooms. A graduate of the U. S. Naval Academy and former Navy pilot, he holds a doctorate degree in human behavior.

Dr. Waitley is the author of over a dozen books, including several international best-sellers like *Seeds of Greatness* and *The Winner's Edge*. He has sold over 10 million audio programs in 14 languages. His album, *The Psychology of Winning*, is the all-time best-selling program on personal and professional excellence.

Dr. Waitley has counseled winners in almost every occupational and professional field. He has conducted stress management seminars for Apollo astronauts and served as Consultant to the President of the Salk Institute. While he was president of the International Society for Advanced Education, Dr. Waitley studied and counseled returning POWs from Viet Nam. Dr. Waitley also served as chairman of psychology on the U.S. Olympic Committee's Sports Medicine Council, responsible for performance enhancement of the country's athletes.

❑ *David Riklan's Favorite Denis Waitley Quotes and Thoughts*

- Expect the best, plan for the worst, and prepare to be surprised.

- Failure should be our teacher, not our undertaker. Failure is delay, not defeat. It is a temporary detour, not a dead end. Failure is something we can avoid only by saying nothing, doing nothing, and being nothing.

- Forget about the consequences of failure. Failure is only a temporary change in direction to set you straight for your next success.

- If you believe you can, you probably can. If you believe you won't, you most assuredly won't. Belief is the ignition switch that gets you off the launching pad.

- Life is the movie you see through your own eyes. It makes little difference what's happening out there. It's how you take it that counts.

- The real risk is doing nothing.

- There are two primary choices in life: to accept conditions as they exist, or accept the responsibility for changing them.

- To establish true self-esteem, we must concentrate on our successes and forget about the failures and the negatives in our lives.

- You must stick to your conviction but be ready to abandon your assumptions.

- You must welcome change as the rule but not as your ruler.

❑ *The Best Way to Get Started with Denis Waitley*

Even though Denis Waitley has written several informative books on success, I recommend that you start by listening to his audio program, *The Psychology of Winning*. The program provides a remarkable set of strategies that can change your life dramatically.

According to Dr. Waitley, there is often only a small difference between the top leaders in every field and those who merely "do well." In *The Psychology of Winning,* he offers simple, profound principles of thought behavior that can guide you to the top in your field of endeavor. He has also identified "the ten most prominent qualities that total winners exhibit in common, that make them so uncommonly successful." They include:

- Positive Self-Awareness (that the world is abundant)
- Positive Self-Esteem (how can you love others if you don't love yourself)
- Positive Self-Control (losers let it happen, winners make it happen)
- Positive Self-Motivation (you'll move toward what you dwell on)
- Positive Self-Expectancy (optimism is the biology of hope)
- Positive Self-Image (the thermostat in your head—set it high)
- Positive Self-Direction (goal-setting is the way to achieve your purpose)

- Positive Self-Discipline   (practicing within when you are without)
- Positive Self-Dimension   (be in control of your time, NOW and it's gone)
- Positive Self-Projection   (persisting again and again as preview of coming attractions)

I truly believe that *The Psychology of Winning* audio program will educate and inspire you to greater success.

TO READ ADDITIONAL BOOK EXCERPTS or ARTICLES or to LISTEN TO DENIS WAITLEY RIGHT NOW, VISIT
http://www.selfgrowth.com/experts

❏ *Books*

- Seeds of Greatness Treasury: Poetry, Prose & Proverbs of Inspiration
- Seeds of Greatness: The Ten Best-Kept Secrets of Total Success
- The Winner's Edge
- Empires of the Mind: Lessons to Lead and Succeed in a Knowledge-Based World
- The Joy of Working: The 30-Day System to Success, Wealth, and Happiness on the Job

❏ *Audio and Video Programs*

- The Psychology of Winning
- The New Dynamics of Goal Setting
- How to Handle Conflict & Manage Anger
- The Platinum Collection *(3 album CD set – 18 CDs, plus bonus music CD)*

❏ *Other Programs and Highlights*

Dr. Waitley was voted business speaker of the year by the Sales and Marketing Executives' Association and Toastmasters' International. He was also inducted into the International Speakers' Hall of Fame. He is a founding director of the National Council on Self-Esteem and the President's Council on Vocational Education and received the Youth Flame Award from the National Council on Youth Leadership.

❏ *Contact Information*

ADDRESS: P.O. Box 197
             Rancho Santa Fe, CA 92067
PHONE: 1-877-769-4625   *(corporate offices)*
             1-800-WAITLEY *(customer service)*

EMAIL: info@waitley.com
WEBSITE: www.waitley.com

MAXWELL MALTZ
(Expert #101)

+---+
| **MAXWELL MALTZ QUICK FACTS** |
| |
| *Main Areas:*   Psycho-Cybernetics; Self-Image; Motivation |
| *Best-Seller:*   "Psycho-Cybernetics" (over 30 million copies sold) |
| *Profile:*   Author; Speaker; Counselor; Researcher; Surgeon; |
| 1899-1975 |
| *Affiliation:*   The Psycho-Cybernetics Foundation, Inc. |
+---+

❑ *Maxwell Maltz Biography*

Maxwell Maltz, M.D. created the Self Improvement phenomenon *Psycho-Cybernetics*. For many years, he had a practice as a reconstructive and cosmetic facial surgeon, but he moved from treating "outer scars" to "inner scars" after observing that some patients were still unhappy despite their new faces. Some claimed that although their appearance changed, they did not feel any different.

Dr. Maltz tried to find out why this was happening. He discovered that your "outer life" was a reflection of how you saw yourself on the inside, what he called "self-image." Dr. Maltz noted that you can never rise higher than your self-image. If your "inner self" is not equal to your "outer self," then you will always revert back to where you think you belong.

After a decade of counseling patients, extensive research, and testing his evolving "success conditioning techniques," Dr. Maltz published his findings in 1960. The *Psycho-Cybernetics* book was an instant best-seller and made him one of the most in-demand motivational speakers throughout the 1960s and the early 1970s. Dr. Maltz wrote over a dozen books, applying *Psycho-Cybernetics* to different purposes, including business success and sex life improvement.

❑ *David Riklan's Favorite Maxwell Maltz Quotes and Thoughts*

- Often the difference between a successful person and a failure is not one has better abilities or ideas, but the courage that one has to bet on one's ideas, to take a calculated risk—and to act.

- Accept yourself as you are. Otherwise you will never see opportunity. You will not feel free to move toward it; you will feel you are not deserving.

- If you make friends with yourself you will never be alone.

- Realizing that our actions, feelings, and behavior are the result of our own images and beliefs gives us the level that psychology has always needed for changing personality.

- We must have courage to bet on our ideas, to take the calculated risk, and to act. Everyday living requires courage if life is to be effective and bring happiness.

- Close scrutiny will show that most "crisis situations" are opportunities to either advance or stay where you are.

- When you see a thing clearly in your mind, your creative "success mechanism" within you takes over and does the job much better than you could do it by conscious effort or "willpower."

- Within you right now is the power to do things you never dreamed possible. This power becomes available to you just as you can change your beliefs.

- What is opportunity and when does it knock? It never knocks. You can wait a whole lifetime, listening, hoping, and you will hear no knocking. None at all. You are opportunity, and you must knock on the door leading to your destiny. You prepare yourself to recognize opportunity, to pursue and seize opportunity as you develop the strength of your personality, and build a self-image with which you are able to live—with your self-respect alive and growing.

- Low self-esteem is like driving through life with your hand-break on.

❑ *The Best Way to Get Started with Maxwell Maltz*

The best way to get started with Maxwell Maltz is to read the original *Psycho-Cybernetics*. This book has sold unbelievably well because it provides real value, is very readable, is based on science, and contains a road map to achieve greater success. Dr. Maltz says that your self-image is your key to a better life because of two important discoveries:

- All of your actions, feelings, behaviors, even your abilities are always consistent with your own self-image.
- The self-image can be changed.

In *Psycho-Cybernetics*, Dr. Maltz teaches you how to change your self-image and achieve that greater success. Some of the areas that he covers in the book include the following:

- Imagination—the first key to your success mechanism.

- Dehypnotize yourself from false beliefs.
- How to utilize the power of rational thinking.
- How to remove emotional scars or how to give yourself an emotional facelift.
- Do-it-yourself tranquilizers that bring peace of mind.

Psycho-Cybernetics provides many practice exercises and specific ideas to improve your life. Even though the book was written in 1960, his assertions, beliefs, and systems still work today.

TO READ ADDITIONAL BOOK EXCERPTS or ARTICLES or to LISTEN TO MAXWELL MALTZ RIGHT NOW, VISIT
http://www.selfgrowth.com/experts

❑ *Books*

- Psycho-Cybernetics
- The New Psycho-Cybernetics: The Original Science of Self-Improvement and Success That Has Changed the Lives of 30 Million People
- Zero-Resistance Selling: Achieve Extraordinary Sales Results Using the World-Renowned Techniques of Psycho-Cybernetics

❑ *Audio and Video Programs*

- Zero Resistance Living *(a full 12-week course of advanced Psycho-Cybernetics principles, with basic and master's level manuals, 14 audio CD's, and other never-before-released Maltz materials)*
- The New Psycho-Cybernetics *(audio tapes and video)*

❑ *Other Programs and Highlights*

The Psycho-Cybernetics Foundation, Inc. is dedicated to creating a new "renaissance" in self-image psychology by making available all of Dr. Maltz's works. The Foundation also develops new publications featuring contemporary authors, speakers, and leaders in the human potential field.

❑ *Contact Information*

ADDRESS: Psycho-Cybernetics, L.L.C.
                    10339 Birdwatch Drive
                    Tampa, FL 33647
PHONE: 813-994-8267
EMAIL: info@psycho-cybernetics.com
WEBSITE: www.psycho-cybernetics.com

APPENDICES

APPENDIX A

Other Valuable Self Improvement Experts

In a book on the Top 101 Self Improvement Experts, we ran the risk of missing experts who have provided tremendous value to the industry but whose name recognition wasn't popular enough to make the Top 101 list yet. In an effort to provide a more complete resource on Self Improvement, we provided this appendix with additional experts who we feel also provide great material to help us improve our lives. These experts are listed in alphabetical order by last name.

Alessandra, Tony – Developer of The Platinum Rule™ (which accommodates the feelings of others—"Treat others the way they want to be treated.")
Website: http://www.alessandra.com

Allen, David – Author, *Getting Things Done: The Art of Stress-Free Productivity*
Website: http://www.gettingthingsdone.com

Ammon-Wexler, Jill – International Success Mentor/Coach and Doctor of Psychology
Website: http://www.quantum-self.com

Andreas, Steve – Author, *Transforming Your Self: Becoming Who You Want to Be*
Website: http://www.steveandreas.com

Andrews, Andy – Author, *The Traveler's Gift: Seven Decisions That Determine Personal Success*
Website: http://www.andyandrews.com

Angier, Michael – Founder of SuccessNet
Website: http://www.successnet.org

Anthony, Robert – Author, *The Ultimate Secrets of Total Self-Confidence*
Website: http://www.total-success-4u.com

Antion, Tom – Author, *Wake 'Em Up! How to use humor and other professional techniques to create alarmingly good Business Presentations*; Tom Antion and Associates Communication Company provides informative and entertaining keynote speeches and educational seminars.
Website: http://www.antion.com

Assaraf, John – Author, *The Street Kid's Guide to Having It All*
Website: http://www.thestreetkid.com

Bach, David – Author, *The Automatic Millionaire: A Powerful One-Step Plan to Live and Finish Rich*
Website: http://www.davidbach.com

Bach, Richard – Author, *Illusions*
Website: http://www.richardbach.com

Bailey, William E. – Personal Coach, Mentor, and Motivational Speaker
Website: http://www.tsinow.net

Bauer, Paul – Creator of the Dream-Minder Software Tool
Website: http://www.dreamsalive.com

Bays, Brandon – Author, *The Journey: A Practical Guide to Healing Your Life and Setting Yourself Free*
Website: http://www.thejourney.com

Becker, Dennis – Speech Improvement Expert
Website: http://www.speechimprovement.com

Bench, Doug – Developer of Science for Success Systems
Website: http://www.scienceforsuccess.com

Berg, Howard – Speed Reading Expert
Website: http://www.mrreader.com

Bhajan, Yogi – A Master of Kundalini Yoga (the Yoga of Awareness) and a dedicated and inspired teacher.
Website: http://www.yogibhajan.com

Billue, Stan – Provides world class sales training, motivation, mentoring, and marketing.
Website: http://www.stanbillue.com

Bissonette, Pete – President, Publisher, and Co-Founder of Learning Strategies Corporation.
Website: http://www.learningstrategies.com

Bjorseth, Lillian – Networking and Communication Skills Training
Website: http://www.duoforce.com

Blair, Gary Ryan – Author, *Goal Setting 101: How to Set and Achieve a Goal!*
Website: http://www.goalsguy.com

Blood, Michele – Creator of MusiVation™ and Host of the Internet TV Show
MPowerTV
Website: http://www.mpowertv.com

Bly, Robert – Author, *Iron John*
Website: http://www.robertbly.com

Bolles, Richard N. – Author, *What Color is Your Parachute? A Practical
Manual for Job-Hunters & Career-Changers*
Website: http://www.jobhuntersbible.com

Bombeck, Erma – Author, *If Life Is a Bowl of Cherries—What Am I Doing in
the Pits?*
Website: http://www.humorwriters.org

Borysenko, Joan – Author, *Minding the Body, Mending the Mind*
Website: http://www.joanborysenko.com

Boyd, Ty – Author, *The Million Dollar Toolbox: A Blueprint for Transforming
Your Life & Your Career with Powerful Communication Skills*; Ty Boyd
Executive Learning Systems' most popular course, The "Excellence in
Speaking Institute," is in its 24th year. They have had attendees from over
30 countries and every state and province in North America.
Website: http://www.tyboyd.com

Breathnach, Sarah Ban – Author, *Simple Abundance: A Daybook of Comfort
and Joy*
Website: http://www.simpleabundance.com

Brescia, Mike – Author, *Today Is Your Day To Win: 99 Laser-Focused, No
Holds Barred Coaching Sessions To Help You Make Today And The Rest
Of Your Life A Stunning Success*
Website: http://www.thinkrightnow.com

Brody, Marjorie – Workplace/Career Expert, Professional Speaker/Executive
Coach, and Author of more than a dozen books on communications topics,
including *Career MAGIC: A Woman's Guide to Reward & Recognition*
Website: http://www.marjoriebrody.com

Brothers, Joyce – Well Known Psychologist
Website: http://www.drjoycebrothers.com

Brown, H. Jackson – Author, *Life's Little Instruction Book®*
Website: http://www.instructionbook.com

Bryan, Mark – Author, *Money Drunk, Money Sober: 90 Days to Financial Freedom*
Website: http://www.markbryan.com

Burg, Bob – Author, *Winning Without Intimidation: How to Master the Art of Positive Persuasion in Today's Real World in Order to Get What You Want, When You Want It*
Website: http://www.burg.com

Burke, Charles – Success Expert
Website: http://www.moreluck.com

Callahan, Roger – Author, *Tapping the Healer Within: Using Thought-Field Therapy to Instantly Conquer Your Fears, Anxieties, and Emotional Distress*
Website: http://www.tftrx.com

Campbell, Joseph – Author, *The Power of Myth* (with Bill Moyers, 1988)
Website: http://www.jcf.org

Carle, Gilda – Author, *Don't Bet on the Prince! How to Have the Man You Want by Betting on Yourself*
Website: http://www.drgilda.com

Carter-Scott, Chérie – Author, *If Life Is a Game, These Are the Rules: Ten Rules for Being Human, As Introduced in Chicken Soup for the Soul*
Website: http://www.drcherie.com

Cassou, Michele – Author, *Life, Paint and Passion: Reclaiming the Magic of Spontaneous Expression* and *Point Zero: Creativity Without Limits*
Website: http://www.michelecassou.com

Cayce, Edgar – Author, *My Life As A Seer: The Lost Memoirs*
Website: http://www.edgarcayce.org

Chironna, Mark – Personal Coach, Mentor, and Physician of the Soul
Website: http://www.markchironna.com

Choquette, Sonia – Author, *Your Heart's Desire: Instructions for Creating the Life You Really Want*
Website: http://www.soniachoquette.com

Cialdini, Robert – Author, *Influence*
Website: http://www.influenceatwork.com

Clements, Alan – Author, *Instinct for Freedom: Finding Liberation through Living*
Website: http://www.worlddharma.com

Clemmer, Jim – Author, *Growing the Distance: Timeless Principles for Personal, Career, and Family Success*
Website: http://www.clemmer.net

Cohen, Herb – Author, *You Can Negotiate Anything*
Website: http://www.herbcohenonline.com

Collins, Susie and Otto – Relationship and Life Success Coaches; Authors, *Should You Stay or Should You Go? Compelling Questions to help you make that difficult relationship decision*
Website: http://www.collinspartners.com

Courtenay, Bryce – Author, *The Power of One*
Website: http://www.brycecourtenay.com

Cutright, Paul and Layne – Founders of The Center for Enlightened Partnership
Website: http://www.enlightenedpartners.com

Davis, Laura – Author, *I Thought We'd Never Speak Again: The Road from Estrangement to Reconciliation*
Website: http://www.lauradavis.net

Dawson, Roger – Author, *Secrets of Power Negotiating*
Website: http://www.rdawson.com

Day, Laura – Author, *The Circle: How the Power of a Single Wish Can Change Your Life*
Website: http://www.practicalintuition.com

de Bono, Edward – Author, *The Use of Lateral Thinking*
Website: http://www.edwdebono.com

de Roos, Dolf – Author, *Real Estate Riches: How to Become Rich Using Your Banker's Money*
Website: http://www.dolfderoos.com

Decker, Bert – Author, *You've Got To Be Believed To Be Heard: Reach the First Brain to Communicate in Business and in Life*
Website: http://www.bertdecker.com

Deep, Sam – Author, *Yes, You Can! 1,200 Inspiring Ideas for Work, Home, and Happiness*
Website: http://www.samdeep.com

Deida, David – Author, *The Way of the Superior Man: A Spiritual Guide to Mastering the Challenges of Women, Work, and Sexual Desire*
Website: http://www.deida.com

Diamond, Claude – Mentor, Coach, and Founder of the Diamond Consulting Group
Website: http://www.claudediamond.com

Dobson, James – Author, *Bringing Up Boys: Practical Advice and Encouragement for Those Shaping the Next Generation of Men*
Website: http://www.family.org

Donahue, Gene – Founder of TopAchievement.com
Website: http://www.topachievement

Dooley, Mike – Developer of the Audio CD *Infinite Possibilities: The Art of Living Your Dreams*
Website: http://www.tut.com

Dowrick, Stephanie – Author, *Intimacy and Solitude*
Website: http://www.stephaniedowrick.com

Drucker, Peter – Author, *The Essential Drucker: The Best of Sixty Years of Peter Druckers Essential Writings on Management*
Website: http://www.peter-drucker.com

Dwoskin, Hale – Author, *Happiness Is Free, The Sedona Method*
Website: http://www.sedona.com

Edward, John – Psychic Medium, Host of the TV Show *Crossing Over with John Edward*, and Author, *After Life: Answers From the Other Side*
Website: http://www.johnedward.net

Eicholz, Marti – Founder and Executive Director of transformation.org and the Institute for Transformation LLC (IFT)
Website: http://www.transformation.org

Eker, T. Harv – Provides peak potentials training through books, tapes, and seminars
Website: http://www.peakpotentials.com

Evans, Paul – Public Speaking Expert
Website: http://www.instantspeakingsuccess.com

Falter-Barnes, Suzanne – Author, *How Much Joy Can You Stand?*
Website: http://www.howmuchjoy.com

Fettke, Rich – Author, *Extreme Success: The 7-Part Program That Shows You How to Succeed Without Struggle*
Website: http://www.fettke.com

Finley, Guy – Author, *The Secret of Letting Go*
Website: http://www.guyfinley.com

Fortgang, Laura Berman – Author, *Living Your Best Life: Discover Your Life's Blueprint for Success*
Website: http://www.laurabermanfortgang.com

Fripp, Patricia – CSP, CPAE Award-Winning Professional Keynote Speaker
Website: http://www.fripp.com

Fritz, Robert – Author, *The Path of Least Resistance: Learning to Become the Creative Force in Your Own Life*
Website: http://www.robertfritz.com

Gage, Randy – Developer of Self Development and Prosperity Products
Website: http://www.randygage.com

Gelb, Michael – Author, *Discover Your Genius: How to Think Like History's Ten Most Revolutionary Minds*
Website: http://www.michaelgelb.com

Gerber, Michael E. – Author, *E-Myth*
Website: http://www.e-myth.com

Gilligan, Stephen – Author, *The Courage to Love: Principles and Practices of Self-Relations Psychotherapy*
Website: http://www.stephengilligan.com

Gitomer, Jeffrey – Author, *The Sales Bible: The Ultimate Sales Resource*
Website: http://www.gitomer.com

Gladwell, Malcolm – Author, *The Tipping Point: How Little Things Can Make a Big Difference*
Website: http://www.gladwell.com

Glasser, William – Author, *Reality Therapy*
Website: http://www.wglasser.com

Goodier, Steve – Author, *Lessons of the Turtle*
Website: http://www.lifesupportsystem.com

Gordon, Jon – Author, *Become an Energy Addict: Simple, Powerful Ways to Energize Your Life*
Website: http://www.energyaddict.com

Harricharan, John – Author, *When You Can Walk on Water, Take the Boat*
Website: http://www.insight2000.com

Harris, Bill – Founder and President of Centerpointe Research Institute
Website: http://www.centerpointe.com

Hartmann, Thom – Author, *The Last Hours of Ancient Sunlight: Waking Up to Personal and Global Transformation*
Website: http://www.thomhartmann.com

Helmstetter, Shad – Author, *What To Say When You Talk To Your Self*
Website: http://www.shadhelmstetter.com

Hendricks, Gay and Kathlyn – Authors, *Conscious Loving: The Journey to Co-Commitment*
Website: http://www.hendricks.com

Hewitt, Les – Co-Author, *The Power of Focus: How to Hit Your Business, Personal and Financial Targets with Absolute Certainty* and *The Power of Focus for Women: How To Live The Life You Really Want*
Website: http://www.achievers.com

Hinds, Josh – Co-Creator of the One Question Project
Website: http://www.joshhinds.com

Houston, Jean – Author, *A Passion for the Possible: A Guide to Realizing Your True Potential*
Website: http://www.jeanhouston.org

Howard, Vernon – Author, *The Power of Your Supermind*
Website: http://www.anewlife.org

Huber, Cheri – Author, *There Is Nothing Wrong With You: Regardless of What You Were Taught to Believe*
Website: http://www.cherihuber.com

Humbert, Philip E. – Author, *Speaker and Coach*
Website: http://www.philiphumbert.com

Hunkin, Allan – Founder of the Success Talk Channel™
Website: http://www.success-talk.com

Jarow, Rick – Author, *Creating the Work You Love: Courage, Commitment and Career*
Website: http://www.anticareer.com

Jeary, Tony – Author, *Life is a Series of Presentations*
Website: http://www.tonyjeary.com

Jeffers, Susan – Author, *Feel the Fear and Do it Anyway*
Website: http://www.susanjeffers.com

Jimenez, Lisa – Personal Coach, Motivational Speaker, and Developer of the Conquer Fear! Program
Website: http://www.lisajimenez.com

Johnson, Vic – Founder of MP3Motivators.com
Website: http://www.mp3motivators.com

Jones, Charlie "Tremendous" – Author, *Life Is Tremendous*
Website: http://www.executivebooks.com

Jong, Erica – Author, *Fear of Flying*
Website: http://www.ericajong.com

Kane, Ariel and Shya – Authors, *Working on Yourself Doesn't Work: A Book About Instantaneous Transformation*
Website: http://www.ask-inc.com

Karrass, Chester A. – Author, *Negotiating Game Rev*
Website: http://www.karrass.com

Kehoe, John – Author, *Mind Power into the 21st Century: Techniques to Harness the Astounding Powers of Thought*
Website: http://www.learnmindpower.com

Keirsey, David – Author, *Please Understand Me II: Temperament, Character, Intelligence*
Website: http://www.keirsey.com

Keller, Jeff – Creator of the *Success from Soup to Nuts* Audio Program
Website: http://www.attitudeiseverything.com

Kidd, Sue Monk – Author, *The Dance of the Dissident Daughter*
Website: http://www.suemonkkidd.com

Kinder, George – Author, *Seven Stages of Money Maturity: Understanding the Spirit and Value of Money in Your Life*
Website: http://www.kinderinstitute.com

Kingston, Karen – Author, *Clear Your Clutter with Feng Shui* and *Creating Sacred Space with Feng Shui*
Website: http://www.spaceclearing.com

Kreidman, Ellen – Author, *Light Her Fire*
Website: http://www.lightyourfire.com

Kubler-Ross, Elisabeth – Author, *On Death and Dying*
Website: http://www.elisabethkublerross.com

Langemeier, Loral – Provides wealth coaching.
Website: http://www.liveoutloud.com

Leonard, Thomas – Author, *The Portable Coach: 28 Sure Fire Strategies for Business and Personal Success*
Website: http://www.thomasleonard.com

Levenson, Lester – Creator of the Sedona Method
Website: http://www.sedona.com

Levine, Mel – Author, *A Mind at a Time*
Website: http://www.allkindsofminds.org

Levine, Terri – Author, *Stop Managing, Start Coaching*, and Creator of the highly acclaimed Coaching Kits. These famous Coaching Kits have been called "the best thing to happen in coaching." Grab one at http://www.terrilevine.com/kits.html.
Website: http://www.terrilevine.com

Linn, Denise – Author, *Sacred Space: Clearing and Enhancing the Energy of Your Home*
Website: http://www.deniselinn.com

Litman, Mike – Author, *Conversations with Millionaires: What Millionaires Do to Get Rich, That You Never Learned About in School!*
Website: http://www.mikelitman.com

Lofholm, Eric – Sales Trainer
Website: http://www.ericlofholm.com

Lorayne, Harry – Author, *The Memory Book*
Website: http://www.harrylorayne.com

Lucado, Max – Author, *Traveling Light: Releasing the Burdens You Were Never Intended to Bear*
Website: http://www.maxlucado.com

Lynch, Pat – Author, *The Five Secrets: What You're NOT Supposed To Know Because It Will Set You Free And Change Your Life Forever!*
Website: http://www.patlynch.com

Mackay, Harvey – Author, *Swim With the Sharks Without Being Eaten Alive: Outsell, Outmanage, Outmotivate, and Outnegotiate Your Competition*
Website: http://www.mackay.com

Marden, Orison Swett – Founder of Success Magazine
Website: http://www.orisonswettmarden.com

Marston, Ralph – Creator of the Thought for the Day and The Daily Motivator
Website: http://www.greatday.com

Matthews, Philippe – A self-empowered and self-motivated entrepreneurial maverick, Philippe Matthews is dedicated to human potential and personal growth and development.
Website: http://www.empowermag.com

Mayer, Jeffrey – Author, *If You Haven't Got the Time to Do It Right, When Will You Find the Time to Do It Over?*
Website: http://www.succeedinginbusiness.com

McColl, Peggy – Author, *On Being a Dog with a Bone*
Website: http://www.destinies.com

McMeekin, Gail – Author, *The 12 Secrets of Highly Creative Women: A Portable Mentor* and *The Power of Positive Choices: Adding and Subtracting Your Way to a Great Life*
Website: http://www.creativesuccess.com

Merton, Thomas – Author, *The Seven Storey Mountain: An Autobiography of Faith*
Website: http://www.merton.org

Meyer, Joyce – Author, *Battlefield of the Mind: Winning the Battle in Your Mind*
Website: http://www.joycemeyer.org

Meyer, Paul J. – Author, *The Five Pillars of Leadership: How to Bridge the Leadership Gap*, and Founder of Success Motivation® International, Inc.
Website: http://www.pauljmeyer.com

Miedaner, Talane – Author, *Coach Yourself to Success: 101 Tips from a Personal Coach for Reaching Your Goals at Work and in Life*
Website: http://www.lifecoach.com

Moore, Thomas – Author, *Care of the Soul: A Guide for Cultivating Depth and Sacredness in Everyday Life*
Website: http://www.careofthesoul.net

Morrissey, Mary Manin – Author, *No Less Than Greatness: The Seven Spiritual Principles That Make Real Love Possible*
Website: http://www.lecworld.org

Moss, Robert – Author, *Conscious Dreaming: A Spiritual Path for Everyday Life*
Website: http://www.mossdreams.com

Nemeth, Maria – Author, *The Energy of Money: A Spiritual Guide to Financial and Personal Fulfillment*
Website: http://www.youandmoney.com

Newberry, Tommy – Author, *Success is Not an Accident: Change Your Choices, Change Your Life*
Website: http://www.1percentclub.com

Nouwen, Henri – Author, *Life of the Beloved: Spiritual Living in a Secular World*
Website: http://www.nouwen.net

Orloff, Judith – Author, *Dr. Judith Orloff's Guide to Intuitive Healing: Five Steps to Physical, Emotional, and Sexual Wellness* and *Positive Energy: Ten Extraordinary Prescriptions for Transforming Fatigue, Stress, and Fear Into Vibrance, Strength and Love*
Website: http://www.drjudithorloff.com

Osho – A well-known philosopher and spiritual leader of the twentieth century, Osho taught his devoted followers to experience meditation and transformation. His influence continues to reach people far and wide; the Osho Meditation Resort, the largest meditation resort in the world, gets visitors of all ages from over 100 countries. Osho is India's best-selling author and has written such books as *The Book of Secrets* and *Courage: The Joy of Living Dangerously.*
Website: http://www.osho.com

Osteen, Joel – Pastor at the Lakewood Church in Houston, Texas. The Lakewood Church television program airs in the United States and on international stations around the world.
Website: http://www.lakewood.cc

Pease, Allan – Author, *Signals: How to Use Body Language for Power, Success, and Love*
Website: http://www.AllanPease.com

Peters, Tom – Author, *In Search of Excellence*
Website: http://www.tompeters.com

Pilzer, Paul Zane – Author, *Unlimited Wealth: The Theory and Practice of Economic Alchemy*
Website: http://www.paulzanepilzer.com

Plumb, Charlie – A former Navy fighter pilot and P.O.W., J. Charles Plumb is now a sought-after motivational speaker.
Website: http://www.charlieplumb.com

Ponder, Catherine – Author, *Dynamic Laws of Prosperity*
Website: http://www.prosperitynetwork.com

Prager, Dennis – Author, *Happiness Is a Serious Problem: A Human Nature Repair Manual*
Website: http://www.dennisprager.com

Qubein, Nido – Author, *How to Be a Great Communicator: In Person, on Paper, and on the Podium*
Website: http://www.nidoqubein.com

Ramsey, Dave – Author, *The Total Money Makeover: A Proven Plan for Financial Fitness*
Website: http://www.daveramsey.com

Reid, Greg S. – Author, *The Millionaire Mentor*
Website: http://www.alwaysgood.com

Robey, Dan – Author, *The Power of Positive Habits*
Website: http://www.thepowerofpositivehabits.com

Robinson, Larry W. – Multi-Media Personality, Inspirational Speaker, and Author, *Get Up and Get Over it!*
Website: http://www.larrywrobinson.com

Robinson, Lynn – Author, *Compass of the Soul: 52 Ways Intuition Can Guide You to the Life of Your Dreams*
Website: http://www.lynnrobinson.com

Rose, Amara – As a "midwife for the soul," Amara offers life purpose coaching, talks, tapes, e-courses, wisdom circles, retreats, and a FREE inspirational monthly newsletter, "What Shines."
Website: http://www.liveyourlight.com

Rowe, Dorothy – Author, *Depression: The Way Out of Your Prison*
Website: http://www.dorothyrowe.com.au

Ruettiger, Rudy – Motivational Speaker and Author, whose life story was portrayed in the TriStar movie *Rudy*
Website: http//www.RudyInternational.com

Rutherford, Darel – Author, *Being The Solution: A Spiritual Path to Personal Power and Financial Independence*
Website: http://www.beingsolution.com

Sayre, Kent – Author, *Unstoppable Confidence*
Website: http://www.unstoppable-confidence.com

Scheele, Paul – Author, *The Photoreading Whole Mind System*
Website: http://www.learningstrategies.com

Scheinfeld, Bob – Author, *The Invisible Path to Success: Seven Steps to Understanding and Managing the Unseen Forces Shaping Your Life*
Website: http://www.invisiblepath.com

Scolastico, Ron – Author, *Doorway to the Soul: How to Have a Profound Spiritual Experience*
Website: http://www.ronscolastico.com

Shawkey, Gary – Founder of Gary Shawkey International
Website: http://www.garyshawkey.com

Sheehy, Gail – Author, *Passages: Predictable Crises of Adult Life*
Website: http://www.gailsheehy.com

Shoshanna, Brenda – Author, *Why Men Leave: Men Talk About Why They Decided to End the Relationship—And What Might Have Changed Their Minds* and *Zen and the Art of Falling in Love*
Website: http://www.brendashoshanna.com

Silva, José – Author, *The Silva Mind Control Method*
Website: http://www.silvamethod.com

Simon, Stephen – Founder/President of Moving Messages: The Institute for Spiritual Entertainment, Inc.; Leading Spokesperson for the Genre of "Spiritual Cinema"
Website: http://www.movingmessagesmedia.com

Sotkin, Joan – Creator of Prosperity Place, which contains information that will help you improve your relationship with money with the Build Your Money Muscles Program.
Website: http://www.prosperityplace.com

Stanley, Charles – Author, *Finding Peace: God's Promise of a Life Free from Regret, Anxiety, and Fear*
Website: http://www.intouch.org

Staples, Walter Doyle – Author, *Think Like a Winner!*
Website: http://www.walterstaples.com

Strachar, Ed – Developer of the Reading Genius Program
Website: http://www.readinggenius.com

Stuberg, Robert – Founder of Success.com and Author, *The 12 Life Secrets: Timeless Wisdom For Living An Extraordinary Life*
Website: http://www.success.com

Sutphen, Dick - Developer of Mind-Programming CDs
Website: http://www.dicksutphen.com

Sylver, Marshall – Author, *PASSION PROFIT & POWER*
Website: http://www.sylver.com

Taylor, Eldon – Foremost authority on subliminal information processing, and Director and Co-Founder of Progressive Awareness Research, Inc.
Website: http://www.innertalk.com

Tice, Lou – Author, *Personal Coaching for Results: How to Mentor and Inspire Others to Amazing Growth*
Website: http://www.pacificinstitute.com.au

Tonay, Veronica – Author, *Every Dream Interpreted*
Website: http://www.veronicatonay.com

Tresidder, Todd R. – Founder of Financial Mentor
Website: http://www.financialmentor.com

Twyman, James F. – Author, *Emissary of Light: A Vision of Peace*
Website: http://www.emissaryoflight.com

Virtue, Doreen – Author, *Healing With the Angels: How the Angels Can Assist You in Every Area of Your Life*
Website: http://www.angeltherapy.com

Vivekananda, Swami – Author, *Raja-Yoga*
Website: http://www.vivekananda.org

Vurnum, Gary – Founder of Our Success Partnership
Website: http://www.oursuccesspartnership.com

Watts, Alan – Author, *The Book: On the Taboo Against Knowing Who You Are*
Website: http://www.alanwatts.net

Weiner-Davis, Michele – Author, *Divorce Busting*
Website: http://www.divorcebusting.com

Wells, Rebecca – Author, *Divine Secrets of the Ya-Ya Sisterhood*
Website: http://www.ya-ya.com

Wenger, Win – Author, *The Einstein Factor: A Proven New Method for Increasing Your Intelligence*
Website: http://www.winwenger.com

Westheimer, Ruth – Relationship Expert
Website: http://www.drruth.com

Wetmore, Donald E. – Time Management Expert
Website: http://www.balancetime.com

White, Robert – Founder of Lifespring, ARC International, and now ARC Worldwide, a transformational leadership training resource for individuals and organizations. Author, *One World, One People* and *Living an Extraordinary Life: Unlocking your potential for success, joy and fulfillment*
Website: http://www.arcworldwide.com

Whyte, David – Author, *The Heart Aroused: Poetry and the Preservation of the Soul in Corporate America*
Website: http://www.davidwhyte.com

Widener, Chris – Speaker, Writer, and President of Made for Success; Focuses on Leadership
Website: http://www.madeforsuccess.com

Wieder, Marcia – Author, *Making Your Dreams Come True*
Website: http://www.marciaw.com

Wilber, Ken – Author, *A Brief History of Everything*
Website: http://www.worldofkenwilber.com

Wood, Andrew – Author, *Traits of Champions*
Website: http://www.traitsofchampions.com

Wright, Judith – Author, *There Must Be Something More Than This*
Website: http://www.wrightlearning.com

Yager, Jan – Author, *When Friendship Hurts: How to Deal With Friends Who Betray, Abandon, or Wound You*
Website: http://www.janyager.com

Yancey, Philip – Author, *Disappointment with God*
Website: http://www.philipyancey.com

Zohar, Danah – Author, *The Quantum Self*
Website: http://www.dzohar.com

Zufelt, Jack – Author, *The DNA of Success: Know What You Want ...To Get What You Want*
Website: http://www.dnaofsuccess.com

APPENDIX B

Other Valuable Self Improvement Companies and Resources

In a book on Self Improvement Experts, we ran the risk of missing major companies that have high quality products but no well-known expert or founder.

Many of the experts on the list have major companies they are directly involved in. Stephen Covey, for example, is president of FranklinCovey, one of the largest companies in the Self Improvement Industry.

I have included a list of some of the main Self Improvement companies that do not have a leader who made the list but that are absolutely worth looking at. These companies are listed in alphabetical order.

Alcoholics Anonymous (AA) – Fellowship of men and women who share their experience, strength, and hope with each other that they may solve their common problem and help others to recover from alcoholism.
Website: http://www.alcoholics-anonymous.org

Alphasonics – Developer of High Quality Subliminal Tape Programs.
Website: http://www.alphasonics.com

American Institute of Stress – Dedicated to the advancement of knowledge of the role of stress in health and disease.
Website: http://www.stress.org

American Management Association International – The world's largest membership-based training organization.
Website: http://www.amanet.org

American Society of Clinical Hypnosis – The largest U.S. organization for health and mental health care professionals using clinical hypnosis.
Website: http://www.asch.net

American Society of Training and Development (ASTD) – Association for training and performance professionals in areas such as HRD, HRM, learning technology, evaluation, EPSS, ROI, and change management.
Website: http://www.astd.org

ARC Worldwide – Offers high impact transformational leadership training programs for individuals and organizations. Its principals have founded and led companies with over 1.2 million satisfied graduates and hundreds of corporate clients. ARC partners with executives and companies facing major challenges or significant opportunities to create extraordinary team focus, alignment and commitment.
Website: http://www.arcworldwide.com

A.R.E. Bookstores – Offers readers a wide variety of new and classic books on holistic health and healing, and all forms of balanced living. A non-profit organization.
Website: http://www.arebookstore.com

Association of Unity Churches – A principle-centered, proactive organization dedicated to spiritual leadership.
Website: http://www.unity.org

Barksdale Foundation – Self Esteem and Self Control Materials and Programs.
Website: http://www.barksdale.org

Beliefnet.com – Spirituality and Religion Internet Portal.
Website: http://www.beliefnet.com

Bennett/Stellar University – Offers professional certification in NLP, hypnosis, Reiki, and personal growth training.
Website: http://www.imagineit.org

Biofeedback Certification Institute of America (BCIA) – Created to establish and maintain standards for practitioners who use biofeedback and to certify those who meet these standards.
Website: http://www.bcia.org

Body and Soul Magazine – Bodyandsoulmag.com and Body & Soul Magazine are all about inspiring you to live a healthy, balanced, and fulfilling life.
Website: http://www.bodyandsoulmag.com

Brain.com – A brain-related Internet Portal.
Website: http://www.brain.com

Canyon Ranch – A health resort that offers fitness and wellness programs, spa treatments, and nutritious gourmet meals.
Website: http://www.canyonranch.com

Centerpointe Research – Powerful Effective Personal Growth, Self Help, Meditation, and Mind Development Tool.
Website: http://www.centerpointe.com

Coach University – A worldwide group of professional business coaches working with clients by phone to reach their special vision of success.
Website: http://www.coachinc.com

CoachVille – The mission of CoachVille is to improve the quality of coaching worldwide.
Website: http://www.coachville.com

ConsciousOne.com – Spiritual-based courses on the Internet.
Website: http://www.consciousone.com

Dailyinbox.com – Publisher of Self Improvement Internet Ezines.
Website: http://www.dailyinbox.com

East West Books – Major provider of spiritual and New Age books and tapes.
Website: http://www.eastwest.com

Emode.com – Self-testing psychology site. Includes tests on personality, IQ, relationships, careers, and health. Also provides a celebrity matchmaker.
Website: http://www.emode.com

Esalen Institute – Known for its blend of East/West philosophies, its experiential/didactic workshops, the steady influx of philosophers, psychologists, artists, and religious thinkers, and its breathtaking grounds with natural hot springs.
Website: http://www.esalen.org

The Expanding Light Retreat – Year-round retreat in the Sierra Nevada foothills of Northern California. Offering workshops in yoga, Ananda Yoga, meditation, spiritual growth, and more.
Website: http://www.expandinglight.org

Fred Pryor Seminars, Careertrak – A complete Training Resource offering a variety of courses in many different subjects.
Website: http://www.pryor.com

Hope Magazine – Humanity making a difference, bi-monthly magazine featuring stories of making the world a better place, and finding our place within it.
Website: http://www.hopemag.com

Innertalk – Patented, independent, and scientifically proven effective technology for products that do something—not just say something. Free MP3s, e-books, and online hypnosis.
Website: http://www.innertalk.com

Institute of HeartMath – Developer of tools for people to use in the moment to relieve stress. Provides training for educators, corporations, and health and human services professionals.
Website: http://www.heartmath.org

Institute of Noetic Sciences – Provides research and education in consciousness and human potential.
Website: http://www.noetic.org

International Coach Federation – Promotes excellence in professional life coaching, business coaching, executive coaching, and corporate coaching.
Website: http://www.coachfederation.org

Kabbalah Centre– Offers online courses, information about the center activities, and teachings for the modern day Kabbalist.
Website: http://www.kabbalah.com

Landmark Education – Offers integrated programs that address one's ability to think beyond what is known and to operate effectively in the fulfillment of new possibilities.
Website: http://www.landmarkeducation.com

Learning Annex – An alternative adult-education organization offering short, inexpensive courses and seminars on personal growth, business, and career.
Website: http://www.learningannex.com

Learning Strategies Corporation – Provides tapes, books, and training to experience your full potential including PhotoReading, Spring Forest Qigong, Paraliminal Tapes, and more.
Website: http://www.learningstrategies.com

Maharishi University of Management – Students learn the Transcendental Meditation program as part of their first course at the university. This simple procedure unfolds inner creativity and intelligence.
Website: http://www.mum.edu

Midwest Center for Stress and Anxiety – Offers a self-help study program to deal with stress and anxiety.
Website: http://www.stresscenter.com

The Monroe Institute – A non-profit research and educational organization founded by Robert Monroe. Has investigated human consciousness for over 40 years.
Website: http://www.monroeinstitute.org

National Association of Personal Financial Advisors – The largest professional association of Fee-Only comprehensive financial planners in the United States.
Website: http://www.napfa.org

National Association of Professional Organizers – A nationwide network of professionals in all areas of organization.
Website: http://www.napo.net

National Sleep Foundation – Non-profit organization supporting public education, sleep-related research, and advocacy related to sleep disorders such as insomnia, apnea, narcolepsy, and excessive daytime sleepiness.
Website: http://www.sleepfoundation.org

National Speakers Association (NSA) – As the leading organization for experts who speak professionally, NSA provides resources and education to advance the skills, integrity, and value of its members and the speaking profession.
Website: http://www.nsaspeaker.org

Network of Alternatives for Publishers, Retailers & Artists (NAPRA) – The oldest trade association promoting communication between publishers, retailers, and others in order to expand their efforts in successfully producing, marketing, and selling products.
Website: http://www.napra.com

New Age Health Spa – The spa dedicated to the art of living well. New Age was created in 1986 as a result of our quest to live in greater harmony with nature and explore new pathways to personal fulfillment.
Website: http://www.newagehealthspa.com

New Age Journal – Offers articles, news of recent events, and business and events listings for New Age interests.
Website: http://www.newagejournal.com

New Leaf Distributing Company – Metaphysical books, audio, and video. Also offers magazines and general merchandise.
Website: http://www.newleaf-dist.com

New York Open Center – Urban holistic learning center. Alternative health and bodywork disciplines, depth psychologies, and sociocultural issues. Website: http://www.opencenter.org

Nightingale-Conant – Offers a variety of resources designed to enhance personal and professional development: audio downloads, audio cassettes, CD programs, and more. Website: http://www.nightingale.com

Omega Institute for Holistic Studies – Exceptional learning vacations and wellness retreats for personal growth led by renowned faculty. Omega Rhinebeck, New York Campus: April through October. Free catalogs. 800-944-1001 or online. Website: http://www.eomega.org

Onespirit.com – Offers inspirational self-help books including psychology and philosophy titles, as well as new age books covering astrology, dreams, and yoga. Website: http://www.onespirit.com

The Option Institute – The Option Institute is a non-profit, international and training center for The Option Process©. For over two decades, the institute has been teaching people to live happier, more self-empowered and successful lives. Website: http://www.option.org

Osho – You can experience meditation, visit a meditation resort, take an online tarot reading, enjoy an online magazine, and buy books all on the Osho website. Website: http://www.osho.com

Outward Bound – Celebrating over 40 years and more than 500,000 alumni, Outward Bound USA is the pioneer and leader in challenging adventure education for youths and adults. Website: http://www.outwardbound.com

Psychology Today – Online and print magazine covering psychology, mental health, therapy, and counseling. Website: http://www.psychologytoday.com

Sedona Training Associates – Discover the simple yet powerful secrets of the Sedona Method that allow you to overcome any fear or anxiety in 60 seconds or less. Website: http://www.sedona.com

Silva Mind Control Method – Formerly known as Silva Mind Control, this self-help program teaches you how to increase your IQ, develop clairvoyance, and use the mind to heal the body and find God.
Website: http://www.silvamethod.com

Spafinders.com – Specializes in the arrangement of spa vacations around the world.
Website: http://www.spafinder.com

Success.com – Personal Development and Success Leadership Community
Website: http://www.success.com

Successories – Motivational products specializing in wall decor, employee gifts and awards, screen savers, success books, and more.
Website: http://www.successories.com

SyberVision – Designs, develops, and markets advanced audio- and video-based personal achievement systems based on a proprietary expert learning technology developed by SyberVision founder Steve DeVore with the Stanford University Neuropsychology Research Laboratory.
Website: http://www.sybervision.com

Thinkrightnow.com – Accelerated Success Conditioning Programs that enable you to have the same core beliefs and take the same actions as people who are already great at what you want to do. An automated system that forces desired changes. Now you can be like the few who regularly enjoy great accomplishments, while most never come close.
Website: http://www.thinkrightnow.com

Toastmasters International – Non-profit organization where members learn public speaking skills by speaking to groups and working with others in a supportive environment.
Website: http://www.toastmasters.org

Tools For Wellness – Whether your interest is cognitive enhancement, peak physical or mental performance, anti-aging, consciousness exploration and expansion, optimal wellness, defense against harmful environmental influences, self-improvement, or simply living smarter, they guide you to products that suit your needs.
Website: http://www.toolsforwellness.com

Wainwright House – Retreat center providing personal and global transformation.
Website: http://www.wainwright.org

Western Spirit Enrichment Center – Spiritual retreat and personal growth center offering individuals and couples journeys of self-discovery and adventurous outdoor experiences in nature.
Website: http://www.westernspiritranch.com

APPENDIX C

Other Valuable Self Improvement Books

This is a single book and has the limitations that are naturally imposed by a single book. When you start with only 101 experts, it's easy to miss some extraordinary people and extraordinary books that have helped countless people improve their lives. We have included an additional quick reference chapter for other Self Improvement books and their authors. These people didn't make the list for a variety of reasons:

A) Their area of expertise is not in Self Improvement. They are well known for something else.
B) They are better known for their books than for their name. They might have been listed as expert #102.

The list below is in alphabetical order.

The 100 Simple Secrets of Happy People: What Scientists Have Learned and How You Can Use It – by David Niven

The 12 Secrets of Highly Creative Women: A Portable Mentor – by Gail McMeekin

17 Lies That Are Holding You Back & The Truth That Will Set You Free – by Steve Chandler

The 80/20 Principle: The Secret to Success by Achieving More with Less – by Richard Koch

Accelerated Learning for the 21st Century: The Six-Step Plan to Unlock Your Master-Mind – by Colin Penfield Rose

Acres of Diamonds – by Russell H. Conwell

After Life: Answers From the Other Side – by John Edward

The Alchemy of Happiness – by Muhummad Al-Ghazali

Analects – by Confucious

The Anxiety & Phobia Workbook – by Edmund J. Bourne

The Art of Loving – by Erich Fromm

Atlas Shrugged and the Fountainhead – by Ayn Rand

Autobiography – by Benjamin Franklin

Awakening Loving-Kindness – by Pema Chodran

The Battered Woman – by Lenore Walker

Battlefield of the Mind: Winning the Battle in Your Mind – by Joyce Meyer

Be Heard Now! Tap into Your Inner Speaker and Communicate with Ease – by Lee Glickstein

Being The Solution – by Darel Rutherford

The Bhagavad-Gita: Krishna's Counsel in Time of War – by Stephen Mitchell (Translator)

The Bible

The Book: On the Taboo Against Knowing Who You Are – by Alan Watts

Born To Win – by Muriel James and Dorothy Jongeward

Bridge to Terabithia – by Katherine Paterson

A Brief History of Everything – by Ken Wilber

Bringing Up Boys: Practical Advice and Encouragement for Those Shaping the Next Generation of Men – by James Dobson

Care of the Soul: A Guide for Cultivating Depth and Sacredness in Everyday Life – by Thomas Moore

The Circle: How the Power of a Single Wish Can Change Your Life – by Laura Day

Clear Your Clutter With Feng Shui – by Karen Kingston

Coach Yourself to Success: 101 Tips from a Personal Coach for Reaching Your Goals at Work and in Life – by Talane Miedaner

Compass of the Soul: 52 Ways Intuition Can Guide You to the Life of Your Dreams – by Lynn Robinson

The Complete C.S. Lewis Signature Classics – by C. S. Lewis

The Complete Collected Poems of Maya Angelou – by Maya Angelou

The Conquest of Happiness – by Bertrand Russell

Conscious Dreaming: A Spiritual Path for Everyday Life – by Robert Moss

Conscious Loving: The Journey to Co-Commitment – by Gay Hendricks and Kathlyn Hendricks

The Consolation of Philosophy (6th C) – by Boethius

Conversations with Millionaires: What Millionaires Do to Get Rich, That You Never Learned About in School! – by Mike Litman

The Courage to Love: Principles and Practices of Self-Relations Psychotherapy – by Stephen Gilligan

Create Your Own Luck: 8 Principles of Attracting Good Fortune in Life, Love, and Work – by Azriela Jaffe

Creating the Work You Love: Courage, Commitment and Career – by Rick Jarow

Crucial Conversations: Tools for Talking When Stakes are High – by Kerry Patterson

The Dance of the Dissident Daughter – by Sue Monk Kidd

Depression: The Way Out of Your Prison – by Dorothy Rowe

The Dhammapada (Buddha's teachings) – by Eknath Easwaran (Translator)

Disappointment with God – by Philip Yancey

Discover Your Genius: How to Think Like History's Ten Most Revolutionary Minds – by Michael Gelb

Divine Secrets of the Ya-Ya Sisterhood – by Rebecca Wells

Divorce Busting – by Michele Weiner-Davis

The DNA of Success – by Jack Zufelt

Don't Bet on the Prince! How to Have the Man You Want by Betting on Yourself – by Gilda Carle

Doorway to the Soul: How to Have a Profound Spiritual Experience – by Ron Scolastico

Dr. Judith Orloff's Guide to Intuitive Healing: Five Steps to Physical, Emotional, and Sexual Wellness – by Judith Orloff

Dynamic Laws of Prosperity – by Catherine Ponder

Dynamic People Skills – by Dexter Yager

The Einstein Factor: A Proven New Method for Increasing Your Intelligence – by Win Wenger

E-Myth – by Michael E. Gerber

The Energy of Money: A Spiritual Guide to Financial and Personal Fulfillment – by Maria Nemeth

The Essential Drucker: The Best of Sixty Years of Peter Druckers Essential Writings on Management – by Peter Drucker

Every Dream Interpreted – by Veronica Tonay

Execution: The Discipline of Getting Things Done – by Larry Bossidy

Extreme Success: The 7-Part Program That Shows You How to Succeed Without Struggle – by Rich Fettke

Facing Codependence: What It Is, Where It Comes from, How It Sabotages Our Lives – by Pia Mellody

Fear of Flying – by Erica Jong

Feel the Fear and Do it Anyway – by Susan Jeffers

Finding Peace: God's Promise of a Life Free from Regret, Anxiety, and Fear – by Charles Stanley

Fish! Tales: Real-Life Stories to Help You Transform Your Workplace and Your Life – by Stephen C. Lundin

Flow: The Psychology of Optimal Experience – by Mihaly Csikszentmihalyi

Forgiveness: The Greatest Healer of All – by Gerald G. Jampolsky

Frames of Mind: The Theory of Multiple Intelligences – by Howard Gardner

The Game of Life and How to Play It – by Florence Scovel Shinn

Games People Play – by Eric Berne

Gandhi: An Autobiography: The Story of My Experiments with Truth – by Mahatma Gandhi

Gestalt Therapy: Excitement and Growth in the Human Personality – by Fritz Perls

Getting Things Done: The Art of Stress-Free Productivity – by David Allen

Getting to Yes: Negotiating Agreement – by Roger Fisher

Goal Setting 101: How to Set and Achieve a Goal! – by Gary Ryan Blair

God and You: Prayer as a Personal Relationship – by William A. Barry

Growing the Distance: Timeless Principles for Personal, Career, and Family Success – by Jim Clemmer

A Guide for the Advanced Soul – by Susan Hayward

Happiness Is a Serious Problem: A Human Nature Repair Manual – by Dennis Prager

Happiness Is Free – by Hale Dwoskin

Healing with the Angels: How the Angels Can Assist You in Every Area of Your Life – by Doreen Virtue

The Heart Aroused – by David Whyte

Heaven and Earth: Making the Psychic Connection – by James Van Praagh

The Hero Within – by Carol Pearson

How I Raised Myself From Failure to Success – by Frank Bettger

How Much Joy Can You Stand? – by Suzanne Falter-Barnes

How Proust Can Change Your Life – by Alain de Botton

How to Be a Great Communicator: In Person, on Paper, and on the Podium – by Nido Qubein

How to Have Confidence and Power in Dealing with People – by Les Giblin

I and Thou – by Martin Buber

I Thought We'd Never Speak Again: The Road from Estrangement to Reconciliation – by Laura Davis

I'm OK, You're OK – by Thomas Harris

The I Ching or Book of Changes – by Richard Wilhelm (Translator)

If Life is a Bowl of Cherries—What Am I Doing in the Pits? – by Erma Bombeck

If Life is a Game, These are the Rules: Ten Rules for Being Human as introduced in Chicken Soup for the Soul – by Chérie Carter-Scott

If You Haven't Got the Time to Do It Right, When Will You Find the Time to Do It Over? – by Jeffrey Mayer

Illusions – by Richard Bach

In Search of Excellence – by Tom Peters

Influence – by Robert Cialdini

Instinct for Freedom: Finding Liberation through Living – by Alan Clements

Intimacy and Solitude – by Stephanie Dowrick

An Intimate History of Humanity – by Theodore Zeldin

The Invisible Path to Success: Seven Steps to Understanding and Managing the Unseen Forces Shaping Your Life – by Bob Scheinfeld

Iron John – by Robert Bly

It Only Takes a Minute to Change Your Life! – by Willy Jolley

Jack: Straight from the Gut – by Jack Welch

The Journey: A Practical Guide to Healing Your Life and Setting Yourself Free – by Brandon Bays

Just As I Am – by Billy Graham

The Language of Letting Go – by Melody Beattie

The Last Hours of Ancient Sunlight: Waking Up to Personal and Global Transformation – by Thom Hartmann

Leadership – by Rudolph W. Giuliani

Lessons of the Turtle – by Steve Goodier

Life is a Series of Presentations – by Tony Jeary

Life Is Tremendous – by Charlie "Tremendous" Jones

Life of the Beloved: Spiritual Living in a Secular World – by Henri Nouwen

Life, Paint and Passion: Reclaiming the Magic of Spontaneous Expression – by Michele Cassou

Life's Little Instruction Book® – by H. Jackson Brown

Light Her Fire – by Ellen Kreidman

The Little Book of Letting Go: A Revolutionary 30-Day Program to Cleanse Your Mind, Lift Your Spirit and Replenish Your Soul – by Hugh Prather

Living an Extraordinary Life: Unlocking your potential for success, joy and fulfillment – by Robert White

Living Deliberately: The Discovery and Development of Avatar – by Harry Palmer

Living Your Best Life: Discover Your Life's Blueprint for Success – by Laura Berman Fortgang

Looking Out For No. 1 – by Robert J. Ringer

Lost in the Cosmos: The Last Self-Help Book – by Walker Percy

Love, Medicine and Miracles: Lessons Learned about Self-Healing from a Surgeon's Experience with Exceptional Patients – by Bernie Siegel

The Magic of Believing – by Claude M. Bristol

The Magic of Thinking Big – by David Joseph Schwartz

The Magic Story – by Frederick Van Rensselaer Day

Making Your Dreams Come True – by Marcia Wieder

Man's Search For Meaning – by Viktor Frankl

The Master Key System – by Charles F. Haanel

Mastery: The Keys to Success and Long-Term Fullfillment – by George Leonard

Meditation: A Simple Eight Point Program for Translating Spiritual Ideals into Daily Life – by Elbert Hubbard

The Meditations of Marcus Aurelius – by Marcus Aurelius

The Memory Book – by Harry Lorayne

A Message to Garcia – by Elbert Hubbard

The Million Dollar Toolbox: A Blueprint for Transforming Your Life & Your Career with Powerful Communication Skills – by Ty Boyd

The Millionaire Next Door – by Thomas Stanley

A Mind at a Time – by Mel Levine

Mind Power into the 21st Century: Techniques to Harness the Astounding Powers of Thought – by John Kehoe

The Mind-Body Makeover Project: A 12-Week Plan for Transforming Your Body and Your Life – by Michael Gerrish

Mindfulness – by Ellen J. Langer

Minding the Body, Mending the Mind – by Joan Borysenko

Miss Manners' Guide to Domestic Tranquility: The Authoritative Manual for Every Civilized Household, However Harried – by Judith Martin

Modern Man in Search of a Soul – by Carl Jung

Money Drunk, Money Sober: 90 Days to Financial Freedom – by Mark Bryan

Motivation and Personality – by Abraham Maslow

My Life As A Seer: The Lost Memoirs: The Visions, The Prophecies, and Life of The Twentieth Century's Leading Psychic as Told in His Own Words – by Edgar Cayce

Negotiating Game Rev – by Chester A. Karrass

A New Beginning I: Handbook for Joyous Survival – by Jerry and Esther Hicks

The New Strategic Selling: Unique Sales System Proven Successful By The World's Best Companies – by Stephen E. Heiman

NLP: The New Technology of Achievement – by S. Andreas and C. Faulkner (eds)

No Less Than Greatness: The Seven Spiritual Principles That Make Real Love Possible – by Mary Manin Morrissey

Now, Discover Your Strengths – by Marcus Buckingham

On Becoming a Leader – by Warren Bennis

On Becoming a Person – by Carl Rogers

On Being a Dog with a Bone – by Peggy McColl

On Death and Dying – by Elisabeth Kubler-Ross

Passages: Predictable Crises of Adult Life – by Gail Sheehy

A Passion for the Possible: A Guide to Realizing Your True Potential – by Jean Houston

PASSION PROFIT & POWER – by Marshall Sylver

The Path of Least Resistance: Learning to Become the Creative Force in Your Own Life – by Robert Fritz

A Path With Heart – by Jack Kornfield

People with MS with the Courage to Give – by Jackie Waldman

Personal Coaching for Results: How to Mentor and Inspire Others to Amazing Growth – by Lou Tice

The Phenomenon of Man – by Pierre Teilhard de Chardin

The Photoreading Whole Mind System – by Paul Scheele

Please Understand Me II: Temperament, Character, Intelligence – by David Keirsey

The Portable Coach: 28 Sure Fire Strategies for Business and Personal Success – by Thomas Leonard

Positive Action for Health and Wellbeing: A Practical Guide to Improving Your Wellbeing – by Brian Roet

The Power of Concentration – by Theron Dumont

The Power of Focus: How to Hit Your Business, Personal and Financial Targets with Absolute Certainty – by Les Hewitt

The Power of Full Engagement: Managing Energy, Not Time, Is the Key to High Performance and Personal Renewal – by Jim Loehr

The Power of Myth (1988) – by Joseph Campbell (with Bill Moyers)

The Power of One – by Bryce Courtenay

The Power of Positive Habits – by Dan Robey

The Power of Your Subconscious Mind – by Joseph Murphy

The Power of Your Supermind – by Vernon Howard

Power Through Constructive Thinking – by Emmet Fox

Prosperity (Unity Classic Library) – by Charles Fillmore

Psychological Foundations of Success: A Harvard-Trained Scientist Separates the Science of Success from Self-Help Snake Oil – by Stephen J. Kraus

Psychosynthesis: A Collection of Basic Writings – by Roberto Assagioli

The Quantum Self – by Danah Zohar

Ragged Dick – by Horatio Alger

Raja-Yoga – by Swami Vivekananda

Real Estate Riches: How to Become Rich Using Your Banker's Money - by Dolf de Roos

Reality Therapy – by William Glasser

The Richest Man in Babylon – by George Clason

Sacred Space: Clearing and Enhancing the Energy of Your Home – by Denise Linn

The Sales Bible: The Ultimate Sales Resource – by Jeffrey Gitomer

The Science of Getting Rich – by Wallace D. Wattles

The Secret of Letting Go – by Guy Finley

Secrets of Power Negotiating – by Roger Dawson

Self-Help – by Samuel Smiles

Self-Mastery Through Conscious Autosuggestion – by Emile Coué

Self-Nurture: Learning to Care for Yourself As Effectively As You Care for Everyone Else – by Alice Domar

Self-Reliance – by Ralph Waldo Emerson

Seth Speaks: The Eternal Validity of the Soul (A Seth Book) – by Jane Roberts

Seven Stages of Money Maturity: Understanding the Spirit and Value of Money in Your Life – by George Kinder

The Seven Storey Mountain: An Autobiography of Faith – by Thomas Merton

A Short Guide to a Happy Life – by Anna Quindlen

Siddhartha – by Hermann Hesse

Signals: How to Use Body Language for Power, Success, and Love – by Allan Pease

The Silva Mind Control Method – by José Silva

Simple Abundance: A Daybook of Comfort and Joy – by Sarah Ban Breathnach

Slowing Down to the Speed of Love: How to Create a Deeper, More Fulfilling Relationship in a Hurried World – by Joseph Bailey

The Soul's Code: In Search of Character and Calling – by James Hillman

Stephanie Winston's Best Organizing Tips: Quick, Simple Ways to Get Organized and Get on with Your Life – by Stephanie Winston

Stop Managing, Start Coaching – by Terri Levine

Stopping: How to Be Still When You Have to Keep Going – by David Kundtz

The Street Kid's Guide to Having It All – by John Assaraf

Success Is Not An Accident: Change Your Choices, Change Your Life – by Tommy Newberry

Success Through a Positive Mental Attitude – by Napoleon Hill and W. Clement Stone

Superlearning 2000: New Triple-Fast Ways You Can Learn, Earn, and Succeed in the 21st Century – by Sheila Ostrander and Lynn Schroeder

Swim With the Sharks Without Being Eaten Alive: Outsell, Outmanage, Outmotivate, and Outnegotiate Your Competition – by Harvey Mackay

The Tao of Pooh – by Benjamin Hoff

Tao Te Ching – by Lao Tzu

Tapping the Healer Within: Using Thought-Field Therapy to Instantly Conquer Your Fears, Anxieties, and Emotional Distress – by Roger Callahan

The 9 Insights of the Wealthy Soul: A Father, A Son and Life's Greatest Treasure – by Michael Norwood

The Five Secrets: What You're NOT Supposed To Know Because It Will Set You Free And Change Your Life Forever! – by Pat Lynch

The Millionaire Mentor – by Greg S. Reid

There Is Nothing Wrong With You: Regardless of What You Were Taught to Believe – by Cheri Huber

There Must Be Something More Than This – by Judith Wright

They Call Me Coach – by John Wooden

Thick Face, Black Heart: The Warrior Philosophy for Conquering the Challenges of Business and Life – by Chin-Ning Chu

Think Like a Winner! – by Walter Doyle Staples

The Tipping Point: How Little Things Can Make a Big Difference – by Malcolm Gladwell

Today Is Your Day To Win: 99 Laser-Focused, No Holds Barred Coaching Sessions To Help You Make Today And The Rest Of Your Life A Stunning Success – by Mike Brescia

The Total Money Makeover: A Proven Plan for Financial Fitness – by Dave Ramsey

Tough Times Never Last, But Tough People Do! – by Robert H. Schuller

Traits of Champions – by Andrew Wood

Transforming Your Self: Becoming Who You Want to Be – by Steve Andreas

Transitions: Making Sense of Life's Changes – by William Bridges

The Traveler's Gift: Seven Decisions That Determine Personal Success – by Andy Andrews

Traveling Light: Releasing the Burdens You Were Never Intended to Bear – by Max Lucado

Unlimited Wealth: The Theory and Practice of Economic Alchemy – by Paul Zane Pilzer

Unstoppable Confidence – by Kent Sayre

The Use of Lateral Thinking – by Edward de Bono

Walden – by Henry David Thoreau

The Way and Its Power: Lao Tzu's Tao Te Ching and Its Place in Chinese Thought – by Arthur Waley

The Way of the Superior Man: A Spiritual Guide to Mastering the Challenges of Women, Work, and Sexual Desire – by David Deida

The Wealthy Barber: Everyone's Commonsense Guide to Becoming Financially Independent – by David Chilton

What Color is Your Parachute? A Practical Manual for Job-Hunters & Career-Changers – by Richard N. Bolles

What Life Could Mean to You – by Alfred Adler

What to Say When You Talk to Your Self – by Shad Helmstetter

When Bad Things Happen to Good People – by Harold Kushner

When Friendship Hurts: How to Deal With Friends Who Betray, Abandon, or Wound You – by Jan Yager

When You Can Walk on Water, Take the Boat – by John Harricharan

Why Am I Afraid to Tell You Who I Am? – by John Powell

Why Men Leave: Men Talk About Why They Decided to End the Relationship—And What Might Have Changed Their Minds – by Brenda Shoshanna

The Will To Believe – by William James

Winning Without Intimidation: How to Master the Art of Positive Persuasion in Today's Real World in Order to Get What You Want, When You Want I, and from Whom You Want It—Including the Difficult People You Come Across Everyday! – by Bob Burg

Women Who Run With the Wolves: Myths and Stories of the Wild Woman Archetype – by Clarissa Pinkola Estes

Working on Yourself Doesn't Work: A Book About Instantaneous Transformation – by Ariel and Shya Kane

Yes, You Can! 1,200 Inspiring Ideas for Work, Home, and Happiness – by Sam Deep

You Can Negotiate Anything – by Herb Cohen

You Just Don't Understand: Women and Men in Conversation – by Deborah Tannen

Your Heart's Desire: Instructions for Creating the Life You Really Want – by Sonia Choquette

Your Perfect Right: Assertiveness and Equality in Your Life and Relationships (Eighth Edition) – by Robert E. Alberti and Michael L. Emmons

You've Got To Be Believed To Be Heard: Reach the First Brain to Communicate in Business and in Life – by Bert Decker

ABOUT SELFGROWTH.COM

SelfGrowth.com is the Internet super-site for Self Improvement and Personal Growth. It is part of a network of websites owned and operated by Self Improvement Online, Inc., a privately held New Jersey-based Internet company.

Our company's mission is to provide informative, quality Self Improvement and Natural Health information to help people improve their lives. We provide information ranging from Goal Setting and Stress Management to Natural Health and Alternative Medicine.

If you want to get a sense for our website visibility in the Self Improvement area on the Internet, you can start by going to Google, Yahoo, AOL, Lycos, or just about any search engine on the Internet. Then type in the words "Self Improvement." SelfGrowth.com consistently comes up as the top or one of the top websites for Self Improvement.

❑ *Other Facts About This Site*

SelfGrowth.com:

- Publishes six informative newsletters on Self Improvement, Personal Growth, and Natural Health.
- Offers over 4,000 unique articles from more than 550 experts.
- Links to over 5,000 websites in an organized Directory.
- Features an updated Self Improvement Store and Events Calendar.
- Gets visitors from over 100 countries.

❑ *Contact Information*

ADDRESS: Self Improvement Online, Inc.
20 Arie Drive
Marlboro, New Jersey 07746
PHONE: (732) 761-9930
EMAIL: webmaster@selfgrowth.com
WEBSITE: www.selfgrowth.com

INDEX

* signifies a Top 101 Expert chapter

S

T

U

V

W

Y

Z

ABOUT THE AUTHOR

David Riklan is the president and founder of Self Improvement Online, Inc., a leading provider of Self Improvement and Personal Growth information on the Internet.

His company was founded in 1998 and now maintains four websites on Self Improvement and Natural Health, including:

1. www.SelfGrowth.com
2. www.SelfImprovementNewsletters.com
3. www.NaturalHealthNewsletters.com
4. www.NaturalHealthWeb.com

Riklan has a degree in chemical engineering from the State University of New York at Buffalo and has 18 years of experience in sales, marketing, management, and training for companies such as Hewlett Packard and The Memory Training Institute. His interest in Self Improvement and Personal Growth began over 20 years ago and was best defined through his work as an instructor for Dale Carnegie.

Riklan is a self-professed Self Improvement junkie. His house is full of Self Improvement books and tapes. He took his first Self Improvement course, Evelyn Wood Speed Reading, when he was 16 years old, and his interest hasn't ceased yet.

He lives and works in New Jersey with his wife and business partner, Michelle Riklan. Together, they run Self Improvement Online, Inc. and are raising three wonderful children: Joshua, Jonathan, and Rachel.